PLATE I.

Fig. 344.

Fig. 353.

BUDDHA DISPUTING WITH THE HERETICS.
(From Grünwedel, *Alt-Buddhistische Kultstätten.*)

History and Doctrines of
THE ĀJĪVIKAS

LALA SUNDERLAL JAIN RESEARCH SERIES

VOLUME XVII

History and Doctrines of THE ĀJĪVIKAS

A Vanished Indian Religion

A. L. BASHAM

With a foreword by
L. D. BARNETT

MOTILAL BANARSIDASS PUBLISHERS
PRIVATE LIMITED • DELHI

Reprint: Delhi, 1981, 2002, 2009
First Edition: London, 1951

ISBN: 978-81-208-1204-8

MOTILAL BANARSIDASS
41 U.A. Bungalow Road, Jawahar Nagar, Delhi 110 007
8 Mahalaxmi Chamber, 22 Bhulabhai Desai Road, Mumbai 400 026
203 Royapettah High Road, Mylapore, Chennai 600 004
236, 9th Main III Block, Jayanagar, Bangalore 560 011
Sanas Plaza, 1302 Baji Rao Road, Pune 411 002
8 Camac Street, Kolkata 700 017
Ashok Rajpath, Patna 800 004
Chowk, Varanasi 221 001

PRINTED IN INDIA
BY JAINENDRA PRAKASH JAIN AT SHRI JAINENDRA PRESS,
A-45, NARAINA, PHASE-I, NEW DELHI 110 028
AND PUBLISHED BY NARENDRA PRAKASH JAIN FOR
MOTILAL BANARSIDASS PUBLISHERS PRIVATE LIMITED,
BUNGALOW ROAD, DELHI 110 007

To

My Revered *GURU*

L. D. BARNETT

CONTENTS

CHAPTER PAGE

Foreword by Prof. Satya Ranjan Banerjee xi
Foreword by Dr. L. D. Barnett xiii
Preface to the Second Edition xv
Abbreviations xxi

PART I. HISTORY OF THE ĀJĪVIKAS

I. Introduction 3
The Historical Background to the Rise of Ājīvikism.

II. The Six Heretics
The Record of the *Sāmañña-phala Sutta* . . . 11
Other Buddhist References to the Doctrines of the Heretics 18

III. Makkhali Gosāla and his Predecessors
Ājīvika Leaders before Makkhali Gosāla . . 27
Nanda Vaccha and Kisa Saṅkicca 27
The Immediate Predecessors of Makkhali Gosāla . 30
Makkhali Gosāla 34
Birth of Makkhali Gosāla 35
The Meeting of Gosāla with Mahāvīra . . . 39
The Peregrinations of the Two Ascetics . . . 41
Gosāla and the Sesamum Plant 47
Gosāla and Vesiyāyaṇa 49
Gosāla Attains Magical Power and becomes the Leader of the Ājīvikas 50

IV. The Last Days of Makkhali Gosāla
The Six *Disācaras* 56
Gosāla is Exposed by Mahāvīra 58
Gosāla Visits Mahāvīra 60
Gosāla's Delirium 61
Ayampula Visits Gosāla 62
Gosāla's Repentance and Death 64

CHAPTER PAGE

The Date of Gosāla's Death 66
The Name and Titles of Makkhali Gosāla . . 78

V. PŪRAṆA AND PAKUDHA
Pūraṇa Kassapa 80
The Death of Pūraṇa 84
Pakudha Kaccāyana 90

VI. THE EARLY ĀJĪVIKA COMMUNITY (I)
The Wandering Philosophers 94
Etymology of the Term Ājīvika 101
The Ājīvika Initiation 104
Ājīvika Nudity 107
Ājīvika Asceticism 109
The Ājīvika *Sabhā* 115
Song and Dance 116

VII. THE EARLY ĀJĪVIKA COMMUNITY (II)
Begging and Dietary Practices 118
Accusations of Worldliness and Immorality . . 123
The Final Penance 127
Ājīvika Laymen 131
Relations between Ājīvikas and Buddhists . . 134
Relations between Ājīvikas and Jainas . . . 138

VIII. ĀJĪVIKAS IN THE NANDA AND MAURYA PERIODS
Mahāpadma 142
Ājīvikism in Maurya Times 145
The Barābar and Nāgârjunī Caves 150

IX. ĀJĪVIKAS IN LATER TIMES
References in Sanskrit Literature 161
Varāhamihira and Utpala . . , . . . 168
Sīlâṅka and the Trairāśikas 174
Nemicandra on the Ājīvikas 181
Lexicographical References 182
The Last References to Ājīvikas 184

X. THE SOUTHERN ĀJĪVIKAS
The Inscriptions 186
Ājīvikas in Tamil Literature 196

APPENDIX TO PART I—THE ICONOCLAST ASCETICS OF KASHMĪR 205

PART II. DOCTRINES OF THE ĀJĪVIKAS

CHAPTER PAGE

XI. ĀJĪVIKA SCRIPTURES

The *Mahānimittas*, the *Maggas*, and the *Onpatu-katir* 213
Pāli and Prākrit Quotations 216
Quotations by the Commentators 220

XII. *NIYATI* 224

Niyativāda Dialectic 228
The Development of the *Niyati* Doctrine . . 235

XIII. ĀJĪVIKA COSMOLOGY

The Categories of the *Sāmañña-phala Sutta* . . 240
The Eight Last Things 254
The Six Inevitables 255
Other Ājīvika Categories 256
Maṇḍala-mokṣa 257

XIV. OTHER DOCTRINES OF THE ĀJĪVIKAS

The Elements 263
Ājīvika Atomism in Relation to other Indian Atomic Doctrines 267
The Soul 270
The Gods 272
Ājīvika Logic 274
The Status of Makkhali Gosāla 275

XV. CONCLUSION

Summary 278
Dr. Barua's Three Questions 279
The Influence of the Ājīvikas 279
The Place of the Ājīvikas in Indian History . . 283

BIBLIOGRAPHY 289
INDEX 301

ILLUSTRATIONS

PLATE | OPPOSITE PAGE

I. Buddha Disputing with Heretics. (From Grünwedel, *Alt-Buddhistische Kultstätten*, figs. 344 and 353.) *frontispiece*

II. The Buddha Meets Upaka the Ājīvika. (From Krom, *The Life of the Buddha*, plate 110.) 94

III. The Buddha's *Parinirvāṇa*. (From Foucher, *L'Art Gréco-Bouddhique*, fig. 278.) 136

IV. Discomfiture of a Naked Ascetic. (From Foucher, *L'Art Gréco-Bouddhique*, fig. 261.) 138

V. Barābar Cave Inscriptions. (From *CII*. vol. i, opposite p. 182.) 150

VI. Nāgârjunī Cave Inscriptions. (From *IA*. xx, opposite p. 365.) 152

VII. Plans of the Barābar and Nāgârjunī Caves. (From Cunningham, *Four Reports* . . . opposite p. 45.) . 154

VIII. Façade of the Lomas Ṛṣi Cave. (From *JBORS*. xii, 1926, following p. 308.) 156

MAPS

I. Bhāratavarṣa, showing places mentioned in the text . *at end*

II. Part of Eastern Deccan, showing places connected with the Ājīvikas 187

FOREWORD

It is gratifying to write a Foreword to *History and Doctrines of the Ājīvikas* written by A.L. Basham. The book exhibits quite clearly the origin and development of the Ājīvikas sect in ancient India. In the sixth century B.C. in Magadha, three unorthodox sects developed almost in the same region. All these three sects were seeking satisfying explanations of the sacrifice and the Upaniṣadic gnosis. The doctrines of these three sects were propagated by Mahāvīra, Buddha and Gosāla. In course of time the doctrines of Mahāvīra and Buddha became famous and the doctrines of Gosāla past into the land of oblivion. Basham has restored this sect in his *The Ājīvikas*. At the time of Mahāvīra, the Ājīvikas were powerful and Mahāvīra had to encounter with the views of the Ājīvikas.

It is a fact worthnoting that the Ājīvika sect was very much alive till the Mauryan period and it was due to the patronage of Aśoka, it reached its zenith. After that the Ājīvikas community dwindled rapidly in Northern India and soon became long-extinct. In South India, it, however, survived for a long period, perhaps, untill the 14th century A.D.

Though A.W.F. Hoernley wrote an article on the Ājīvikas in the *Encyclopedia of Religion and Ethics* (Vol. I) edited by Hastings, and Rockhill in the *Life of Buddha*, Appendix II, R.G. Bhandarkar and K.P. Pathak in the Indian Antiquary, Vol. XL, 1912, Basham's contribution to the subject is the best till now.

Basham in his book *The Ājīvikas* has nicely delineated the history and the doctrines of the Ājīvikas and has restored quite authentically one of the vanished Indian religion. Every statement of Professor Basham is authenticated with lots of supporting documents culled from different fields of studies: literary, inscriptional, and even from the art pictures. A book like this has a perennial source of information.

It is quite in the fitness of things that this book is being reprinted again for the benefit of the scholars, so that this lost religion is kept alive from generation to generation.

SATYA RANJAN BANERJEE
Quondam Professor of Linguistics
Calcutta University

A FOREWORD

BY DR. L. D. BARNETT

Both in religious and in social life movements of extreme intensity are apt to engender opposite forces. This rule of human nature is strikingly exemplified by the development of religion in Ancient India. Here history began with the dominance of Vedism, a group of polytheistic cults autocratically engineered by the Brāhmaṇs, who vigorously claimed that the welfare and indeed the very existence of the world, including even the gods, depended upon the maintenance of their systems of sacrifice, which grew to immense size and complexity. Dissent from this crude creed first appeared in the Upaniṣads, in which a few liberal-minded Brāhmaṇs, perhaps supported by some of the military aristocracy, put forward speculations of an elementary monistic idealism, while leaving the edifice of Vedism intact for the use of the unenlightened. But a far greater peril to Brāhmaṇic ritualism arose about this time, and spread far and wide, affecting some few of the Brāhmaṇs themselves; for now the very foundations of Brāhmaṇic orthodoxy were uncompromisingly denied, and preachers of what they claimed to be new and true doctrine arose on many sides. This radical movement assumed many phases. In some circles, Brāhmaṇic and non-Brāhmaṇic, it appeared in the form of a coarse atheistic materialism associated with the name of Cārvāka. Elsewhere it took a less crude shape. Among the aristocratic clans of the North two noblemen came under its influence, and created great churches: they were Gautama Buddha, the founder of Buddhism, and Mahāvīra Vardhamāna, whom the Jains revere as their twenty-fourth Tīrthaṅkara. But besides these and some other less successful leaders of gentle birth there was a multitude of men of humble origin noisily preaching their heresies in various wise; and among these the Ājīvikas played a part of some importance, if not of great glory.

The history of this queer sect is reconstructed by Dr. Basham in the following pages with much skill and scholarly thoroughness. As he shows, their reputation has been somewhat unfairly blackened by the *odium theologicum* of their rivals, the Buddhists and the Jains ; and they deserve some credit for the obstinate consistency and intellectual honesty with which they clung to their doctrine of predestination, to the exclusion of all other principles. Logically, of course, one may ask how believers in that dismal creed can submit themselves voluntarily to self-torture and even to death in pursuance of it. But man is not a logical creature : he does not abstain from effort although he may believe the issue to be predetermined, as the example of Calvin and his Church shows.

For a long period, extending from early classical times to the middle of the Medieval period, our knowledge of Ājīvika history is a blank, for no records of those years have survived. Then the curtain rises again, and we find abundant documents in inscriptions of the Tamil and Kanarese areas and in a few works of southern literature. These show that in the intervening centuries the Ājīvikas had undergone changes such as are usual in the development of Indian religious bodies : the little congregation had hardened into a caste-community of considerable size, and the figure of its founder had assumed features of divinity. The story that is here narrated is indeed a highly interesting and instructive chapter in the vast record of Indian thought.

L. D. Barnett.

PREFACE TO THE SECOND EDITION

The original edition of *History and Doctrines of the Ājīvikas* is now nearly thirty years old, and for some years it has been out of print. In introducing this reprint I am acutely conscious of the long period which has elapsed since, as a lecturer at the School of Oriental and African Studies, London University, I completed the thesis on which the book is based. In that period many new texts have appeared in print, and much fresh work has been done on the age which saw the rise of the Ājīvikas; hence it may be that a completely new edition of this book is required. Unfortunately I have been so deeply involved in other fields of teaching and research that I cannot myself undertake such a task at present, and the demand for a reprinted edition grows, as interest in Indian religions and philosophy increases throughout the world. Thus I am compelled to allow the book to be published as it stands, without alteration.

I can, however, draw the reader's attention to significant reviews which put forward alternative interpretations and correct definite mistakes. These I list below :

Walther Schubring : *ZDMG*, civ. pp. 256-63. The late Professor Schubring, with his unparallelled knowledge of the Jaina sources, here discusses and elucidates several very knotty points.

Helen M. Johnson, *Journal of the American Oriental Society*, lxxv, (1954), pp. 63-65. Corrects several minor errors and makes valuable suggestions.

D. Maskell, *Philosophy* xxxii (1957), pp. 82-84. Makes valuable suggestions.

H. C. E. Zacharias, *Anthropos* xlviii, (1953), pp. 323-24. Severely (and perhaps justly) criticizes my anthropological approach, which is 'Victorian'.

The late Professor Jayatilleke in his *Early Buddhist Theory of Knowledge*, (London, Allen & Unwin, 1963), criticized certain of my interpretations rather forcibly. I am quite unconcerned and unrepentant, but the reader should be aware of these criticisms.

One of the most serious attacks on my interpretation was made by Dr. B. Sitaraman ("Asuvika and Ājīvikas", ed. S.Ritti and B. R. Gopal, *Studies in Indian History and Culture* (*Prof. P. B. Desai Felicitation Volume*) Dharwar, 1971, pp. 483-87). Dr. Sitaraman maintains that the *Ācuvi-kācu* (or similar formula) of the South Indian inscriptions was not a tax on Ājīvikas. This suggestion is not new, and is contraverted by considerable evidence, which I have dealt with on pp. 191 ff. below.

It is unfortunate that I am unable at this stage to provide a detailed examination of all these and other criticisms. Perhaps one day I shall be able to produce a completely new edition of this book, introducing new data and with many paragraphs rewritten. Meanwhile I can but hope that this reprint will be of some use to younger scholars throughout the world, wherever the history of Indian religious life is studied.

As an explanation of my methods I cannot do better than quote from the preface to the first edition :

"In this study I have attempted, by a further examination of the better known sources, and by the use of material derived from sources hitherto untapped in this connection, to provide a more detailed and thorough study of Ājīvikism than has existed hitherto.

"While I may claim to have added something to the work of Hoernle, Barua, and the other authorities, the account presented in this work, based mainly on the passing references of the Ājīvikas' religious opponents, is inevitably fragmentary, and not always definite. To the lacunae in our knowledge must be added many uncertainties arising from contradictions in the sources themselves and from the imponderable but very real effect upon their authors of *odium theologicum*, which is usually clearly apparent, and which must often have led to exaggerations, and perhaps to deliberately false statements. This being the case I have frequently been compelled to state my conclusions in hypothetical or provisional terms. The reader is asked to forgive the many occasions on which such irritating words and phrases as "probably", "possibly", "perhaps", "it may be that", or "we may tentatively conclude", etc., occur in the text. Such provisional conclusions are inevitable in the study of a subject such as this, and most Indologists would agree that they are better than no conclusions at all, or than categorical

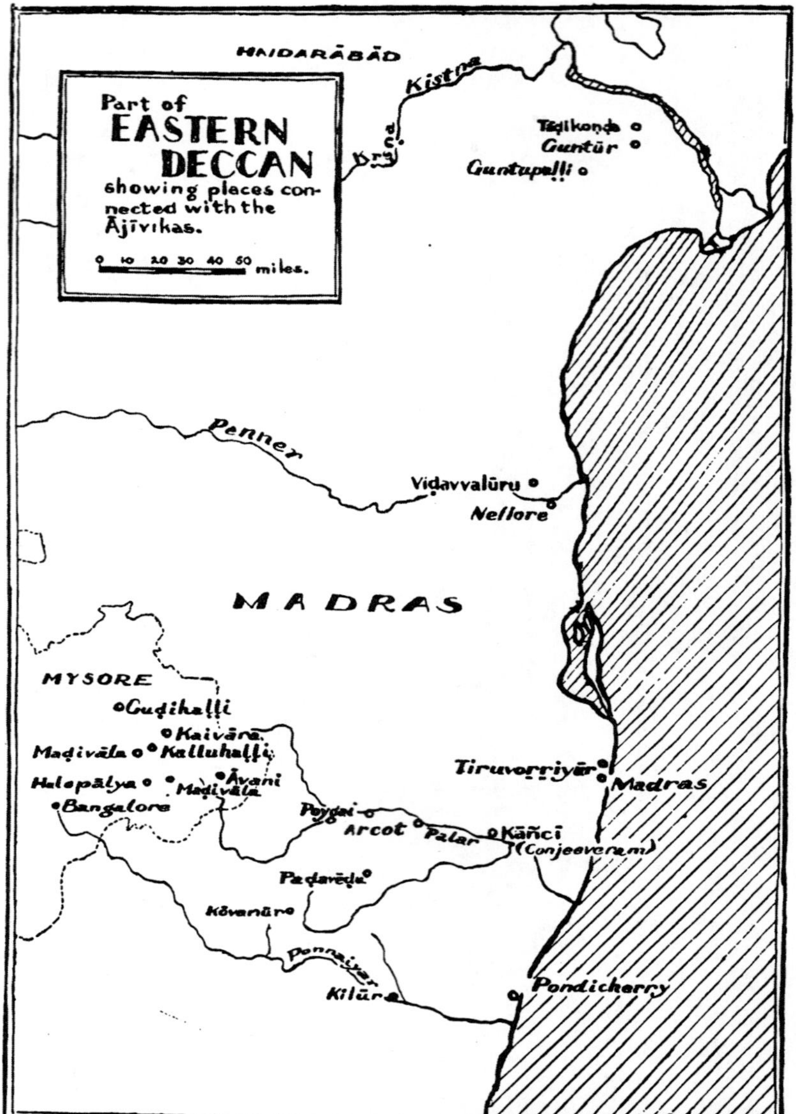
Part of
EASTERN
DECCAN
showing places connected with the Ājīvikas.
0 10 20 30 40 50 miles.
HAIDARĀBĀD
Kistna
Tāḍikoṇḍa
Guntūr
Guntupalli
Penner
Viḍavvalūru
Nellore
MADRAS
MYSORE
Guḍihalli
Kaivāra
Maḍivāla
Kalluhalli
Halepālya
Āvani
Maḍivāla
Bangalore
Poygai
Arcot
Palar
Kāñci
(Conjeeveram)
Tiruvorriyūr
Madras
Paḍavēḍu
Kōvanūr
Ponnaiyar
Kilūr
Pondicherry

[*facing p.* 187

assertions based on inadequate evidence. Although in this and in other respects my picture of the rise, development, and decline of the Ājīvika sect is still lamentably defective, I trust that my work will throw a little new light on an interesting and significant aspect of India's past, and will encourage further research.

"I must ask the reader's indulgence for certain very speculative paragraphs which have found their way into the final chapter. It is not for the research worker to usurp the privileges of the philosopher and theorize at length on the pattern of history. Nevertheless every facet of the world's history must stand in some relationship to every other and to the whole, and it seems to me to be legitimate, in a study of this character, that an effort should be made to establish such a relationship. Since history is not an exact science, any such attempt must inevitably be to some extent speculative. In the main body of my work I have attempted to keep firmly to my subject, and the digressions which from time to time occur, on such subjects as the age of a source, or the location of a town, should be found to have a significant bearing upon the main theme, or to be necessary for the full appreciation of its background. But, with the natural exuberance which arises with the knowledge of a long task nearing completion, I have allowed myself more latitude in the final chapter. The more speculative parts of that chapter, together with some passages of the introduction, I offer to the reader in the hope that they may stimulate him to further thought on the relation of religion and philosophy to sociology and politics.

"The more important passages from the sources have been translated or paraphrased in the course of the work. I have here and there allowed myself considerable liberty in translation, mainly with a view to rendering the passages in readable English, rather than in the Sanskritized style of a close translation. For the reader who wishes to refer to them I have included in footnotes the romanized originals of the most important phrases of these passages, whether Sanskrit, Pāli, Prākrit, or Tamil. I have usually broken up the longer compounds with hyphens, and as far as possible have simplified the junction of words by the use of the apostrophe to mark a dropped vowel or one which has coalesced with that following, and of the circumflex accent to mark vowels long by *sandhi*. Except in this particular the system employed for the Sanskrit passages is orthodox. In those Pāli texts wherein ŋ is used for *anusvāra* this sign has been regularly replaced by ṃ; otherwise the transliteration of Pāli passages is that of the Pāli Text Society. In all transliterations, *anusvāra*, when occurring within the word before any of the twenty-five *sparśa* consonants, has usually been expressed by the appropriate nasal letter; this, though it may offend some linguistic purists, is a common practice with modern Indian vernaculars, and avoids such ugly combinations as *Maṃkhali*, *aṃta*, etc. In Tamil transliterations I have used the rule-of-thumb system of the Madras University Tamil Lexicon. This has normally been adhered to even in the case of Sanskrit words occurring in Tamil, and in the Sanskrit titles of Tamil works, wherever *grantha* characters are not used in the texts to express them—thus *Civañānacittiyār* appears in the place of the more usual hybrid form *Śivajñāna-siddhiyār*. Occasional inconsistencies in these systems of transliteration, if found, are unintentional.

"In the hope that this work may be of some interest to students of religion and philosophy who have no special knowledge of Ancient India, I have included in the index a few brief definitions of less familiar Indian terms used in the text."

Of the scholars included in the acknowledgements of help in the first edition, five of the most important—Dr. L... D. Barnett, who supervised the original thesis, Mr. M. S. H. Thompson, who painstakingly guided me through the very difficult Tamil literary sources, Mr. C. A. Rylands and Dr. W. Stede, who taught me Sanskrit and Pāli respectively, and Professor V. R. R. Dikshitar, who was instrumental in obtaining copies of South Indian Inscriptions, are, to my knowledge, dead. I remember them still, and also those still living who helped me, with affection and respect. I think particularly, in writing this preface, of my supervisor, Dr. L. D. Barnett. He was already in his 80s when this thesis was completed, but was still as intellectually alert as ever. This was the last thesis to be completed of the many that he supervised.

Perhaps the most important contribution that I have made to scholarship is indirect, in the work of the hundred or so research students whom I have supervised, wholly or partially, since completing my own thesis. Many of their theses have been published, and are known wherever Indian history is studied, and many of my former students are now themselves widely recognized for their scholarship. For my success in helping so many young scholars I have nobody to thank but those young scholars themselves and Lionel David Barnett. It was his unfailing and evident interest in his students' progress, his willingness to spend time and trouble on them, his special care for the needs of his Indian students, writing in a language which was not their own, his careful checking of his students' note-making and writing methods, which set the example which I have tried to follow. I hardly knew him personally. He never invited me to his home, and I never invited him to mine. At our weekly meetings we rarely discussed anything except the work in hand. Yet I felt that this old man genuinely cared for me, as I genuinely cared for him, and that if I were in serious trouble he would unfailingly do his best to help me. There were times when the problems involved in my research seemed too much for me, and I was inclined to give up in despair. My weekly meeting with Dr. Barnett invariably restored my confidence. He had an aura about him; a sincerity and repose emanated from him, which gave unfailing encouragement, a kind of psychological help as well as practical help in historical method and interpretation. I record this in order that this reprint of my book may help to keep alive the memory of a truly great man, to whom I, and many others with me, owe an incalculable debt.

In connexion with this Indian edition, I have to thank Mr. S. L. Jain of Messrs Motilal Banarsidass, Delhi, for his initiative and enterprise, and also for his patience; and Messrs Luzac & Co., London, and the School of Oriental and African Studies, London University, owners of the copyright of the first edition, for permitting the publication of this reprint.

A. L. BASHAM

Canberra, 1980

ABBREVIATIONS

Abh. Rāj.	*Abhidhāna Rājendra.*
ABORI.	*Annals of the Bhandarkar Oriental Research Institute*, Poona.
Aṅg.	*Aṅguttara Nikāya.*
AR.	*Annual Report on South Indian Epigraphy.*
ASI.	Archæological Survey of India.
Bh. Sū.	*Bhagavatī Sūtra.*
BSOAS.	*Bulletin of the School of Oriental and African Studies.*
CHI.	*Cambridge History of India.*
CÑC.	*Civañāṉa-cittiyār Parapakṣam.*
Comm.	Commentary.
Dhp. Comm.	Buddhaghosa's *Dhammapad'-aṭṭha-kathā.*
Dīgha.	*Dīgha Nikāya.*
DPPN.	Malalasekera, *Dictionary of Pāli Proper Names.*
Ed.	Edited by.
Edn.	Edition.
Epi. Ind.	*Epigraphia Indica.*
ERE.	*Encyclopædia of Religion and Ethics.*
IA.	*Indian Antiquary.*
IHQ.	*Indian Historical Quarterly.*
IS.	Weber's *Indische Studien.*
JA.	*Journal Asiatique.*
Jāt.	*Jātaka.*
JBORS.	*Journal of the Bihar and Orissa Research Society.*
JDL.	*Journal of the Department of Letters*, Calcutta University.
JRAS.	*Journal of the Royal Asiatic Society.*
Majjh.	*Majjhima Nikāya.*
Maṇi.	*Maṇimēkalai.*

Mbh.	*Mahābhārata.*
Nīl.	*Nīlakēci.*
PHAI.	Raychaudhuri, *Political History of Ancient India*, 4th edn.
PTS.	Pāli Text Society.
Saṃ.	*Saṃyutta Nikāya.*
SBE.	*Sacred Books of the East.*
SII.	*South Indian Inscriptions.*
Sū.	*Sūtra.*
Sū. kṛ.	*Sūtrakṛtâṅga.*
Sum. Vil.	*Sumaṅgala Vilāsinī*, Buddhaghosa's comm. to the *Dīgha.*
Therīg.	*Therīgāthā.*
Tr.	Translated by.
Uv. Das.	*Uvāsaga Dasāo.*
Vin.	*Vinaya Piṭaka.*

PART ONE

HISTORY OF THE ĀJĪVIKAS

CHAPTER I

INTRODUCTION

The Historical Background to the Rise of Ājīvikism

The range of philosophical speculation in Ancient India went beyond the bounds laid down by Hinduism in its various branches, and even beyond those fixed by the great heterodox sects of Buddhism and Jainism. The presence of fully materialist groups, Cārvākas or Lokāyatas, which denied the existence of the soul, the gods, and the future life, is very well known. Besides these, however, were other sects which, while not denying human immortality or the existence of the gods, would not accept any of the more popular interpretations of these doctrines, but preferred explanations which were not consistent with Hinduism, Buddhism, or Jainism. That teachers of such heretical doctrines were the contemporaries of the Buddha is proved by the *Sāmañña-phala Sutta*, the starting point of our researches. It is clear that several such teachers gathered groups of followers together and founded *saṅghas*, perhaps in some cases loosely linked one with another; and from some of these developed Ājīvikism, the subject of our present study, which survived the death of its founder for nearly two thousand years, and was, at least locally, a significant factor in ancient Indian religious life.

Ājīvikism was, in fact, a third heretical sect, beside those of Buddhism and Jainism, with both of which its relations seem to have been often far from cordial. The cardinal point of the doctrines of its founder, Makkhali Gosāla, was a belief in the all-embracing rule of the principle of order, *Niyati*, which ultimately controlled every action and all phenomena, and left no room for human volition, which was completely ineffectual. Thus Ājīvikism was founded on an unpromising basis of strict determinism, above which was developed a superstructure of complicated and fanciful cosmology, incorporating an atomic theory which was perhaps the earliest in India, if not in the world. The ethics of the sect were often said by its opponents to be antinomian, but it is certain that, whatever their ethics, the Ājīvikas practised asceticism of a severe type which often terminated, like that of the Jainas, in death by starvation.

Ājīvika determinism emerged, together with the atomism with which it was later associated, in conditions of rising civilization in the Ganges valley, when political power was rapidly being consolidated. By the sixth century B.C. at least part of India had enjoyed some two thousand years of urban culture. The industrious and uninspiring civilization of the Indus cities, with its chthonic religion, had been replaced by the more barbaric culture of the Āryans, with a disorderly pantheon of celestial deities. The Āryans, no doubt heirs to the residuum of the Indus civilization, gradually expanded southwards and eastwards from the Panjāb. By the tenth century B.C., when they had occupied Kurukṣetra and the Doāb, the first steps in philosophical speculation had been taken, and sceptics were already asking whether it was possible to know the ultimate basis of the universe.[1] But at this period of small tribal kingdoms most of the mental energy of the best minds seems to have been devoted to a sterile effort at providing a satisfying symbolic interpretation of the elaborate and costly sacrificial rituals of the time.

Penetration down the Ganges probably proceeded slowly; but the records of the period have left little direct indication of the process of Āryan expansion, or of the culture of the people whom the Āryans met. It is not likely that that culture was at the lowest stages of barbarism. It must have been able to exert a counter-influence on the Āryan polytheism which was imposed upon it, for it is difficult otherwise to account for the emergence of the doctrine of transmigration and of mystical monism in the period of the Upaniṣads, which probably dates from the seventh century B.C.[2] By this time we find that Āryan influence had reached as far as Magadha and Videha, where reigned the great king Janaka, an enthusiastic patron of the hermits and wandering sophists who propagated the new ideas.[3] We cannot be certain

[1] *Ṛg Veda* x, 129, 7.
[2] Macdonnell, *History of Sanskrit Literature*, p. 226.
[3] *CHI.* i, pp. 122, 127.

that the earliest teachers of the Upaniṣadic doctrines were Āryan by blood. The theory of transmigration must have been developed from older animist theories very widespread among primitive peoples, and its first propagators may have been non-Āryans, stimulated by the invaders to develop their cruder ideas of metempsychosis by giving them an ethical basis in the form of *karma.*

In the time of the Buddha, which was also the time of Makkhali Gosāla, we find the territory of what is now Utta Pradesh and South Bihār occupied by two great kingdoms, Kosala and Magadha. Both were expanding, and had recently absorbed lesser states on their borders, Kāsī (the district of Benares) having fallen to Kosala,[1] and Aṅga (E. Bihār and N.-W. Bengal) to Magadha.[2] To the north of the two great kingdoms were small tribal oligarchies, precariously maintaining their existence against the greater states. The most famous of them, that of the Śākyas, was already tributary to Pasenadi or Prasenajit of Kosala, and was soon to be devastated by his son Viḍūḍabha[3]; while the largest of the so-called republics, the confederacy of the Vajjis, which seems to have superseded the kingdom of Janaka in Videha, was also soon to be conquered by Viḍūḍabha's contemporary, Ajātasattu, the son of king Bimbisāra of Magadha.[4]

The people of the time and region seem to have called themselves Āryans; Buddha knew the word well, and used it in the sense of "good" or "noble". But the non-Āryan element, both in culture and race, must still have been strong. It has even been suggested that the whole development of religion and philosophy in this period, from Upaniṣadic gnosis to complete materialism, was but a reflection of the non-Āryan reaction to the Āryan sacrificial system and to the rigid Āryan social order of the four *varṇas.*[5]

By this time a city civilization had developed in the Ganges valley, beside the immemorial culture of the villages; numerous towns, which must have existed at the time of the Buddha, are mentioned in the earliest Buddhist scriptures. A high standard of luxury was enjoyed by kings, nobles, and

[1] *PHAI.*, pp. 130–1.
[2] Ibid., p. 167.
[3] Ibid., pp. 162–3.
[4] Ibid., pp. 171–4. V. infra, pp. 69 ff.
[5] *CHI.* i, p. 144, and references in n. 1 of that page.

merchants, and many of the latter had amassed very large fortunes. Punch-marked coins were probably in use, and writing was known, but not widely used.

The three heterodox sects which arose in this cultural climate, Buddhism, Jainism, and Ājīvikism, had much in common. All three alike rejected the sacrificial polytheism of the Āryans and the monistic theories of the Upaniṣadic mystics. The personified natural forces of the former, and the world-soul of the latter were replaced by cosmic principles, and the supernatural powers were relegated to an inferior or even negligible position. In fact the three new religions represent a recognition of the rule of natural law in the universe, and the work of their founders may in this respect be compared with that of their approximate contemporaries, the natural philosophers of Ionia. Of the three systems that of the Ājīvikas, based on the principle of *Niyati* as the only determining factor in the uinverse, perhaps represents a more thorough recognition of the orderliness of nature than do the doctrines of either of its more successful rivals.

The religious reformer rarely devises the central tenets of his new faith without any basis of older belief on which to build; rather he restates, modifies, or throws a fresh light upon earlier teaching, and this restatement has for his contemporaries the force and novelty of a new revelation. We may feel confident that fatalist teachings, out of which the doctrine of *Niyati* developed, had existed before the time of Makkhali Gosāla, as indeed is indicated by various references in both Buddhist and Jaina texts.[1] A belief in fate, the inevitability of important events, or of events with dire consequences, seems to arise at an early stage of religious development in many cultures. Parallel with it arises the belief in the efficiency of magic, spells, sacrifice, and prayer, to circumvent the effects of fate.[2] Certain peoples, notably the earlier Semites, almost consistently rejected determinism and fatalism. Thus for the Babylonians " . . . the fates . . . were not believed to have been fixed from the beginning, but were pictured as in hourly process of development under the personal supervision of the supreme deity ".[3] Similarly

[1] V. infra, pp. 27 ff.
[2] V. *ERE*. v, p. 772 s.v. Fate.
[3] *ERE*. v, p. 779.

Hebrew monotheism, while based firmly on the almightiness of God, asserted, implicitly and explicitly, the power of the individual to affect his own destiny by pursuing courses of conduct pleasing to the Almighty. The early development of astrology in the Middle East does not seem to have led to the logical conclusion that the fortune of the individual, if predictable and correlated to the regular movements of the stars, must be rigidly determined.

On the other hand the Indo-European peoples may have entertained a belief in an inevitable destiny at a very early period. Admittedly the hymns of the *Ṛg Veda* do not suggest a fatalistic attitude to life. One's destiny is influenced by propitiating the gods, who are the arbiters of human fortune, and can be induced to show favour, or to relent in their anger. This seems to have been the general priestly theory of all the Indo-European peoples in the earlier stages of their development. But there is evidence of another line of thought. Though a wholly fatalist attitude may not be found in the religious tradition, as depicted for instance in the *Ṛg Veda,* such an attitude does appear in the martial tradition of the epics. Widespread in Indo-European epic literature is the hero who, well knowing that he and his comrades are fated to defeat and death, goes boldly into battle because it is " the thing to do ", the right and natural conduct of the warrior. As examples of this doomed warrior we may cite Karṇa in the *Mahābhārata,*[1] both Hector and Achilles in the *Iliad,*[2] Hagen in the *Nibelungenlied,*[3] and Ferdiad in the Cuchullain Saga.[4] No doubt other examples may be found. From its widespread occurrence it seems probable that this grim tradition of the doomed hero was known to the Indo-European peoples before their separation, and we may infer that it existed in India long before the final recension of the

[1] *Mbh. Udyoga,* 141–3.

[2] *Iliad* vi, 447–9, 486–9 (Hector); xix, 420–3 (Achilles).

[3] *Nibelungenlied,* ed K. Bartsch, xxvi, 1587–9.

[4] *Táin Bó Cúalnge,* ed. E. Windisch, pp. 456–7, v. 8. Although before and during his protracted duel with Cuchullain Ferdiad blusters and threatens, these are the conventional boasts of the warrior, and he recognizes his fate at the last (pp. 526–9). The whole of the *Táin,* from the words of Fedelm the prophetess (pp. 26–39), to the death of the wonderful bull, which had been the bone of contention between the opposing parties, is permeated with epic fatalism. Even in the last sentence of the story we read: " So war seine Geschichte und seine Schicksal " (*Deired*) (pp. 908–9).

Mahābhārata. May it have had any influence on the development of Ājīvika fatalism? In eastern India at the time of Makkhali Gosāla were *vrātyas*, bands of nomadic Āryans who had fallen away from the priestly religion, and might be received back into the Āryan fold only after purification ceremonies.[1] Their chief centre was Magadha, a kingdom which Makkhali Gosāla visited in the course of his wanderings with Mahāvīra before his "enlightenment".[2] At that time Magadhans were famous as bards,[3] and sang the martial songs out of which the epic tradition grew at the courts of chieftains all over Āryāvarta. Makkhali Gosāla, before his association with Mahāvīra, was, according to the Jaina story, a *maṅkha*; this word is equated by Hemacandra with *māgadha*, a bard.[4] Thus a very slender chain of relations connects the founder of Ājīvikism with the Āryan fatalist tradition, and his determinism may in part have been inspired by ideas derived from the renegade Āryan singers of martial songs.

But the Ājīvika doctrine of *Niyati* may also have had a non-Āryan ancestry. Admittedly rigid determinism is not natural to the thought of most Indian religions; according to the usual form of the *karma* theory a man's present state is determined by his past conduct, whether in this life or a previous one, but he has a sufficient measure of free will to permit him to modify his future by choosing the right course of action. Yet the climate and geography of India are such as to encourage a fatalist attitude to life. The phenomena of nature are impressive in their grandeur and regularity. Natural catastrophes such as flood, drought, and famine occur from time to time on such a scale that no human effort, even at the present day, can prevent them, or do more than mitigate their effects. In the time of Makkhali

[1] *CHI*. i, 146. If we accept the theory of J. W. Hauer (*Der Vrātya*, Stuttgart, 1927) that the *vrātyas* were a class of heterodox nomadic holy-men, whose religious practices included sympathetic magic, exorcism, ritual dancing, and cursing their opponents, it may be suggested that they had some influence upon the Ājīvikas. The latter were also given to religious dancing and singing, and their leader had the reputation of a wonder worker whose ready imprecations were most effective in their operation. Hauer himself has compared the unstrung bow of the *vrātya* with the *daṇḍa* or staff of the orthodox ascetic of later times (op. cit., p. 132). The Ājīvikas also appear to have carried staves (v. infra, p. 99).

[2] V. infra, pp. 39 ff.

[3] *PHAI*., p. 96.

[4] V. infra, pp. 33–36.

Gosāla the dependence of man upon nature must have been felt by the Indian even more strongly than at present. The slogan of the Ājīvika sect, " Human effort is ineffectual," [1] may have been a very widespread and popular phrase, in time of distress often on the lips of the ordinary people of the Ganges valley. It is the typical cry of the peasant everywhere, when his crops are ruined by storm or drought, or when his livestock dies of pestilence. Significant in this connection is the *Mahābhārata* story of Maṅki, who, it is said, became a fatalist after the accidental loss of two steers.[2]

Here then we have two possible sources of the Ājīvika creed, which must have provided gloomy and despairing comfort both to the warrior fighting a losing battle and to the peasant impoverished by the failure of his crops or herds. Probably both elements, as well as the personal genius of Makkhali Gosāla and of others, contributed to the finished Ājīvika doctrine, which for two millennia filled a small place in the religious life of India, and attempted to provide, however inadequately, for the spiritual needs of a small fraction of her people.

[1] *N'atthi purisakāre.* V. infra, p. 14.
[2] V. infra, pp. 38-39.

CHAPTER II

THE SIX HERETICS

The Record of the *Sāmañña-phala Sutta*

Throughout the Pāli canon the teaching of the Buddha and the activities and discipline of his Order are contrasted with the doctrines and practices of six other teachers and their followers, who are represented as the Buddha's contemporaries, and were doubtless, like the Buddha himself, inspired by the wave of dissatisfaction with the system of orthodox Brāhmaṇism, which seems to have swept over the Ganges valley in the sixth and fifth centuries B.C.

The six heretics, as portrayed in the Pāli texts, have little individuality. Occasional brief references to an individual teacher may be found, but they are usually referred to as a group.[1] Their character as real human beings is often very tenuous; for instance in the *Milinda Pañha* they are represented as still surviving centuries after the Buddha's death,[2] and have become mere lay figures, representative of non-Buddhist heterodoxy. Their teachings are often confused, and the doctrines attributed in a given reference to any one teacher may elsewhere be ascribed to another. Much of the information about the six that is contained in the Buddhist texts, like the references to Gosāla in those of the Jainas, is to be treated very cautiously; for it is evident that the authors had but a limited knowledge of the teachings of the heretics, and what knowledge they had was warped by *odium theologicum*. Nevertheless these Buddhist and Jaina texts are the only source of our knowledge of the origin of the Ājīvikas, and must be the starting point for any study of the sect.

In the Pāli scriptures the lengthiest and most detailed passage on these men and their doctrines is contained in the *Sāmañña-*

[1] E.g. *Majjh.* i, 198, 250; *Saṃ.* i, 66; *Jāt.* i, 509, iv, 398 ff.; *Vin.* ii, 111 ff.
[2] pp. 4 ff. V. infra, p. 21.

phala Sutta of the *Dīgha Nikāya*.[1] The philosophies there ascribed to them contain much that was included in later Ājīvika teaching, and the passage in which the heretical ascetic Makkhali Gosāla propounds his determinist view of the universe [2] has been taken by both Hoernle and Barua as a basis for their studies on the Ājīvikas. The philosophical implications of the *Sutta* will be considered in the second part of this work [3]; meanwhile it merits careful consideration from the historical viewpoint.

The narrative framework of the *Sāmañña-phala Sutta* may be summarized as follows :—

While the Buddha, accompanied by 1,250 *bhikkhus*, was staying at Rājagaha, then the Magadhan capital, King Ajātasattu felt in need of spiritual guidance. One after another six of his ministers came forward, each suggesting one of the six heretical teachers as a person capable of resolving the King's doubts. The names of the six were :—

1. Pūraṇa Kassapa,
2. Makkhali Gosāla,
3. Ajita Kesakambalī,
4. Pakudha Kaccāyana,
5. Sañjaya Belatthiputta, and
6. Nigaṇṭha Nātaputta.

Each is described in the same stock terms, a formula applied elsewhere to the six heretics in the Pāli canon.[4] The phrases have a certain importance since they at least indicate the celebrity and influence which the early Buddhist tradition attributed to the six teachers. Each is referred to as the leader of an order (*gaṇâcariyo*), well known, famous, the founder of a sect (*titthakāro*), respected as a saint (*sādhu-sammato*), revered by many people, a homeless wanderer of long standing (*cira-pabbajito*), and advanced in years.

Each minister urged the King to visit one or other of the ascetics, who would set his mind at rest, but at each suggestion the King remained silent. Finally Jīvaka, the "children's doctor" (*komārabhacco*), suggested a visit to the Buddha. The suggestion was acceptable to Ajātasattu, who left for Jīvaka's mango grove, where the Master was staying with his followers.

[1] *Dīgha* i, pp. 47 ff.
[2] V. infra, pp. 13-14.
[3] V. infra, pp. 224 ff, 240 ff.
[4] E.g. *Jāt.* i, 509 ; *Dīgha* ii, 150.

On his arrival he asked the Buddha to answer the question which had been troubling him: "The fruits of various worldly trades and professions are obvious, but it is possible to show any appreciable benefit to be derived from asceticism? (*sandiṭṭhikaṃ sāmañña-phalaṃ*)." He declared that he had previously put the same question to other ascetics and brāhmaṇas, but had so far received no satisfactory answer. At the Buddha's request he repeated the replies given to his inquiry by the six heretics. None of them had tried to give a logical answer to the King's question, but each had prevaricated, repeating what seems to be the set formula of the school which he had founded. After hearing Ajātasattu's account of his interviews with the six heretics the Buddha preached a sermon on the advantages of the homeless life, and the King was duly consoled and impressed.

From this, and from many other passages in the Pāli canon, it is quite clear that Buddhism in its early stages had to contend not only with the orthodox brāhmaṇas and with the adherents of the twenty-fourth *tīrthaṅkara* of Jainism, who is the sixth teacher of the above list, but also with the followers of several other religious leaders. The six heretics must have been the most important members of a class which contained many lesser men, with smaller more localized followings, whose names and doctrines have now completely vanished. There is no need to accept the view which, both implicitly and explicitly, is to be found expressed in Dr. B. M. Barua's *Pre-Buddhistic Indian Philosophy*, that these men were philosophers or theologians in a modern sense. Rather it seems probable that in the sixth century B.C. the mental life of India was in ferment, and was permeated by a mass of mutually contradictory theories about the universe and man's place therein, some verging on the bizarre in their fancifulness, others more capable of a logical justification. The chief mouthpieces of the new ideas were Buddha and Mahāvīra, but many others, including the six heretics, must have made some contribution to the thought of their time.

While the three unorthodox systems of Buddhism, Jainism, and Ājīvikism crystallized round the names of Buddha, Mahāvīra, and Makkhali Gosāla respectively, it seems, in the case of the latter sect at any rate, that other teachers beside the reputed founder contributed to the finished doctrinal system. This will be made clear by a study of the doctrines attributed to the six teachers in various parts of the Pāli canon. To commence with our *locus classicus*, the teachings of the six, as narrated by Ajātasattu to the Buddha in the *Sāmañña-phala Sutta*, may be paraphrased as follows :—

1. *Pūraṇa Kassapa*

" He who performs an act or causes an act to be performed . . . he who destroys life, the thief, the housebreaker, the plunderer . . . the highway robber, the adulterer and the liar . . . commit no sin. Even if with a razor-sharp discus a man reduce all the life on earth to a single heap of flesh, he commits no sin . . . . If he come down the south bank of the Ganges, slaying, maiming, and torturing, and causing others to be slain, maimed, or tortured, he commits no sin, neither does sin approach him. Likewise if a man go down the north bank of the Ganges, giving alms and sacrificing, and causing alms to be given and sacrifices to be performed, he acquires no merit, neither does merit approach him. From liberality, self-control, abstinence, and honesty is derived neither merit, nor the approach of merit." [1]

2. *Makkhali Gosāla*

There is neither cause nor basis for the sins of living beings ; they become sinful without cause or basis. Neither is there cause or basis for the purity of living beings ; they become pure without cause or basis. There is no deed performed either by oneself or by others (which can affect one's future births), no human action, no strength, no courage, no human endurance or human prowess (which can affect one's destiny in this life).[2] All beings,

[1] *Karato kho kārayato . . . pāṇaṃ atimāpayato, adinnaṃ ādiyato, sandhiṃ chindato, nillopaṃ harato . . . paripanthe tiṭṭhato, paradāraṃ gacchato, musā bhaṇato karoto na karīyati pāpaṃ. Khura-pariyantena ce pi cakkena yo imissā paṭhaviyā pāṇe . . . eka-maṃsa-puñjaṃ kareyya, n'atthi tato-nidānaṃ pāpaṃ, n'atthi pāpassa āgamo. Dakkhinañ ce pi Gaṅgā-tīraṃ āgaccheyya hananto ghātento chindanto chedāpento pācanto pācento, n'atthi tato-nidānaṃ pāpaṃ, n'atthi pāpassa āgamo. Uttarañ ce pi Gaṅgā-tīraṃ gaccheyya dadanto dāpento yajanto yajāpento n'atthi tato-nidānaṃ puññaṃ, n'atthi puññassa āgamo. Dānena damena saṃyamena sacca-vajjena n'atthi puññaṃ, n'atthi puññassa āgamo.* Op. cit., p. 52.

[2] This paraphrase is expanded on the basis of Buddhaghosa's commentary, *Sumaṅgala Vilāsinī* : *A t t a k ā r e ti atta-kāro. Yena attanā kata-kammena ime sattā devattam . . . pi pāpuṇanti, tam pi paṭikkhipati. . . . N'atthi p u r i s a - k ā r e ti yena purisa-kāreṇa sattā vuttappakāra-sampattiyo pāpuṇanti, tam pi paṭikkhipati. Sum. Vil.* i, pp. 160–1.

all that have breath, all that are born, all that have life, are without power, strength, or virtue, but are developed by destiny, chance, and nature, and experience joy and sorrow in the six classes (of existence).

There are 1,400,000 chief uterine births, 6,000 and 600 ; 500 *karmas*, 5 *karmas*, 3 *karmas*, a *karma*, and half a *karma* ; 62 paths ; 62 lesser *kalpas* ; 6 classes (of human existence) ; 8 stages of man ; 4,900 means of livelihood (?) ; 4,900 ascetics ; 4,900 dwellings of *nāgas* ; 2,000 faculties ; 3,000 purgatories ; 36 places covered with dust (?) [1] ; 7 sentient births ; 7 insentient births ; 7 births from knots (?) [1] ; 7 gods ; 7 men ; 7 *pisāca* (births ?) ; 7 lakes ; 7 knots (?),[1] and 700 ; 7 precipices, and 700 ; 7 dreams, and 700 ; and 8,400,000 great *kalpas* through which fool and wise alike will take their course, and make an end of sorrow. There is no question of bringing unripe *karma* to fruition, nor of exhausting *karma* already ripened, by virtuous conduct, by vows, by penance, or by chastity. That cannot be done.[2] *Saṃsāra* is measured as with a bushel, with its joy and sorrow and its appointed end. It can neither be lessened nor increased, nor is there any excess or deficiency of it. Just as a ball of thread will, when thrown, unwind to its full length, so fool and wise alike will take their course, and make an end of sorrow.[3]

[1] These and several other cruxes in Makkhali's catalogue are provisionally rendered in the light of Buddhaghosa's commentary (*Sum. Vil.* i, pp. 163–4). For a fuller consideration of them v. infra, pp. 240 ff.

[2] Here I have taken the liberty of inserting a full stop which does not occur in the PTS. edition of the text. If we read *H'evaṃ n'atthi* with *doṇa-mite* we have a definite contradiction of Makkhali's doctrine as expressed elsewhere. Buddhaghosa agrees in associating the phrase with the preceding sentence : *H ' e v a ṃ n ' a t t h ī ti evan n' atthi taṃ hi ubhayaṃ pi na sakkā kātun ti dīpeti. Sum. Vil.* i, p. 164.

[3] *N'atthi . . . hetu, n'atthi paccayo sattānaṃ saṃkilesāya, ahetu-appaccayā sattā saṃkilissanti. N'atthi hetu, n'atthi paccayo sattānaṃ visuddhiyā, ahetu-apaccayā sattā visujjhanti. N'atthi atta-kāre, n'atthi para-kāre, n'atthi purisa-kāre, n'atthi balaṃ, n'atthi viriyaṃ, n'atthi purisa-thāmo, n'atthi purisa-parakkamo. Sabbe sattā, sabbe pāṇā, sabbe bhūtā, sabbe jīvā, avasā abalā aviriyā niyati-saṅgati-bhāva-pariṇatā chass' ev' âbhijātisu sukha-dukkhaṃ paṭisaṃvedenti.*

Cuddasa kho pan' imāni yoni-pamukha-sata-sahassāni, saṭṭhiñ ca satāni, cha ca satāni ; pañca ca kammuno satāni, pañca ca kammāni, tīṇi ca kammāni, kamme ca, aḍḍhı-kamme ca ; dvaṭṭhi paṭipadā ; dvaṭṭh' antarakappā ; chaḷ âbhijātiyo ; aṭṭha purisa-bhūmiyo ; ekūna-paññāsa ājīva-sate ; ekūna-paññāsa paribbājaka-sate ; ekūna-paññāsa nāgâvāsa-sate ; vise indriya-sate ; tiṃse niriya-sate ; chattiṃsa rajo-dhātuyo ; satta saññi-gabbhā ; satta asaññi-gabbhā ; sattā nigaṇṭhi-gabbhā ; satta devā ; satta mānusā ; satta pesācā ; satta sarā ; satta paṭuvā, satta paṭuvā-satāni ; satta papātā, satta papāta-satāni ; satta supinā, satta supina-satāni ; cull-âsiti mahākappuno sata-sahassāni, yāni bāle

3. *Ajita Kesakambalī*

There is no (merit in) almsgiving sacrifice or offering, no result or ripening of good or evil deeds. There is no passing from this world to the next.[1] No benefit accrues from the service of mother or father.[2] There is no after-life, and there are no ascetics or brāhmaṇas who have reached perfection on the right path, and who, having known and experienced this world and the world beyond, publish (their knowledge). Man is formed of the four elements; when he dies earth returns to the aggregate of earth, water to water, fire to fire, and air to air, while the senses vanish into space. Four men with the bier take up the corpse; they gossip (about the dead man) as far as the burning-ground,[3] (where) his bones turn the colour of a dove's wing, and his sacrifices end in ashes. They are fools who preach almsgiving, and those who maintain the existence (of immaterial categories) speak vain and lying nonsense. When the body dies both fool and wise alike are cut off and perish. They do not survive after death.[4]

ca paṇḍite ca sandhāvitvā saṃsaritvā dukkhass' antaṃ karissanti. Tattha n'atthi: "imin' âhaṃ sīlena vā vatena vā tapena vā brahmacariyeṇa vā aparipakkaṃ vā kammaṃ paripācessāmi, paripakkaṃ vā kammaṃ phussa-phussa vyanti-karissāmî" ti. H'evaṃ n'atthi. Doṇa-mite sukha-dukkhe pariyanta-kaṭe saṃsāre, n'atthi hāyana-vaḍḍhane, n'atthi ukkaṃs'-âvakaṃse. Seyyathā pi nāma sutta-guḷe khitte nibbeṭhiyamānam eva phaleti, evam eva bāle ca paṇḍite ca sandhāvitvā saṃsaritvā dukkhass' antaṃ karissanti. Dīgha i, pp. 53–4.

[1] This paraphrase on the basis of Buddhaghosa: *N'atthi ayaṃ loko ti para-loke ṭhitassa pi ayaṃ loko n'atthi. N'atthi para-loko ti idha loke ṭhitassa pi para-loko n'atthi. Sabbe tattha tatth' eva ucchijantî ti dasseti* (*Sum. Vil.* i, p. 165). Buddhaghosa seems to imply that Ajita admitted the existence of a world beyond, but one which it was impossible for mortals to enter; certainly he did not deny the existence of the material world.

[2] Again an expansion of the text, based on Buddhaghosa: *N'atthi mātā n'atthi pitā ti tesu sammā-paṭipattim icchā-paṭipattim phal'-âbhāva-vasena vadati. Sum. Vil.* i, p. 165.

[3] Accepting Buddhaghosa: *Padān' îti, "ayam evaṃ sīlavā ahosi, evaṃ dussīlo" ti, ādinā nayena pavattāni guṇâguṇa-padāni. Sum. Vil.* i, p. 166. Chalmers translates tho same passage as it occurs in *Majjh.* i, p. 515, as "whose remains are visible as far as the charnel ground" (*Further Dialogues* i, p. 364).

[4] *N'atthi . . . dinnaṃ, n'atthi yiṭṭhaṃ, n'atthi hutaṃ, n'atthi sukaṭa-dukkaṭā-naṃ kammānaṃ phalaṃ vipāko, n'atthi ayaṃ loko, n'atthi paro loko, n'atthi mātā, n'atthi pitā, n'atthi sattā-opapātikā, n'atthi loke samaṇa-brāhmaṇā sam-maggatā sammā-paṭippannā, ye imañ ca lokaṃ parañ ca lokaṃ sayaṃ abhiññā sacchikatvā pavedenti. Cātum-mahābhūtiko ayaṃ puriso; yadā kālaṃ karoti paṭhavī paṭhavi-kāyaṃ anupeti anupagacchati, āpo āpo-kāyaṃ . . ., tejo tejo-kāyaṃ . . ., vāyo vāyo-kāyaṃ anupeti anupagacchati, ākāsaṃ indriyāni saṃka-manti. Āsandi-pañcamā purisā mataṃ ādāya gacchanti, yāva āḷāhanā padāni pañ-ñāpenti, kāpotakāni aṭṭhīni bhavanti, bhass-ant' âhutiyo. Dattu-paññattaṃ yad idaṃ dānaṃ, tesaṃ tucchaṃ musā vilāpo ye keci atthikavādaṃ vadanti. Bāle ca*

4. *Pakudha Kaccāyana*

The seven elementary categories are neither made nor ordered, neither caused nor constructed; they are barren, as firm as mountains, as stable as pillars. They neither move nor develop; they do not injure one another, and one has no effect on the joy, or on the sorrow, or on the joy and sorrow of another. What are the seven? The bodies of earth, of water, of fire, and of air, and joy and sorrow, with life as the seventh . . . . No man slays or causes to slay, hears or causes to hear, knows or causes to know. Even if a man cleave another's head with a sharp sword, he does not take life, for the sword-cut passes between the seven elements.[1]

5. *Nigaṇṭha Nātaputta*

A *nigaṇṭha* is surrounded by the barrier of fourfold restraint. How is he surrounded? . . . He practises restraint with regard to water, he avoids all sin, by avoiding sin his sins are washed away, and he is filled with the sense of all sins avoided.[2] . . . So surrounded by the barrier of fourfold restraint his mind is perfected,[3] controlled, and firm.[4]

6. *Sañjaya Belatthiputta*

If you asked me, "Is there another world?" and if I believed that there was, I should tell you so. But that is not what I say.

paṇḍite ca kāyassa bhedā ucchijjanti vinassanti, na honti param maraṇā. Dīgha i, p. 55. A remarkable parallel to this passage is to be found in *Sūtrakṛtâṅga* (*Sū. kṛ.* II, i, 9, fol. 275 ff., in *SBE.* xlv, II, i, 15–17).

[1] *Satt' ime . . . kāyā akaṭā akaṭa-vidhā animmitā animmātā vañjhā kūṭaṭṭhā esika-ṭṭhāyi-ṭṭhitā. Te na iñjanti na vipariṇamanti na aññam-aññam vyābādhenti n' âlam aññam-aññaesa sukhāya vā dukhāya vā sukha-dukkhāya vā. Katame satta? Paṭhavi-kāyo āpo-kāyo tejo-kāyo vāyo-kāyo sukhe dukkhe jīva-sattame . . . . Tattha n'atthi hantā vā ghātetā vā sotā vā sāvetā vā viññātā vā viññāpetā vā. Yo pi tiṇhena satthena sīsaṃ chindati na koci kiñci jīvitā voropeti, sattannaṃ yeva kāyānaṃ antareṇa sattha-vivaraṃ anupatati. Dīgha* i, p. 56. With this compare *Sū. kṛ.* II, i, 10, fol. 280 ff. (*SBE.* xlv, II, i, 20–4). Here a five-element theory is outlined in very similar terms.

[2] This doubtful interpretation on the basis of Buddhaghosa: *Sabba-vāri-yuto ti sabbena pāpa-vāraṇena yutto. Sabba-vāri-dhuto ti sabbena pāpa-vāraṇena dhuta-pāpo. Sabba-vāri-phuṭṭho ti sabbena pāpa-vāraṇena phuṭṭho. Sum. Vil.* i, p. 168.

[3] Buddhaghosa: *Gatatto ti koṭippatta-citto.* Op. cit., loc. cit.

[4] *. . . Nigaṇṭho cātu-yāma-saṃvara-saṃvuto hoti. Kathañ ca . . . saṃvuto hoti? . . . Nigaṇṭho sabba-vārī-vārito ca hoti, sabba-vārī-yuto ca, sabba-vārī-dhuto ca, sabba-vārī-phuṭṭho ca . . . . Yato . . . evam . . . saṃvuto hoti, ayam vuccati . . . nigaṇṭho gatatto ca yatatto ca ṭhitatto ca ti. Dīgha* i. p. 57.

I do not say that it is so; I do not say that it is otherwise; I do not say that it is not so; nor do I say that it is not not so [1]... (The same formula is repeated after various hypothetical questions.)

Of these six statements of doctrine three have little relevance to the study of the Ājīvikas. That which is here ascribed to Ajita Kesakambalī is a clear expression of materialism, and its author, whether Ajita or another, must have been a forerunner of the later Cārvākas. The teaching ascribed to Nigaṇṭha Nātaputta is very obscure, but, as Jacobi has pointed out,[2] while it is not an accurate description of the Jaina creed it contains nothing alien to it. We may accept the identification of Nigaṇṭha with Vardhamāna Mahāvīra, the twenty-fourth *tīrthaṅkara* of Jainism. The passage ascribed to Sañjaya Belatthiputta is probably satirical, a tilt at agnostic teachers who were unwilling to give a definite answer to any metaphysical question put to them. Dr. Barua holds another view, and believes that the statement of Sañjaya represents a doctrine which was held in good faith by a school of Pyrrhonists.[3] Whatever the authenticity of this passage, its agnosticism was never a part of the Ājīvika creed, and it may be omitted from further consideration.

We are left with the passages ascribed to Pūraṇa, Makkhali, and Pakudha. The doctrines of all three, and the names of two of these teachers are connected with later Ājīvikism. The authenticity of the ascription of *niyativāda* to Makkhali Gosāla may be confirmed by reference to the Jaina scriptures, wherein Gosāla Maṅkhaliputta propounds a very similar doctrine.[4] Pakudha's fantastic atomism and his Parmenidean doctrine of immobility, which follows logically from Makkhali's determinism, are integral parts of the teaching of the Dravidian Ājīvikas as described in Tamil texts.[5] Pūraṇa is mentioned by name and apparently held in high respect by these later Ājīvikas,[6] and his

[1] "*Atthi paro loko?*" *ti iti ce taṃ pucchasi,* "*atthi paro loko*" *ti iti ce me assa,* "*atthi paro loko*" *ti te naṃ vyākareyyaṃ. Evam pi me no. Tathā ti pi me no. Aññathā ti pi me no. No ti pi me no. No no ti pi me no* .... *Dīgha* i, p. 58.

[2] Introduction to *Gaina Sūtras*, pt. ii, *SBE*. xlv, pp. xx–xxi.

[3] *Pre-Buddhistic Indian Philosophy*, pp. 325 ff.

[4] V. infra, pp. 218–19.

[5] V. infra, pp. 235 ff., 262 ff.

[6] V. infra, pp. 80–81.

antinomian ethics are quite consistent with Makkhali's metaphysics.

Other Buddhist References to the Doctrines of the Heretics

In certain other passages of the Pāli canon the distribution of doctrines among the six teachers is significantly altered, in a way which strongly suggests that the credos ascribed in the *Sāmañña-phala Sutta* to Makkhali, Pūraṇa, and Pakudha were aspects of a single body of teaching.

Thus in *Mahābodhi Jātaka*[1] King Brahmadatta of Benares has five heretical councillors, who are respectively an *ahetukavādi*, an *issarakāraṇavādi*, a *pubbekatavādi*, an *ucchedavādi*, and a *khattavijjavādi*. The doctrines maintained by these five are stated in versified form, and are in part paraphrases of the *Sāmañña-phala Sutta* passages which we have quoted. At the conclusion of the story the five ministers are stated to have been previous incarnations of Pūraṇa, Makkhali, Pakudha, Ajita, and Nigaṇṭha. Thus, assuming that the doctrines were thought to have been held in the order named, the fatalist teaching ascribed in the *Sāmañña-phala Sutta* to Makkhali is here attributed to Pūraṇa; Makkhali himself becomes a theist[2]; Pakudha maintains an obscure doctrine which seems to approximate to the orthodox theory of *karma*[3]; Ajita upholds materialism, as in the *Sāmañña-phala Sutta* reference; while Nigaṇṭha, in fact the apostle of *ahiṃsā*, is here the teacher of a Macchiavellian doctrine, resembling the antinomianism of Pūraṇa, as described in the *Sutta* passage.[4]

A further account of heterodox teachings occurs in the *Sandaka Sutta* of the *Majjhima Nikāya*.[5] Here the *bhikkhu* Ānanda describes to the wanderer Sandaka the four "antitheses to the higher life" (*abrahmacariyavāsā*). These are:—

(1) The materialist teacher, who denies the existence of an

[1] *Jāt.* v, pp. 227 ff.

[2] *Ayaṃ loko issara-nimmito ti. Jāt.* v, p. 228.

[3] *Imesaṃ sattānaṃ sukhaṃ vā dukkhaṃ vā uppajjamānaṃ pubbekaten' eva uppajjatī, ti.* Ibid.

[4] *Mātā-pitaro pi māretvā attano va attho kāmetabbo.* Ibid.

[5] *Majjh.* i, pp. 513 ff.

after-life. The passage describing his teaching is a word-for-word transcription of Ajita Kesakambalī's doctrine as given in the *Sāmañña-phala Sutta*.[1] Here, however, no teacher is named.

(2) The antinomian—a repetition of Pūraṇa's doctrine.[2]

(3) The fatalist—repeating the teachings of Makkhali as given in the *Sāmañña-phala Sutta* up to " . . . experience, joy, and sorrow in the six classes (of existence) ".[3]

(4) The atomist. Here the atomic theory of Pakudha[4] is repeated, but appended to it we are given the second half of Makkhali's determinist teaching, including the obscure list of categories.[5]

Ānanda then describes the four " comfortless vocations (*anassāsikāni brahmacariyāni*). These are :—

(1) The teacher claiming omniscience.
(2) The traditionalist.
(3) The rationalist, and
(4) The sceptic.

To the latter is ascribed the passage given in the *Sāmañña-phala Sutta* to Sañjaya,[6] but the other three teachers of the second group are referred to in terms not suggesting any of the six famous heretics.

The conclusion of the *Sutta* is surprising. Sandaka realizes that all the teachers are false guides, and that if their doctrines are true all self-control is a work of supererogation. He is converted to the true *Dhamma*, and declares : " These Ājīvikas . . . are children of a childless mother ; they extol themselves and disparage others, yet they have only produced three shining lights, to wit Nanda Vaccha, Kisa Saṅkicca, and Makkhali Gosāla." [7]

It will be seen that the fatalist teaching, in the *Sāmañña-phala Sutta* ascribed to Makkhali, is here divided, and the second

[1] V. supra, p. 15. [2] V. supra, p. 13. [3] V. supra, pp. 13–14.
[4] V. supra, p. 16. [5] V. supra, p. 14. [6] V. supra, pp. 16–17.

[7] *Ime pan' ājīvikā puttamatāya puttā, attānañ c' eva ukkaṃsenti pare ca vambhenti, tayo c' eva niyyātāro paññāpenti, seyyath' idaṃ Nandaṃ Vacchaṃ, Kisaṃ Saṅkiccaṃ, Makkhali Gosālan ti. Majjh.* i, p. 524.

I adopt Lord Chalmers' translation (*Further Dialogues* i, p. 371), which is based on Buddhaghosa's commentary, *Papañca-sūdanī* : *P u t t a - m a t ā y a p u t t â ti so kira imaṃ dhammaṃ sutvā ājīvikā matā nāmâ ti saññī hutvā evam āha. Ayaṃ h'ettha attho. Ājīvikā matā nāma, tesaṃ mātā puttamatā hoti iti ājīvikā puttamatāya puttā nāma honti.* Op. cit., iii, p. 235.

half linked with the doctrine of Pakudha. The propagators of all the objectionable teachings are classed together under the broad title of Ājīvikas, and two new names, those of Nanda Vaccha and Kisa Saṅkicca, are introduced; these two shadowy figures we shall consider in the following chapter.[1]

Further confusion is to be found in a passage in the *Petavatthu*,[2] where a verse paraphrase of parts of the doctrines ascribed in the *Sāmañña-phala Sutta* to Makkhali, Pūraṇa, Ajita, and Pakudha, together with certain new teachings which are to be found among the doctrines of the later Ājīvikas, are placed in the mouth of the *peta*, Nandaka. Similar verse passages occur in *Mahānārada-kassapa Jātaka*,[3] where various doctrines elsewhere ascribed to the six heretics are spoken by the ascetic Guṇa.

Two remarkable references, strongly indicating the confusion of the various doctrines, are to be found in the *Saṃyutta Nikāya*. In one of these[4] Mahāli, a Licchavi, approaches the Buddha while the latter is residing at Vesāli, and declares: "Pūraṇa Kassapa says, 'there is neither cause nor basis for the sins of living beings; they become sinful without cause or basis. Neither is there cause or basis for the purity of living beings; they become pure without cause or basis.'" The same phrase is repeated in the second passage,[5] but here the words "ignorance and lack of discernment"[6] are substituted for "sins", and their antitheses for "purity". These passages indicate quite clearly that Pūraṇa was thought of as holding doctrines very similar to those of Makkhali, to whom the words are ascribed in the *Sāmañña-phala Sutta*.

In the *Aṅguttara Nikāya*[7] the six *abhijātis*, or classes of humanity, ascribed in the *Sāmañña-phala Sutta* to Makkhali, are stated by the monk Ānanda to be a distinctive part of Pūraṇa's teaching. Here the six classes are described in detail, and, significantly, Pūraṇa is said to include in his highest category (*paramasukk'-âbhijāti*) none other than the three shining lights of the *Majjhima* passage,[8] Nanda Vaccha, Kisa Saṅkicca, and Makkhali Gosāla. Thus we have no less than three passages in which parts of Makkhali's doctrine are ascribed to Pūraṇa,

[1] V. infra, pp. 27 ff.
[2] iv, 3, pp. 57 ff.
[3] *Jāt.* vi, pp. 219 ff. V. infra, pp. 217, 263.
[4] *Saṃ.* iii, p. 69.
[5] *Saṃ.* v, p. 126.
[6] *Aññāṇāya adassanāya.*
[7] *Aṅg.* iii, p. 383 f.
[8] V. supra, p. 19.

and one in which the latter is purported to proclaim the former to be in the highest rank of spiritual attainment.

The six are mentioned together in the *Milinda Pañha*, as contemporaries of the Greco-Indian King. Here doctrines are ascribed only to the two most important members of the group, Makkhali and Pūraṇa, and their statements are of the most brief description. When the King asks Pūraṇa " Who rules the world ? " the latter replies " The earth rules the world ".[1] Makkhali's brief speech implies an antinomian and fatalistic doctrine, but also states a view not to be found elsewhere ascribed to the Ājīvikas, to the effect that brāhmaṇas, kṣattriyas, vaiśyas, śudras, and outcastes would all retain their original status in future births.[2] This doctrine is quite inconsistent with all statements of the Ājīvika theory of transmigration to be found elsewhere ; in fact the whole passage, with its obscurity and blatant anachronism, seems to be lacking in all significance as a source for reconstructing Ājīvika history and theology, and merely indicates that, by the time of the composition of the text, Ājīvikism was very imperfectly known in northern India.

The Tibetan version of the *Sāmañña-phala Sutta*, quoted by Rockhill,[3] shows even further confusion. The *Dulva* ascribes to Pūrṇa Kāśyapa not only the antinomianism of the Pāli version, but also a denial of life after death, a view attributed in the Pāli to Ajita. " Maskarin son of Gośālī " maintains the same doctrine as in the Pāli ; " Sañjayin son of Vairattī " acquires an antinomianism very like that of Pūraṇa in the original text ; " Ajita Keśakambala " here maintains not only Pakudha's doctrine of the seven elements, but also the second half of Makkhali's fatalistic catechism, including the long list of obscure categories ; " Nirgrantha son of Djñātī " retains his authentic teaching of *karma* wiped out by penance ; and " Kakuda Kātyāyana " usurps the place of Sañjaya as the prevaricating sceptic.

Rockhill also quotes two Chinese versions of the *Sutta*.[4] In the first of these, the translation of which is dated A.D. 412–13,

[1] " *Ko lokam pāleti* " *ti*. " *Paṭhavī . . . lokam pāleti* " *ti*. *Milinda Pañha*, p. 4.

[2] *N'atthi . . . kusalâkusalāni kammāni, n'atthi . . . kammānaṃ phalaṃ vipāko . . . ye te idhaloke khattiyā . . . brāhmaṇā vessā suddā caṇḍālā pukkusā te paralokaṃ gantvā pi puna brāhmaṇā* (etc.) . . . *bhavissanti*. Op. cit., p. 5.

[3] *The Life of the Buddha*, p. 99 f.

[4] Op. cit., app. ii, p. 255 f.

we find Pūraṇa maintaining his original doctrine of guiltlessness; Makkhali has acquired part of Ajita's materialism; "Kakuda Kātyāyana" has a portion of Makkhali's determinism; Sañjayin remains a sceptic; while the Nirgrantha Jñātrīputra claims omniscience, as did the historical Mahāvīra.

The second version is a little earlier, the date of its translation, as given by Rockhill, being A.D. 381–395. Here Pūraṇa becomes the materialist; Maskarin Gośāla declares "there is no present world nor the world to come, nor power nor powerlessness, nor energy. All men have obtained their pleasure and pain (?)"—an obscure doctrine, clearly owing much to Ajita's pronouncement in the Pāli, but evidently implying fatalism in its last phrase. The prevaricating sceptic is here Ajita; "Kakuda's" teaching is almost unintelligible in the translation—"If there be a man who has been cut off and who sees with his eyes, there can be no dispute (about the question). If the life of the body comes to an end there is nothing to grieve about in the death of life"; Sañjayin declares that there is no reward of sin or virtue—Pūraṇa's doctrine in the Pāli *Sutta*; and Nirgrantha maintains that all is the effect of *karma*.

The various ascriptions of doctrine to be found in the Buddhist scriptures may be conveniently summarized in tabular form:—

	Dīgha i, 47.	*Jāt.* v, 227.	*Majjh.* i, 513.[1]	*Saṃ.* iii, 69.	*Saṃ.* v, 126.	*Aṅg.* iii, 383.	*Milinda Pañha*, 4–5.	*Dulva.*	Chinese, A.D. 412–13.	Chinese, A.D. 381–395.
Pūraṇa Kassapa	A	D_1	(A)	D_1	D_1^2	D_2^2	X	M	A	M
Makkhali Gosāla	D_1D_2	T	(D_2)				D[3]	D	M[2]	D[2]
Ajita Kesakambalī	M	M	(M)					ED_2	M[2]	S
Pakudha Kaccāyana	E	K	(ED_2)					S	D_1	?
Nigaṇṭha Nātaputta	R	A						P	O	A
Sañjaya Belatthiputta	S		(S)					A	S	K

ABBREVIATIONS

A. Antinomianism, the doctrine of no rewards or penalties.
D_1. Determinism, the first part of Makkhali's doctrine.

[1] Here the teachers are not named, but they may be inferred.
[2] In a partial or garbled form.
[3] In a partial form, with the additional doctrine that caste status does not change from life to life.

D_2. The second part of Makkhali's doctrine, including the list of categories.
M. Materialism.
E. The theory of the seven elemental substances.
R. The doctrine of fourfold restraint.
S. Prevaricating scepticism.
T. Theism.
K. The doctrine of *karma*.
O. The doctrine of the omniscient teacher.
P. The doctrine of salvation by penance.
X. "The earth rules the world."

It is clear that some of these passages are more reliable than others. That in the *Dīgha Nikāya* shows a completeness and consistency lacking in the rest, and perhaps represents the original source of the other references. The Tibetan and Chinese versions, which have undergone translation, are most suspect, although it is to be noted that the Chinese versions are of a date probably little later than the final recension of the Pāli canon. Yet, despite the very evident textual confusion and corruption, a striking degree of consistency is shown in some particulars.

Of the doctrines here considered those most characteristic of the later Ājīvikas are Makkhali's determinism and Pakudha's theory of unchanging elemental substances. It will be seen from the above table that determinism is in five places attributed to Makkhali, in four to Pūraṇa, and in two to Pakudha. The theory of the elements occurs only once in its isolated form, and is there ascribed to Pakudha, but it is twice found combined with determinism. In the Tibetan version, where the ascriptions are most confused, these two theories together are ascribed to Ajita. It may be suggested that the Tibetan version is based not on the *Dīgha* but on the *Majjhima* reference, where the two doctrines are also combined in the same manner. The debt of the Tibetan version to the *Majjhima* is also indicated by the new doctrine devised for Nigaṇṭha, which is perhaps based on direct knowledge of Jaina practice; the doctrine of fourfold restraint, which is ascribed to him in the *Dīgha*, is omitted in the *Majjhima* passage. The remarkable confusion of the Tibetan version may also be accounted for on the assumption that it is derived from the *Majjhima*, for in the latter the names of the teachers are not explicitly stated, and misattribution might thus easily have arisen. The ascription of determinism and the theory of the seven elemental substances to Ajita in the Tibetan version seems certainly erroneous, and may be ignored.

Thus we find that Buddhist tradition ascribes Ājīvika teachings not only to Makkhali but also to Pūraṇa and Pakudha and, with the exception of the doubtful Tibetan reference, to no other of the six heretical teachers. It seems therefore that all three had some hand in the development of Ājīvikism.

Before leaving the *Sāmañña-phala Sutta* a further point must be considered. The passage there ascribed to Makkhali Gosāla employs the Māgadhī *-e* termination almost consistently for the masculine nominative singular. In Ajita's catechism the termination occurs only twice, in the phrase *bāle ca paṇḍite*, and may there be a corrupt reading, resulting from the proximity of the same phrase in Makkhali's statement. In the teaching of Pakudha we find the termination only in the phrase *sukhe dukkhe jīva-sattame*. The statements of the other three ascetics contain no Māgadhisms.

The Māgadhī forms in Makkhali's doctrinal statement must surely be of some significance. They have been noticed by Franke,[1] who suggests two possibilities: either that the Māgadhisms have been deliberately introduced in order to make the speaker seem ludicrous, or that they represent reminiscences of the language of the original teachers. The former hypothesis can scarcely be correct. While the Māgadhī dialect was reserved for lowly and humorous characters in the Sanskrit drama, the Māgadhī *-e* termination was regularly employed in the great body of early Jaina literature, and we have no reason to believe that it made a ludicrous impression on the contemporary listener. If the intention had been purely ludicrous the *-e* termination would surely have been employed in the speeches of all six heretics.

It may be inferred that most of the passage ascribed to Makkhali has a provenance different from that of the others. The first paragraph of this passage, which retains the regular masculine nominative in *-o*, and where the Māgadhī *-e* only occurs in the phrase *n'atthi atta-kāre, n'atthi parakāre, n'atthi purisa-kāre*, may emanate from another source. Different sources of the two parts of this passage are also indicated by the fact that in the *Majjhima* and *Dulva* versions[2] it is broken up,

[1] *Dīgha Nikāya in Auswahl Übersetzt*, p. 56, n. 5.
[2] V. supra, p. 22.

and the second half incorporated with the theory of the seven elements and attributed in the former to an unnamed teacher suggesting Pakudha, and in the latter to Ajita.

Further evidence that the first passage of Makkhali's teaching in the *Sāmañña-phala Sutta* emanates from a source different from that of the second is supplied by the *Praśnavyākaraṇa Sūtra*.[1] Here we find a description of the doctrines of the *nāstikavādins*, which shows remarkable parallels to the teachings ascribed in the *Sāmañña-phala Sutta* to Ajita and Makkhali; for example such phrases as "there is no mother nor father, neither is there human action".[2] Throughout this passage, besides the regular Ardha-māgadhī masculine ending in *-e*, occurs the Pāli *-o*. This fact suggests that this passage, and the first part of Makkhali's teaching in the *Sāmañña-phala Sutta*, look back to a common source in Pāli or in some dialect with masculine endings in *-o*, while the second part of the *Sāmañña-phala Sutta* passage is taken from a Māgadhī source. On this hypothesis, however, the three anomalous Māgadhisms (i.e. the compound nouns ending in *-kāre*) in the first part of the Makkhali passage are difficult to explain, especially as the corresponding word in the *Praśnavyākaraṇa* has the *-o* ending. We can only suggest that they occur as the result of contamination from the second part of the passage, where the nominative singular masculine in *-e* is to be found throughout.

The brief Māgadhī phrase in the Pakudha passage of the *Sāmañña-phala Sutta*[3] is unexpected. The first four elements, earth, water, fire, and air, are given the regular Pāli *-o* endings, but the fifth, sixth, and seventh, joy, sorrow, and life respectively, have the Māgadhī *-e*, where *-aṃ* would be expected. It may be suggested that the three latter elements have been interpolated by a different hand in a statement of doctrine which originally taught only four elemental substances, as did the Buddhists and Cārvākas. As will be shown in our second part,[4] the three latter elements of Pakudha's list have other points of difference from the four former, and joy and sorrow do not seem to have been accepted as elements by all Ājīvikas.[5]

[1] *Sūtra* 7, fols. 26–8.

[2] *Ammā-piyaro n'atthi, na vi atthi purisakāro.* For further comparisons between the two texts v. infra, pp. 217–18.

[3] V. supra, p. 16. [4] V. infra, pp. 262 ff. [5] V. infra, p. 265.

To sum up the conclusions of this chapter: Ājīvika doctrine emanated from at least two sources; the mainstay of early Ājīvikism, the doctrine of *Niyati*, was probably first propagated in a Magadhan dialect; and the component doctrines of Ājīvikism were early associated with the names of Makkhali, Pūraṇa, and Pakudha.

CHAPTER III

MAKKHALI GOSĀLA AND HIS PREDECESSORS

Ājīvika Leaders before Makkhali Gosāla

According to the *Bhagavatī Sūtra* Makkhali Gosāla considered himself to be the twenty-fourth *tīrthaṅkara* of the current *Avasarpiṇī* age.[1] The passage in which this is stated may indeed be a Jaina interpolation, but numerous other indications are to be found both that ascetics referred to as Ājīvikas existed before their greatest leader, Makkhali Gosāla, and that the Ājīvika order preserved recollections of prophets who preceded him. Both in the Buddhist and Jaina texts names are mentioned which apparently refer to his predecessors.

Nanda Vaccha and Kisa Saṅkicca

These names are linked with that of Makkhali Gosāla in a stock phrase which, as we have seen,[2] occurs in various contexts in the Pāli scriptures.

Thus in the *Aṅguttara* [3] the *bhikkhu* Ānanda is purported to have declared that the heretical leader Pūraṇa Kassapa believed in the Ājīvika theory of the six classes of men (*chaḷâbhijātiyo*); according to his classification the highest class, the most white (*paramasukka*), contained only three members, namely Nanda Vaccha, Kisa Saṅkicca, and Makkhali Gosāla. Buddhaghosa apparently plagiarized this passage for his commentary to the reference to the six classes in the *Sāmañña-phala Sutta*,[4] and added: "They are the purest of all." [5]

In the *Majjhima Nikāya* the same names are given by the *nigaṇṭha* Saccaka or Aggivessana as the leaders of his order.[6] To this Buddhaghosa comments that the three had achieved leadership over the extreme ascetics.[7]

[1] *Bh. Sū.* xv, *sū.* 554, fol. 679. V. infra, pp. 64, 68.
[2] V. supra, pp. 19–20.
[3] *Aṅg.* iii, p. 383.
[4] *Sum. Vil.* i, p. 162.
[5] *Te kira sabbehi paṇḍaratarā.*
[6] *Majjh.* i, p. 238.
[7] *Te kira kiliṭṭhatapānaṃ matthakappattā ahesuṃ.* *Papañca Sūdanī* ii, p. 285.

Again in the *Sandaka Sutta* of the *Majjhima* the three names occur [1] when the ascetic Sandaka, on his conversion by the Buddha, declares them to be the only great leaders [2] produced by the Ājīvikas.

Hoernle [3] suggests that Kisa and Nanda were probably Makkhali's contemporaries. " There were indeed other groups of ascetics of a similarly dubious character who also bore the name of Ājīvikas . . . but they lived apart under separate leaders, the names of two of whom, Nanda Vaccha and Kisa Saṅkicca, are recorded in the Buddhist scriptures." That in the days of the Buddha more than one school of ascetics was given the title of Ājīvika seems very probable, but that the two teachers Nanda and Kisa were the contemporaries of Makkhali Gosāla cannot be definitely established. If Nanda Vaccha and Kisa Saṅkicca were altogether independent of Makkhali Gosāla, as Hoernle asserts, it is surprising that the three are so frequently mentioned together, when another teacher, Pūraṇa Kassapa, who was certainly revered with Makkhali by the later Ājīvikas,[4] is referred to as the leader of a separate school. Despite these objections the view of Hoernle is shared by A. S. Gopani.[5]

Barua,[6] on the other hand, believes that Nanda Vaccha and Kisa Saṅkicca represent previous leaders of the Ājīvikas. Nanda, he states categorically, was succeeded by Kisa, and Ḳisa by Makkhali. He is in this respect guilty of some inconsistency, since he proceeds to interpret the seven reanimations of Gosāla Maṅkhaliputta, as described in the *Bhagavatī Sūtra*,[7] as " a genealogical succession of seven Ājīvika leaders ", concluding with Gosāla. In maintaining the priority in time of Nanda and Kisa to Makkhali he supports Jacobi, who first put the view forward.[8]

Barua's arguments for elevating Nanda and Kisa to the status of earlier *tīrthaṅkaras* of the Ājīvika order are by no means conclusive. They are based on two *Jātaka* stories in which the chief characters bear names suggesting those of the two hypothetical Ājīvika *arhants*.

[1] *Majjh.* i, p. 524.
[2] *Niyyātaro*, in Lord Chalmers' translation " shining lights " (v. supra, p. 19).
[3] *ERE.* i, p. 265. [4] V. infra, pp. 80 ff. [5] *Bhāratīya Vidyā* ii, p. 202.
[6] *JDL.* ii, p. 2. [7] V. infra, pp. 30 ff.
[8] Introduction to *Gaina Sūtras* ii; *SBE.* xlv, p. xxxi.

In the first of these, *Sarabhaṅga Jātaka*,[1] the Bodhisatta is born as Sarabhaṅga, also referred to as Jotipāla and Kondañña. He is a famous hermit in the Kaviṭṭha forest, on the banks of the Godhāvarī. Among his chief pupils is one Kisa Vaccha, whose name appears to be a telescoped version of those of the two Ājīvika *arhants*. Kisa is said to have left the hermitage with the permission of his teacher, and to have moved to the city of Kumbhavatī, whose king was Daṇḍaki. Here he obtained the reputation of a scapegoat (*kālakaṇṇi*), who would remove ill-luck when spat upon, and as a result was shamed and insulted by the populace. After some time he was recalled by his teacher Sarabhaṅga, and the King and his kingdom were destroyed by the gods in punishment for the ignominies borne by the saint. Soon after this Kisa Vaccha is said to have died; innumerable ascetics attended his cremation, and the ceremony was marked by a rain of heavenly flowers.

A second *Jātaka* [2] tells of the ascetic Saṅkicca, another incarnation of the Bodhisatta. He is the son of the chief brāhmaṇa of Brahmadatta, the semi-legendary and ubiquitous King of Benares, and is represented as converting a regicide prince by a long description of purgatory. Among the inhabitants of the nether world he mentions King Daṇḍaki, who is suffering there on account of his subjects' persecution of the passionless (*araja*) Vaccha Kisa.

Barua does not value too highly the evidence of the similarity of the names of these two ascetics and those of the Ājīvika leaders. After summarizing the references above quoted he admits that "by no stretch of the imagination can Kisa Vaccha be transformed into Nanda Vaccha .... There is no other ground to justify the identification of Kisa Vaccha with Nanda Vaccha or of Saṃkicca with Kisa Saṃkicca than the fact that the views of Sarabhaṅga . . . bear *a priori*, like those of the hermit Saṃkicca, a close resemblance to the ethical teaching of Makkhali Gosāla at whose hands the Ājīvika religion attained a philosophical character".[3]

It is difficult to trace on what Barua bases his last assertion. Sarabhaṅga is an ascetic of the typical *Jātaka* type, with no distinctive ethical views, while the only special characteristic of

[1] *Jāt.* v, pp. 125 ff. [2] *Jāt.* v, pp. 261 ff. [3] *JDL.* ii, p. 4.

Saṅkicca is the possession of a lively sense of the reality of the infernal regions, and of the torments experienced there by sinners. There seems no reason to believe that Makkhali Gosāla made the fear of hell a special feature of his doctrine.

Despite Dr. Barua's doubts it is perhaps legitimate to conclude that Kisa Vaccha, or Vaccha Kisa, was a hermit, long dead in the Buddha's day, around whom a body of legend had grown. His fame is made clear by another *Jātaka* reference,[1] wherein he is mentioned as an inhabitant of Brahmaloka, among an exalted company of *ṛṣis*, including such famous sages as Aṅgiras and Kaśyapa. A second ascetic, Saṅkicca, seems to have been connected in the folk memory with Kisa Vaccha. As Barua points out,[2] Saṅkicca was thought to have been posterior in time to Kisa Vaccha, for in the *Jātaka* reference he is described as mentioning the latter. The two ascetics were perhaps looked upon with reverence by the early Ājīvikas and the Buddhists alike, and the popular floating traditions about them adapted to the needs of the respective sects. In the course of the adaptation the names seem to have been confused.

The reference to Kondañña, as the family name of the teacher Sarabhaṅga or Jotipāla, the preceptor of Kisa Vaccha, suggests Udāī Kuṇḍiyāyaṇīya, the first of the strange series of reanimations quoted in the *Bhagavatī Sūtra*.[3] Perhaps we have here another garbled version of an Ājīvika tradition going back to one Kauṇḍinya, but the theory rests on such a slender basis that much importance cannot be attached to it.

It seems clear, however, that the Ājīvikas, like the Buddhists and the Jainas, had a tradition of earlier teachers who had spread the true doctrine in the distant past; and, like those of the Buddhists and Jainas, these traditions may have contained a small kernel of historical truth.

The Immediate Predecessors of Makkhali Gosāla

In the *Bhagavatī Sūtra*[4] Gosāla Maṅkhaliputta, as the Ājīvika leader is called by the Jainas, is said to have made a remarkable statement, which perhaps indicates the existence of a line of

[1] *Jāt.* vi, p. 99. [2] *JDL.* ii, p. 3. [3] V. infra, p. 31.
[4] *Bh. Sū.* xv, *sū.* 550, fol. 674.

Ājīvika teachers whose spiritual mantle had fallen upon his shoulders.

It is stated that Gosāla and Mahāvīra, after the ending of their collaboration in asceticism, were parted for sixteen years, during which the former gained a high reputation for his sanctity, and gathered a large following in the city of Sāvatthi. At the end of this period Mahāvīra visited the city, and denounced his former colleague as a charlatan; whereupon Gosāla, surrounded by his followers, proceeded to the *caitya* where Mahāvīra was staying, and angrily declared that he was not the Gosāla who had been Mahāvīra's associate, but that the original Gosāla was dead, and that the soul now inhabiting the apparent Gosāla was that of Udāī Kuṇḍiyāyaṇīya, which had passed through seven bodies in succession, finally taking up its abode in that of the dead Gosāla, which it had reanimated. He declared further that his soul had travelled through all the eighty-four lakhs of great *kalpas*, which must necessarily elapse before it could end its journey, and had occupied all forms of body in determined order. It had attained its final birth as Udāī, an auspicious and beautiful infant; at an early age Udāī had become an ascetic; and the soul nearing perfection had passed from one body to another as the soul which had been the original occupant of that body had been separated from it by death.

These reanimations Gosāla endowed with the technical title of *paüṭṭa-parihāra* (abandonments of transmigration), and declared that such a series of reanimations was the fated lot of every soul in the final stages of its rigidly determined passage through *saṃsāra*. At the moment, however, we are not concerned with reanimation as a point of doctrine, but with its significance historically. The *Sūtra* quotes with remarkable circumstantial detail the names of the previous occupants of the seven bodies inhabited in turn by the soul of Udāī, together with the length of time during which they were thus inhabited, and the place at which the soul transferred itself from one body to another. According to the text the soul of Udāī passed from body to body as follows:—

(1) Ẹnejjaga (Skt. Ṛṇañjaya), outside Rāyagiha, at the Maṇḍiyakucchi *caitya*; the soul remained incarnate in Eṇejjaga's body for twenty-two years.

(2) Mallarāma, at the Candoyaraṇa *caitya* outside Uddaṇḍapura, for twenty-one years.

(3) Maṇḍiya, at the Aṅgamaṇḍira *caitya* outside Campā, for twenty years.

(4) Roha, at the Kāmamahāvaṇa *caitya* outside Vāṇārasī, for nineteen years.

(5) Bhāraddāī, at the Pattakālagaya *caitya* outside Ālabhiyā, for eighteen years.

(6) Ajjuṇa Goyamaputta, at the Koṇḍiyāyaṇa *caitya* outside Vesālī, for seventeen years.

(7) Gosāla Maṅkhaliputta, at Hālāhalā's pottery at Sāvatthī, for sixteen years.

This fantastic catalogue has been interpreted by Hoernle[1] as an effort on the part of Gosāla to live down his past connection with Mahāvīra. For Barua "the only legitimate inference to be drawn . . ." is that "in this . . . enumeration . . . there is preserved a genealogical succession of seven Ājīvika leaders, together with a list of . . . successive geographical centres of their activities . . . ."[2]

It is not easy to accept Barua's theory without question. If the list is actually that of a succession of ascetic teachers, leaders of the same order, it is surprising that each one makes his headquarters in a different town. The progressive diminution by one year of the period of each reanimation also gives strong ground for suspicion that the scheme is artificial. Even if we admit that the list may represent a succession of seven teachers (or eight, if Udāī, the originator of the process, be included), little reliance may be placed on the total of 117 years between the commencement of the ministry of Eṇejjaga and that of Gosāla.

Two disorderly features of the list suggest, however, that it is not wholly a monkish fiction. The immediate predecessor of Gosāla, Ajjuṇa Goyamaputta, is distinguished by a *gotra* name or patronymic, as is Udāī Kuṇḍiyāyaṇīya, in whose body the migrant soul was originally born; but the other five names are given without patronymics. This fact suggests that Ajjuṇa was a real person, the period of whose life overlapped with that of

[1] *ERE.* i, p. 263. [2] *JDL.* ii, p. 5.

Gosāla, and whose name was well known to his contemporaries. The others, on the other hand, seem to have been earlier and more shadowy figures, whose family names had been forgotten. The fame of the original Udāï, the first of the line, may have been such that his *gotra* name survived over several generations. Had the list been completely artificial it might be expected that all the names would have received *gotra* titles.

The six predecessors of Gosāla are reported to have lived and taught at named *caityas* outside various cities of the Ganges basin. Gosāla, on the other hand, made his headquarters in the workshop of a potter woman. Had the list been a mere fiction, invented by an Ājīvika theologian to add dignity to his master's life-story, the residences of the six earlier reanimations would surely have been of the same type as that of the last. Consistency might also have been expected if the list had been the slanderous creation of a Jaina author.

These two marked inconsistencies in the list point in favour of its reliability. The names are probably those of a succession of teachers from whom Gosāla obtained some elements of his doctrine. Less reliance can be placed on the names of the *caityas* and cities, which change with an automatic regularity and never repeat themselves. The periods given for the successive ministeries of the seven teachers seem certainly false, with the exception of the sixteen years attributed to Gosāla. This may represent an accurate tradition, on the basis of which the ministeries of his six predecessors were arrived at by the mechanical addition of one year each.

References in Buddhist or Hindu texts to confirm the historicity of these names are not to be found. Numerous seers and teachers of the Bhāradvāja *gotra* are referred to in the Pāli and later Vedic texts, but there is no reason to believe that the Bhāraddāï of the *Bhagavatī Sūtra* represents any one of them. Ālabhiyā, the city near which he is said to have resided, is not mentioned in Sanskrit literature. but is thought by Hoernle [1] to be identical with the town of Ālavi mentioned in the Pāli scriptures, and identified by Cunningham with the modern Newal, nineteen miles south-east of Kanauj. For the names prior to that of Bhāraddāï no counterparts can be found, but a possible connec-

[1] *Uv. Das.* ii, app. iii, pp. 51–3.

tion with Gosāla's immediate predecessor, Ajjuṇa Goyamaputta, occurs in the *Lalitavistara*.[1] Here the preceptor of the future Buddha during his youth at Kapilavastu is Arjuna, a great master of mathematics. As a Śākyan this teacher would belong to the Gautama *gotra*,[2] and his generation, according to the Buddhist tradition, was that immediately preceding the Buddha's, and therefore also that of Makkhali Gosāla. An interest in number and a tendency to classify numerically is clearly to be found in Gosāla's teaching as described in the *Sāmañña-phala Sutta* and in the *Bhagavatī Sūtra*. It is not intrinsically impossible that the Śākyan mathematician became in his later life a wandering ascetic, teaching in the neighbourhood of Vesāli, where he came in contact with the young Gosāla, and strongly influenced his views.

Makkhali Gosāla

The teacher to whom the later Ājīvikas looked back with the greatest respect, and whom earlier investigators have considered to be the sole founder of the Ājīvika order, was Makkhali Gosāla. The name appears thus in the Pāli canon. In Buddhist Sanskrit works it usually becomes Maskarin Gośāla, but the *Mahāvastu* and some other texts have the forms Gośālikāputra,[3] and Gośālīputra.[4] The Jaina scriptures reverse the two names and refer to the Ājīvika teacher as Gosāla Maṅkhaliputta, while the Tamil sources give his name as Maṟkali. No references to him can be found in Hindu Sanskrit literature, with the doubtful exception of a shadowy figure in the *Mahābhārata* called Maṅki,[5] who may represent a corrupt and distorted recollection of the historical Makkhali or Maṅkhaliputta.

The most valuable source for the reconstruction of the story of his life and works is the Jaina *Bhagavatī Sūtra*, the fifteenth section of which gives a lengthy description of his breach with Māhāvīra and the circumstances of his death.

[1] Ed. Lefmann, p. 146.
[2] V. Malalasekera, *DPPN*., s.v. *Gotama*.
[3] Ed. Senart i, pp. 253, 256.
[4] Ibid., iii, p. 383.
[5] V. infra. pp. 38–39.

Birth of Makkhali Gosāla

Two stories of the origin of the Ājīvika leader are to be found, the one in the *Bhagavatī Sūtra*, and the other in Buddhaghosa's commentary to the *Sāmañña-phala Sutta*. Neither is worthy of unqualified credence, but both are of importance, if only for the evidence they give of the dislike and scorn which was felt by both Buddhist and Jaina for the Ājīvikas and their founder.

In the Jaina text[1] Mahāvīra is represented as declaring to his disciple Indabhūī Goyama the birth and parentage of Gosāla Maṅkhaliputta. His father, according to Mahāvīra, was a *maṅkha* named Maṅkhali, and his mother's name was Bhaddā.[2] The word *maṅkha* is interpreted by the commentator Abhayadeva as a type of ascetic " whose hand is kept busy by a picture board ".[3] Hoernle declares that " the . . . word . . . has not been found anywhere but in the passage of the Bhagavatī Sūtra which adduces it as the source of the name Maṅkhali, and it is presumably an invention *ad hoc* ".[4] Whatever the meaning of the word, this is certainly not the case. In the standard description of prosperous cities, used throughout the Ardha-māgadhī scriptures, the word *maṅkha* is to be found.[5] Hemacandra, in his commentary on the *Abhidhāna-cintāmaṇi*, equates it with *māgadha*, a bard.[6] It is not impossible that the *maṅkha* filled both the functions of an exhibitor of religious pictures, and a singer of religious songs. That such mendicants existed in Ancient India is proved by Viśākhadatta's *Mudrārākṣasa*, one of the minor characters of which is a spurious religious mendicant described as a " spy with a Yama-cloth " (*yama-paṭena carah*), that is one carrying a picture of the god Yama painted upon a cloth. He habitually enters the houses of his patrons, where he displays his Yama-cloth, and sings songs, presumably of a religious type.[7]

1 *Bh. Sū.* xv, *sū.* 540, fol. 659 f.

2 Ratna-Prabha Vijaya (*Śramaṇa Bhagavān Mahāvīra*, vol. ii, pt. i, pp. 373 ff.) gives a long paraphrase of a Jaina account of the life of Maṅkhali, the father of Gosāla. The story is evidently fictitious, and the author does not quote his source.

3 *Citraphalaka-vyagrakaro bhikṣāka-viśeṣaḥ.* Op. cit., fol. 660.

4 *ERE.* i, p. 260.

5 V. *Antagaḍa Dasāo*, tr. Barnett, p. 2, n. 3, and many references in Ratnacandrajī *Ardha-māgadhī Dictionary*, s.v. *maṅkha*.

6 *Abhidhāna-cintāmaṇi*, comm. to v. 795, p. 365 (Böhtlinck and Rieu edn.).

7 *Jāva evaṃ gehaṃ pavisiā jama-paḍaṃ daṃsaānto gīāiṃ gāāmi. Mudrārākṣasa* i, 17, ed. Karmarkar, p. 14. V. also p. 20 of the same text.

Moreover the word seems to have been used in Kashmīr as a proper name, and two Maṅkhas appear in the *Rājataraṅgiṇī*,[1] the second being a poet well known to students of later Sanskrit literature. Thus there is no justification for Hoernle's contention that the word is meaningless. This point has been recognized by Charpentier, who, on the strength of a *sūtra* of Pāṇini, admits the possibility that Gosāla's father was a mendicant bearing a picture board displaying a representation of the god Śiva.[2]

The details of the *Bhagavatī Sūtra's* account of Gosāla's birth, while not intrinsically impossible, seem to have been constructed in order to provide an etymology for his personal name. While Bhaddā was pregnant, she and her husband Maṅkhali the *maṅkha* came to the village (*sannivesa*) of Saravaṇa, where dwelt a wealthy householder Gobahula. Maṅkhali left his wife and his luggage (*bhaṇḍa*) in Gobahula's cowshed (*gosālā*), and tried to find accommodation in the village. Since he could find no shelter elsewhere the couple continued to live in a corner of the cowshed, and it was there that Bhaddā gave birth to her child. His parents decided to call him Gosāla, after the place of his birth.

No great value can be attached to the details of this story. The account of Gosāla's parentage and birth fits too closely to his name and patronymic to allow unqualified credence. His mother, Bhaddā, has a name used in the Jaina texts to designate the mother of many mythological figures,[3] which in this context seems devoid of all historical significance. In some respects the story recalls that of the birth of Jesus, as recorded in Saint Luke's gospel, and should therefore be of some interest to the student of comparative religion and mythology. Historically it is almost valueless.

Mahāvīra is reported to have told this story with the avowed intention of bringing Gosāla's reputation into disrepute. This being the case it is improbable that the legend represents an authentic Ājīvika tradition about the birth of their leader. Both Buddhist and Jaina hagiologists provided exalted origins for the founders of their respective sects, and it is likely that the

[1] *Rājataraṅgiṇī* viii, 969, 995, 3354.
[2] *JRAS.* 1913, pp. 671–2.
[3] V. Ratnacandrajī, *Ardha-māgadhī Dictionary*, s.v. *Bhaddā*.

Ājīvikas did the same for Gosāla. The one feature in the story which may be authentic is the name of the village of Gosāla's birth, Saravaṇa. In this connection it is to be noted that he is not the only figure in Indian legend to have been born in a *śaravana*, or thicket of reeds. Gosāla shares that honour with the god Kārttikeya, who is sometimes referred to by the epithets *śaravana-bhava*,[1] and *śaravan'-ôdbhava*.[2] Is it possible that the Ājīvikas taught that their teacher was born or found, not in a village called Saravaṇa, which as a place-name is not to be found elsewhere, but in a thicket of reeds ? The Moses-in-the-bullrushes theme is to be found elsewhere in Indian legend, notably in the story of the hero Karṇa.[3]

About Gosāla's early life, before his meeting with Mahāvīra, the *Bhagavatī Sūtra* tells us only that he maintained himself by the profession of a *maṅkha*, with a picture-board in his hand.[4] A further tale is provided by Buddhaghosa, in his commentary to the *Sāmañña-phala Sutta*.[5] He agrees with the *Bhagavatī* in stating that Gosāla acquired his name on account of his birth in a cowshed, and further states that Gosāla was a slave who, while walking over a patch of muddy ground carrying a pot of oil, was hailed by his master with the words "don't stumble, old fellow !" (*tāta mā khal' iti*). Despite the warning he carelessly tripped and spilt the oil. Fearing his master's anger he made off, but his master pursued and overtook him, catching him by the edge of his robe (*dāsakaṇṇa*). Leaving his garment behind him Gosāla escaped in a state of nudity. Hence he became a naked mendicant, and acquired the name of Makkhali from the last words, "*Mā khali*," spoken to him by his master.

This story is a patent fiction constructed, probably by Buddhaghosa himself, to provide an etymology for the names of the Ājīvika leader, to account for his nudity, and to pour scorn on his order by attributing to him a servile origin. It is even less credible than the Jaina account, especially if read in connection with a similar story told by Buddhaghosa about Pūraṇa

[1] *Meghadūta*, 45.

[2] *Mbh.* iii, 14635 (Calcutta edn., 1835. The verse does not occur in the Poona edn.).

[3] *Mbh. Adi.* 111, 13–14.

[4] *Cittaphalaga-hatthagaë maṅkhattaṇeṇaṃ appāṇaṃ bhāvemāṇe viharati. Bh. Sū.* xv, *sū.* 540, fol. 660.

[5] *Sum. Vil.* i, pp. 143–4.

Kassapa, to whom a servile origin is also attributed, and for whose name a similar fantastic etymology is devised.[1]

Hoernle, without explicitly accepting either story, suggests that a kernel of truth may be extracted from them. He writes: "the two accounts . . . are quite independent of each other . . . . All the more valuable are the two accounts, both in respect of the points in which they agree and in which they differ. They agree on two points: first, that Gosāla was born of low parentage in a cowshed . . . and secondly, that (his profession) . . . was not sincere, but adopted merely for the sake of getting an idle living."[2] In our opinion the correspondences are less striking than the differences, and prove nothing. The provision of fanciful etymologies for proper names was a common practice in Ancient India, and many other examples are to be found. The name Gosāla would inevitably suggest birth in a cowshed to the ancient etymologist. Both Buddhist and Jaina opposed the Ājīvikas, and it is not surprising that both tried to establish Gosāla's base lineage and insincerity. The fact is that neither story belongs to the Ājīvika tradition, and even if that tradition could be re-established we should still be far from the true story of the birth and early life of Makkhali Gosāla. The Jaina story is of the nature of an exposure, and the Buddhist is obviously created *ad hoc*. Both clearly show the intense *odium theologicum* which almost invariably attached itself to the Ājīvikas and to their founder. We can only admit that the Jaina account is not inherently impossible. It may be that Gosāla was born at a village called Saravaṇa of mendicant parents; even the story of his birth in a cowshed may be based on fact. But the evidence with which to establish this with any degree of certainty is lacking.

It is just possible that a very garbled and corrupt reference to Makkhali Gosāla is to be found in the *Mahābhārata*.[3] Among the episodes of the *Śānti Parvan* is the story of one Maṅki, who, after repeated failures in all his ventures, purchased a couple of young bulls with the last of his resources. One day the bulls broke loose, and were both killed by a camel. Maṅki thereupon

[1] *Sum. Vil.* i, p. 142. V. infra, pp. 82–83.
[2] *ERE.* i, p. 260.
[3] *Mbh.*, *Śānti*, 176, v. 5 ff. (Kumbhakonam edn.).

uttered a long chant on the power of destiny, and the advisability of desirelessness and inactivity. The *adhyāya* concludes with the statement that, in consequence of the loss of his two bulls, Maṅki cast off all desires and attained immortality.

The hymn of Maṅki contains Sāṅkhya *guṇa* teaching, and perhaps shows Buddhist influence also, but of the varied influences which it betrays that of Ājīvikism seems most prominent.[1] The name of the hero of the story may well be an anomalous corruption of the Prākrit Maṅkhali or of the Pāli Makkhali. These facts suggest that we have here a garbled reference to the leader of the Ājīvikas. The strange story of the two bulls is possibly a very confused version of a legend about their teacher which was current among the Ājīvikas themselves.

THE MEETING OF GOSĀLA WITH MAHĀVĪRA

In the *Bhagavatī Sūtra* the story of Gosāla's association with Mahāvīra is put into the mouth of Mahāvīra himself, as a continuation of his exposure of his rival, and it is narrated with much circumstantial detail.[2] In the third year of his asceticism Mahāvīra had taken up temporary quarters in a corner of a weaving-shed (*tantuvāya-sālā*) at Nālandā, near Rāyagiha. Thither came Gosāla Maṅkhaliputta, and, finding no other accommodation, took shelter in the same shed. On completing a month's fast, Mahāvīra went to Rāyagiha (Skt. Rājagṛha) to beg his food. There he and his patron Vijaya were greeted by a miraculous rain of flowers, and by other auspicious omens, amid the acclamations of the citizens. Hearing of these great events Gosāla waited outside Vijaya's house until Mahāvīra emerged, circumambulated him three times, and begged to become his pupil in asceticism. Mahāvīra gave him no answer, but returned to the weaving shed, where he performed a further month's fast, after which the same phenomena were repeated, with a different patron. The miracles occurred again, after a third fast. At the conclusion of a fourth month's penance Mahāvīra visited a brāhmaṇa named Bahula, at Kollāga, a village near Nālandā.

On finding that Mahāvīra had left the weaving-shed Gosāla

[1] V. infra, p. 218.

[2] *Bh. Sū.*, xv, *sū.* 541, fol. 660–3.

searched for him high and low in Rāyagiha. Unable to find him, he returned to the weaving-shed, where he stripped off his upper and lower garments, and gave them, with his waterpots, slippers, and picture-board, to a brāhmaṇa.[1] He then shaved his hair and beard and went away. As he passed Kollāga he heard the cheering of a crowd, and concluded that it was applauding Mahāvīra. So he made a further search, and found Mahāvīra at Paṇiyabhūmī, outside Kollāga. He once more begged Mahāvīra to accept him as a disciple. This time his request was granted, and for six years after the meeting at Paṇiyabhūmī the two shared the hardships and joys of the ascetic life.[2]

The story so far, if deprived of its supernatural incidents, is not incredible, and, with Hoernle, we may believe that it is essentially true. The Pāli texts refer to all six heretical teachers together in such a manner as to suggest that their relations were by no means always mutually antagonistic,[3] and numerous points of similarity in Jaina and Ājīvika doctrine and practice suggest the early interaction of the two teachings. But the account of the circumstances of the meeting seems by no means reliable. The earnest entreaties of Gosāla and Mahāvīra's steadfast refusal to accept him as a disciple are just such elements as would be introduced into the story by an author wishing to stress the inferiority of Ājīvikism to Jainism and of Gosāla to Mahāvīra. Therefore we believe that the text is not to be trusted when it states that the former was formally a disciple of the latter.

The reference to Paṇiyabhūmī in the text of the *Bhagavatī Sūtra* has given some trouble to the medieval commentator Abhayadeva, and to both Hoernle and Barua. Abhayadeva was in doubt whether the word in the text [4] should be taken as in the ablative or the locative.[5] Hoernle[6] found difficulty in accepting the ablative, which would involve an unusual construction, but

[1] *Sāḍiyāo ya pāḍiyāo ya kuṇḍiyāo ya pāhaṇāo ya cittaphalugaṃ ca māhaṇe āyāmettā.* Op. cit., fol. 662.

[2] *Bh. Sū.*, xv, *sū.* 541, fol. 663.

[3] E.g. at the great miracle contest at Sāvatthi. V. infra, pp. 84 ff.

[4] *Ahaṃ . . . Gosāleṇaṃ . . . saddhiṃ Paṇiyabhūmīe chavvāsāiṃ vihariṭṭhā.* *Bh. Sū.* xv, *sū.* 541, fol. 663.

[5] *P a ṇ i y a b h ū m ī e tti Paṇitabhūmer ārabhya, pranītabhūmau vā—manojñabhūmau vihṛtavān iti yogaḥ.* Op. cit., fol. 664.

[6] *Uv. Das.*, vol. ii, p. 111, n.

recognized that the locative interpretation implied an unresolved anomaly, since the *Kalpa Sūtra* states that Mahāvīra spent only one rainy season in Paṇiyabhūmī.[1] Barua,[2] ignoring the clear statement of the *Bhagavatī* that Paṇiyabhūmī was near Kollāga, which was a settlement near Nālandā,[3] located it in Vajrabhūmi, on the strength of Vinayavijaya's commentary to the relevant passage of the *Kalpa Sūtra.*[4] The *Ācārâṅga Sūtra* states that Mahāvīra did in fact visit Vajjabhūmī, which the commentator Śīlâṅka describes as a district of Lāḍha, or Western Bengal.[5]

It seems probable that the crucial passage in the *Bhagavatī* must be interpreted to mean that Gosāla and Mahāvīra spent six years together after their meeting at Paṇiyabhūmī, and not that the six years were spent at that place. The weight of Jaina tradition suggests that Mahāvīra was a wanderer and that, except during the rainy seasons, he frequently changed the scene of his activities. This tradition is confirmed by Jinadāsa Gaṇī's *cūrṇī* to the *Āvaśyaka Sūtra,* which purports to give a complete itinerary of the journeys of Mahāvīra and Gosāla during the six years in question. Although this source, which is considered below, is no earlier than the seventh century A.D.,[6] and must be treated very cautiously, it strengthens the traditions of the *Ācārâṅga* and *Kalpa Sūtras* that the six years were mainly spent in wandering.

The Peregrinations of the Two Ascetics

Jinadāsa's *cūrṇī* to the *Āvaśyaka Sūtra* contains a full account of Mahāvīra's early career, in the course of which are described the journeys which he made in the company of Gosāla. The author repeats the account of Gosāla's birth and early life, as given in the *Bhagavatī.*[7] He tells the story of the meeting of the two ascetics, and adds a significant incident which is said to have taken place just before Mahāvīra's final acceptance of Gosāla

[1] *Sū.* 122, ed. Jacobi, p. 64.
[2] *JDL.* ii, pp. 56–7.
[3] *Bh. Sū.*, fol. 662–3.
[4] To *sū.* 122, Bombay edn., fol. 187.
[5] *Ācārâṅga* i, 9.3.2. fol. 301–2 (Bombay edn.): in Jacobi's edn. and *SBE.* xxvi, i, 8, 3, 2.
[6] Schubring, *Die Lehre der Jainas,* p. 60.
[7] V. supra pp. 35–36.

as his associate.[1] Gosāla, about to go on a begging expedition, asked Mahāvīra what alms he would receive that day. The latter [2] replied that, besides the usual alms of food, he would be given a counterfeit coin. The prophecy was fulfilled, and thus Gosāla decided that what was to be could not be otherwise.[3]

After the two ascetics had departed together a further prophecy of Mahāvīra's greatly increased his belief in the power of *Niyati*. This was made at a village called Suvaṇṇakhalaya, and concerned the breaking of a pot of milk, the property of certain cowherds. Gosāla is said to have done his utmost to prevent the fulfilment of the prophecy.[4]

Then the two proceeded to Bambhaṇagāma, where Gosāla cursed the house of Uvaṇanda, a village headman, who refused him alms. His words, " If my master has any ascetic power may this house burn ! " were fulfilled immediately, not by virtue of his own asceticism, but by *devas*, desirous of vindicating Mahāvīra's fame.[5]

The third rainy season of Mahāvīra's asceticism was spent at Campā in severe penance. After this the two visited a settlement called Kālāya, where they sheltered for the night in an empty house which was resorted to by two lovers. In the darkness the ascetics were not detected, until Gosāla's prurience betrayed him, and he was soundly beaten by the man. A similar incident occurred at another village called Pattakālaya.[6]

At a settlement called Kumāraya Gosāla was involved in an altercation with a group of ascetic followers of Pārśva. He tried to destroy their settlement by the same process as that which he had employed on the house of Uvaṇanda, but the superior virtue of the proto-Jaina ascetics prevented his curse from taking effect.[7] At another settlement called Coraga the two were suspected of being hostile spies and were thrown into a well, but were recognized by two female followers of Pārśva,

[1] *Āvaśyaka Sūtra* (Ratlam edn.), vol. i, p. 282.

[2] Or rather, according to Jinadāsa, the *Vyantara* god Siddhatthaka, who seems to have employed the meditating Mahāvīra as a medium on several occasions when he was addressed by Gosāla.

[3] *Jahā bhavitavvaṃ ṇa taṃ bhavaï annahā.* Op. cit., p. 283.

[4] Ibid., loc. cit.

[5] Ibid., pp. 283–4.

[6] Ibid., pp. 284–5.

[7] Ibid., pp. 285–6.

and were released. The second rainy season of their association was spent at Piṭṭhicampā.[1]

Thence the two proceeded to Kataṅgala, and stopped in the meeting house of a settlement of *daridda-theras*, householder ascetics, with wives and families. It was a night of festival, during which the *theras* gathered for religious singing in their meeting house. The puritanical Gosāla roundly reproached them for their lax habits, and was thrown out into the cold of the winter night. Latecomers to the festival, sympathizing with his plight, brought him back into the hall, only for the process to be repeated twice more. At last the ascetics gave up attempting to exclude their censorious guest, and decided to put up with him for the sake of Mahāvīra, and to drown his protests with their drums.[2]

Outside the city of Sāvatthi Gosāla once more asked Mahāvīra to forecast the results of the day's begging expedition, and was told that he would receive human flesh. In the city a woman who had recently lost her child had been told by a fortune-teller that her next child would live if she gave some of the flesh of her dead child, mixed with rice, to a mendicant. Gosāla happened to be passing at the time, and received and ate the alms without knowing that they contained the human flesh prophesied by Mahāvīra. When he returned Mahāvīra asked him to vomit, and he realized that the prophecy had been fulfilled. As he could not again find the woman's house, in his anger he cursed the whole district by the same formula as before, and it was burnt to the ground.[3]

Near the village of Haledutā the ascetics spent the night in meditation under a tall tree. Merchants camping nearby started a fire, which spread through the undergrowth and approached their resting place. Shouting to Mahāvīra to follow him, Gosāla retreated, but the imperturbable Mahāvīra held his ground, although his feet were scorched by the flames.[4]

At the village of Maṅgala the two rested in the temple of Vāsudeva. Gosāla was irritated by the village children playing in the temple precincts, and angrily chased them away. For this display of bad temper he received a beating from the villagers.

[1] Ibid., pp. 286–7. [2] Ibid., p. 287. [3] Ibid., pp. 287–8. [4] Ibid., p. 288.

A similar incident occurred in the temple of Baladeva at the village of Āvattā.[1]

At a place called Corāya Gosāla, begging alone, was lured by the rich food which was being prepared for a festival. He was seen lurking in the vicinity of the festival pavilion, and was thought to be a spy sent by brigands. This resulted in another beating, after which Gosāla cursed the pavilion, which was promptly burnt to the ground.[2]

At Lambuya the ascetics were seized by one of the village headmen, but were recognized and released. Thence they proceeded to Lāḍha (W. Bengal), called in the text a non-Āryan country. Here at the village of Punnakalasā they were attacked by two robbers, and were only saved by the intervention of the god Sakka, who killed their assailants. The fifth rainy season of Mahāvīra's asceticism was spent at the city of Bhaddiyā.[3]

At the village of Kadalī, Gosāla, while begging alone, found an almsgiving ceremony in progress. He accepted much more rice than he could eat, and the villagers, disgusted at his greediness, poured what was left in his bowl over his head. The same treatment was meted out to him at a village called Jambusanda. At Tambāya he was again involved in a quarrel with the followers of Pārśva.[4]

Then the two proceeded to Vesāli. On the way Gosāla violently upbraided Mahāvīra for refusing to come to his assistance when attacked. He decided that his lot would be easier if he travelled alone, and the two ascetics parted company. Soon after this Gosāla fell in with a band of 500 robbers, by whom he was mercilessly teased, carried pick-a-back (?), and called "Grandfather".[5] He then determined to rejoin Mahāvīra, since in his company he had always been freed from his persecutors by some pious person who recognized Mahāvīra's sanctity. He was left at last by the robbers, and after searching for six months found Mahāvīra, who was spending the sixth rainy season of his asceticism at the city of Bhaddiyā.[6]

The following year was spent in uneventful wanderings in Magadha, and the seventh rainy season was passed at Ālabhiyā.[7]

[1] Ibid., p. 289. [2] Ibid., p. 290. [3] Ibid., loc. cit. [4] Ibid., p. 291
[5] *Pañcahi vi corasaehiṃ vāhito mātulo tti kāuṃ.* Ibid., p. 292.
[6] Ibid., p. 293. [7] Ibid., loc. cit.

At Kuṇḍaga the two ascetics sheltered in the temple of Vāsudeva. Here Gosāla obscenely insulted the ikon, was seen by a villager, and was severely beaten. A similar event occurred at the village of Maddaṇā, in a temple of Baladeva.[1]

At Lohaggala, described as the capital of King Jiyasattu, the couple were arrested as spies, but later identified and released. At Purimatāla they passed a bridal procession, and Gosāla received another beating for mocking the bride and bridegroom for their ugliness. Later at a place called Gobhūmi, he quarrelled with a company of cowherds, whom he called *mlecchas*, and was given the same treatment at their hands. The eighth rainy season was spent at Rāyagaha.[2]

In his ninth year of asceticism Mahāvīra decided to visit non-Āryan countries, in order to invite persecution and thus to work off his *karma*. Accompanied by Gosāla he journeyed to Lāḍha and Vajjabhūmi (W. Bengal), where both were put to great ignominy by the uncouth inhabitants. There they spent the ninth rainy season.[3]

In Mahāvīra's tenth year of wandering they left the non-Āryan lands and went to Siddhatthagāma. Soon after this the incident of the sesamum plant occurred, which led to their final separation. This is described in full in the *Bhagavatī Sūtra*, and will be considered below.

In another time and place Jinadāsa's terse Prākrit narrative would have been expanded by its author into a picaresque novel. In it Gosāla fills rather the rôle of a Sancho Panza than that of a Judas, for his misfortunes, while in part due to his loyalty to his master, and in part to his arrogance, are mainly the result of a lewd and surly clownishness, which can scarcely have been a significant element in the character of the founder of an important religious sect. The story as it stands is evidently fiction.

Nevertheless it is of some value to the historian. The frame-

[1] Ibid., pp. 293–4. This is the interpretation of Muni Ratna-Prabha Vijaya (*Śramaṇa Bhagavān Mahāvīra*, vol. ii, pt. i, p. 440). The phrases *Vāsudeva-paḍimāe adhiṭṭhāṇaṃ muhe kāuṃ ṭhito*, and *tassa* (i.e. *Baladevassa*) *muhe sāgāritaṃ* are obscure. It might be possible to interpret the former as meaning " laid his face (in reverence) on the base of the ikon of *Vāsudeva* ". The *Païa-sadda-mahaṇṇavo* gives *maithuna* as a possible meaning of *sāgāriya* in the second phrase.

[2] Ibid., pp. 295–6.

[3] Ibid., p. 296.

work of the account of Mahāvīra's peregrinations is based on a very ancient tradition, for otherwise Lāḍha would not be described as a non-Āryan country. The visit of Mahāvīra to this district is confirmed by the early *Ācārāṅga Sūtra*.[1] The *Kalpa Sūtra* confirms that Mahāvīra passed rainy seasons in the places specified by Jinadāsa,[2] with the exception of that spent in Lāḍha and Vajjabhūmi; this discrepancy is explained by the commentator Vinayavijaya, who states that Paṇiyabhūmi, where Mahāvīra is said by the *Kalpa Sūtra* to have spent a rainy season, is in Vajrabhūmi.[3] Thus it is evident that Jinadāsa did not invent the whole of his story.

In respect of the length of the period of the association of the two ascetics Jinadāsa's account differs from that of the *Bhagavatī Sūtra*. The latter source states that the two were associated for a period of six years.[4] According to the former their meeting took place at the end of the second rainy reason of Mahāvīra's asceticism, which was spent at Nālandā, and the two parted in the season of Śarada, after the ninth rainy reason. The period of their association is thus seven years. We prefer, however, to accept the *Bhagavatī's* six years, as being found in the earlier and more reliable source.

We suggest that the inspiration of many of the incidents of this story was obtained from Ājīvika legends about their founder, which were adapted by Jinadāsa to display Gosāla in a ludicrous light. The episode of the broken pot, which strengthened his faith in the power of destiny, reminds us that Buddhaghosa also wrote of the spilling of the contents of a pot at a crucial moment of Gosāla's career.[5] We may believe that the Ājīvikas had legends in which Gosāla was said to have called down fire from heaven upon his adversaries by the virtue of his austerities, and that these were utilized by Jinadāsa to provide further episodes of his story.

It is significant that four of Gosāla's adventures are said to have taken place in Vaiṣṇavite temples. Jinadāsa may indeed have been guilty of anachronism in these episodes, for it is by no means certain that temple worship and iconolatry had developed in India in the sixth century B.C. But the gods involved, Vāsudeva

[1] V. supra, p. 41.
[2] *Kalpa Sūtra*, *sū*. 122, ed. Jacobi, p. 64.
[3] Fol. 187 (Bombay edn.).
[4] V. supra, p. 40.
[5] V. supra, p. 37.

and Baladeva, are among the earliest Vaiṣṇavite divinities known to us. Vaiṣṇavite tendencies are to be found in Ājīvika doctrine at a much later date,[1] and Ājīvikas are by one commentator explicitly identified with *ekadaṇḍins*, or Vaiṣṇava ascetics.[2] The association of Gosāla with Vaiṣṇavite temples and his expulsion from them may conceal an attempt of Jinadāsa to explain away a legend of the later Ājīvikas in which their founder was depicted as breaking away from some more orthodox system. The same may be the case with the story of Gosāla and the *daridda-theras*, with whom he was allowed to remain on sufferance. These suggest the devotees of some Vaiṣṇavite *bhakti* cult, and we have evidence that, like these, the Ājīvikas employed music in their religious practice.[3]

Thus, although Jinadāsa gives us little reliable information about the life of Gosāla, it may be that he gives a few hints on what the Ājīvikas themselves believed about their master.

Gosāla and the Sesamum Plant

Still addressing his disciple Indabhūī Goyama, Mahāvīra is said by the *Bhagavatī Sūtra* to have told of two significant incidents which led to the separation of the two ascetics.

During the season of *Śarada* the couple left the *vihāra* at the village of Siddhatthagāma, and set out for Kummāragāma. Neither of these places can be located, but we may assume that they were somewhere in Magadha. On the way to Kummāragāma they passed a flourishing sesamum shrub in full bloom. Looking at it, Gosāla asked Mahāvīra a question, apparently designed to test the latter's intuitive knowledge. "Sir," he asked, "will this sesamum bush bear fruit or not, and what will become of these seven sesamum flowers?"[4] Mahāvīra replied that the shrub would develop, and that the

[1] V. infra, p. 276.

[2] V. infra, pp. 168 ff.

[3] V. infra, pp. 116–17.

[4] *Esa ṇaṃ Bhante tila-thambaë kiṃ nipphajjissaī, no nipphajjissati? Eë ya satta tila-puppha-jīvā udāïttā udāïttā kahiṃ gacchihinti, kahiṃ uvavajjihinti?* *Bh. Sū.* xv, *sū.* 542, fol. 664. In the above paraphrase we take *nipphajjissaī* to mean "develop" or "bear fruit". This seems to make much better sense in the context than "perish", the interpretation of Hoernle (*ERE.* i, p. 263), and Barua (*Pre-Buddhistic Indian Philosophy*, p. 301).

seven sesamum flowers would produce seven seed-pods in one cluster.[1]

This very definite answer displeased Gosāla, and he determined to prove Mahāvīra a liar; so he quietly dropped behind and pulled up the sesamum bush. But at that moment a shower of rain fell, the plant took root again,[2] and so the flowers ripened and seven sesamum pods were produced in one cluster, just as Mahāvīra had prophesied.

Soon afterwards the couple returned by the same road.[3] As they drew near the spot where the sesamum plant grew Gosāla reminded Mahāvīra of his forecast, and declared that he would find that the plant had not ripened and the seeds had not formed. Mahāvīra, on the other hand, stood firm by his prophecy. He declared that he had been aware all the time of what Gosāla had done. The plant had been pulled up, and had temporarily died, but it had been reanimated by the shower and was once more living, while the seven pods had developed in the cluster. Plants, Mahāvīra added, were capable of *paüṭṭa-parihāra*, or reanimation without transmigration.[4]

Gosāla would still not believe Mahāvīra's word. But, on approaching the sesamum cluster, he found that it contained the seven seed-pods, just as Mahāvīra had prophesied. The revival of the sesamum plant made such an impression upon him that he became convinced that all living things were likewise capable of reanimation. And on this point he and Mahāvīra parted company, and their association came to an end.

The strange story of Gosāla and the sesamum plant is possibly the adaptation of an Ājīvika parable connected with a particular point of Gosāla's doctrine. The early Ājīvikas may well have had a favourite simile resembling the story—that just as an uprooted

[1] *Esa naṃ tilatthaṃbhaë nipphajjissaï, no na-nipphajjissaï, eë ya satta tila-puppha-jīvā . . . egāë tila-saṅguliyāë satta tilā paccāyāissanti.* Op. cit., loc. cit. In this context the meaning of the word *saṅgulikā*, which I have translated "cluster", is uncertain. Abhayadeva interprets it as *phalikā* seed-pod. Each sesamum flower produces a pod, and in this case seven pods would therefore be expected; yet the text mentions only one *saṅgulikā*, which I therefore take to mean a cluster of pods or flowers. A single sesamum pod contains many more than seven seeds, and the *satta tilā* here seem to be not single seeds, but pods.

[2] According to Jiṇadāsa's version of the story, the sesamum was replanted by the foot of a passing cow, sent by the *devas*. (*Āvaśyaka cūrṇī* i, p. 297.)

[3] *Bh. Sū.* xv, *sū.* 544, fol. 666.

[4] *Vaṇassaïkāïyā paüṭṭa-parihāraṃ pariharanti.* Loc. cit.

sesamum plant may revive after rain, so a dead body may, given certain favourable conditions, be reanimated. This was certainly part of the Ājīvika creed,[1] and since its technical term, *paüṭṭa-parihāra*, is also used here in the story of the sesamum shrub, it would seem that the story and the theory are in some way connected. Thus the Jaina account in the *Bhagavatī Sūtra* may have been devised on the basis of the Ājīvika simile to discredit the latter sect. On the other hand we have no other evidence that the Ājīvikas used such a simile, and the possibility that the story has some basis of fact cannot be excluded.

Gosāla and Vesiyāyaṇa

A further event which took place at the end of the period of Gosāla's association with Mahāvīra is also mentioned in the *Bhagavatī Sūtra.*[2] The incident occurred on the journey to Kummāragāma, after Gosāla had uprooted the sesamum plant. As they proceeded on their way the couple met a foolish ascetic (*bāla-tavassī*) named Vesiyāyaṇa, outside the village of Kuṇḍaggāma; he was seated on the ground facing the sun, with his arms raised above his head, and was engaged in a series of fasts, each of three days' duration. His body was covered with insects, born of the heat of the sun, and out of pity for all living things he would not interfere with them. Gosāla approached him and derisively asked him, " Sir, are you a *muni* or a host for lice ? " (*jūyā-sejjayaraë*). Vesiyāyaṇa did not reply, and Gosāla twice repeated the same question. After the third insult Vesiyāyaṇa's wrath was thoroughly aroused. In order to encompass Gosāla's destruction he stepped back seven or eight paces and released against him the magical heat which he had accumulated by his asceticism. But Mahāvīra, taking pity on his companion, counteracted the attack by releasing a flow of cooling magical power (*sīyaliyaṃ teyalessaṃ*). When Vesiyāyaṇa saw that Gosāla was in no way injured by his attack he was pacified, and recognized Mahāvīra's superior psychic power.

After Mahāvīra had explained to Gosāla what had happened the latter, filled with terror and awe at his colleague's miracle, did him homage, and asked how he too might obtain similar

[1] V. supra, p. 31. [2] *Bh. Sū.* xv, *sū.* 543, fol. 665–6.

powers. Mahāvīra replied that such powers could only be obtained after a six months' course of strict penance.

This story, like that of the sesamum shrub, may be a Jaina travesty of an authentic Ājīvika tradition, in this case of a psychic duel between Gosāla and another ascetic, Vesiyāyaṇa. In its present form it seems to be an attempt on the part of the author of the *Bhagavatī* at discrediting the Ājīvikas by attributing unworthy motives to Gosāla in his asceticism, and is of little importance.

Gosāla Attains Magical Power, and becomes the Leader of the Ājīvikas

After his experiences with the sesamum plant and with Vesiyāyaṇa Gosāla seems to have determined to acquire magic power and superhuman insight equal to those of Mahāvīra. He therefore practised penance in the manner which Mahāvīra had laid down, seated facing the sun in the vicinity of a lake, with his hands raised above his head, and eating only one handful of beans every three days.[1] Thus, at the end of six months, he acquired magic power (*saṅkhitta-viula-teyalesse jāe*).

If we accept the tradition of the six years spent with Mahāvīra,[2] this event must be placed about seven years after Gosāla's abandonment of the profession of a *maṅkha*. As Hoernle has pointed out,[3] Gosāla claimed to have attained *jina*-hood some two years before Mahāvīra. He is said to have spent sixteen years at Sāvatthi as a pseudo-*jina* before his death,[4] which Mahāvīra survived for sixteen and a half years.[5] But Mahāvīra is said to have lived as a *jina* for a little less than thirty years.[6] If the Jaina scriptures give approximately accurate figures the events here described must have taken place some two or three years before Mahāvīra laid claim to *jina*-hood.

The *Bhagavatī Sūtra* gives us no further information about Makkhali Gosāla's activities until the twenty-fourth year of his

[1] *Bh. Sū.* xv, *sū.* 545, fols. 666–7. Jiṇadāsa (*Āvaśyaka cūrṇī* i, p. 299) states that Gosāla performed this penance in the pottery at Sāvatthi, and adds that he tested his newly acquired power on a passing serving-girl, whom he reduced to ashes.

[2] V. supra, p. 40. [3] *Uv. Das.* ii, p. 108, n. [4] V. supra, p. 32.

[5] V. infra, p. 67. [6] *Kalpa Sūtra, Sū.* 147.

career as an ascetic,[1] when he had made his headquarters at Sāvatthi in the workshop of the potter-woman Hālāhalā, and was surrounded by many disciples. At this time, according to the *Bhagavatī* account, he was visited by six *disācaras*, in consultation with whom he codified the Ājīvika scriptures ; and his denunciation by Mahāvīra and subsequent death took place soon after this. Thus of the total of twenty-four years of Gosāla's life as an ascetic six were spent with Mahāvīra at Paṇiyabhūmī, and sixteen as a religious leader at Sāvatthi. The two years intervening between these two periods were no doubt filled by the journey to Kummāragāma,[2] the six months' penance,[3] and preliminary wanderings before making Sāvatthi his headquarters.

Gosāla's acquisition of magic power must represent an Ājīvika tradition similar to those of the Jainas and Buddhists, in which the enlightenment of the founders of the respective sects is described. Between this and the meeting with the *disācaras*, something over sixteen years must have elapsed. In this period it is not likely that Gosāla resided continuously at Sāvatthi ; probably, like his greater rivals Buddha and Mahāvīra, he travelled from place to place among the towns and villages of the Ganges valley, preaching and gathering converts. There is evidence that Ājīvikas of a sort, both ascetics and laymen, existed already at the time,[4] and his mission probably consisted largely in knitting together locally influential Ājīvika holy men and their followers, regularizing their doctrines, and gaining converts by the display of pseudo-supernatural powers. The Jaina tradition about Gosāla agrees with that of the Buddhists concerning the six heretics, that magical performances were part of his stock in trade, and it appears that he was capable, either honestly or by fraud, of producing psychic phenomena.

No doubt Sāvatthi was his headquarters, where he spent the rainy seasons, and where he obtained strongest support. The habits of the Sāvatthi Ājīvikas are vividly described in the *Jātaka* [5] ; and it would seem that the Kosalan king Pasenadi was more favourably disposed to them than was his contemporary, Bimbisāra of Magadha.[6]

[1] *Caüvvīsa-vāsa-pariyāye*, interpreted by Abhayadeva as *caturviṃśati-varṣa-pramāṇa-pravrajyā-paryāyaḥ*. *Bh. Sū.* xv, *sū.* 539, fol. 658.

[2] V. supra, pp. 47–48. [3] V. supra, p. 50. [4] V. infra, pp. 94 ff.

[5] *Jāt.* i, p. 493. V. infra, p. 110. [6] V. infra, p. 86.

During this period Gosāla seems to have acquired a reputation for his taciturnity, as well as for his asceticism. This is shown by a verse in the *Saṃyutta Nikāya*, wherein he is described as "having abandoned speech" (*vācam pahāya*),[1] and by Buddhagosa, who, in his version of the Ājīvika classification of the eight stages of the ascetic's career, states that the ascetic in the highest stage does not speak.[2] Gosāla's silence is confirmed by the Tamil text *Nīlakēci*, which states that the deified Maṟkali never speaks for fear of injuring living creatures.[3] On the other hand, both the *Bhagavatī Sūtra* and the *Uvāsaga Dasāo* refer to Gosāla as speaking, even at the time of his death,[4] so we must conclude that his silence was by no means absolute.

The sources give few indications of Makkhali Gosāla's movements and activities during his career as a religious leader. That he sometimes left Sāvatthi is shown by the *Uvāsaga Dasāo*,[5] which describes the conversion by Mahāvīra of a wealthy Ājīvika layman of Polāsapura, Saddālaputta the potter. Hearing of the defection of his disciple, Gosāla is said to have visited Polāsapura soon after Mahāvīra's departure, attended by a crowd of followers. He went first to the *Ājīviya-sabhā*, where he left his begging bowl, and then, accompanied only by a few of his chief followers, visited Saddālaputta. The latter greeted him without the reverence due from a disciple to his spiritual master. After some discussion Gosāla is purported to have admitted that Mahāvīra was a *mahā-māhaṇa*,[6] and to have praised him in Jaina terms. Saddālaputta then asked him whether he felt himself competent to dispute with Mahāvīra, and he admitted that he did not. Finally the potter offered him hospitality, but only because he had praised his new teacher Māhavīra. For some time Gosāla resided in the potter's workshop, but Saddālaputta, in spite of much persuasion, was unable to convert him to Jainism.

The town of Polāsapura is referred to only in the Jaina scriptures, and no clear indications of its location are given.[7] We may assume that it was a small town somewhere in the

[1] *Saṃ.* i, p. 66. V. infra, p. 217.

[2] *Sum. Vil.* i, p. 163. V. infra, p. 246.

[3] *Nīl.* v, 672. V. infra, p. 276.

[4] V. infra, p. 64.

[5] *Uv. Das.* ed. Hoernle i, pp. 105 ff. V. infra, p. 132.

[6] *Māhaṇa* is usually translated "a brāhmaṇa". In this context this cannot be the literal meaning, since Mahāvīra was a *kṣattriya*.

[7] V. infra, p. 133.

Ganges watershed. The description of Gosāla, attended on his journeyings by many disciples, bears a generic likeness to the stories of the progresses of Buddha and Mahāvīra as recorded in the Buddhist and Jaina scriptures. It is to be noted that the town is depicted as having already an *Ājīviya-sabhā*, or meeting-place of the Ājīvikas,[1] but that Gosāla did not reside in it, but in the workshop of one of his local supporters; he followed the same practice at Sāvatthi, where his usual place of residence was in Hālāhalā's pottery. These two instances suggest that he gave his special patronage to the potter caste.

The adulatory terms in which Gosāla is said to have praised Mahāvīra may have no basis of fact. This passage, like many others in the Jaina scriptures, seems to have been composed with the disparagement of Gosāla and the Ājīvikas in view; but if it has any historical significance it is as an indication that the rift between the two teachers was by no means so profound as the *Bhagavatī Sūtra* indicates. Saddālaputta, even after his conversion by Mahāvīra, continued to give some patronage to Gosāla, thus anticipating the practice of Aśoka and other Indian monarchs of later times, who, while maintaining one specially favoured doctrine, were quite ready to support the representatives of several others.

Our doubts as to the reliability of the story of Gosāla's praise of Mahāvīra are strengthened by a reference in the *Sūtrakṛtâṅga*,[2] wherein he speaks of his former comrade in far less friendly terms. Here Gosāla is involved in discussion with a certain Adda, an earnest disciple of Mahāvīra, and criticizes his rival on various grounds. Mahāvīra had formerly been a solitary ascetic, but was now surrounded by monks, to whom he taught the law. One or other of these courses must be wrong.[3] He was afraid to stay in public guest-houses or gardens for fear of meeting skilful men, whether base or noble, talkative or taciturn, who might put awkward questions to him.[4] Finally Gosāla alleged that

[1] V. infra, pp. 115–16.

[2] *Sū. kṛ.* ii, 6, 1 ff., fol. 388 ff.

[3] *Egantam evaṃ aduvā vi iṇhiṃ, do-v annam-annaṃ na sameti jamhā.* Loc. cit., v. 3.

[4] *Mehāviṇo sikkhiya buddhimantā suttehi atthehi ya ṇicchayannā.*
Pucchiṃsu mā ṇe aṇagāra anne iti saṅkamāṇe ṇa uveti tattha. Loc. cit., v. 16, fol. 392.

Mahāvīra was a mercenary teacher, vending his wares like a merchant.[1]

We have no reliable information about the circumstances of this discussion. Adda, the Jaina protagonist, is said in the *niryukti* to the passage to have been the son of one Adda, of Addapura [2]—a statement which adds nothing to our knowledge, but rather casts doubt on the reliability of the account. If the story has any historical significance it is to suggest that the relations of Gosāla and Mahāvīra worsened with the passage of time. Details of the account of the incident of Saddālaputta suggest that it took place soon after Mahāvīra's "enlightenment", when he was not so widely known as he later became. Gosāla's debate with Adda, on the other hand, presupposes a strong Jaina community, defending itself against all comers.

A brief and obscure reference is contained in the *Vihimaggapavā* of Jinapaha Sūri,[3] to the effect that Gosāla was disappointed that no gifts had been received, and therefore his followers did not accept (alms) from their female relatives.[4] This phrase by a late Jaina writer may refer to a lost Ājīvika story of the prophet being without honour in his own country.

Turning to the Pāli scriptures we can find few references to the Ājīvika leader except in conjunction with the five other heretical teachers of the Buddhist canon. Two passages, however, make it clear that the Buddha knew of Makkhali Gosāla, and thought his doctrine exceedingly pernicious. In the *Aṅguttara Nikāya* [5] he declares that Makkhali is a stupid man (*mogha-puriso*), and that he knows of no other person born to the detriment grief and disadvantage of so many people, or to such disadvantage and sorrow of gods and men. Makkhali is like a fisherman, casting his net at the mouth of a river, for the destruction of many fish.

In another passage of the *Aṅguttara* [6] the Buddha expresses

[1] *Pannaṃ jahā vaṇië udayaṭṭhī āyassa heüṃ pagareti saṅgaṃ.*
Taūvame samaṇe Nāyaputte icc' eva me hoti matī viyakkā. Ibid., v, 19, fol. 394.

[2] V., 187, fol. 385.

[3] Quoted in Weber, *Verzeichniss*, vol. ii, MS. 1944, p. 870. I have been unable to procure a copy of this text.

[4] *Gosālo jaī dattīhiṃ aladdhiyāhiṃ uvahaō c'eva ahava have jogavāhiṇo to heto ṇa sambandhiṇīo gheppanti.*

[5] *Aṅg.* i, p. 33; cf. *Aṅg.* i, p. 287.

[6] *Aṅg.* i, p. 286.

a very forcible opinion on the value of Makkhali's teaching. Just as a hair blanket (*kesakambala*) is the worst of all fabrics in texture, appearance, and utility, so of all unorthodox doctrines (*samaṇa-ppavādānaṃ*) that of Makkhali is the worst. It seems that this attack was originally levelled against Ajita Kesakambalī, since the striking simile is especially appropriate to him. But the change of the name to Makkhali is itself significant; it must have been made at a time when Ajita was almost forgotten, and the forces of Buddhism needed further ammunition against the Ājīvikas.

These severe strictures of the Buddha upon Makkhali, and the simile of the fisherman in particular, seem to indicate the great success of the latter's mission. Rather than Mahāvīra it is Makkhali Gosāla who emerges as the Buddha's chief opponent and most dangerous rival.

CHAPTER IV

THE LAST DAYS OF MAKKHALI GOSĀLA

THE SIX *DISĀCARAS*

The history of Gosāla is resumed in the *Bhagavatī Sūtra*[1] in the twenty-fourth year of his asceticism. He was then living at Sāvatthi in the workshop of his devoted disciple Hālāhalā the potter-woman, surrounded by a community (*saṅgha*) of Ājīvikas.

At this time he was visited by six *disācaras*, named Sāṇa, Kalanda, Kaṇiyāra, Acchidda, Aggivesāyaṇa, and Ajjunna Gomāyuputta. According to the text the six ascetics " extracted the eightfold *Mahāṇimitta* in the *Puvvas*, with the *Maggas* making the total up to ten, after examining hundreds of opinions ". After briefly considering this eightfold *Mahāṇimitta* Gosāla declared the six inevitable factors in the life of every being—gain and loss, joy and sorrow, life and death.[2] Thenceforward he claimed to be a *jina*, an *arhant*, a *kevalin*, and a possessor of omniscience.

The passage describing the visit of the *disācaras* is of great obscurity. The author introduces into the story six new characters, who seem to have been responsible for the collation of the Ājīvika scriptures from earlier material. The character of the newcomers is obscure, and the compound *disācara* seems unique. It is not quoted either in the St. Petersburg Lexicon or in the Dictionary of the Pāli Text Society, and seems not to occur elsewhere in the Jaina texts, this being the only reference given in Ratnacandrajī's *Ardha-māgadhī Dictionary*.

The *disācaras* were obviously wandering ascetic philosophers

[1] *Bh. Sū.* xv, *sū.* 539, fols. 658–669.

[2] *Te cha disācarā aṭṭhaviham puvvagayaṃ maggadasamaṃ satehiṃ satehiṃ mati-daṃsaṇehiṃ nijjuhanti. . . . Gosālaṃ Maṅkhaliputtaṃ uvaṭṭhāiṃsu. Taë ṇaṃ se Gosāle . . . teṇaṃ aṭṭhaṅgassa mahāṇimittassa keṇaï ulloya-metteṇaṃ savvesiṃ pāṇāṇāṃ . . . imāiṃ cha aṇaïkkamaṇijjāiṃ vāgareti. Bh. Sū.*, loc. cit.

of some sort, but the uncommon name given to them suggests that they were of a special type. They were evidently on good terms with Gosāla, and appear to have shared his doctrines. Their names, like those of most of the lesser figures associated with Gosāla, cannot well be connected with any of those in Pāli and Sanskrit literature. Sāṇa, Kaṇiyāra, and Acchidda seem to have no counterparts whatever; Kalanda, however, is in some manuscripts called Kaṇanda,[1] which suggests the Vaiśeṣika philosopher Kaṇāda. The name of Ajjunna Gomāyuputta suggests that of Ajjuṇa Goyamaputta,[2] the teacher whose mantle possibly fell upon Gosāla, but who must have died sixteen years previously.[3] Barua [4] suggests that he was "the same as the Ājīvika Pāṇḍuputta, son of a repairer of old carts".[5] Since the epic Arjuna was the son of Pāṇḍu, Pāṇḍuputta and Ajjuna may be taken as synonyms of the same name, but the argument is extremely tenuous. Even though we accept the very doubtful equivalence of the two names, Pāṇḍuputta of the Pāli reference may equally well have been Ajjuṇa Goyamaputta, the previous host of the soul of Udāï, from whose body that soul was said to have passed to that of Gosāla in its last *pauṭṭa-parihāra*.[6]

The surname Aggivessana occurs here and there in the Pāli scriptures. Saccaka Nigaṇṭhaputta, who visited the Buddha at Kūṭâgāra-sālā near Vesāli, and was converted by him, is referred to by this title.[7] The same Saccaka is elsewhere referred to as a furious debater of Vesāli, who was defeated in argument by the Buddha.[8] Another Aggivessana is Dīghanakha the *paribbājaka*, nephew of the *bhikkhu* Sāriputta, and also converted by the Buddha.[9] It is hardly probable that either of these two have any connection with the *disācara* Aggivesāyaṇa; the name seems certainly that of a clan or *gotra*.

The *disācara* Aggivesāyaṇa may also be connected with Agniveśa, the semi-legendary physician upon whose doctrines the *Caraka Saṃhitā* is based.[10] The text states that Atreya, who had

[1] Teste, *JDL.* ii, p. 41, n.
[2] V. supra, pp. 32–34.
[3] The patronymic appears in the form *Goyamaputta* in at least one MS.—India Office Cat. No. 7447, fol. 201.
[4] *JDL.* ii, p. 41. [5] V. infra, pp. 126–27. [6] V. supra, p. 32.
[7] *Majjh.* i, pp. 237 ff. [8] *Majjh.* i, pp. 227 ff. [9] *Majjh.* i, pp. 497 ff.
[10] Hoernle, *Studies in the Medicine of Ancient India* i, p. 1.

learned *ayurveda* from Bharadvāja, imparted his knowledge to six disciples, Agniveśa, Bhela, Jatūkarṇa, Parāśara, Hārīta, and Kṣūrapāṇi, each of whom produced a *sūtra*.[1] The names of the five fellow-students of Agniveśa bear no resemblance to those of the five other *disācaras*, their number and this one name being the only points common to the two groups. We may note, however, that Bharadvāja is here two generations removed from Agniveśa; the same may be said of Bhāraddāï in the list of the *paüṭṭa-parihāras* of Udāï[2]; here Bhāraddāï is two generations removed from Gosāla, and therefore presumably from Aggivesāyaṇa the *disācara*. This further tenuous similarity is probably coincidental and we must conclude that there are no certain references to any of the six *disācaras* outside the *Bhagavatī Sūtra*.

It is probable that the *disācaras* were Gosāla's chief disciples, and that the meeting at Sāvatthi was a conference at which the doctrines of the Ājīvikas were codified and the claims of their leader to omniscience and perfection were explicitly stated. The *disācaras* may have been wandering evangelists, to whom Makkhali Gosāla had assigned dioceses corresponding to the six quarters (*diśā*) of early Hinduism and Buddhism.[3] On this hypothesis, however, it is not easy to suggest the functions of the *disācaras* representing the upward and downward directions.

The scriptures and doctrines which formed the agenda of this important meeting will be considered at greater length in the second part of this work.[4]

Gosāla is exposed by Mahāvīra

At that time Mahāvīra was in the neighbourhood of Sāvatthi, and the visit of the six *disācaras* to Gosāla was reported to him by his chief disciple Indabhūï Goyama.[5] Mahāvīra then told his followers the story of the birth of Gosāla and of the early association of the two ascetics, which we have paraphrased above. The news of Mahāvīra's exposure of Gosāla rapidly spread through

[1] *Caraka Samhitā*, ed. Sastri i, 29 ff., p. 13.
[2] V. supra, p. 32.
[3] *Śatapatha Brāhmaṇa* xiv, 6, 11, 5. *Siṅgālovāda Sutta*, *Dīgha* iii, pp. 188–9. *Sthānāṅga* vi, *sū*. 499.
[4] V. infra, pp. 213–15.
[5] *Bh. Sū*. xv, *sū*. 540, fols. 659–660.

the city, and seems to have resulted in a popular demonstration against the latter. Gosāla, who at the time was at the penance-ground (*āyāvaṇa-bhūmī*), returned to Hālāhalā's workshop with his followers, his eyes blazing with rage.[1]

Shortly afterwards Āṇanda, a simple-minded ascetic disciple of Mahāvīra, was passing the pottery. On seeing him Gosāla called to him, and told him a cautionary story of a company of merchants, who, while passing with their caravan through a desert, found that their water supply was exhausted. In their search for water they found a large anthill, which had four heaps (*vappu*) rising from its base. On breaking the first they found an abundant supply of clear water, while the second yielded gold, and the third jewels. Delighted at their discovery they decided to break down the fourth and last. A worthy and thoughtful member of the company tried to restrain them, saying that the breaking of the last heap would cause their destruction. But his warning was not heeded, and the merchants proceeded to demolish it. From it there emerged a fiery serpent, which burnt the whole company to ashes, sparing only the cautious merchant, who had tried to prevent the demolition of the last heap of the anthill. Gosāla threatened that if Mahāvīra continued to slander him he would reduce him to ashes in the same manner as the serpent had destroyed the merchants.[2]

The story of the merchants is important in that it indicates that Gosāla, like the Buddha, was in the habit of employing folk-tales in his preaching. This story is repeated with but slight variation in the *Jātaka*,[3] where, perhaps significantly, the merchants are said to have come from Sāvatthi.

The terrified Āṇanda returned and repeated the story to Mahāvīra, who calmed his fears and forbade for the future all association of his followers with Gosāla.[4]

The facts that Āṇanda was ready to listen to Gosāla's story, and that Mahāvīra was compelled to forbid all communications between his disciples and the Ājīvika leader, tend to strengthen the suspicion that the rift between the two sects was not at first so profound as the *Bhagavatī* account suggests.[5]

[1] Ibid., *sū*. 546, fols. 666–7.

[2] *Bh. Sū*. xv, *sū*. 547, fols. 668–670.

[3] *Jāt*. iv, p. 350.

[4] *Bh. Sū*. xv, *sū*. 549, fol. 671.

[5] V. supra, p. 53.

Gosāla visits Mahāvīra

After this incident Gosāla, filled with anger, visited Mahāvīra at the Koṭṭhaga *caitya*, attended as usual by a band of followers. Here he explained that he was not really Gosāla Maṅkhaliputta, the former colleague of Mahāvīra, but Udāï Kuṇḍiyāyaṇīya,[1] and expounded fully his doctrine of transmigration under the control of *Niyati*.[2] After this long lecture Mahāvīra replied that Gosāla was like a thief chased by villagers, feverishly trying to hide himself. "It won't do, Gosāla!" he said, "that shadow is your own, and nobody else's!"[3]

Thereupon Gosāla's anger flared into fury, and he roundly cursed Mahāvīra.[4] This horrified the disciple Savvāṇubhūti, who reproached Gosāla sternly for so reviling his former teacher.[5] Gosāla promptly turned his anger upon the faithful disciple, and immediately reduced him to a heap of ashes by the magic force which he had accumulated from his asceticism. When a second disciple, Suṇakkhatta, remonstrated with him, he also suffered the same fate, although he survived long enough to pay a final homage to his master Mahāvīra.

Gosāla once more turned to Mahāvīra and repeated his curses. The latter reproached him in terms the same as those used by his two dead disciples. Gosāla then stepped back and attempted to destroy his adversary by his magic power; but on so perfect an ascetic as Mahāvīra the magic was quite ineffectual. The stream of supernatural force rebounded, and penetrated the body from which it had emanated.

Apparently Gosāla was unaware of what had happened. "You are now pervaded by my magic force," he said to Mahāvīra, "and within six months you will die of bilious fever (*pittajjara*)."

Unperturbed, Mahāvīra replied that the magic power of Gosāla had had no effect on him, but that Gosāla himself would die of bilious fever within seven nights, smitten by his own powers. He, Mahāvīra, on the other hand, would live on earth as a *jina* for another sixteen years.[6]

[1] V. supra, pp. 30 ff.

[2] *Bh. Sū.* xv, *sū.* 550, fols. 673–4. V. infra, pp. 219, 249 ff.

[3] *Taṃ mā evaṃ Gosālā n' ārihasi . . . . Sacc' eva te sā chāyā, no annā. Bh. Sū.* xv, *sū.* 551, fol. 677.

[4] Op. cit., *sū.* 552, fol. 677.

[5] Op. cit., *sū.* 553, fol. 677.

[6] *Bh. Sū.* xv, *sū.* 553, fol. 678.

The news of this magic duel spread through the city. The whole populace was aroused to a high pitch of excitement, and the partisans of one or other of the ascetics fiercely maintained their masters' causes.

Now Mahāvīra permitted his disciples to approach Gosāla and dispute with him. Already the latter began to feel the effects of the magic power, and his complexion changed its hue. Many of his disciples left him, and went over to Mahāvīra's faction, but a few remained faithful to their old master. Staring about him, tearing his beard, and stamping the ground, Gosāla cried "Alas, I am ruined!"[1] and returned to the potter-woman's workshop.

The circumstantial details of this story give it a measure of credibility. After extracting the supernatural element we have the record of a violent quarrel which took place between Gosāla and Mahāvīra, shortly before the death of the former, in the course of which two followers of the latter lost their lives. This is Hoernle's interpretation of the story.[2] Barua, on the other hand, suggests that the account of the deaths of the two disciples may be a veiled admission that they betrayed their leader and joined the faction of Gosāla.[3] This is by no means impossible, but in view of the explicit statement of the text we prefer the former explanation.

It would seem that, prior to this incident, the two teachers had generally tolerated one another, and the followers of the two sects had been often on not unfriendly terms. The quarrel at the Koṭṭhaga *caitya* apparently changed the situation, and from now on the relations of the Ājīvikas and the Nirgranthas became openly hostile, tempered only by the vows of *ahiṃsā* which the members of the latter sect maintained, as probably did the Ājīvikas also.

Gosāla's Delirium

The discomfited Gosāla, once more at his headquarters in Hālāhalā's pottery, appears to have lapsed into a state bordering on delirium. He clutched a mango stone in his hand, drank

[1] *Hā hā aho, haō 'ham assi.* Op. cit., fol. 679. [2] *ERE.* i, p. 259.
[3] *JDL.* ii, pp. 34 ff.

spirits, sang continuously, danced, did reverence to his patron Hālāhalā,[1] and sprinkled his fevered limbs with the cool muddy water in which the potter's clay had been mixed.[2]

Here the thread of the story is broken by another pronouncement of Mahāvīra to his disciples.[3] He declared that the magic heat (*teye*) which was destroying Gosāla was sufficient to reduce the sixteen great regions (*jaṇavayā*) to ashes. He further stated that, to hide the shame of his objectionable conduct (*vajja*), Gosāla would lay down the doctrine of the eight last things (*carimāiṃ*),[4] and of the four drinks (*pāṇagāiṃ*) and the four substitutes for drink (*apāṇagāiṃ*).[5]

The interpolation of Mahāvīra's prophecy is very significant. The writer of the *Bhagavatī* seems to have composed this passage with the same motive as he did that on the sesamum plant [6]—to discredit the Ājīvikas by attributing an unworthy origin to points of Ājīvika doctrine. Thus in its details the account may be unreliable; but the essential import of the passage, that Gosāla during his last illness laid down certain new doctrines based on his own actions and on the events of the time,[7] is by no means incredible, and may be accepted for want of contrary evidence.

Ayampula visits Gosāla

The *Bhagavatī Sūtra's* account returns to the dying Gosāla.[8] In Sāvatthi there dwelt Ayampula, an earnest lay adherent of the Ājīvika order. In the early part of the night he was suddenly troubled by an important question: "What is the form of the *hallā*?" [9] He decided to put this question to his omniscient teacher, so he rose and went to the potter's workshop. There he found Gosāla in the shameful condition already described. Ayampula was about to retire, but was intercepted by some of the Ājīvika disciples who surrounded Gosāla. They informed him that their master had just propounded his new doctrines of the

[1] *Añjalikammaṃ karemāṇe*. There seems no reason to interpret the phrase, as does Hoernle, in a sexual sense. It may imply that Gosāla commanded his followers to revere Hālāhalā after his death.

[2] *Bh. Sū.* xv, *sū.* 553, fol. 679.

[3] Ibid., *sū.* 554, fol. 679 ff.

[4] V. infra, pp. 68 ff.

[5] V. infra, pp. 127 ff.

[6] V. supra, pp. 47 ff.

[7] V. infra, pp. 68 ff.

[8] *Bh. Sū.* xv, *sū.* 554, fols. 680–1.

[9] *Kiṃsaṇṭhiyā hallā paṇṇattā?* Ibid., loc. cit.

eight finalities, the four drinks, and the four substitutes for drink; and they added that Gosāla was quite able to answer Ayampula's question. While they kept him out of sight of Gosāla they made a sign to the latter to throw aside his mango stone before giving audience to Ayampula. At last the credulous Ayampula was allowed to approach. The master's words to him were of the strangest character: "This is not a mango stone, but a mango skin. Of what form is the *hallā*? It is like a bamboo root. Play the *vīṇā*, old fellow, play the *vīṇā*, old fellow!"[1]

After this remarkable utterance we are told that Ayampula was fully satisfied, and went home.

The nature of the *hallā*, about which Ayampula's mind was so troubled, is uncertain. The commentator Abhayadeva confidently defines the *hallā* as "a certain insect, the form of which is like that of the *govālikā* grass",[2] and on Gosāla's reply to Ayampula's question, Abhayadeva remarks, "it is well known in the world that the form of the *govālikā* grass is that of a bamboo root."[3] The explanation of Abhayadeva is the only one available. But the reader asks whether Ayampula would go to the trouble of visiting Gosāla at night if his inquiry were of a purely entomological nature. The explanation of Abhayadeva may disguise the fact that the commentator himself was unaware of the meaning of this rare word.

The incident may have been inserted by the author of the *Bhagavatī Sūtra* with satirical intention. It seems certain that the later Ājīvikas held surprising theories about the *jīva*, for instance that it was of eight parts and five hundred *yojanas* in size.[4] The question of Ayampula is possibly the ludicrous counterpart of a serious question put to Gosāla concerning the size of the soul, and Gosāla's reply may be similarly ludicrous in intention.

Gosāla's statement that the object which he had been holding was not a mango stone but a mango skin is probably to be read in the context of the four substitutes for drink, as laid down by Gosāla in his delirium. The ascetic undertaking the final Ājīvika

[1] *No khalu esa ambakūṇaë, ambacoyaë ṇaṃ ese. Kiṃsaṇṭhiyā hallā paṇṇattā? Vaṃsī-mūla-saṇṭhiyā hallā paṇṇattā! Vīṇaṃ vāëhi re vīragā! 2.* Ibid., loc. cit.

[2] *Govālikā-tṛṇa-samān'-âkāraḥ kīṭaka-viśeṣaḥ.* Ibid., fol. 684.

[3] *Idaṃ ca vaṃśī-mūla-saṃsthitatvaṃ tṛṇa-govālikāyā loka-pratītam.* Ibid., loc. cit.

[4] V. infra, pp. 270 ff.

penance, which involved ritual suicide by slow starvation, was permitted to hold a raw mango in his mouth, without sucking its juice or eating it.[1] The presence of a mango stone in Gosāla's hand would have indicated to Ayampula that he had broken his own rule by eating the flesh of the fruit. Hence he is purported to have denied that it was a mango stone. His exhortation to Ayampula to play the *vīṇā* is perhaps connected with the two *mārgas*, stated by the commentator to be song and dance, which he is said to have ordained at the conference with the six *disācaras*.[2] There is reason to believe that we have here a further Jaina attempt to ascribe an unworthy origin to later Ājīvika practice.

Gosāla's Repentance and Death

When Gosāla realized that his end was near he gave orders to his disciples for the preparation of a sumptuous funeral. They were to bathe his body in scented water, anoint it with sandal paste, array it in a rich robe, and bedeck it in all his ornaments. They were then to mount it on a bier drawn by a thousand men, and to proceed through the streets of Sāvatthi, proclaiming that the *jina* Gosāla Maṅkhaliputta, the last *tīrthaṅkara* of the twenty-four *tīrthaṅkaras* of this *Avasarpiṇī* had passed away. After this his body was to be cremated.[3]

Towards the end of the seventh night Gosāla came to his senses. He fully realized how evil had been his past conduct, and was afflicted with the most lively remorse. He told his disciples that he was no *jina*, but a fraud, a murderer of *śramaṇas*, a betrayer of his teacher, dying from the effects of his own magic power. He recognized Mahāvīra as the true *jina*, cancelled his former instructions, and told his disciples to desecrate his body on his death. They were to tie a rope to his left foot, to spit thrice into his face, and to drag his body round the streets of Sāvatthi, proclaiming that he was not a *jina* but a cheat and a murderer, and that Mahāvīra was the only true *jina*. After this they were to dispose of his body without respect.[4]

On his death the Ājīvika monks kept only the letter of his instructions. Upon the floor of the pottery they traced a plan

[1] V. infra, p. 128.
[2] V. supra, pp. 56–58, and infra, p. 117.
[3] *Bh. Sū.* xv, *sū.* 554, fol. 681.
[4] *Bh. Sū.* xv, *sū.* 555, fols. 681–2.

of the city of Sāvatthi, and over this they dragged the body by its left foot, proclaiming all the while that Gosāla was not the true *jina*. Then they unfastened the rope from the ankle of the dead man, opened the door of the pottery, and, adorning the body according to Gosāla's first instructions, performed the funeral with great pomp.[1]

Hoernle interprets the *Bhagavatī* story as follows: "The taunts of his rivals and the consequent distrust of the townspeople made Gosāla's position at Sāvatthi untenable. It preyed on his mind so much that it became utterly unhinged and throwing aside all ascetic restraint he gave himself up to drinking . . . . Six months of this riotous living brought on his end." [2] The period of six months, which Hoernle gives for the last phase of Gosāla's life, seems to be based on the duration of the final penance which he is said to have ordained shortly before his death.[3] Yet the *Sūtra* states categorically that his death occurred on the seventh night from the magic duel. Barua [4] has noted the discrepancy, and does not accept the Jaina story, but believes that Gosāla died voluntarily at the end of a penance of six months' duration.

Whatever inaccuracy there may be in the details of the account there seems no reason to disbelieve the broad outline of the story, which is narrated with a vividness and a wealth of circumstantial detail rare in canonical Jaina literature. After an illness which involved fever and delirium, and which was perhaps induced by his penances, Gosāla died, and was given a sumptuous funeral by his followers. The story of his deathbed repentance is so gratifying from the Jaina point of view that it is hard to accept. Accounts of similar last-minute conversions and edifying last words are common in the popular religious literature of all places and periods, and can rarely be authenticated. It requires little critical acumen to realize that this part of the story is quite unreliable.

Dr. A. S. Gopani appears to accept the accuracy of the whole of the *Bhagavatī Sūtra* story of Gosāla, including even the account of his deathbed conversion, without criticism.[5] In this course we

[1] Ibid., *sū*. 556, fol. 682.
[2] *ERE*. i, p. 259.
[3] V. infra, pp. 127 ff.
[4] *JDL*. ii, p. 36.
[5] *Bhāratīya Vidyā*. ii, pp. 201–210, and iii, pp. 47–59, passim.

cannot follow him. The whole chapter is pervaded by sectarian prejudice, and, as we have seen, many of its episodes seem to have been devised in order to provide an ignominious origin for certain elements of Ājīvika belief and custom. On the other hand it seems probable that the author used as material for his biography of Gosāla authentic Ājīvika traditions, which he adapted to suit his own purposes. It is not impossible, after critical examination, tentatively to separate this hypothetical Ājīvika tradition from the Jaina interpolations and corruptions. This we have attempted to do in our treatment of the several episodes of Gosāla's life-story. There remains, however, the question: even after the most careful sifting, how much of this residue of authentic tradition is itself historically reliable? We cannot answer this question, for both Buddhist and Hindu sources are completely silent on the most important incidents of the *Bhagavatī Sūtra* story, and therefore we have no independent confirmation of it. For want of contradictory evidence we can but provisionally accept these unconfirmed traditions wherever they are not inherently improbable, all the while bearing in mind the fact that they are based on the slender authority of a single text, compiled by the opponents of the protagonist of the story; we must also remember that the final recension of the text in question took place over a millennium after the events it purports to describe, and was carried out by men who had scant regard for historical accuracy.

The Date of Gosāla's Death

Certain indications in the *Bhagavatī Sūtra*, taken together with references elsewhere in the Jaina canon and in the Buddhist scriptures, may be used tentatively to fit the year of Gosāla's death into a framework provided by those of his great contemporaries, Buddha and Mahāvīra.

As we have seen [1] Gosāla is said to have lived as an ascetic for twenty-four years, the first six of which were spent with Mahāvīra, and the last sixteen as a pseudo-*jina* at Sāvatthi. It seems that the whole of the twenty-four year period occurred during the lifetime of his two greater rivals.

[1] V. supra, pp. 50–51.

Reliable synchronisms of the events of Gosāla's life with that of the Buddha do not exist. The *Sāmañña-phala Sutta* depicts him, together with the other five heretical teachers, as being alive during the reign of King Ajātasattu of Magadha,[1] but this statement is of little value as a synchronism, especially when it is remembered that all six are referred to in the *Milinda Pañha* as the contemporaries of King Menander of Śākala.[2] In the *Saṃyutta Nikāya*[3] King Bimbisāra, Ajātasattu's father and predecessor, is reported to have told the Buddha that the six heretics were well established in their status as teachers,[4] while the Buddha was young and had but recently become a mendicant.[5] This suggests that Makkhali Gosāla was considerably older than the Buddha, but no value can be placed on the statement, for the heretics seem here obviously introduced as representatives of older and well-established philosophic schools, and not as individuals.

Two important statements in the *Bhagavatī Sūtra* itself do, however, give a clue to the approximate date of Makkhali Gosāla's death. These are, firstly, Mahāvīra's prophecy that he would survive the death of Gosāla by sixteen or sixteen and a half years. This statement was made twice, the first time to Gosāla himself after the magic duel at the Koṭṭhaga *caitya*,[6] when the duration of Mahāvīra's survival of Gosāla is given as sixteen years; and again soon after the death of Gosāla, when Mahāvīra was taken ill at the town of Meṇḍhiyagāma.[7] Remembering Gosāla's curse, the disciple Sīha feared that his master would die within six months as a result of the magic duel, but Mahāvīra calmed his fears, and stated that he had yet sixteen and a half years to live on earth as a *jina*. Mahāvīra quickly recovered, after eating the flesh of a cockerel killed by a cat.

At a distance of over two thousand years the discrepancy of six months in the two statements is not very significant, but of the two the second seems the more probably accurate. It may be suggested that the extra half-year is the insertion of a meticulous copyist who had access to early records now lost to us and desired greater accuracy for Mahāvīra's forecast.

[1] V. supra, pp. 11–12. [2] V. supra, p. 21. [3] *Saṃ.* i, p. 68.
[4] *Saṅghino gaṇino ñātā yassassino titthakārā.*
[5] *Daharo c' eva jātiyā, navo ca pabbajāyā.*
[6] V. supra, p. 60 [7] *Bh. Sū.* xv, *sū.* 557, fols. 685–6.

A second point of synchronism is contained in the list of the eight finalities proclaimed by Gosāla in his last illness.[1] These are :—

1. The last drink (*carime pāṇe*).
2. The last song (*carime geye*).
3. The last dance (*carime naṭṭe*).
4. The last greeting (*carime añjalikamme*).
5. The last great stormcloud (*carime pokkhala-saṃvaṭṭaë mahāmehe*).
6. The last sprinkling scent-elephant (*carime seyaṇaë gandha-hatthī*).
7. The last battle with large stones (*carime mahāsilākaṇṭaë saṅgāme*).
8. The twenty-fourth and last *tīrthaṅkara* of this *Avasarpiṇī* (*imīse Osappiṇīë caüvīsāë titthakarāṇaṃ carime tittha-kare*), who was Gosāla himself.

Abhayadeva explains three of these eight finalities as having been laid down by Gosāla to impress his followers with the cataclysmic quality of his own impending death[2]; the first four, on the other hand, were put forward with the even more reprehensible motive of excusing his own delirious conduct in singing, dancing, drinking muddy water, and saluting Hālāhalā.[3] The eighth and last was, of course, Gosāla himself. All of them were supposed inevitably to occur at a *jina*'s *nirvāṇa*, according to Ājīvika teaching.

This very plausible explanation of the strange list is accepted with modifications by Hoernle. " The *raison d'être* of this curious doctrine," he writes " . . . is that the dubious death of their master was felt by his disciples to require investment with some kind of rehabilitating glamour." [4]

The first four of the eight finalities were obviously suggested by the behaviour of Gosāla in his delirium.[5] For the sixth and seventh Hoernle has found striking parallels.[6] The *Nirayāvalikā* [7]

[1] *Bh. Sū.* xv, *sū.* 554, fol. 679. V. supra, pp. 62-63.

[2] *Puṣkala-saṃvarttak'-âdīni tu trīṇi bāhyāni prākṛt'-ânupayoge 'pi carama-sāmānyāj jana-citta-rañjanāya caramāṇy uktāni.* Ibid., fol. 684.

[3] V. supra, pp. 61–62. *Pānak'-âdīni catvāri svagatāni. . . . Etāni kila nirvāṇa-kāle jinasy' âvaśyam-bhāvīn' îti n' âsty eteṣu doṣa ity asya . . . avadya-pracchādan'-ârthāni bhavanti.* Abhayadeva to *Bh. Sū.*, fols. 683–4.

[4] *ERE.* i, p. 263.

[5] V. supra, pp. 61–62.

[6] *Uv. Das.* ii, app. i, p. 7.

[7] Gopani and Chokshi edn., pp. 19 ff.

contains the account of a splendid rutting elephant called "Sprinkler" (*Seyaṇaä*), because he was in the habit of sprinkling the ladies of the Magadhan court with water from his trunk while they were bathing. This elephant, together with a priceless necklace, was given by King Seṇiya (Bimbisāra of the Buddhist texts), to his younger son Vehalla.

On the accession of Prince Kūṇiya (Ajātasattu), Seṇiya's wicked son, the new king desired this fine elephant and the necklace. Inspired by his covetous wife Paümāvaï, Kūṇiya demanded the treasures of Vehalla, who, disinclined to give them up and fearful for his life, fled with them to the court of his maternal uncle, Ceḍaga, who was chieftain of Vesāli, and head of the clan of the Licchavis, the chief element of the Vajjian confederacy of the Pāli texts. After some negotiation war broke out between Magadha and the Licchavis over the two treasures, and a great battle took place. The outcome is not clearly stated in the text, but the battle is said to have been very fiercely fought, and in it a prince Kāla was killed by Ceḍaga and the forces under his command were completely routed. It would seem therefore that all did not go well for the Magadhan invaders. The battle is referred to as *Rahamusala*, and is said to have taken place during the lifetime of Mahāvīra, who, according to the text, knew telepathically of the death of the prince Kāla. These events seem certainly to be those which inspired the sixth and seventh of the finalities, the sprinkling scent elephant and the battle with great stones.

Although Hoernle seems to have been unaware of the fact, the story of Kūṇiya's war with the Licchavis is told elsewhere in Jaina literature. The *Bhagavatī Sūtra* itself [1] gives an account of the campaign, with significant differences of detail. Here two battles are fought, called *Mahāsilākaṇṭaë* and *Rahamusale* respectively. Kūṇiya is said to have gone out to the *Mahāsilākaṇṭaë* battle only after the engagement had commenced, when he heard that the fortunes of his armies were declining. Ceḍaga, a mighty archer, shot Kūṇiya's ten brothers on ten successive days, and his success seemed assured until, on the eleventh day, the god Indra presented Kūṇiya with a great war-engine, which struck down the Licchavis with great stones. The second defeat

[1] *Bh. Sū.* vii, *sū.* 299 ff., pp. 576 ff.

of Ceḍaga, at the *Rahamusala* battle, took place in similar circumstances, after Kūṇiya had received from Camara, the Indra of the Asuras, a wonderful chariot armed with a great club, which worked havoc among the Licchavis.

Jinadāsa's *Āvaśyaka Cūrṇī*[1] continues the story. The *gaṇarājas*, or chieftains of the confederate clans, demoralized by the two defeats, abandoned Ceḍaga and returned to their own cities. Ceḍaga retreated on Vesāli, and prepared for a siege. The city held out for twelve years, when it was betrayed by the treachery of the ascetic Kūlavālaya, the force of whose religious merit had formerly protected it. He was won over by a beautiful prostitute in the employ of Kūṇiya, and persuaded to break his vows and to betray the city. Ceḍaga committed suicide by drowning, and the Licchavis emigrated to Nepal.[2]

Thus we have two synchronisms for the date of Gosāla's death, the first being the tradition of its occurence sixteen and a half years before that of Mahāvīra, and the second that of its taking place during the war between Magadha and Vesāli in the reign of Ajātasattu-Kūṇiya. Of the two the latter seems the more reliable. It is probable that the author of the *Bhagavatī* made use of an authentic Ājīvika tradition, for the occurrence of the great battle and the death of their leader in the same year would make a great impression upon Gosāla's followers, and the memory of the synchronism might well be accurately preserved. On the other hand the tradition of the sixteen and a half years between the deaths of the two teachers is of a type more easily corrupted. The author of the *Bhagavatī* seems to have had a predilection for certain numbers. For instance the number six occurs in this chapter in various contexts. Thus Gosāla lives with Mahāvīra for six years,[3] he performs a six months' penance,[4] he confers with the six *disācaras*,[5] he proclaims the six inevitables,[6] he threatens Mahāvīra with death in six months' time.[7] A period of sixteen years has already been introduced once into the story, when it is stated that Gosāla spent sixteen years in the pottery

[1] *Āvaśyaka Cūrṇī*, vol. ii, pp. 172 ff.

[2] The elliptical account of the *Āvaśyaka Cūrṇī* is expanded in a *bhāṣya* to the *Uttarādhyayana Sūtra*, which is not available, but is paraphrased in *Abhidhāna Rājendra*, vol. iii, s.v. *Kūlavālaya*.

[3] V. supra, p. 40. [4] V. supra, p. 50. [5] V. supra, p. 56 ff.

[6] V. supra, ibid. [7] V. supra, p. 60.

at Sāvatthi as leader of the Ājīvika order,[1] and, as will be shown, certain evidence indicates that Mahāvīra did not survive Gosāla by so long a period.[2] Although this evidence is inconclusive, and although we accept the tradition of the sixteen years between the deaths of the two men as a working hypothesis, the possibility must be recognized that the author of the *Bhagavatī* may have introduced the period of sixteen or sixteen and a half years into his account of Mahāvīra's prophecy with his former statement in view. It would indeed be an edifying act of cosmic justice if Mahāvīra, threatened with rapid death by Gosāla, were portrayed as surviving his adversary by the length of the latter's career as a false prophet. In our efforts to fix the date of Gosāla's death we must therefore give the greatest credence to the synchronism of this event with the war between Magadha and Vesāli, and our first efforts must be towards settling the approximate date of the war.

Dr. H. C. Raychaudhuri [3] has identified the war of the *Nirayāvalikā Sūtra* with that referred to in the Pāli scriptures as having taken place soon after the Buddha's death. The account of the preparations for this war is to be found in the *Mahāparinibbāna Sutta*, and that of the war itself in Buddhaghosa's commentary thereon. Much of the story is therefore contained in a comparatively late source, but it must be remembered that Buddhaghosa was himself a Magadhan, and may have had access to trustworthy records or traditions about the earlier history of his own country.

According to the Pāli record the war is said to have arisen, not over a wonderful elephant, but over an unnamed river-port (*Gaṅgāyam ekaṃ paṭṭana-gāmam*),[4] half of which was in Magadhan territory and half in that of the Licchavis. There, from the foot of a mountain, descended a very costly fragrant material.[5] When King Ajātasattu went to claim this strange substance he found that the Licchavis had preceded him, and had removed it; he therefore planned the war in order to gain possession of the scent-producing mountain. Plans seem to have been laid very carefully; according to the *Mahā-parinibbāna Sutta*

[1] V. supra, p. 32. [2] V. infra, p. 75. [3] *PHAI*. pp. 171 ff.

[4] *Sum. Vil.* ii, p. 516.

[5] *Tatr' âpi ca pabbata-pādato mahagghaṃ gandhabhaṇḍaṃ otarati.* *Sum. Vil.*, loc. cit.

Ajātasattu's first step was to send the minister Vassakāra to the Buddha, to inquire as to the probable outcome of an immediate attack.[1] Vassakāra's visit is said to have been made while the Buddha was at Gijjhakūṭa near Rājagaha, the Magadhan capital, just before his journey northwards, at the end of which he died. According to Buddhaghosa it was on the Buddha's advice that Ajātasattu decided not to wage immediate war on the Vajjis, but to bide his time.[2] The *Sutta* further states that the Buddha, as he proceeded northwards, once more met the minister Vassakāra, who, together with another minister named Sunīdha, was supervising the erection of a fort at Pāṭaligāma,[3] and that he correctly prophesied the future greatness of the city that would arise on the site.

Buddhaghosa completes the story by stating that Ajātasattu, not confident of his ability to overcome the Vajjis by force, sent the unscrupulous Vassakāra, in the guise of a refugee, to sow dissension among the Licchavi clansmen. Three years were spent by Vassakāra in preparing the ground for Ajātasattu's invasion, at the end of which period the latter crossed the Ganges and occupied Vesāli with little opposition.[4]

If the tradition is accurate Vassakāra's visit to the Buddha must have taken place within a year of the latter's death. Three years were spent in preparing the ground for the invasion, which must therefore have occurred some two years or more after the death of the Buddha. If we allow a few months to cover the duration of the actual campaign, and the time taken for the news of the war to reach Sāvatthi, and if we accept Raychaudhuri's equation of the Pāli and Jaina accounts, we may place the death of Gosāla approximately three years after that of the Buddha.

On a careful examination of the two stories, however, it seems by no means certain that they refer to the same campaign. The *gandha-hatthī* of the Jaina account reminds the reader of the *gandha-bhaṇḍaṃ* of the Pāli and we may suggest that the author of the *Nirayāvalikā* and Buddhaghosa both worked on the same tradition, but that one of the two, probably the latter, had

[1] *Dīgha* ii, pp. 72 ff.
[2] *Sum. Vil.* ii, p. 522.
[3] *Sunīdha-Vassakārā Magadha-mahāmattā Pāṭaligāme nagaraṃ māpenti Vajjīnaṃ paṭibāhāya. Dīgha* ii, pp. 86 ff.
[4] *Sum. Vil.* ii, pp. 522–4.

received it in a garbled form. The obscure perfumed material of the Pāli account is less plausible than the tame elephant of the *Nirayāvalikā*, and the latter therefore seems more reliable in this particular. The two stories agree on the break-up of the confederation, and on the betrayal of Vesāli by an agent of Magadha. Otherwise they have little in common.

In the Jaina story the war is said to have taken place at some unspecified time after the self-inflicted death of the imprisoned King Seṇiya. No definite statement is given of the time which elapsed between the death of Seṇiya and the war, but between the two events there occurred the repentance of King Kūṇiya (Ajātasattu), the funeral ceremonies of his father, and the removal of the court from Rājagṛha to Campā. Although the interval does not appear to have been very great it may have lasted for one or two years. This probability is strengthened by the Buddhist account of a war with Kosala soon after Ajātasattu's accession.[1] In the Buddhist story the visit of Vassakāra which initiated Ajātasattu's schemes against the Vajjis and was the first in a chain of events culminating in the Buddha's death, must have taken place at least six or seven years after the death of Bimbisāra-Seṇiya, since the *Mahāvaṃsa* states that the Buddha's *nirvāṇa* occurred in the eighth year of the reign of Ajātasattu-Kūṇiya.[2]

The accounts of the progress of the war in the two stories are also discrepant. The *Nirayāvalikā* tells of a fierce battle in which at least part of Ajātasattu-Kūṇiya's forces was defeated by Ceḍaga.[3] The other Jaina accounts speak of protracted warfare. The Pāli story, on the other hand, makes no mention of any severe fighting, but suggests that the resistance of the Vajjis was slight, since they had been previously weakened by the intrigues of Vassakāra.[4] Yet the building of the fort at Pāṭaligāma suggests not that Ajātasattu-Kūṇiya contemplated the invasion of the territory of a comparatively weak enemy, but that he was himself expecting invasion; this indeed is explicitly stated to be the motive in fortifying the village.[5]

[1] *PHAI.* p. 170.
[2] *Ajātasattuno vasse aṭṭhame muni nibbuto. Mahāvaṃsa* ii, 32, p. 15.
[3] V. supra, p. 69.
[4] V. supra. p. 72.
[5] *Vajjīnaṃ paṭibāhāya. Dīgha* ii, p. 86.

The similarities and differences in the two accounts, if taken together, indicate that the war was a protracted one and had at least two phases, which are suggested by the Jaina tradition of two great battles, and of the lengthy siege of Vesāli.

In the first, which took place soon after the accession of Ajātasattu-Kūṇiya, and with which the Jaina tradition of the elephant is connected, the Magadhan invasion was frustrated, and it would even seem that Magadha itself was in danger of a counter-invasion from the Vajjis. In the second phase of the war it was decided favourably to Ajātasattu through the intrigues of Vassakāra, some two or three years after the death of the Buddha. On the strength of the Jaina story, it may well be that the final capture of Vesāli did not take place until an even later date.

If we accept *c.* 483 B.C. as the date of the Buddha's *nirvāṇa*,[1] on the basis of the *Mahāvaṃsa* synchronism the accession of Ajātasattu must have occurred in the year *c.* 491 B.C., and his second campaign against the Vajjis *c.* 481–480 B.C. The first campaign, soon after which the death of Gosāla occurred, must have taken place at some time between the date of Ajātasattu's accession and the year preceding the Buddha's death. We suggest that the first campaign occurred *c.* 485 B.C., and the death of Gosāla in that year, or in 484 B.C., if we allow a year for the news of the " Battle of Great Stones " to spread to Sāvatthi and to become fixed in the popular consciousness. On the strength of the *Bhagavatī* statement that Mahāvīra survived Gosāla for sixteen and a half years,[2] this date would place that of Mahāvīra's death in 468–467 B.C. which agrees with the date suggested by Jacobi on the basis of Hemacandra's *Pariśiṣṭa-parvan*,[3] and supported by Charpentier.[4] Whatever our interpretation of the discrepant traditions, however, it seems clear that the death of Gosāla was not far removed in time from that of the Buddha.

There are two difficulties at least in the acceptance of the above theory. The first is a statement in the *Kalpa Sūtra* to the effect that the kings of the Licchavis instituted a festival in memory

[1] De la Vallée Poussin (*Indo-européens et Indo-iraniens*, pp. 238 ff.) outlines various theories at some length. With de la Vallée Poussin I provisionally support Geiger's date (*Mahāvaṃsa* translation, p. xxviii), which is consistent with my general chronological scheme.

[2] V. supra, p. 67.

[3] *The Kalpasūtra of Bhadrabāhu*, p. 8.

[4] *CHI.* i, p. 156.

of Mahāvīra's *nirvāṇa*.[1] This implies that they were still influential at the time of his death, and could not then have been completely overthrown by Ajātasattu-Kūṇiya. Yet the latter is said to have threatened to root out, destroy, and utterly ruin the Vajjis.[2] We must assume that Ajātasattu did not carry out his threats, but that the chiefs of the Vajjis were merely reduced to subordination, and allowed a degree of local autonomy. The marriage of Candra Gupta I to the Licchavi princess Kumāradevī,[3] and the rise of a Licchavi dynasty in Nepal,[4] indicate that the chief clan of the Vajjian Confederacy retained its individuality for some eight hundred years after the war with Ajātasattu.

More serious is the fact that the Pāli scriptures record the death of Mahāvīra or Nigaṇṭha Nātaputta as taking place at Pāvā during the Buddha's lifetime, and as being accompanied by serious confusion and quarrelling among his supporters. The event was reported to the Buddha by the novice Cuṇḍa, who expressed the hope that on the death of the Buddha similar quarrels would not arise in his order.[5] This fact indicates that Mahāvīra's death was thought of as having taken place towards the end of the Buddha's life, when the Buddhist *bhikkhus* were very concerned about the future of the community on the death of its founder. We suggest that the Pāli record may not in fact refer to the death of Mahāvīra at Pāvā, but to that of Gosāla at Sāvatthi, which the *Bhagavatī Sūtra* also mentions as having been accompanied by quarrelling and confusion.[6] At a later date, when the chief rival of Buddhism was no longer Ājīvikism but Jainism, the name may have been altered to add to the significance of the account.

A further objection might be raised that the Śvetâmbara Jaina tradition places the date of Mahāvīra's *nirvāṇa* in the year 470 before Vikrama, or 528 B.C., while the Digambara traditional date is even earlier—the impossible year of 605 before Vikrama.[7] The wide divergence of the two traditions tends to make even the more plausible date suspect. It is to be noted that the Sinhalese

[1] *Kalpa Sūtra*, *sū*. 123. *SBE*. xxii, p. 266.
[2] *Dīgha* ii, pp. 72–3.
[3] *PHAI*. p. 445. De la Vallée Poussin, *Dynasties* . . ., pp. 33–5.
[4] De la Vallée Poussin, *Dynasties* . . ., p. 173.
[5] *Majjh*. ii, pp. 243 ff.
[6] V. supra, pp. 58 ff.
[7] *PHAI*. p. 173, n.; *CHI*. i, p. 155.

tradition of the Buddha's *nirvāṇa* occurring in 544 B.C. is almost certainly some sixty years too early.[1] But the Buddhist and Jaina traditions taken together confirm Jacobi's contention that the Buddha predeceased Mahāvīra by about sixteen years.[2]

Yet another argument against the theory that Mahāvīra predeceased the Buddha may be derived from the account of the war between Magadha and the Licchavis in the *Nirayāvalikā Sūtra*. Mahāvīra was alive at the time, and in contact with the Magadhan court. If we reject the Jaina tradition of his death sixteen and a half years after that of Gosāla, and accept the Buddhist record of its occurrence before that of the Buddha, we must assume that he too died very shortly after the first campaign of Ajātasattu-Kūṇiya. This must have occurred at some time between 491 and 484 B.C., on the basis of our calculations, which are founded on the assumption that the Buddha died in 483 B.C.[3] Now Mahāvīra was seventy-two years old at the time of his death, and must have been at least in his late sixties at the time of the war, if we assume that he predeceased the Buddha. But Ceḍaga, the chieftain of the Licchavis, was his maternal uncle, and therefore was probably considerably older than Mahāvīra. Although he was thus a very old man, on the hypothesis of Mahāvīra's advanced age at the time, he is yet described as leading the Licchavi forces in battle and taking a full part in the campaign. Moreover, according to Jinadāsa, he survived the twelve-year siege of Vesāli which followed the battle. Such elderly leadership is by no means impossible, but at least very improbable, and points to an inaccuracy in one or other of the stories.

Hoernle has made two attempts to fix the date of Gosāla's death. In the first he suggests 483 B.C., arrived at by counting back sixteen years from Jacobi's date for Mahāvīra's *nirvāṇa*.[4] His second and revised estimate involves more complicated calculations.[5] He accepts 482 B.C. as the "practically certain" date of the Buddha's *nirvāṇa*. The father and predecessor of Ajātasattu, King Bimbisāra, was murdered by his son eight years before the *nirvāṇa*, or in 490 B.C. Hoernle believes that for some

[1] De la Vallée Poussin, *Indo-européens*, p. 240.
[2] *Kalpasūtra of Bhadrabāhu*, p. 9.
[3] V. supra, p. 74. [4] *Uv. Das.* ii, p. 111, n. [5] *ERE.* i, pp. 260–1.

years before this Ajātasattu was *de facto* ruler, and that the war took place not in the year of his legal, but of his *de facto* accession, which cannot have been long before the murder of Bimbisāra. Jacobi's theory of the later date of Mahāvīra's death he now rejects, in order to devise a chronological scheme according to which Mahāvīra may predecease the Buddha; but the *Bhagavatī* tradition of the sixteen years' interval between the deaths of Mahāvīra and Gosāla he accepts without question. He therefore suggests 484 B.C. for the death of Mahāvīra and 500 B.C. for that of Gosāla, and for the war and the *de facto* accession of Ajātasattu.

Hoernle's second calculation has the one advantage that it allows the acceptance of the Buddhist tradition of Mahāvīra's death being prior to that of the Buddha. For the sake of the acceptance of this one story other statements equally probable have been rejected. The *Mahā-parinibbāna Sutta's* record, that preparations for a campaign against the Vajjis were made in the last year of the Buddha's life, is not brought into relation with the chronological scheme. Hemacandra's statement that the *nirvāṇa* of Mahāvīra occurred 155 years before the accession of Candragupta Maurya,[1] which the Jaina tradition places in 313 B.C.,[2] is rejected.

Hoernle's interpretation of the chronology of the war cannot be accepted. No statement that it took place in the first year of Ajātasattu's reign, whether legal or *de facto*, can be found in either Buddhist or Jaina sources. Though Hoernle believes that it occurred during the lifetime of Bimbisāra-Seṇiya, both the *Nirayāvalikā* and the *Mahā-parinibbāna Sutta* make it clear that it took place after his suicide or murder, not after his abdication. Whatever the accuracy of other calculations, Hoernle's theory is untenable.

In our opinion the synchronism of Gosāla's death with the war with the Vajjis is by far the most reliable of any indications of the date of the former event. Illiterate and semi-literate people all over the world retain accurate memories of the years of births and deaths by this naturally arising system of synchronism with important historical events, and there is far less danger of error in such a method than in the memory of the

[1] *Pariśiṣṭaparvan* viii, 341. [2] *CHI.* i, p. 164.

number of years elapsing between one event and another. Therefore we believe that the death of Gosāla occurred soon after the great war between Magadha and the Vajjis, and this war could not have taken place in 500 B.C., if we maintain the general accuracy of both Buddhist and Jaina traditions.

The Name and Titles of Makkhali Gosāla

Before leaving the most famous of the Ājīvika leaders the question of his name and titles calls for further consideration. As we have seen, the name appears in various forms.[1] In the Pāli texts it is Makkhali Gosāla; in Buddhist Sanskrit, Maskarin Gośāla, Gośālīputra, or Gośalikāputra; in Jaina Prākrit, Gosāla Maṅkhaliputta; and in Tamil, Maṟkali.

Of these forms the Pāli seems the best. Although the word *maṅkha*, which Hoernle believed to be a nonce-word, does exist outside the *Bhagavatī Sūtra*,[2] and even although Gosāla's father may have been a religious mendicant called by that term,[3] the nasal which has found its way into the Jaina form *Maṅkhaliputta* seems anomalous, and cannot well be the linguistic ancestor of the *ṟ* in the Tamil form *Maṟkali*. That this element of the name is a patronymic, as is implied by the Jaina form, is improbable, since it is refuted by the joint testimony of Pāli and Tamil sources. The *Mahāvastu's* metronymic forms, *Gośālī-* and *Gośālikā-putra*, are nowhere confirmed by Pāli sources, but are if anything disproved by the dubious Jaina statement that the name of Gosāla's mother was Bhaddā.[4] It is probable that the personal name of the teacher was Gosāla, and that Makkhali, or Maskarin, a fairly common appellation of a staff-bearing ascetic, was rather a title than a proper name.

The etymology of this word has been established by Hoernle. "It describes Gosāla," he writes, "as having originally belonged to the Maṅkhali or Maskarin class of religious mendicants."[5] The word is explained by Pāṇini as a mendicant who bears a *maskara*, or bamboo rod.[6] His commentator Patañjali disagrees with this interpretation. "A mendicant," he says,

[1] V. supra, p. 34. [2] V. supra, pp. 35–36. [3] V. supra, *ibid.* [4] V. supra, p. 36.
[5] *ERE.* i, p. 260.
[6] *Maskara-maskariṇau veṇu-parivrājakayoḥ. Aṣṭādhyāyī* vi, 1, 154.

"is not called *maskarin* because he has a *maskara* . . . but because he says 'don't perform actions, quietude is the best for you!'"[1] Patañjali's etymology on the basis of the slogan "Don't perform actions" (*Ma kṛta karmāṇi*) is of the same class as that of Buddhaghosa,[2] and does not need lengthy consideration from the linguistic point of view, although it may contain a genuine religious slogan which was used by ascetics of a heterodox type, perhaps by the Ājīvikas. Patañjali's etymology is, however, supported by Vāmana, as a possible derivation, and substantially the same slogan is repeated. "An ascetic, being habitually inactive, is called *maskarin*, from his denial of *karma*. He says 'don't perform actions, quietude is best for you!'"[3]

Despite the testimony of Patañjali and Vāmana we cannot accept this fantastic derivation in the face of Pāṇini. It must be assumed that the name Maskarin, Makkhali, or Maṅkhali was connected with the fact that its owner carried a bamboo staff. That such staff bearing ascetics existed is clear from various references to *maskarins* and *ekadaṇḍins*, which will be considered in a later chapter.[4]

The title Maskarin seems to have been that by which Gosāla was most widely known among his followers, for the Tamil texts have no apparent knowledge of his personal name, which seems to have been neglected or forgotten. It seems that, as with the names of the founders of Buddhism and Jainism, growing reverence for the Ājīvika leader led to the gradual disuse of his personal name in favour of the title. Apparently he was also known by other titles of a more exalted type. Both the *Bhagavatī Sūtra* and the *Sāmañña-phala Sutta* mention him as claiming the title of *tīrthaṅkara*.[5] The former text adds that he called himself *jina*, *arhant*, and *kevalin*.[6] In the Tamil we find *Maṟkali* referred to as *Āptaṉ*,[7] a rather unusual title which may have had a specifically Ājīvika connotation.

[1] *Na vai maskaro 'sy' âst' îti maskarī parivrājakaḥ. . . . Mā kṛta karmāṇi, mā kṛta karmāṇi, śāntir vaḥ śreyas' îty āh' âto maskarī parivrājakaḥ. Mahābhāṣya*, ed. Kielhorn iii, p. 93.

[2] V. supra, p. 37.

[3] *Mākaraṇa-śīlo maskarī karm'-âpavāditvāt parivrājaka ucyate. Sa tv evam āha*: "*Mā kuruta karmāṇi, śāntir vaḥ śreyas' iti. Kāśikā*, ed. Balasastri, p. 522.

[4] V. infra, pp. 99–100. [5] V. supra, pp. 68, 11. [6] V. supra, p. 56.

[7] V. infra, p. 276.

CHAPTER V

PŪRAṆA AND PAKUDHA

Pūraṇa Kassapa

That Pūraṇa, the antinomian of the *Sāmañña-phala Sutta*, played a not unimportant part in early Ājīvikism is evident from a number of references in the Pāli canon and from two other references of a much later date.

A verse in the *Saṃyutta Nikāya* [1] mentions four of the six heretics together. Of these the names *Pakudhako Kātiyāno* and *Nigaṇṭho* stand as separate singular nouns, but those of Makkhali and Pūraṇa are combined in the form *Makkhali-Pūraṇāse.* No doubt the exigencies of the metre must have had some influence in inspiring the poet to compound the names, but the fact that he did so suggests that he looked upon the two as closely connected. It is also perhaps significant that all four are mentioned as leaders of a single school (*gaṇassa satthāro*), and that the name of Makkhali precedes that of Pūraṇa. The conclusions we derive from this verse are strengthened by those passages in the Pāli canon in which Pūraṇa is said to have maintained the doctrine of the six classes of men, and other teachings elsewhere ascribed to Makkhali.[2] Conclusive evidence of Pūraṇa's important status in Ājīvikism is provided by the two later references, the Jaina Tamil poem *Nīlakēci*, and Guṇaratna's *Tarka-rahasya-dīpikā.*

The first of these texts depicts a demi-goddess, Nīlakēci, converted to Jainism and travelling from one teacher to another to dispute on points of doctrine. Her opponents include among others the Buddhist elder Maudgalyāyana and the Buddha himself, Parāśara, who is the protagonist of Sāṅkhya metaphysics, and Pūraṇa, the leader of the Ājīvikas.[3] He is described as the

[1] *Saṃ.* i, p. 66. V. infra, p. 217, where the verse is quoted.
[2] V. supra, p. 20.
[3] V. infra, pp. 199–200.

chief of a monastery of Ājīvika monks at a place called Kukkuṭanagara, "the Lord Pūraṇaṉ, without comparison in intelligence."[1] He receives Nīlakēci, and expounds his doctrine to her, stating that Maṟkali is the Ājīvikas' Lord (*iṟai*).[2] Thus it is plain that the Tamil Ājīvikas looked upon Pūraṇa as a great leader, the contemporary of the Buddha, and second only to Maṟkali himself. The name Pūraṇaṉ may by this time have become a title, for it seems in one verse to be applied not to the teacher, but to the deified Maṟkali.[3] The location of Kukkuṭanagara, where Pūraṇa is said to have taught, may be of some significance, and is considered in a later chapter.[4]

The other two Tamil works containing outlines of Ājīvika teaching do not refer to Pūraṇa, although in *Maṇimekalai* the anonymous teacher with whom the heroine discusses Ājīvika philosophy has the epithet of Purāṇaṉ, "the Elder."[5] This word is employed in place of the name Pūraṇa at least twice in the Pāli scriptures.[6] The *Civañāṉa-cittiyār*, which is later than the two first-mentioned works, mentions neither Pūraṇa nor Maṟkali. These works, in so far as they give information about the Ājīvikas, will be considered more fully in due course.[7]

Meanwhile we have evidence that, at an even later period, Pūraṇa was not forgotten. In the *Tarka-rahasya-dīpikā*, Guṇaratna's commentary on Haribhadra's *Ṣaḍdarśana-samuccaya*, the author presents in his preface a list of theories on the nature of the world, which is interesting from many points of view. "Various theorists," writes Guṇaratna, "propound various theories on the nature of the world. For instance some declare the world to be born of Nārīśvara; others maintain that it arose from Soma and Agni; . . . some that it is made by Time; . . . the Sāṅkhyas, that it arose from *prakṛti*; the Buddhists, that it is a mere conception (*vijñaptimātram*); Pūraṇa, that it is born of Destiny (*Pūraṇo niyati-janitaṃ*); Parāśara, that it

[1] *Pūraṇaṉ eṉpāṉ puruvara-k-kaṟṟavaṉ*. *Nīl.* v, 668. V. also v. 673.
[2] *Nīl.* v, 671.
[3] Ibid., v, 673.
[4] V. infra, pp. 201–2.
[5] *Ācīvaka-nūl-ariṇṭa-Purāṇaṉai*. *Maṇi.* xxvii, 108.
[6] *Tadā pañca diṭṭhi-gatikā Purāṇa-Kassapa,-Makkhali-Gosāla,-Pakudha-Kaccāna,-Ajita-Kesakambali,-Nigaṇṭha-Nāthaputtā ahesuṃ*. *Jāt.* v, p. 246. V. also *Jāt.* i, 509.
[7] V. infra, pp. 196 ff.

arises by natural evolution (*pariṇāma-prabhavam*); the Turks, that it comes into existence through a wholly divine man from among their religious teachers.[1] These and other teachers of various doctrines are to be found."[2] Guṇaratna's list proves that the memory of Pūraṇa survived as late as *c*. A.D. 1400.[3] It is surprising that he did not quote Gosāla as the representative of the *niyativādins*, for he must have known the name from its frequent occurrence in his own Jaina literature, which makes only one dubious reference to Pūraṇa. By this time it is doubtful whether Ājīvikas survived in northern India, and those members of the sect with whom Guṇaratna may have come in contact had perhaps deified Makkhali and looked upon Pūraṇa only as their human prophet. As will be shown in a later chapter, at least some of the Dravidian Ājīvikas seem to have held this view.[4]

These two references establish without reasonable doubt that Pūraṇa was an important figure among the later Ājīvikas; and the Pūraṇa of these texts must surely be none other than Pūraṇa Kassapa of the Pāli scriptures. It is surprising that no detailed reference to him occurs in the Jaina canon, where several Pūraṇas are mentioned, but none certainly suggesting the heretic Pūraṇa of the Buddhist scriptures. For this reason our knowledge of Pūraṇa's life is more fragmentary than that of the life of Makkhali Gosāla, for in the case of Pūraṇa we have not two independent sets of sources upon which to work.

Of Pūraṇa's birth and origin Buddhaghosa gives a fanciful story,[5] bearing the same stamp as that provided by him to account for Makkhali Gosāla's initiation into asceticism.[6] He was born, says Buddhaghosa, as a slave, the hundredth in the household of his master; from the fact that he made up the total of one hundred slaves he was given the name Pūraṇa, "the Completion."[7] His birth was considered auspicious, and he was

[1] *Turuṣkā, gosvāminām aika-divya-puruṣa-prabhavam.* Guṇaratna seems to refer to the Christians. *Turuṣka* was a very loosely used term, and the passage suggests Christ rather than Allah or Muhammad.

[2] *Ṣaddarśana-samuccaya*, ed. Suali, p. 20.

[3] Glasenapp, *Der Jainismus*, p. 108.

[4] V. infra. p. 276.

[5] *Sum. Vil.* i, p. 142.

[6] V. supra, p. 37.

[7] *Dāsa-sataṃ pūrayamāṇo jāto. Sum. Vil.*, loc. cit.

treated well and never scolded. Despite this he ran away from his master. In his flight his garments were stolen by thieves. Pūraṇa had not the sense to cover himself with leaves or grass, and entered a certain village as naked as on the day of his birth (*jāta-rūpeṇ' eva*). The villagers thought that he was a holy man, and gave him liberal alms. Pūraṇa was so impressed by the ease with which he gained a living in the state of nudity that even when offered a garment he would not put it on. Gradually his reputation grew and he gained a following of five hundred disciples.

The story is scarcely worthy of serious consideration. Its only value is to show that Pūraṇa, like Makkhali, was habitually naked. This fact is confirmed by the *Divyâvadāna*,[1] where he is described as a *nirgrantha*, clothed in the garment of righteousness (*dharma-śāta-praticchanna*); the phrase is obviously an euphemism for a state of total nudity.

We have little information about the events of Pūraṇa's life. The *Mahāvastu* [2] states that he met the Buddha, before the latter's enlightenment, at the village of Uruvilvā, and that while the latter received liberal alms from the villagers, Pūraṇa's bowl remained empty. A certain Pūraṇa who may be the Pūraṇa Kassapa of Buddhist tradition, is described in the Jaina *Bhagavatī Sūtra*.[3] He is said to have been a foolish ascetic (*bālatavassī*), who had previously been a householder in an unidentifiable place called Bebhela. On his begging rounds he made use of a bowl divided into four sections, and gave the contents of the first section to travellers, the second to crows and dogs, and the third to fish and tortoises, keeping only the contents of the fourth section for himself. He is said to have died by self-starvation after twelve years of asceticism, in the eleventh year of Mahāvīra's ascetic career. In their details the two stories are not consistent, for, according to our synchronisms,[4] the eleventh year of Mahāvīra's asceticism fell in *c.* 500–499 B.C., the year following his breach with Gosāla. If Pūraṇa's mendicancy commenced only twelve years before this date the Buddha must then have been in the thirteenth or fourteenth year of his enlightenment, and could not have met the mendicant Pūraṇa while still

[1] Ed. Cowell and Neil, p. 165.
[2] Ed. Senart, vol. ii, p. 207.
[3] *Bh. Sū.* iii, *sū.* 143, p. 304 f.
[4] V. supra, p. 74.

a *bodhisattva*. We suggest that the twelve years in the Jaina story refer in fact not to Pūraṇa's whole career as a mendicant, but to the period of his claim to *jina*-hood. Thus the two stories may be harmonized.

The evidence of the Pāli texts indicates that Pūraṇa's doctrines and practices did not differ greatly from those of Makkhali Gosāla, and that considerable confusion existed in the minds of the authors of the *Nikāyas* concerning the teachings of the two. In no less than four references Pūraṇa is described as maintaining part of the doctrine of determinism attributed in the *Sāmañña-phala Sutta* to Makkhali.[1] In one of these he is said to hold the doctrine of the six classes of men (*abhijāti*) and even to place Makkhali Gosāla, together with the shadowy Nanda Vaccha and Kisa Saṅkicca, in the highest class.[2]

There can be little doubt that, with differences of approach and emphasis, Pūraṇa and Makkhali taught what was virtually the same doctrine. Pūraṇa's reference to Makkhali as belonging to the highest of the six classes, and the passage in *Nīlakēci* above-mentioned,[3] suggest that he may have looked up to Makkhali as his spiritual superior, at least during part of his career. But he appears to have claimed omniscience,[4] and his very title suggests that he was looked upon by his followers as perfect.

The Death of Pūraṇa

While our knowledge of the events of Pūraṇa's life is negligible, we have an account of his death which contains interesting features, and, existing as it does in more than one version, may have a basis of truth. The sources agree that Pūraṇa died by his own hand. The Buddhist accounts add that his death took place at Sāvatthi, after a great miracle contest in which he and his fellow heretics were worsted by the Buddha. The event was a popular subject for illustration by Buddhist sculptors and artists.[5]

[1] V. supra, pp. 18, 20–21.
[2] *Aṅg.* iii, p. 383. V. supra, p. 20.
[3] V. supra, p. 81.
[4] *Aṅg.* iv, p. 428.
[5] Foucher, *L'Art Gréco-Bouddhique . . .*, vol. i, pp. 534–7.

The description of Pūraṇa's suicide is contained in the commentary to the *Dhammapada*,[1] and in the *Divyâvadāna*.[2] A Tibetan version of the story also exists.[3] The first version differs from the two latter in several particulars, and is considerably briefer. In the Pāli version an unnamed *seṭṭhi* of Rājagaha is said to have suspended a bowl by a cord sixty feet in the air, and to have invited holy-men of all sects to fly up and bring it down, offering to become the disciple of the successful competitor. On six successive days the six heretics tried to persuade the *seṭṭhi* to give them the bowl, but refused to put their magic powers to the test. On the seventh day the bowl was retrieved by the *bhikkhu* Piṇḍola Bhāradvāja, who gave a remarkable display of levitation. On hearing the news of his disciple's feat the Buddha reproached him, and forbade the repetition of such miraculous displays.

The heretics were delighted at the news, thinking that the cessation of Buddhist miracles would leave them masters of the field. But their hopes were dashed when they heard that the Buddha had told King Bimbisāra that his injunction was binding on the *bhikkhus* only, and not on himself, and that if the heretics attempted to display their powers he too would perform a miracle. He further declared that in four months' time he would give such a performance at Sāvatthi. The heretics decided to pursue him unremittingly, in the hope of shaking his equanimity and thus weakening his magic powers. They followed him to Sāvatthi, and there obtained from their disciples one hundred thousand pieces of money, with which they erected a pavilion. King Pasenadi offered to have a similar pavilion erected for the Buddha, but he refused, stating that he had a pavilion-builder, and would perform his miracle under the mango tree of Gaṇḍa, the King's gardener. The heretics, hearing of his promise, uprooted all the mango trees for a league around.

On the full moon of the month Āsāḷhi the Buddha was presented with a mango fruit by Gaṇḍa. He told the latter to dig a hole and plant the mango stone. No sooner had the Buddha washed his hand over the spot where the stone was planted than a tree

[1] *Dhammapad'-aṭṭhakathā* iii, pp. 199 ff.
[2] *Divyâvadāna*, pp. 143 ff.
[3] Rockhill, *The Life of the Buddha*, p. 80.

sprang up, fifty cubits high and covered with flowers and fruit. The populace, realizing the evil stratagems of the six heretics, began to pelt them with mango stones.

The god Sakka then took a hand in the contest. He ordered the wind to uproot the heretics' pavilion, the sun to scorch their naked bodies, and the wind to cover them with dust and to cause countless drops of rain to fall on them. Looking like mottled cows (*kabara-gāvi-sadisā*) they fled in all directions.

Meanwhile a peasant who was a devotee of Pūraṇa Kassapa had unyoked his oxen, and, taking a vessel of gruel and a cord, had set out for Sāvatthi, intending to watch the miracle-contest. On the way he met Pūraṇa in his flight, and said : " I set out, sir, to see my noble masters perform a miracle. Where are you going ? " " What is a miracle to you ? (*Kin te paṭihāreṇa* ?)," replied Pūraṇa, " Give me that pot and cord ! " He then took the pot and cord, went to the bank of a river, tied the pot round his neck, and jumped into the stream. Raising bubbles in the water, he died, and was reborn in the Avīci hell.

The *Divyâvadāna* tells a slightly different story. The instigator of the miracle-contest is here said to be the tempter, Māra. In the form of Pūraṇa he suggested to Maskarin that the Buddha should be challenged to a contest ; in the form of Maskarin he repeated the suggestion to Sañjayin, and so on from one of the six heretics to another. The six then asked King Bimbisāra to arrange the contest, but, mindful of the Buddha's orders, he refused. Thereupon the heretics left for Śrāvasti, followed by the Buddha, who knew of their plans by virtue of his superhuman insight. King Prasenajit of Kosala was more favourable to the ascetics' proposal than had been Bimbisāra, and he carried the challenge to the Buddha, who was staying at the Jetavana. The Buddha agreed to take part in a miracle contest after an interval of seven days. Meanwhile the heretics gathered their supporters together and laid their plans.

On the seventh day the contest took place outside the city, where each teacher was provided with a specially prepared pavilion. The Buddha performed several spectacular miracles, but the six heretics were powerless, and their discomfiture was completed by a violent rainstorm, caused by Pañcika, the general of the *yakṣas*. The heretics ran in all directions, but the Buddha was untouched by the rain, and his rivals were put to the final humiliation of having to take refuge in his pavilion.

Then Pūraṇa, fearing that the Buddha would win over his disciples, began to discuss philosophical questions with them, and tempers rose high. Metaphysical slogans—"The world is eternal!" "The world is transient!" "The world is both!" "The world is neither!" "Body and soul are one!" "Body and soul are different!"—were bandied from one to another of the ascetics and their followers, and they left the scene of the contest a quarrelling rabble.[1]

The terrified Pūraṇa took to flight. On his way he was met by a hermaphrodite (*paṇḍaka*), who disrespectfully asked him where he was going. He replied that the time had come for his departure from the body, his faculties being somewhat impaired. The sun, he said, had given him a thirst, and he asked the whereabouts of the nearest pond.[2] The hermaphrodite, addressing Pūraṇa by uncomplimentary epithets such as *śramaṇ'-âdhama* and *hīn'-âsat-puruṣa*, pointed to a nearby lotus pond. There Pūraṇa tied a pot full of sand about his neck, jumped into the water, and was drowned.

The other ascetics (*nirgranthāḥ*) made a search for Pūraṇa, and while seeking him they met a prostitute. They asked her whether she had seen Pūraṇa, "clothed in the garment of righteousness"; she replied scornfully with an obscene verse, and would give them no information. Ultimately they found him lying dead in the lotus pond. They pulled out his body, and, leaving it on one side, they went away.

The Tibetan version of the story, as summarized by Rockhill,[3] appears to agree in essentials with the *Divyâvadāna* version.

These stories clearly contain elements inserted for the edification of the Buddhist community, but the central fact of both

[1] "*Antavāl lokaḥ,*" "*Anantaḥ,*" "*Antavāṃś c' ânantavāṃś ca,*" "*N'aiv' ântavān n'ânantavān,*" "*Sa jīvas tac charīram,*" "*Anyo jīvo 'nyac charīram*" *iti te kalahajātā viharanti bhaṇḍana-jātā vigṛhītā vivādam āpannāḥ. Divyâvadāna*, p. 164.

[2] The words of Pūraṇa are very obscure. *Gamanāya me samayaḥ pratyupasthitaḥ kāyasya me balavīryaṃ kiñcit spṛṣṭhaś ca bhāvaḥ sukhaduḥkhate me. Anāvṛtaṃ jñānam ih' ârhatāṃ dūr âpagato 'smi. Paratimir'-âpanudaś ca tṛṣaṃ patati. Ācukṣva me dūṣika etam artham—śītôdakā kutra sā puṣkiriṇī?* Op. cit., p. 165. The editors of the text remark, "Much of this page is evidently in verse, but is too corrupt to be so arranged." Op. cit., p. 706.

[3] *The Life of the Buddha*, p. 80.

versions, the suicide of Pūraṇa, is by no means incredible. Death by ritual suicide was the common end of the Jaina ascetic who felt his faculties begin to fail, and similar suicides by Ājīvikas are well attested.[1] It is probable, as the *Bhagavatī Sūtra* suggests,[2] that Pūraṇa's followers developed a legend of their master ending his life by suicide in an odour of sanctity, and that this story was twisted by the Buddhists into the complimentary forms paraphrased above.

Certain elements of the two Buddhist stories differ, but their common features are more numerous. Both agree that, after a miracle contest at Sāvatthi, in which Pūraṇa and his fellow ascetics were worsted, and which was followed by a violent storm, he committed suicide by drowning, with a pot tied about his neck.

The pot occurs in both accounts; this fact strengthens the probability that this feature of the story has some basis of fact. We are reminded of the potter's shop in which Makkhali Gosāla died, and also that Dravidian Ājīvika ascetics seem to have been in the habit of performing fatal penance in large funerary urns (*tāḻi*).[3]

Other incidents in the stories of Pūraṇa's death remind us of the *Bhagavatī Sūtra's* account of the death of Gosāla. Both events take place in Sāvatthi, both follow a contest at which miraculous powers are displayed, and both take place in an atmosphere of great excitement and tension among the ascetic communities. The great storm which preceded Pūraṇa's death suggests the Last Great Storm Cloud, one of the eight finalities declared by Gosāla in his last illness.[4] Pūraṇa's frantic flight from the scene of the contest and his violent thirst may be parallelled by the delirium of Gosāla, when he bathed in muddy water used for mixing the potter's clay.[5] Mango stones occur in both stories.[6] The strange figure of the prostitute in the *Divyâvadāna* version of the story tenuously suggests Hālāhalā the potter-woman, for it would seem, in the light of the numerous references to the licentious conduct of the early Ājīvikas,[7] that the author of the *Bhagavatī Sūtra* intended to insinuate that her relations with Gosāla were closer than those of a hospitable lay disciple.

[1] V. infra, pp. 127 ff.
[2] V. supra, p. 83.
[3] V. infra, pp. 111–12.
[4] V. supra, p. 68.
[5] V. supra, p. 62.
[6] V. supra, pp. 61–64.
[7] V. infra, pp. 123 ff.

Probably certain elements of the story of Gosāla's death have found their way, in a corrupt form, into the Buddhist story of Pūraṇa's suicide. If this be the case the credibility of the former story is strengthened without by any means invalidating the latter. We may provisionally accept the historicity of the suicide of Pūraṇa at Sāvatthi, at the same time recognizing that the details of both versions of the story are unreliable.

The event is said to have taken place during the reigns of King Bimbisāra of Magadha and Pasenadi of Kosala. Rockhill, basing his view on the Tibetan version, believes that it occurred in the sixteenth year of the Buddha's ministry.[1] This date seems definitely too early. As Malalasekera has pointed out,[2] it would exclude the possibility of King Ajātasattu visiting Pūraṇa,[3] since the former could have been only a small child at the time of the death of the latter. There are other weighty objections to Rockhill's figure. Buddha's ministry lasted forty-four years. If we retain 483 B.C. as the date of his *nirvāṇa*,[4] on Rockhill's theory Pūraṇa's suicide must have occurred *c.* 511 B.C. But, on the basis of our synchronisms,[5] and of the *Bhagavatī Sūtra's* statement that Gosāla's ministry lasted for sixteen years,[6] the latter's ministry must have commenced *c.* 501 B.C., or ten years after Pūraṇa's death. This invalidates the strong Buddhist tradition that the ministries of the six heretical teachers were contemporary, and renders it quite impossible that Pūraṇa could have been in any way subordinate to Makkhali Gosāla.

We suggest that Pūraṇa's death took place towards the end of the reigns of Bimbisāra and Pasenadi; thus it must have occurred at least nine or ten years before that of the Buddha, on the basis of the Sinhalese Chronicle,[7] and eight years or more before that of Makkhali, on the basis of our previous calculations.[8] The Jaina statement that Pūraṇa died in the eleventh year of Mahāvīra's asceticism[9] is not unplausible. It would place the event in the year *c.* 500–499 B.C., immediately after Makkhali Gosāla's claim to enlightenment. This does not invalidate the framework of the *Sāmañña-phala Sutta*, wherein King Ajātasattu states that he had sought guidance from Pūraṇa as well as from

[1] *The Life of the Buddha*, p. 79.
[2] *DPPN.*, s.v. *Pūraṇa*.
[3] V. supra, pp. 11–12.
[4] V. supra, p. 74, n. 1.
[5] V. supra, p. 74.
[6] V. supra, p. 32.
[7] V. supra, p. 73, n. 2.
[8] V. supra, p. 74.
[9] V. supra, p. 83.

the other five heretics, since he may well have visited Pūraṇa before his usurpation of the throne of Magadha. This date for Pūraṇa's death does, however, somewhat lessen the probability that he was a follower of Makkhali Gosāla. That he died in the first or second year of Makkhali's *jina*-hood, after what seems to have been a long ascetic career, indicates that he was Makkhali's senior. But it is not impossible for an older teacher to respect a considerably younger man as his spiritual superior, and a comparatively young man may acquire a reputation of great sanctity. Despite Pūraṇa's probable seniority to Makkhali our conclusion is by no means invalidated.

We may tentatively reconstruct the relations of the two prophets as follows :—Pūraṇa, a heretical leader of long standing, maintaining a fatalistic doctrine with tendencies to antinomianism, came in contact with Makkhali Gosāla, a younger teacher with doctrines much the same as his own, but with a more successful appeal to the public. Recognizing his eclipse, he admitted the superiority of the new teacher, and accepted the sixfold classification of men, which placed Makkhali Gosāla and his forerunners Nanda Vaccha and Kisa Saṅkicca in the highest category.[1] Soon after this he decided that his star had set, and ended his own life.

A passing reference to an Āpūraṇa the son of Kaśyapa is to be found in the *Mahābhārata*, where the word occurs in the enumeration of the names of *nāgas* inhabiting the subterranean city of Bhogavatī.[2] This is probably a coincidence, but it is not wholly impossible that the name found its way into the catalogue through an early editor who had heard of Pūraṇa ; on this hypothesis the extra syllable prefixed to the name might be accounted for by the necessity of avoiding an iambic cadence, which would otherwise occur throughout the *pāda*.

Pakudha Kaccāyana

The relations of this ascetic teacher to the later Ājīvikas are less clear than those of Pūraṇa Kassapa, but there is evidence

[1] V. supra, pp. 27 ff.

[2] *Nāgānām eka-vaṃsānāṇ yathā-śreṣṭhaṃ tu me śṛṇu*, 8 . . .
Bāhyakuṇḍo, Maṇir, Nāgas, tath' aiv' Āpūraṇaḥ, Khagaḥ,
Vāmanaś c' Ailapatraś ca, Kukuraḥ Kukuṇas tathā, 10 . . .
Ete c' ânye ca bahavaḥ Kaśyapasy' âtmajāḥ smṛtāḥ, 17.
Mbh., Udyoga, 101.

to show that he too had some influence on the finished doctrine of the sect. We have already seen that he is praised with Makkhali Pūraṇa and Nigaṇṭha in a significant verse of the *Saṃyutta Nikāya*.[1]

His doctrine, according to the *Sāmañña-phala Sutta*, was one of seven eternal and immutable elements, earth, water, fire, air, life, joy, and sorrow.[2] The *Majjhima Nikāya*[3] incorporates with this doctrine part of Makkhali Gosāla's fatalist creed, and one of the Chinese versions of the *Sāmañña-phala Sutta* makes of Pakudha a determinist.[4] His characteristic teaching is, however, a very primitive atomism, perhaps the earliest of Indian atomic theories.[5]

As we hope to establish in our second part, the Southern Ājīvikas held a theory of elements very similar to that of Pakudha. The three chief Tamil sources, *Maṇimēkalai*,[6] *Nīlakēci*,[7] and *Civañāṉa-cittiyār*,[8] all declare that, according to Ājīvika doctrine, there are five immutable atomic elements (*aṇu* or *poruḷ*) : earth, air, water, fire, and life (*uyir* or *cīvam*). *Maṇimēkalai*, however, the oldest of these sources, adds " but joy and sorrow, these too are atoms ".[9] *Nīlakēci* leaves the total of the elements at five, but *Civañāṉa-cittiyār* states, " Our Lord has declared to us the seven which we must consider, including these two which are joined with them, namely good and evil." [10] This is surely the seven-element theory of Pakudha Kaccāyana, with the more moral categories *puṇya* and *pāpa* substituted for the hedonistic *sukha* and *duḥkha*.

A further point in which Pakudha suggests the conduct of the Ājīvikas of later times is to be found in Buddhaghosa's commentary on the *Sāmañña-phala Sutta*. His brief remarks on Makkhali Gosāla and Pūraṇa Kassapa have already been dis-

[1] V. supra, p. 80, and infra, p. 217.
[2] V. supra, p. 16, and infra, pp. 262 ff.
[3] *Majjh.* i, pp. 513 ff. V. supra, p. 19.
[4] Rockhill, op. cit., pp. 255 ff. V. supra, p. 22.
[5] Ui, *The Vaiśeṣika Philosophy*, p. 25. V. infra, pp. 269–70.
[6] *Uyir oḷ' oru nāl vakai-y aṇu. Maṇi.* xxvii, 113. V. infra, pp. 263–65.
[7] *Nīl.* vv, 674–5. V. infra, p. 265.
[8] *CÑC.*, ed. Mudaliyar, p. 256, v. 2. V. infra, pp. 265–66.
[9] *Iṉpam um tuṉpam um ivaiy um aṇu-v eṉa. Maṇi* xxvii, 163. V. infra, p. 263.
[10] *Puṇṇiya-pāvam eṉṉum iraṇṭiṉ um porunt' avaittē-y eṇṇiya-v iv aṟṟiṉ ōṭum ēḻ' eṉa-v eṅkaḷ ōṭu naṇṇiya-v oruvaṉ kūṟum. CÑC.*, p. 266, v. 10.

cussed,[1] and certainly do not give us reason to accept his statements on Pakudha without question. For the names of Makkhali and Pūraṇa Buddhaghosa supplies fantastic and derogatory derivations, but in the case of Pakudha he contents himself with stating that he avoided cold water. Even after excretion he did not perform a ritual ablution, unless he obtained hot water or rice-gruel (*kañjiya*). To cross a stream, Buddhaghosa continues, was a breach of his vows, for which he atoned by making a mound of sand.[2] The *kañji* and the mound of sand suggest practices of the Ājīvikas. Some southern Ājīvika ascetics seem to have used *kañji* as their regular food,[3] while the heap of sand is parallelled by a heap of red powder, which was part of the religious paraphernalia of an Ājīvika ascetic mentioned in the *Jātaka*.[4] These points of contact are admittedly very slight, but they tend to strengthen the conclusion derived from the similarity of Pakudha's doctrines to those of the later Ājīvikas, that he and his followers had some hand in the development of the sect.

About Pakudha's life and works we have no certain information. Dr. Malalasekera states that his followers did not hold him in high esteem, and that he did not lay claim to full enlightenment,[5] but the references on which he bases his statement [6] repeat the same phrases for each of the six heretical leaders, and therefore do not carry conviction. Elsewhere the six are referred to as being held in great respect,[7] and Nigaṇṭha Nātaputta and Makkhali Gosāla certainly seem to have laid claim to full enlightenment, although in the passages referred to they, along with the four other heretics, are said not to have done so.

Dr. Barua [8] has equated Pakudha (called Kakudha in Buddhist Sanskrit texts) with Kabandhin Kātyāyana, one of the questioners of the sage Pippalāda in the *Praśna Upaniṣad*. He believes that the names Kakudha and Kabandhin, which both indicate that

[1] V. supra, pp. 37, 82–83.

[2] *Sīt'-udaka-paṭikkhitto esa. Vaccaṃ katvā pi udakakiccaṃ na karoti, unhôdakam vā kañjiyaṃ vā labhitvā karoti. Nadiṃ vā magg'-ôdakaṃ vā atikkamma, 'sīlam me bhinnan' ti vālika-thūpaṃ katvā sīlaṃ adhiṭṭhāya gacchati. Sum. Vil., i,* p. 144.

[3] *IA*. xli, pp. 88–9. V. infra, p. 204.

[4] V. infra, p. 113.

[5] *DPPN*., s.v. *Pakudha*.

[6] *Majjh*. i, 240 ; ii, 4 ; *Saṃ*. i, 68.

[7] V. supra, p. 11.

[8] *Pre-Buddhistic Indian Philosophy*, p. 281.

PLATE II.

THE BUDDHA MEETS UPAKA THE ĀJĪVIKA.
(From Krom, *The Life of the Buddha on the Stūpa of Barabuḍur.*)

their owner was a humpback, are equivalent. There are no further points of contact, however. The *Upaniṣad* merely states that Kabandhin asked Pippalāda whence all beings came,[1] and received the reply that they were produced by Prajāpati from matter (*rayi*) and breath (*prāṇa*).[2] If the equivalence be accepted, it probably implies that Pakudha or Kakudha was the senior of the Buddha and of the other heretics, and that he was closer to the main current of Indian philosophy than were Makkhali and Pūraṇa.

In any case we may infer that Pakudha was less influential than were either of the two ascetics we have previously considered. In the Jaina texts Makkhali Gosāla appears as a real human being; Pūraṇa Kassapa emerges as a personality in the two accounts of his suicide; Nigaṇṭha Nātaputta was the founder of an enduring sect; and the materialist Ajita Kesakambalī seems to have been singled out by the Buddha for scathing condemnation.[3] On the other hand the two remaining members of the group of six heretics, Pakudha Kaccāyana the atomist and Sañjaya Belatthiputta the agnostic, are never more than shadowy lay figures, nowhere individualized, not worthy of a special mention apart from their fellow ascetic leaders. We may therefore conclude that they made but a slight impression upon contemporary religious life.

1 *Kuto ha va imāḥ prajāḥ prajāyanta? Praśna*, Poona edn., p. 3.
2 Śaṅkara interprets these terms as Soma and Agni. Op. cit., p. 4.
3 V. supra, p. 55.

CHAPTER VI

THE EARLY ĀJĪVIKA COMMUNITY (I)

THE WANDERING PHILOSOPHERS

It is now generally agreed that the ground for the development of non-brāhmaṇic religious sects in India was prepared before the days of the great reforming leaders of the sixth and fifth centuries B.C. In the case of the Ājīvikas there is evidence which points to the fact that Makkhali Gosāla found already in existence ascetic groups following a more or less common way of life and looking back to teachers of previous generations. By knitting these local groups together under his own leadership he established the Ājīvika sect. The tradition, preserved in the Buddhist scriptures, linking Makkhali Gosāla's name with those of Nanda Vaccha and Kisa Saṅkicca,[1] and that of the *Bhagavatī Sūtra*, which seems to record a succession of religious teachers preceding Gosāla,[2] are evidence pointing strongly in that direction.

As Charpentier recognized,[3] Ājīvika ascetics are met in the Pāli scriptures at a time when Makkhali Gosāla cannot have commenced his ministry, if we accept the chronology suggested in a previous chapter.[4] The most striking of these is Upaka the Ājīvika, who, as a symbol of benevolent incredulity, has found a small but significant place in the legends of Buddhism. Upaka is said to have encountered the Buddha on the road to Gayā, immediately after the latter's enlightenment. He noticed the supernal calmness and peace in the bearing of the great teacher, and asked who he was, who was his instructor, and what were his doctrines. When the Buddha told Upaka of his enlightenment he merely said " It may be so, sir ! " (*hupeyya āvuso*), and went on by another way. The historicity of this story is perhaps strengthened by the fact that it is mentioned no less than four

[1] V. supra, pp. 27 ff.
[2] V. supra, pp. 30 ff.
[3] *JRAS.* 1913, pp. 673–4.
[4] V. supra, p. 74.

times in the Pāli texts [1] with little variation, and occurs also in the Mahāyāna scriptures.[2]

Upaka the Ājīvika does not vanish from the scene after his meeting with the Buddha. In the *Therīgāthā*,[3] where he is called Kāla, he is said to have fallen madly in love with a hunter's daughter Cāpā, whom he married and by whom he had a son, Subhadda. His wife appears to have treated him badly, continually taunting him for his earlier Ājīvika connections. One day he remembered his meeting with the Buddha, left his wife, and went to the Buddha at Sāvatthi. There he entered the Buddhist order, and later became an *anāgāmī*. On his death he was reborn in the Avīha heaven.

Upaka was a Magadhan. According to the *Therīgāthā* Commentary [4] he was born at the village of Nāla, near the Bodhi Tree, and lived there with Cāpā after abandoning his asceticism for the life of a householder. If the legend of Upaka be accepted it must be taken to imply that Ājīvika mendicants roamed the roads of Magadha at least a generation before the commencement of Gosāla's ministry.

The towns mentioned in connection with the seven reanimations of Udāī in the *Bhagavatī Sūtra* [5] also suggest that, even before Gosāla's ministry, the regions of Kosala, Magadha, Kāsī, Videha, and Campā were the homes of peripatetic naked philosophers of the Ājīvika type. It is probable that these travelling philosophers, however abstruse their metaphysical doctrines, aimed at gaining the support of the populace, and very often obtained it. An interesting picture of the conditions which must have prevailed at the time is given in *Neru Jātaka*,[6] where we find a certain Buddhist *bhikkhu* preaching in an unnamed frontier village, and winning considerable support from the villagers. On his departure his place is taken by an "eternalist" (*sassatavādi*), then by an "annihilationist" (*ucchedavādi*), and

[1] *Jāt.* i, p. 81; *Vin.* i, p. 8; *Majjh.* i, pp. 170–1; *Dhammapad'-aṭṭhakathā* iv, pp. 71–2.

[2] E.g. *Lalitavistra* xxvi, p. 405, where Upaka's words "*Tad bhaviṣyasi Gautama!*" are couched in the future tense in place of the Pāli optative, and seem to imply faith rather than doubt.

[3] *Therīg.*, 291–311, with comm., pp. 220 ff.

[4] *Paramattha Dīpanī* v, p. 225.

[5] V. supra, pp. 31–32.

[6] *Jāt.* iii, pp. 246 ff.

finally by a naked ascetic (*acelaka*), who in turn gain the temporary loyalty of the villagers.

The religious atmosphere of the time is perhaps comparable to that which prevailed in the Roman Empire, when many people had lost their implicit faith in traditional verities, and were ready to support any new cult which offered a more plausible and attractive system of belief. In Rome the changing spiritual requirements were met in large measure by mystery cults imported from the East. In India, in the sixth and fifth centuries B.C., the wandering ascetics filled the need.

It is quite evident that these wanderers maintained a wide range of doctrines and varied rules of conduct. They were known by various titles, which usually denoted loosely knit classes of ascetic rather than regularly organized orders, as the Buddhist *bhikkhus* and the Jaina *samaṇas* later became. Beside these two terms we find others such as *acelaka*, *nigaṇṭha*, and of course *ājīvika*, which are used quite loosely, and obviously do not imply membership of any organized religious body. Thus in the *Majjhima Nikāya* [1] the Buddha declares that in his long experience of transmigration he has known no Ājīvika to go to heaven but one, and that one was a believer in *karma* and the efficiency of works.[2] This suggests either that all the early Ājīvikas did not accept Makkhali Gosāla's quietist determinism and that the term was sometimes used to denote a wider class of heretical mendicant with varying beliefs, or that there were early schisms of Makkhali's sect which rejected the cardinal doctrine of the founder. The former is the more probable explanation.

In some texts Ājīvikas are clearly distinguished from *nigaṇṭhas*,[3] but the *Sandaka Sutta* seems to embrace all six of the heretical teachers, including the great leader of the *nigaṇṭhas*, Nigaṇṭha Nātaputta or Mahāvīra, in the general category of Ājīvikas.[4] In the *Dhammapada* Commentary [5] Buddhaghosa describes the ascetic with unsettled mind (*anavaṭṭhita-citto*), who may start as an *acelaka*, then become an *Ājīvaka*, then a *nigaṇṭha*, and finally

[1] *Majjh.* i, 483.
[2] *So p' āsi kammavādī kiriyavādī.* Loc. cit.
[3] E.g. *Sutta-nipāta*, 381. *Ye ke c' ime titthiyā vādasīlā, Ājīvikā vā yadi vā nigaṇṭhā.*
[4] *Majjh.* i, pp. 513 ff. V. supra, pp. 18 19.
[5] *Dhp. Comm.* i, p. 309.

a *tāpasa*. Yet in the same work he tells the story of Migāra,[1] the banker of Sāvatthi, who is a follower of naked ascetics (*nagga-samaṇā*), but who falls foul of them when his daughter-in-law becomes a devotee of the Buddha. Here the five hundred ascetics who besiege him in his house are referred to indiscriminately as *nagga-samaṇā*, *acelakā*, and *ājīvikā*. Similarly the *Divyâvadāna*, in the story of Aśoka, seems to use the terms *Ājīvaka* and *Nirgrantha* synonymously.[2]

The significance of this apparent confusion may perhaps be explained by reference to another story in the *Dhammapada* Commentary,[3] in which the boy Jambuka is handed by his parents to a community of Ājīvikas and initiated into their order; but his asceticism takes a form too loathsome even for the Ājīvikas to tolerate, and he is expelled from the community. After this he obtains a great reputation for sanctity as a "wind-eater" (*vāta-bhakkho*), until he is ultimately converted by the Buddha. Buddhaghosa states that his career as a wind-eater lasted for fifty-five years, thus giving a further indication of the existence of Ājīvikas before Makkhali Gosāla. But the significance of the story in this context lies in the fact that even fifty-five years after his expulsion from the order of Ājīvikas he is still referred to by the Buddha as "Jambuka the Ājīvika". We have here a clear indication that the term was used not only for the organized ascetic order of Makkhali, but for free-lance ascetics of a similar type, or for followers of other leaders who later merged with the Ājīvika order.

This has been recognized by Barua in his latest work on the subject.[4] "The term Ājīvika," he writes, "is used in Indian literature; (1) in its widest sense to denote the Parivrājakas or Wanderers as distinguished from the Tāpasas or hermits; (2) in its narrower sense to denote the religious orders represented by the five Tīrthaṅkaras, Pūraṇa Kassapa, Makkhali Gosāla and the rest, considered heretics by the Buddhists; and (3) in its narrowest sense to denote the disciples and followers of Makkhali or Maṅkhaliputta Gosāla."

We are doubtful about Dr. Barua's first category, although in the *Jānakī-haraṇa* the term may have been intended in this

[1] Ibid. i, pp. 390 ff.
[2] V. infra, pp. 147–48.
[3] *Dhp. Comm.* ii, pp. 52 ff.
[4] *ABORI*. viii, p. 183.

sense.[1] We have seen that the second usage is very common in early Buddhist literature. But we must add a rider to Barua's statement, to the effect that some at least of the heretical *tīrthaṅkaras* seem to have been loosely allied, and to have had many points of doctrine in common.

Dr. Barua has attempted to provide an ancestry for the Ājīvikas. "I cannot but strongly feel that all possible inquiries concerning Nanda Vaccha and Kisa Saṅkicca are sure to lead the historian back to a typical representative of the Vānaprastha or Vaikhānasa order of Indian Hermits."[2] In his latest article he is even more definite. "The Ājīvika as a religious order and school of philosophy is known in the Vedic hymns, the Brāhmaṇas, the Āraṇyakas, and other ancient Sanskrit compilations and treatises that can safely be regarded as literary products of a pre-Jaina and pre-Buddhistic age."[3] Unfortunately he gives no references to or quotations from any of these works. This being the case we can only regret that Dr. Barua did not develop his surprising theory more fully, and declare that no statements known to us in pre-Buddhist literature suggest the existence of any such order. To the best of our knowledge the earliest non-Buddhist and non-Jaina reference suggesting the Ājīvikas occurs in the *Śvetāśvatara Upaniṣad*,[4] which is of comparatively late date.[5] Our own views on the origin of Ājīvikism have already been expressed—we do not believe that it derived from Vedic or Brāhmaṇical sources.[6]

We must also disagree with Dr. Barua's first statement, which implies that the Ājīvikas derived from the forest hermits. Whatever the status of the mysterious predecessors of Makkhali Gosāla, the first Ājīvika of whom the Buddhist scriptures bear record, Upaka, is not a hermit with a settled *āśrama* in the forest, but a mendicant, wandering from place to place. We believe also that Barua is mistaken in suggesting that the *vānaprasthas* were an order, in the sense of a body of ascetics with an organized system of practice and doctrine. Rather we believe that the terms *vānaprastha* and *vaikhānasa* were approximately synonymous and of broad connotation, both implying a forest

[1] V. infra, pp. 165 ff. [2] *JDL.* ii, p. 4. [3] *ABORI.* viii, pp. 183-4.
[4] V. infra, pp. 228–29. [5] Macdonnell, *Sanskrit Literature*, pp. 233–4.
[6] V. supra, pp. 6–9.

hermit of the third *āśrama* ; the diversity of the doctrines and disciplines of these hermits is clear from the *Upaniṣads* and from the Pāli scriptures.

Hoernle, in his discussion of the origin of the Ājīvikas, pins his faith on the derivation of the name Makkhali. " It describes Gosāla as having originally belonged to the Maṅkhali or Maskarin class of religious mendicants . . . The Maskarin, as a rule, led a solitary life and the adoption of this manner of life was open to very grave abuses. Hence some men of commanding personality conceived the task of regulating the tendency (to abuses) . . . by organizing the mendicants into communities governed by strict rules of conduct." [1]

Much of Hoernle's statement seems correct. He appears, however, to imply by the word " class " a degree of precision only slightly less than Barua's " order ". The term *maskarin* was in fact a very loose one. Pāṇini's etymology [2] seems only to imply that the word means a mendicant bearing a staff, of whatever class or order. Admittedly there is evidence, beside that of Makkhali's name, to show that the early Ājīvikas carried staves. Hoernle himself quotes *Tittira Jātaka*,[3] the twelfth and thirteenth verses of which describe a mendicant, said in the commentary to be an Ājīvika, as carrying a bamboo staff (*vetâcāra*). " The verses occurring in the Buddhist Jātakas," Hoernle adds, " embody the most ancient folklore—of a much older date than Buddhism itself," thereby implying that long before Makkhali a body of staff-bearing ascetics existed, from which the later Ājīvikas developed.

The Ājīvika Upaka is also referred to as bearing a staff.[4] Indeed staves probably became a regular mark of the Ājīvika order. But it must be noted that, except for its employment in the *sūtra* of Pāṇini, and as an epithet of Gosāla, the word *maskarin* is not to be found until the classical period of Sanskrit literature, and then seems to be used with very varied connotations. Kumāradāsa equates *maskarin* and *ājīvika*,[5] but the *Bhaṭṭikāvya*, of the sixth or seventh century A.D.[6] uses the word in a sense which certainly does not suggest a follower of Gosāla.[7] Bāṇa describes

[1] *ERE.* i, p. 260. [2] V. supra, p. 78. [3] *Jāt.* iii, p. 542.
[4] *Laṭṭhi-hattho, Therīg.*, 291.
[5] *Jānakī-haraṇa* x, 76. V. infra, p. 165, n 4.
[6] Keith, *History of Sanskrit Literature*, p. 116. [7] V. infra, p. 166.

a *maskarin* with a skull for a begging-bowl and wearing a red robe, who must surely have been a Śaivite.[1] The commentator Utpala seems to equate the words *ājīvika* and *ekadaṇḍin*,[2] the latter certainly meaning an ascetic with a single staff as part of his insignia. But Halâyudha the lexicographer quotes the word *ājīvika* as a member of a class containing various other terms for a heretical ascetic,[3] while *maskarin* occurs in the same verse as do the names of more orthodox and respectable ascetics, such as *tapasvin*, *parivrājaka*, *tāpasa*, etc.[4] Hemacandra also includes the word *maskarin* with *vaikhānasa vānaprastha* and *yati* in a group not including *ājīvika*.[5] In fact we have no reason to believe that the term *maskarin* ever meant more than a staff-bearing mendicant of any order. Certainly it was sometimes used to designate the Ājīvikas, but it included a group much wider than they, as Dr. Barua ultimately recognized.[6] This being the case we cannot believe that an " order " of *maskarins* existed before Gosāla's day, and that the Ājīvikas developed from them.

It seems, in fact, an anachronism to suggest that any organized *saṅghas* existed before the time of Buddha, Mahāvīra, and Makkhali Gosāla. Certainly there existed hermits, either solitary or living in colonies, and wandering mendicants. We suggest that the hermit colonies gathered round locally respected leaders, the fame of some of whom probably spread far beyond the locality of their hermitages and often survived their deaths. But the picture painted by the Buddha, when describing his search for truth among the forest teachers,[7] and the flourishing and often fantastic speculations of the *Upaniṣads*, suggest that even within local groups there existed considerable differences of doctrine. In fact India at the time of the emergence of the heterodox sects seems to have been in a state of theological anarchy, mitigated only by orthodox Brāhmaṇism, which was by no means satisfying to the best minds of the times.

[1] *Harṣa-carita* ed. Führer, pp. 152–3. V. infra, p. 167.
[2] V. infra, pp. 169 ff.
[3] *Abhidhāna-ratnamālā* ii, 189–190. V. infra, p. 182.
[4] Ibid. ii, 254.
[5] *Abhidhāna-cintāmaṇi*, 809–810. V. infra, p. 182.
[6] *ABORI*. viii, p. 184. For a further consideration of the term *maskarin* v. infra, pp. 163 ff.
[7] *Jāt*. i, pp. 66 ff.

The solitaries, whether hermits or wanderers, must by their very nature have been laws unto themselves. That they often held certain doctrines and followed certain practices in common might be expected from the basic similarity of human temperaments and the imitative propensities of the human animal. But there is no reason to believe that they were bound by any rules other than self-made ones, such as vows taken on embarking on their careers of mendicancy. The disciplinary innovations of the reforming leaders consisted partly in persuading some of these independent roving philosophers to accept common rules, and in linking them to hermit communities and giving them coherence by insisting on their residence in *vihāras* during the rainy reason. We believe that these wandering sophists and ascetics, rather than hermits or non-existent ascetic "orders", played the biggest part in the development of the heretical *saṅghas* of Buddhism, Jainism, and Ājīvikism.

Etymology of the term Ājīvika

Among the earliest views on the derivation of the word Ājīvika are those of Burnouf and Lassen. The former [1] believed that the term had no derogatory significance, but meant "one who lives on the charity of others", deriving it from *a-jīva*, "the absence of livelihood," with the addition of the suffix *-ka* and the consequent lengthening by *vṛddhi* of the initial vowel. As an alternative explanation Burnouf supported Lassen, who, on the basis of a similar etymology, believed that the word meant an ascetic who ate no living or animal food.[2] Neither of these interpretations is acceptable. The presence of the alternative form *Jīvaka*, attested by the lexicographers [3] and by the astrologer Vaidyanātha Dīkṣita,[4] proves that the first syllable of the word cannot be a privative.

The most widely accepted theory is that the term *Ājīvika* or *Ājīvaka* is derived from the word *ājīva*. This, in Hoernle's words, means "the mode of life, or profession, of any particular class of people, whether they live as householders . . . or as

[1] *Le Lotus de la Bonne Loi* (2nd edn.), ii, p. 777.
[2] *Indische Altertumskunde* ii, p. 107, n. 2, quoted Burnouf, op. cit., loc. cit.
[3] V. infra, pp. 182–83.
[4] V. infra, pp. 184–85.

religious mendicants". Hoernle adds that "the word *ājīvika*, being a derivative of *ājīva*, means one who observes the mode of living appropriate to his class . . . . There is some ground for believing that Gosāla held peculiar views as to the *ājīva* of a mendicant who is truly liberated from the fetters of *karma*. It was probably for this reason that he and his adherents came to be known as *Ājīvika*, or the men who held the peculiar doctrine of *ājīva* . . . . The name 'Ājīvika', it appears, was originally meant to stigmatize Gosāla and his followers as 'professionals'; though, no doubt, in later times, when it became the distinctive name of a mendicant order, it no longer carried that offensive meaning".[1]

Hoernle's hypothesis requires some qualification. From the examples given above[2] it is obvious that the term *ājīvika*, like *nirgrantha*, originally had a wider connotation than the organized followers of Makkhali Gosāla, and might be applied to almost any non-brāhmaṇical naked ascetic. Furthermore it is possible to suggest an alternative etymology.

Admittedly religion offers a number of examples of derogatory nicknames ultimately becoming the regular titles of heterodox sects—the words "quaker" and "methodist" come immediately to mind. In this connection the story of *Paṇḍara Jātaka* may be of some significance.[3] A man suffers shipwreck and is cast ashore near the port of Karambiya in a state of nudity (*nagga-bhoggo*). Like Makkhali Gosāla and Pūraṇa Kassapa in Buddhaghosa's stories,[4] he is mistaken for an ascetic, and is given alms. Thereupon he declares with relief: "I've found a way to make a living!" (*Laddho me jīvik'-opāyo*). This story surely indicates that the connection between the words *ājīva* and *ājīvika* was recognized in ancient India, at least by the Ājīvikas' opponents.

An alternative explanation of the term is provided in the *Dīgha Nikāya*.[5] It is said that the Buddha met at Vesāli a certain ascetic named Kandara-masuka, who maintained seven lifelong vows. The first of these is: "As long as I live I will be naked, and will not put on a garment" (*Yāvaj-jīvam acelako assaṃ, na vatthaṃ paridaheyaṃ*). The second vow is one of perpetual chastity; by the third, surprisingly enough, the ascetic

[1] *ERE*. i, p. 259.
[2] V. supra, pp. 96–98.
[3] *Jāt.* v, pp. 75 ff.
[4] V. supra, pp. 37, 82–83.
[5] *Dīgha* iii, p. 9.

undertakes to beg only spirits and meat, and not to eat gruel or broth; while the last four are vows of a Jaina type, delimiting the area in the four directions beyond which he undertakes not to travel. The ascetic Kandara-masuka is regularly referred to as *acela*, but nowhere as *ājīvika*, and we have no evidence that any of his vows, with the exception of the first, were taken by the organized Ājīvika community. Nevertheless the formula *yāvajjīvam*, which precedes each of the seven vows, may be significant. It suggests the possibility that the word *ājīvika* may be derived from some such phrase as *ā jīvāt*, "as long as life." This view was put forward by Kern,[1] but seems not to have been noticed by later workers in the field, perhaps because the author gave little weight to his theory, and does not appear to have provided references to back it.

Admittedly the preposition *ā* has more often the force of "until" than "as long as", but "it may denote the limit 'to', 'until', 'as far as', 'from', either including the object named or excluding it",[2] and therefore this interpretation is by no means illegitimate.

The adjective *yāvajjīvika* meaning "lifelong" is to be found in the *Āśvalāyana Śrauta Sūtra*,[3] composed at a very early period, perhaps before Gosāla's ministry. It is significant that it is there used in reference to the duration of vows to be taken in penance for errors in sacrificial ritual. The same term, in its Prākrit form *jāvajjīvāë*, with the same connotation, is to be found in the *Bhagavatī Sūtra*.[4] It is by no means impossible that the word *ājīvika* had a similar connotation with the religious community using it, and indicated the lifelong character of the vows taken by the followers of Makkhali Gosāla and by the free-lance Ājīvikas, in contrast to the temporary vows of the Buddhist *saṅgha*. In this case the derogatory etymology from *ājīva* must have been devised by the opponents of the sect, in the same manner as that in which Buddhaghosa devised derogatory etymologies for *Makkhali* and *Pūraṇa*.

To this theory it may be objected that at least one Ājīvika,

[1] *Der Buddhismus und seine Geschichte in Indien* ii, p. 7, n. 2.
[2] Monier Williams, *Sanskrit–English Dictionary*, s.v. *ā*.
[3] *Āśvalāyana Śrauta Sūtra* iii, 14, Poona edn., p. 156. *Etat sāṃvatsaraṃ vrataṃ, yāvaj-jīvikaṃ vā.*
[4] *Bh. Sū.* iii, *sū.* 133, fol. 286.

Upaka, is said to have given up his asceticism.[1] But this fact by no means invalidates our etymology, for even lifelong vows may be broken.

The Ājīvika Initiation

New members seem normally to have been inducted into the Ājīvika order after an initiation ceremony. Before the ministry of Makkhali Gosāla, among local Ājīvika groups and independent mendicants, the ceremony seems to have varied considerably from one group to another. We have already met unscrupulous men who initiated themselves into a profitable career of asceticism by the simple process of losing their clothes.[2] Many spurious mendicants of this type, often loosely called Ājīvikas, must have existed both before and after the days of Makkhali Gosāla. We may, however, assume that Makkhali's organization of the loosely knit ascetics was effective in introducing some regularity into the procedure of admission to the order and initiation.

Two Pāli references give us some indication of the processes of entry into the Ājīvika mendicant fraternity. *Tittira Jātaka* [3] tells of an unfortunate false ascetic (*niggatiko duṭṭha-tāpaso*), who, after a career of chicanery and fraud, is judged and executed by a lion. The tiger who prosecutes him at the lion's court describes the prisoner in a few lines of verse of considerable interest; among other things, says the tiger, he has "burnt his hands by grasping a lump".[4] The commentary elucidates the phrase: "At the time of his going forth as an Ājīvika his hands were burnt by grasping a heated lump." [5] This seems a reliable indication that the early Ājīvika was sometimes initiated by a painful ordeal, and there are faint suggestions of the survival of the practice at a much later date.

In *Mahānāradakassapa Jātaka* [6] the ascetic Guṇa is described as an "ignorant, naked, wretched, and blindly foolish Ājīvika".[7]

[1] V. supra, p. 95.
[2] V. supra, pp. 37,82–83, 102.
[3] *Jāt.* iii, pp. 536–543.
[4] *Hatthā daḍḍhā piṇḍapaṭiggahaṇena.* Op. cit., p. 541.
[5] *Ājīvika-pabbajjaṃ-pabbajjita-kāle uṇha-piṇḍa-paṭiggahaṇena hatth' âpi kir' assa daḍḍhā.* Op. cit., p. 542.
[6] *Jāt.* vi, pp. 219 ff.
[7] *Ajānantaṃ nagga-bhoggaṃ nissirīkam andha-bālam Ājīvikaṃ.*

The word used in this phrase to express his nudity is *nagga-bhogga*, which the Pāli Text Society's Dictionary interprets as " one whose goods are nakedness ". The term is thrice employed in the *Jātakas*,[1] the first and second instances describing the condition of castaways, one of whom became a false ascetic,[2] and the third being an epithet of Guṇa. Very similar compound adjectives are to be found in use much later than the time of the *Jātakas*' composition. An inscription at Belagāmi, Mysore,[3] dated A.D. 1162, catalogues the types of ascetic to whom alms were given at the Koḍiya *maṭh* ; as well as the Jaina *kṣapaṇakas* and the Hindu *paramahaṃsas*, who seem to have been habitually naked,[4] the visitors to the *maṭh* included *nagna-bhagnas*.[5] The *Rājataraṅgiṇī* refers to *rugṇa-nagnâṭaka* ascetics, with emaciated or decayed noses, feet, and hands,[6] who have many points in common with, and may have been, Ājīvikas. We therefore believe that the Pāli word *nagga-bhogga* should be read as a *dvandva* adjective, rather than as a *bahuvrīhi*, and that its second member is equivalent to the Sanskrit *bhugna* (" bent "), rather than *bhogya* (" property ") ; thus the meaning of the term would be not " one whose goods are nakedness ", but " one naked and crippled ". The Ājīvika initiatory ordeals may well have resulted in such mutilation and deformity as to qualify the ascetic for these titles.

Another element in the Ājīvika initiation, for which there is confirmation in a later source, is described in the *Dhammapada* Commentary, in the story of Jambuka, to which we have already referred.[7] The events there described ostensibly refer to the unorganized pre-Makkhali Ājīvikas, but the details of the account of Jambuka's initiation may have been provided by Buddhaghosa, and perhaps apply to the organized community of Makkhali. Jambuka's habits are so disgusting that his parents

[1] *Jāt.* iv, p. 160 ; v, p. 75 ; vi, p. 225.
[2] V. supra, p. 102.
[3] *Epi. Carn.* vii, Shikarpur no. 102.
[4] V. infra, p. 114.
[5] Professor B. A. Saletore (*Mediæval Jainism*, p. 219), following Rice's translation, believes that this word represents two classes of ascetic, the *nagnas* and the *bhagnas*. This we do not accept in view of the existence of similar terms in the Pāli and in the *Rājataraṅgiṇī*, which cannot apply to more than a single class.
[6] *Rājataraṅgiṇī* vii, 1092–4. V. infra, p. 206.
[7] *Dhp. Comm.* ii, p. 52. V. supra, p. 97.

decide that he is not fitted for ordinary life, but only for the Ājīvikas (*Ājīvikānam esa anucchaviko*). Therefore they take him to a local group of Ājīvika ascetics, apparently while he is still a child, and request that he be initiated into their community. The boy is placed in a pit up to his neck, planks are laid over the pit, above his collar-bones, and, sitting on the planks, the Ājīvikas pull out his hair with a piece of the rib of a palm-leaf.[1] It seems that the early Ājīvikas, like the Jainas, extracted the hair by the roots, and that the custom persisted among them is attested by the Tamil text *Civañāṉa-cittiyār*.[2]

Yet Gosāla Mankhaliputta is described as tearing his beard in his last delirium, and in Kumāradāsa's *Jānakī-haraṇa* the Ājīvika's head, like that of the orthodox Hindu ascetic, is covered with a pile of matted locks.[3] The Ājīvikas depicted at Borobudur have hair (Plate II).[4] Thus it seems that Ājīvikas were not always tonsured or clean-shaven. The extraction of the hair by the roots, like the grasping of the heated lump, was probably an ordeal intended to render the novice oblivious to physical pain, and to test his resolution, and, as with the Jainas,[5] was not usually repeated after initiation, or was only repeated at distant intervals.

The other feature of Jambuka's initiation, burial up to the neck, is mentioned in Japanese Buddhist sources as being part of the Ājīvika's ascetic technique.[6] The pit in which the novice was placed may have symbolized his spiritual rebirth from the womb of Mother Earth, or, since burial was not unknown in Ancient India, his " death to the world ".

Two further points connected with entry into Ājīvika asceticism may here be noted. The story of Jambuka indicates that, as with the Buddhists and Jainas, novices were accepted by the Ājīvikas while still children. And the Ājīvika sixfold classification of men, as described in the *Aṅguttara Nikāya* and by Buddhaghosa, shows that women were permitted to enter the Ājīvika order,

[1] *Gala-ppamāṇe āvāṭe thapetvā, dvinnaṃ jattūnaṃ upari padarāṇi datvā, tesaṃ upari nisīditvā, tāl'-aṭṭhi-khaṇḍena kese luñciṃsu.*

[2] *CÑC.* ed. Mudaliyar, p. 255. V. infra, p. 202.

[3] *Dambh'-âjīvikam uttuṅga-jaṭā-maṇḍita-mastakaṃ Kañcin maskariṇaṃ Sītā dadarś' âśramam āgatam. Jānakīharaṇa* x, 76. V. infra, pp. 150 ff.

[4] V. infra, p. 108.

[5] Schubring, *Die Lehre der Jainas*, p. 159.

[6] V. infra, p. 112.

and that their status was not significantly lower than that of the male members of the sect.[1]

ĀJĪVIKA NUDITY

The ascetics called Ājīvika in the Pāli texts, whether the pre-Makkhali mendicants and hermits whom we may call proto-Ājīvikas, or members of the organized Ājīvika sect, appear usually to have lived in a state of nakedness. Makkhali Gosāla and Pūraṇa Kassapa are described as completely unclothed,[2] and it would seem that in the early days of Ājīvikism the lesser members of the community were also habitually naked.[3]

In later times the rule of nudity does not seem to have been so regularly followed. The *Bhagavatī Sūtra* states that on his death the corpse of Gosāla Maṅkhaliputta was arrayed in a splendid robe and bedecked with ornaments,[4] which suggests that some form of pontifical finery was not unknown to the leaders of Ājīvikism. The *Dhammapada* Commentary seems sometimes to distinguish between the words *ājīvika* and *acelaka*,[5] the latter of which was a term of wide connotation and was probably used to refer to any unclothed ascetic. The Ājīvikas depicted at Borobudur wear clothes,[6] and Canarese texts confuse the Ājīvikas with yellow-robed Buddhists.[7] There is ample evidence that wide differences of doctrine existed within the later Ājīvika community,[8] and with some of its sub-sects, as with the Jainas, the cult of nakedness may have tended to die out at an early date.

Pictorial and sculptural representations of Ājīvikas contribute little to our knowledge of the usual Ājīvika garb. Representations of naked ascetics occur occasionally in Buddhist art, but in most cases there is no evidence that these are Ājīvikas and not members of the Digambara Jaina order. A figure in one of the Ajantā frescos has been identified by Foucher as Pūraṇa Kassapa at the great miracle contest at Sāvatthi,[9] and this is completely

[1] *Ājīvikā ājīviniyo ayaṃ sukk'-âbhijātī 'ti vadati*. *Sum. Vil.* i, p. 162; *Aṅg.* iii, p. 383. V. infra, p. 243.
[2] V. supra, pp. 37, 40, 83, 87 [3] V. supra, pp. 97, 102. [4] V. supra, p. 95.
[5] *Dhp. Comm.* i, p. 309. V. supra, p. 96.
[6] V. infra, p. 108. [7] V. infra, pp. 203–4. [8] V. infra, pp. 279–280.
[9] *L'Art Gréco-Bouddhique*, vol. ii, p. 264; also *JA.*, 1909, pp. 21–3. V. supra, pp. 84 ff.

naked. Certain sculptures of the Gandhāra school, depicting the Buddha's *parinirvāṇa*, also show a naked ascetic, who seems to be the Ājīvika in the act of informing the *bhikkhu* Mahākassapa of the great event (Plate III) [1]; but a similar character in other works of the same school depicting the same subject is dressed in a garb resembling that of the orthodox Hindu ascetic.[2]

Representations of Ājīvikas exist outside India. A sculpture at Borobudur shows the encounter of the newly enlightened Buddha with Upaka the Ājīvika; Upaka is here accompanied by two fellow Ājīvikas, and all three wear a peculiar skirt-like garment and have carefully arranged hair (Plate II).[3] Krom is of the opinion that no reliance can be placed on the accuracy of these figures,[4] but it must be remembered that at the time of the building of the Borobudur *stūpa* the Javanese were in contact with Cōḻamaṇḍalam, and that Ājīvikas were to be found in that region. Therefore it is not wholly impossible that the Javanese sculptor was working from personal knowledge, or from an authentic report, of the appearance of Dravidian Ājīvikas.

Central Asian frescos show the Buddha disputing with the heretical leaders.[5] Of the latter some are partly naked, but he whom Grünwedel identifies as Makkhali Gosāla, by virtue of his staff (Plate I, ii), is attired in the garb of the orthodox ascetic, and wears the typical *sannyāsī's* topknot.[6]

It is generally agreed that Mahāvīra founded his order upon a looser group of ascetics, wearing clothing and by no means strict in their chastity, who looked back to the shadowy Pārśva Nātha, the twenty-third *tīrthaṅkara* of Jaina hagiology. Jainism in its later form, it is suggested, was but a development of the older proto-Jainism of Pārśva.[7] It seems, moreover, that the early Jaina monk, although called *acela*, was not normally completely nude, but wore a loincloth [8]; while Mahāvīra himself was habitually naked, he permitted his followers to wear a

[1] Foucher, *L'Art Gréco-Bouddhique*, vol. i, pp. 568 ff. V. infra, p. 136.
[2] Foucher, *L'Art Gréco-Bouddhique*, vol. ii, pp. 259 ff.
[3] Krom, *The Life of the Buddha*, plate 110; also *Barabuḍur*, vol. i, pp. 220–1. V. supra, p. 94.
[4] Krom, *Barabuḍur*, vol. ii, p. 203.
[5] Grünwedel, *Alt-Buddhistische Kultstätten*, figs. 344, 353. V. plate I.
[6] Grünwedel, *Alt-Kutscha* ii, pp. 21–2.
[7] Hoernle, *ERE.* i, p. 265. Full references in Shah, *Jainism in N. India*, pp. 1–12.
[8] *Ācārāṅga Sūtra* i, 7, 7, 1.

minimum of covering to avoid embarrassment and the accusation of indecency. On the other hand the nudity of the Ājīvika seems usually at this period to have been total. This point has been clearly made by Hoernle,[1] who shows that in the Ājīvika sixfold classification of men [2] the white class (*sukk'-âbhijāti*) consisted of Ājīvikas and Ājīvinīs, while the red (*lohit'-âbhijāti*), two stages below it, contained *niganṭhas* wearing one cloth (*ekasāṭakā*). The complete nudity of the Ājīvika is further made clear from the description of Pūraṇa in the *Divyâvadāna*, which precludes the wearing even of a loincloth.[3] Thus the Ājīvika seems to have gone further in his nudity than the early Jaina. We may assume that his motive was the same as that which inspired Mahāvīra in instituting the custom in the Jaina order, the acquisition of complete indifference to all physical sensation.[4]

If our synchronisms are correct,[5] and if we can accept the indications given by the stories of Upaka and Jambuka,[6] it would seem that neither Mahāvīra nor Gosāla was the originator of the cult of nudity, which must have existed before either reformer commenced his ministry. If we accept the existence of the clothed proto-Jainas we can only assume with Hoernle that Mahāvīra introduced his reform in their dress under the influence of Gosāla and the proto-Ājīvikas, adopting the latter's views on the necessity of nakedness for salvation, but making slight concessions to public opinion and human frailty. Gosāla, in this respect more extreme than his former colleague, seems to have insisted on the maintenance of total nudity.

Thus, although later developments may have led to some relaxations in the rules, we may envisage the typical Ājīvika of the early period as usually completely naked, no doubt covered with dust and dirt, perhaps bent and crippled, and armed with a bamboo staff.

Ājīvika Asceticism

Whatever relaxation of discipline may have taken place in private, the early Ājīvika performed penance of the most

[1] *ERE*. i, p. 262.
[2] *Sum. Vil.* i, p. 162 ; *Aṅg*. iii, p. 383. V. infra pp. 243 ff.
[3] *Purastāl lambate daśā. Divyâvadāna*, p. 165.
[4] *Ācārâṅga Sūtra*, loc. cit. [5] V. supra, p. 74. [6] V. supra, pp. 94. 97.

rigorous nature in public. Significant descriptions of his asceticism occur in the Pāli texts, but in reading them it must be borne in mind that some of the penances described may not have been regularly practised by the organized followers of Makkhali Gosāla, but are rather indicative of the activities of the free-lance proto-Ājīvikas.

For instance in *Lomahaṃsa Jātaka* [1] it is stated that the Bodhisatta himself had once become an Ājīvika. Naked and solitary, he fled like a deer at the sight of men. He ate refuse, small fish, and dung. In order that his austerities should not be disturbed he took up his abode in the depths of the jungle. In winter he would leave his thicket and spend the night exposed to the bitter wind, returning to the shade as soon as the sun rose. By night he was wet with melted snow (*himodakena*), and by day with the water dripping from the branches of trees. In summer he reversed the process, and was scorched by the sun all day, while at night the thicket shielded him from the cooling breeze.

This account seems not to represent a typical member of the Ājīvika order, although it is possible that certain solitary hermits were loosely affiliated to it. The figure here described, however, seems to be that of a forest hermit of the most psychopathic type, and the passage is yet another example of the very loose manner in which the term Ājīvika was used in the Pāli texts. It does indicate, however, how closely the word was connected in the popular mind with extreme asceticism.

A picture of Ājīvika penances which seems more probably to apply to the regular order is contained in the prologue to *Naṅguṭṭha Jātaka*.[2] Here it is stated that a company of Ājīvikas was stationed behind the Jetavana at Sāvatthi, and performed false penances (*micchā-tapam*) of various types. These penances included " exerting themselves in a squatting posture " (*ukkuṭika-ppadhāna*), the bat-penance (*vagguli-vata*),[3] lying on beds of thorns (*kaṇṭaka-ppasaya*), and the penance of the five fires (*pañca-tapana*). The acts of self-mortification here named seem to be those practised by Indian ascetics of all periods, but we have no reason to believe that they were not also practised by the

[1] *Jāt.* i, p. 390.
[2] *Jāt.* i, p. 493.
[3] Cowell (*The Jātaka* i, p. 307) translates this phrase on the basis of the commentary as " swinging in the air like bats ".

Ājīvika *saṅgha*. At Sāvatthi Gosāla seems to have made use of a "penance-ground", as well as the pottery in which he regularly resided.[1] It is possible that this adjoined the Jetavana, and that the Ājīvikas described in the Jataka were the train of followers with which Gosāla was usually surrounded.

The Jaina *Aupapātika Sūtra* contains a significant list of the types of Ājīvika mendicant.[2] These include *dugharantariyā*, who, according to Abhayadeva's commentary, were in the habit of begging food at every third house only; *tigharantariyā*, who begged at every fourth house; *sattagharantariyā*, who begged at every eighth house; *uppala-beṇṭiyā*, who, Abhayadeva explains, under a special vow employed lotus stalks in begging,[3] and who perhaps used lotus leaves as begging receptacles; *gharasamudāṇiyā*, those who begged at every house; *vijju-antariyā*, who would not go begging when lightning was seen[4]; and finally *uṭṭiyā-samaṇā*, who, according to Abhayadeva, were ascetics who entered large earthen pots in order to do penance.[5] It is difficult to provide a satisfactory alternative explanation of the last term, which seems meaningless if interpreted according to the primary meaning of *uṣṭrikā* (she-camel).

For the last item of the list we have partial confirmation from a Tamil source. Naccin̲ārkkin̲iyar, the fourteenth century commentator on the early Tamil grammar, *Tolkāppiyam*, quotes as an example an unidentified verse which mentions the existence of ascetics who perform penances in *tāḻi*, or funerary urns.[6] Dr. K. R. Srinivasan, who has noticed this reference,[7] states categorically that these ascetics were Ājīvikas, who, he seems to believe, were identical with Jainas. In fact the text does not give any information on the sectarian affinities of the ascetics in question, but since we know that Ājīvikas were

[1] V. supra, p. 59.

[2] *Aupapātika Sūtra*, *sū*. 41, fol. 196.

[3] *Utpala-vṛṇṭāni niyama-viśeṣād grāhyatayā bhaikṣatvena yeṣāṃ santi te utpalavṛṇṭikāḥ.*

[4] *Vidyuti satyām antaraṃ bhikṣa-grahaṇasya yeṣām asti te vidyud-antarikāḥ. Vidyut-sampāte bhikṣāṃ n' âṭant' îti bhāv'-ârthaḥ.* Abhayadeva to *Aupapātika*, loc. cit.

[5] *Uṣṭrikā mahā-mṛṇmayo bhājana-viśeṣas. Tatra praviṣṭā ye śrāmyanti tapasyant' îti uṣṭrikā-śramaṇāḥ.* Ibid.

[6] *Tāḻi-kavippa-t-tavañ-ceyvar maṇṇāka*
Vāḻiya norraṉai māl varai.
Tolkāppiyam Poruḷ-atikāram, ed. Pillai i, p. 182.

[7] *Ancient India* ii, p. 9.

present in the Tamil country, and since this strange system of penance is ascribed to them in the Jaina text, we may assume that the ascetics referred to in the Tamil verse were Ājīvikas.

The *Sthānāṅga Sūtra* gives a further list of Ājīvika ascetic practices, which are said to be severe penances, terrible penances, the abstention from liquids (*rasa,* which the commentator Abhayadeva interprets as ghee, etc.),[1] and indifference to the pleasures of the sense of taste.[2] Unfortunately we are given no detailed explanation of the distinction between the first and second forms of *tapas*, and the list is only of value as confirmation of the statements of other sources to the effect that, at least in public, the Ājīvikas were given to severe self-mortification.

The Ājīvikas' reputation for asceticism apparently reached the Far East. Chinese and Japanese Buddhist Literature classes the *Ashibikas* (i.e. Ājīvikas) with the *Nikendabtras* or Nirgranthas as practising severe penance. "They both hold that the penalty for a sinful life must sooner or later be paid and since it is impossible to escape from it it is better that it be paid as soon as possible so that the life to come may be free for enjoyment. Thus their practices were ascetic—fasting silence immovability and the burying of themselves up to the neck were their expressions of penance." [3]

That the Ājīvikas continued to practise severe asceticism at a late period is shown by one of our most recent sources, the Tamil *Civañāṉa-cittiyār*, which speaks of them as prescribing great suffering to all souls (as a necessary means of salvation).[4]

A reference in *Tittira Jātaka* [5] indicates that the early Ājīvikas performed secret magical rites of a repulsive tantric type. The unfortunate Ājīvika is there said by his prosecutor the tiger to have "removed blood at midnight".[6] The commentary elucidates this cryptic phrase thus: "*Pupphakam* means

[1] *Ghṛt'-âdi-rasa-parityāgaḥ.*

[2] *Ājīviyāṇaṃ caüvvihe tave . . . uggatave, ghoratave, rasa-nijjūhaṇatā, jibbh'-indiya-paḍisaṃlīṇatā. Sthānāṅga* iv, 309.

[3] Sugiura, *Hindu Logic as Preserved in China and Japan*, p. 16, quoting *Hyaku-ron So* i, 22. The passage has been noticed by Hoernle (*ERE.* i, p. 269) who, adhering to his own theory, identifies the Ashibikas with the Digambara Jainas.

[4] *Pār mēṉ maṉṉ uyir evaṟṟinukkum varunta vēyaṟaṅkaḷ collum. CÑC.* ed. Mudaliyar, p. 255, v. 1.

[5] *Jāt.* iii, pp. 541–2. V. supra, p. 104.

[6] *Abbhūhitaṃ pupphakaṃ aḍḍharattaṃ.*

blood. . . . He cut off the hands and feet of offenders against the king for his living, took them away, threw them into a room, and let the blood run out from the openings of the wounds; going there at midnight he made a heap of red rice-powder."[1] Francis and Neil, in their translation of this *Jātaka* ignore the commentary, and give :—

> " . . . in midnight fray
> wounded, he washed the blood away."[2]

This is a brilliantly imaginative interpretation, but is by no means consistent with the commentary. Whatever the meaning of the strange phrase in the text, the commentary indicates that the wicked Ājīvika was thought of as performing magical ceremonies. This single reference is not reliably confirmed by other sources, although a significant passage in the *Vāyu Purāṇa* also suggests that the Ājīvikas performed mysterious secret rites.[3]

Whatever may have been the practices of the primitive solitary Ājīvika in *Lomahaṃsa Jātaka*,[4] the organized Ājīvika community does not seem to have countenanced the performance of ascetic practices of the most repulsive type. The boy Jambuka, to whom we have already referred,[5] developed a propensity to nudity and the eating of ordure at a very early age, and for this reason his parents had him initiated into the Ājīvika *saṅgha*. As he was quite satisfied by his repulsive diet he refused to go on the usual begging rounds with his fellow mendicants, who, when they learned of the disgusting behaviour of the boy in their absence, promptly expelled him from the community. The *Dhammapada* commentary gives as their motive for his expulsion the fear that the Buddhist monks might discover Jambuka's evil habits and expose the Ājīvikas to scorn and ridicule. But

[1] *Pupphakaṃ ti lohitaṃ, idaṃ vuttaṃ hoti; iminā kira jīvikaṃ nissāya rājâparādhikānaṃ hattha-pāde chinditvā te ānetvā sālāyaṃ nipajjāpetvā vaṇa-mukhehi paggharantaṃ lohitaṃ aḍḍharatta-samaye tattha gantvā kaṇuka-thupaṃ katvā thapitan ti.* I prefer Fausböll's variant reading to that in the text, *kuṇḍakadhūmaṃ nāma datvā*, which does not make good sense. It is possible that the word *te* in the commentary refers to the criminals themselves, in which case it seems that the Ājīvika stanched their wounds with rice-powder, but in this case a magical ceremony is also suggested.

[2] *The Jātaka*, vol. iii, p. 322.

[3] V. infra, pp. 162 ff.

[4] V. supra, p. 110.

[5] V. supra, pp. 97, 105–6.

it seems probable that the Ājīvikas, extremists in asceticism though they were, had definite rules of ascetic conduct, and that their penances were exceeded in repulsiveness by those of some independent ascetics.

That the Ājīvikas lived in communities is clear from this and numerous other references. But it is probable that some Ājīvikas at any rate withdrew themselves from human contacts. Hoernle,[1] on the strength of Weber's paraphrase of the *Paramahaṃsa Upaniṣad*,[2] has pointed out the existence of two classes of mendicant among the *ekadaṇḍins*, of which the higher, or *paramahaṃsa*, abandoned his loincloth, staff, and begging bowl, and lived absolutely unimpeded by worldly possessions. Some such distinction may have existed among the Ājīvikas, who were sometimes looked upon as a species of the genus *ekadaṇḍin*.[3] But we have seen that even Gosāla, although he seems to have been habitually naked, did not discard his begging bowl [4]; and the mendicants described in the *Paramahaṃsa Upaniṣad* are evidently orthodox Hindu ascetics; thus the conclusion is by no means certain.

The strange Bodhisatta Ājīvika to whom reference has already been made,[5] may be such a solitary, although it seems more probable that he was not thought of as being in any way affiliated to the order of Gosāla. A more striking indication of the existence of such solitary ascetics is to be found in the *Sūtrakṛtâṅga*, in the course of the debate between Gosāla and Adda.[6] Gosāla attacks Mahāvīra, who, he declares, was formerly a solitary ascetic (*egantacārī samaṇe*), but is now surrounded by disciples. One or other course must be wrong. To this Adda replies that there is no sin in preaching the *dhamma* to others.[7] Gosāla then changes the subject and maintains that, according to his doctrine, there is no sin for the *egantacārī* in drinking cold water, eating seeds, accepting food specially prepared, or in women.[8]

1 *ERE*. i, p. 260.
2 *IS*. ii, pp. 174–5.
3 V. infra, pp. 169 ff.
4 V. supra, p. 52.
5 V. supra, p. 110.
6 V. supra, p. 53.
7 *Sū. kṛ*. ii, 6, vv. 1–5, fols. 388–9.
8 *Sīodagaṃ sevaū bīyakāyaṃ, āhāyakammaṃ taha itthiyāo.*
Egantacāriss' iha amha dhamme, tavassiṇo n' ābhisameti pāvaṃ. Ibid., v. 7, fol. 390.

We have here a definite indication of lonely wanderers, not gathered in communities, living according to the ascetic rules laid down by Gosāla.

The later Dravidian Ājīvikas developed the concept of Maṟkali, whom they confused with Pūraṇa, as remote, motionless, and silent—the Lord who, although he knew all things, did not speak.[1] He appeared and disappeared mysteriously, " like the rainbow, of incomprehensible form, by nature without defect, Pūraṇaṉ, famed for his perfect knowledge." [2] These passages suggest that the superior grade of Ājīvika monk, the leaders of the *saṅgha*, lived in almost inapproachable solitude, perhaps somewhat relaxing their ascetic discipline, and very occasionally bestowing a theophany upon the lesser members of the community. That " fasting silence and immovability " were among the ascetic practices of the Ājīvikas is confirmed by the Far Eastern sources.[3] Yet our authorities speak with two voices. The consensus of the Buddhist and Jaina references seems to indicate that both Makkhali Gosāla and Pūraṇa were often surrounded by crowds of disciples, and freely conversed with their lay supporters.

The Ājīvika *Sabhā*

It would appear that the Ājīvikas had regular places for meetings and religious ceremonies. The *Uvāsaga Dasāo* [4] refers to an *Ājīviya-sabhā* at the town of Polāsapura. When Gosāla visited this town, attended by the *Ājīviya-saṅgha*, he went first to the *sabhā*, where he deposited his begging-bowl (*bhaṇḍaga-nikkhevaṃ kareï*), and from whence he issued, attended by only a few followers, to visit his backsliding lay disciple Saddālaputta.

From this it is evident that, whatever may have been the habits of free-lance Ājīvika ascetics, the organized sect of Makkhali Gosāla was a religious body with a normal corporate and social life, a *saṅgha* in fact, as were the Buddhist and Jaina orders, with a regular meeting place. The use of the word *sabhā*

[1] *Aṟintāṉ iṟaivaṉ avaṉ ākutalāṟ ceṟintāṉ*. . . *Nīl.* v, 672.

[2] . . . *terivill-uruvam-*
Varaiyā-vakai- vāṉ-iṭu-vill-aṉaiyaṉ,
Puraiyā-v-aṟiviṟ-pukaḻ-Pūraṇaṉē. Ibid. v, 673.

[3] V. supra, p. 112.

[4] V. supra, p. 52.

in this connection is striking, since the term seems to imply a building of the type used for royal courts or for folk-moots of the free tribes, and is rarely used to designate a religious edifice. Of the latter usage the Pāli texts seem to present only one example.[1] The word may mean " a public rest house or hostelry ",[2] and it may therefore be suggested that the *Ājīviya-sabhā* at Polāsapura was merely a rest house for ascetics of the order. But it seems more appropriate to accept the word in its more usual meaning of " an assembly hall ". Its use suggests that the Ājīvika community employed their meeting-place not only for religious ceremonies but for secular meetings, and was tending, even at this early date, to cut itself off from other communities. In the Dravidian Deccan, at a much later period, it appears with some of the attributes of a caste,[3] and it is possible that it began to develop caste characteristics very early. A closely knit corporate life, embracing monk and layman alike, may have arisen as a reaction to the opposition and scorn levelled at the community by other Indian sects, both orthodox and heretical, and the rarity of references to Ājīvikism in later Sanskrit literature may in part be due to the isolation in which the Ājīvika community existed.

As well as the *Ājīvika-sabhā*, we read in the *Vinaya* of an *Ājīvika-seyyā*, inhabited by Ājīvika ascetics who enticed the Buddhist *bhikkhunīs* settled near by.[4] This seems to have been in the nature of a small monastery or *vihāra*, probably a collection of huts. Further the *Bhagavatī Sūtra* refers to Gosāla as returning to the pottery of Hālāhalā from the " penance-ground " (*āyāvaṇa-bhūmī*).[5] This place, we suggest, was merely an open space on the borders of the city, where ascetics of all types congregated to perform their austerities, and had no specifically Ājīvika connection.

Song and Dance

Cryptic passages in the *Bhagavatī Sūtra* suggest that Ājīvika ceremonial may have contained elements of a contemporary

[1] *Dhamma-sabhā*, *Jāt.* vi, p. 333, teste *PTS. Dictionary*, s.v. *sabhā*.
[2] *PTS. Dictionary*, s.v. *sabhā*. The Dictionary gives only one reference in this sense, to *Jāt.* i, p. 302.
[3] V. infra, p. 193. [4] *Vin.* iv, p. 223. V. infra, pp. 124–25. [5] V. supra, p. 59.

popular religious cult, which are found later in devotional Hinduism.

It will be remembered that, when in his last delirium, Gosāla was visited at night by the lay disciple Ayampula, with a question on the size of the *hallā*.[1] The teacher, in reply to Ayampula's question, is reported to have given the inconsequential answer: " Play the *vīṇā*, old fellow ! Play the *vīṇā*, old fellow ! " Most of the actions and words of Gosāla in his last delirium seem to have been inserted in the story in order to provide alleged origins for later Ājīvika practices and doctrines, and the strange phrases of the teacher may indicate that the Ājīvika community was given to the singing of religious songs and to the use of music for religious purposes.

The suspicion is strengthened by Abhayadeva's definition of the two paths (*magga*), which the six *disācaras* extracted from the *Puvvas*, together with the eight *mahānimittas*, at the conference with Gosāla shortly before his death.[2] These paths, according to the commentator, are those of song and dance.[3] Two of the eight finalities of the Ājīvikas are said to be *carime geye* and *carime natte*, the last song and dance,[4] and Gosāla himself is said to have sung and danced in his last delirium.[5]

From these indications we infer that singing and dancing played an important part in Ājīvika religious practice. Possibly the Ājīvikas, in their *Ājīviya-sabhā*, held meetings for ecstatic religious singing and dancing, such as are to-day held by such sects as the Caitanyas. This at least seems the most probable interpretation of these obscure passages.

[1] V. supra, pp. 62–63.
[2] V. supra, p. 56.
[3] *Tathā mārgau gīta-mārga-nṛtya-mārga-lakṣaṇau sambhāvyete.* *Bh. Sū.*, fol. 659.
[4] V. supra, p. 68.
[5] V. supra, p. 62.

CHAPTER VII

THE EARLY ĀJĪVIKA COMMUNITY (II)

BEGGING AND DIETARY PRACTICES

While it is certain that Ājīvika ascetics normally begged their food, like their Buddhist and Jaina counterparts, the sources speak with two voices on Ājīvika begging practices and dietary vows, just as they do on the ascetic customs of the sect.

The most detailed description of the begging customs of naked mendicants is contained in the *Mahāsaccaka Sutta* of the *Majjhima Nikāya*. In it the Buddha asks the *nigaṇṭha* Saccaka Aggivesana how the Ājīvikas maintain themselves. He replies that " the *acelakas*, Nanda Vaccha, Kisa Saṅkicca, and Makkhali Gosāla ", are men of loose habits, who lick their hands (after eating). They do not obey when one says to them " Come Sir ! " or " Stay Sir ! " They do not accept food brought to them, or food specially cooked for them, nor do they accept invitations to dine. They do not eat food from the mouth of a pot or pan, nor on the threshold, nor among faggots or pestles. They do not accept food from two people eating together, from a pregnant woman, from a nursing mother, or from a woman (who has recently been ?) *in coitu*. They will not take gleanings, nor accept food if a dog is standing near or if flies are buzzing round it. They will not take fish, meat, spirits, wine, or other strong drink. They are one-house men, taking one mouthful, two-house men taking two mouthfuls, or seven-house men, taking seven mouthfuls. They live on one saucer (of food daily), or on two, or on seven. They take one meal every day, or every two days or every seven. So they exist (even), eating food at fortnightly intervals.[1]

[1] *Majjh.* i, p. 238. The paraphrase is somewhat expanded and adapted on the basis of Chalmers' translation and Buddhaghosa's commentary (*Papañca Sūdanī* ii, pp. 43 ff.). The original is as follows : "*Seyyath' idaṃ Nando Vaccho, Kiso Saṅkicco, Makkhali Gosālo, ete hi bho Gotama acelakā muttâcārā hatth'-âpalekhanā na ehibhadantikā na tiṭṭhabhadantikā, na abhihaṭaṃ, na uddissakaṭaṃ*

When the Buddha asks Aggivesana how these ascetics survived on so meagre a diet the latter replies that they ate enormous meals in secret.

This passage seems to give a convincing picture of the begging habits of Makkhali Gosāla and his two shadowy predecessors, who are named with him in the text; it might be inferred that it also applies to the community which he established. But its reliability, as applying to the Ājīvika order, is questionable. In another passage of the *Majjhima* [1] the same words are put into the mouth of the Buddha himself, when he describes his own ascetic conduct before his enlightenment. In fact the ascetics here described do not seem to be members of the organized Ājīvika community, despite the inclusion of the name of Makkhali Gosāla; the description of ascetic begging practice applies to the wide class of *acelakas*, or naked ascetics, which class seems to have included not only organized Ājīvikas, but free-lance Ājīvikas and *nirgranthas* or Jainas, as well as independent ascetics and members of the smaller mushroom communities of the time. Some of the practices referred to may have been followed by Makkhali Gosāla's Ājīvikas, but there is no reason to believe that they followed all of them.

Dr. Barua [2] has pointed out the parallel between the series one-house men (*ekâgārikā*), two-house men (*dvâgārikā*), and seven-house men (*sattâgārikā*), in the above passage, and that in the *Aupapātika Sūtra* already quoted,[3] describing the seven types of Ājīvika mendicant. These include *dugharantariyā*, *tigharantariyā*, and *sattagharantariyā*, and on the strength of this similarity Barua has suggested that the two passages may have a common source in an Ājīvika text.

The parallel is not very striking. The *dugharantariya*, who

na nimantaṇaṃ sādiyanti. Te na kumbhī-mukhā patigaṇhanti, na kaḷopimukhā paṭigaṇhanti, na eḷakamantaraṃ, na daṇḍamantaraṃ, na musalamantaraṃ, na dvinnaṃ bhuñjamānānaṃ, na gabbhiniyā, na pāyamānāya, na purisantara-gatāya, na saṅkittisu, na yattha sā upaṭṭhito hoti, na yattha makkhikā saṇḍasaṇḍacārinī; na macchaṃ na maṃsaṃ na suraṃ na merayaṃ na thusoda-kaṃ pipanti. Te ekâgārikā vā honti ekâlopikā, dvâgārikā vā honti dvâlopikā, sattâgārikā honti sattâlopikā. Ekissā pi dattiyā yāpenti, dvīhi pi dattīhi yāpenti, sattahi pi dattīhi yāpenti. Ekâhikam pi āhāraṃ āhārenti, dvīhikam pi āhāram āhārenti, sattâhikam pi āhāram āhārenti, iti evarūpam addhamāsikam pi pariyāya-bhattabhojanânuyogam anuyuttā viharanti.

[1] *Majjh.* i, p. 77.

[2] *JDL.* ii, p. 48.

[3] V. supra, p. 111.

on his begging round misses two houses and calls at every third. is probably not the same person as the *dvâgārika* of the *Majjhima* passage, who, on the obvious interpretation which is confirmed by Buddhaghosa, confines his begging to two patrons only. The long *Majjhima* list makes no reference to the *uppalabeṇṭiyā*, the *vijju-antariyā*, or the *uṭṭiyā-samaṇā* of the *Aupapātika*.

The statement of the *Majjhima* passage above quoted, that the Ājīvikas do not accept invitations (to meals) is particularly suspect, for the *Vinaya*[1] tells of a relative of King Bimbisāra who had become an Ājīvika monk and who persuaded the King to invite all heretical communities to dine in turn, his own, we may presume, being included. A few pages further on[2] we find the Buddhist *saṅgha* provided with a superfluity of food and inviting ascetics of other communities to come and partake of it; on this occasion Ājīvikas seem to have made good use of the invitation. The *Arthaśāstra*[3] finally shakes our faith in the applicability of the *Majjhima* passage to the organized Ājīvika community, by stating that Ājīvikas may not be invited to *śrāddha* feasts; the ban would have been unnecessary if cases had not occurred in which Ājīvikas did attend such functions.

Barua, however, takes the passage as applicable to the followers of Makkhali Gosāla. "An Ājīvika," he writes, "never incurred the guilt of obeying another's command. He refused to accept food which had been specially prepared for him. He did not accept food from people when they were eating, lest they should go short or be disturbed. He did not accept food collected in time of drought. . . . He did not accept food where a dog was standing by or flies were swarming round lest they lose a meal. He did not eat fish or meat, nor use intoxicants."[4] We cannot agree with Barua that such rigid conduct was demanded of the Ājīvika, in view of the numerous references which tell a different story. The passage in the *Majjhima* on which he bases his statement must clearly contain a catalogue of the habits of non-Buddhist mendicants of all types, and cannot have applied *in toto* to the Ājīvikas.

[1] *Vin.* iv, p. 74. V. infra, p. 136.
[2] *Vin.* iv, p. 91. V. infra, pp. 136–37.
[3] *Arthaśāstra* iii, 20, p. 199. V. infra, p. 161.
[4] *Pre-Buddhistic Indian Philosophy*, pp. 167–8.

Hoernle, in his study of the Ājīvikas,[1] has interpreted the phrase *hatth'-âpalekhana* in this crucial passage to imply that the Ājīvika monk had no begging-bowl, but received his alms of sticky rice direct into his hand. This statement is open to the criticism that Gosāla himself is depicted in the *Uvāsaga Dasāo* as carrying a begging-bowl (*bhaṇḍaga*).[2] Further, the *Sūtrakṛtâṅga* has a remarkable passage, which, according to the commentator Śīlâṅka, describes Ājīvikas or Digambaras, wherein they are stigmatized for eating out of vessels, presumably those of householders.[3]

Both in this passage and in the dialogue of Adda and Gosāla in the same book,[4] the Ājīvika is accused of being willing to eat what is specially prepared, and thus the lie is given to another item of the Pāli list.[5] In fact, if the Buddhist thought that the fantastic dietary rules of the *acelakas* useless, or even ridiculous, to the Jaina the conduct of the Ājīvika was little better than that of a householder, lax in the extreme. Gosāla is also said to have disagreed with the pious Adda on the question of the propriety of the ascetic's drinking cold water, eating seeds, and having intercourse with women. The earlier *Sūtrakṛtâṅga* passage, which Śīlâṅka applies to the Ājīvikas, records yet another practice in which the heterodox ascetic did not come up to Jaina standards of behaviour. The unnamed victim of Jaina condemnation was accused of begging food on behalf of sick members of the community and of taking it to them,[6] whereas the Jaina mendicant was not allowed to take more than he required for his own use. The Ājīvikas are accused of "wavering between two ways of life" (*duppakkhaṃ c'eva sevaha*), a taunt similar to that levelled by an

[1] *ERE*. i, p. 265.

[2] V. supra, p. 52.

[3] *Sū. kṛ*. i, 3, 3, 12, fol. 91. *Tubbhe bhuñjaha pāesu.*

[4] *Sū. kṛ*. ii, 6, fol. 388 ff. V. supra, pp. 53–54, 114.

[5] This according to Jacobi's interpretation (*Gaina Sūtras SBE*. xlv, pp. 267, 441). The phrases are " . . . *bhuñjaha* . . . *tam uddissādi jaṃ kaḍaṃ* (*Sū. kṛ*. i, 3, 3, 12, fol. 91), and *āhāyakammaṃ* . . . *paḍisevamāṇā* (*Sū. kṛ*. ii, 6, 8, fol. 390). Both verses are very obscure. Jacobi's first interpretation is based on Śīlâṅka. In the second case Śīlâṅka's brief comment (. . . *ādhākarma* . . .) is as ambiguous as the text.

[6] *Sambaddha-samakappā u, annamannesu mucchiyā*
Piṇḍavāyaṃ gilāṇassa, jaṃ sāreha dalāha ya.
Sū. kṛ. i, 3, 3, 9, fol. 90.

unnamed Ājīvika at the Buddha, whom he called a "shaven householder" (*muṇḍa-gahapatika*).[1]

One minor rule of Ājīvika begging practice is that recorded by Jiṇapaha Sūri, already noted in another context.[2] His *Vihimaggapavā* states that the ascetic followers of Gosāla did not beg food of their female relations, because Gosāla himself was once disappointed at not receiving alms, presumably from his own kin.

Our conclusion on the begging and dietary habits of the Ājīvikas must be that in general they were somewhat less lax than those of the Buddhists and less strict than those of the Jainas. Indeed if a passage in the *Bhagavatī Sūtra*[3] is to be believed they even went so far as to permit the eating of animal food. "This is laid down in the Ājīvika rule, that all beings whose (capacity for) enjoyment is unimpaired obtain their food by killing, cutting, cleaving, lopping, amputating, and attacking." It is noteworthy, however, that the same passage mentions the names of twelve Ājīvika laymen whose lives were led on the principles of strict *ahiṃsā* approved by Jainism, and who were destined for reincarnation in heaven.

The *Vāyu Purāṇa*, in a cryptic passage, refers to the Ājīvikas as using wine and meat, among other things, in their religious ceremonies.[4] This indicates that they were not averse to eating animal food, at least on religious occasions. Yet *Nīlakēci* states that the silence of Maṟkali is due to his solicitude for the lives of animalcules. "If he did not remain silent, by his speech he would destroy. He is of such a nature that he checks himself, otherwise he would be enmeshed in illusion."[5] This the commentator Vāmana Muni explains as: ". . . by speaking he would destroy several living beings as with a sword . . . and, becoming sinful, he would be reborn in *saṃsāra*, be deluded with passions, and perish indeed."[6] *Nīlakēci*, in common with the two

[1] *Vin.* iv, p. 91. V. infra, p. 137.
[2] V. supra, p. 54.
[3] *Ājīviya-samayassa ṇaṃ ayaṃ atthe paṇṇatte: akkhīṇa-paḍibhoīṇo savva-sattā se hantā chettā bhettā lumpittā vilumpittā uddavaïttā āhāraṃ āharenti. Bh. Sū.* viii, *sū.* 329, fol. 369.
[4] *Vāyu*, 69, 286–7. V. infra, pp. 162 ff.
[5] *Ceṟiyāt' uraippiṉ eṟintāṉ; aṉaiya-viyalp' ākutalāṉ maṟintāṉ ṟaṭumāṟ ṟakattē mayaṅki. Nīl.* v, 672.
[6] *Ivaṉ pēccāl aṟaiyuṇṭu anēkam pirāṇi maṟikkum ātaliṉ vāḷiṭṭu-c cilarai veṭṭiṉāṉ pōlum pāpam uṭaiyaṉ ātalil samsārattu-p piṟantu rākâtiyāṉ mayaṅki-k kēṭṭāṉ ē.*

other chief Tamil sources, appears to attempt a logical and unbiassed outline of Ājīvika teaching before refuting it, and therefore seems to carry more weight than the two northern sources, which suggest that the Ājīvikas were addicted to meat-eating. We therefore conclude that the Ājīvikas, like the Buddhists and Jainas, were believers in *ahiṃsā*, and usually vegetarians. It is not impossible that, as the *Vāyu Purāṇa* indicates, some of their number practised magical rites which involved the shedding of blood. But it is unlikely that the Ājīvikas were unaffected by the doctrines of *ahiṃsā* which prevailed among other non-Brāhmaṇical sects. It is probable that in the period of the formation of these sects no community practised vegetarianism as strictly as in later times; both the Buddha [1] and Mahāvīra [2] are said to have eaten meat at least once in the course of their careers as religious leaders.

ACCUSATIONS OF WORLDLINESS AND IMMORALITY

By the Buddhist the Ājīvika ascetic was accused of secret indulgence in rich foods behind a cloak of false austerity, while by the Jaina he was often condemned for his unchastity.

The first accusation is best expressed in the *Mahāsaccaka Sutta*, part of which has been quoted above.[3] When the ascetic Saccaka has completed his description of the extravagant fasts of the *acelakas* the Buddha asks him: "How can they survive on such fare?" To this Saccaka replies: "From time to time they eat excellent food, spice it with excellent spices, and drink excellent beverages. Thus they increase their bodily strength and grow fat." [4]

As has been shown, the passage seems intended to apply to extreme ascetics generally, and not to the Ājīvikas alone. It has already been made clear that Ājīvika practices were not as strict as the *Mahāsaccaka Sutta* suggests. The story of the princely Ājīvika mendicant, who persuaded the Buddha to relax his rule

[1] *Dīgha* ii, p. 127.
[2] V. supra, p. 67.
[3] V. supra, pp. 118–19.
[4] *App' ekadā bho Gotama uḷārāni uḷārāni khādaniyāni khādanti, . . . bhojanāni bhuñjanti, . . . sāyaniyāni sāyanti, pānāni pivanti; te imehi kāyaṃ balaṃ gāhenti nāma brūhenti nāma, medenti nāma.* Majjh. i, p. 238.

forbidding common meals in the order, and invited him and his *bhikkhus* to a meal provided by his relative King Bimbisāra,[1] suggests a freedom of discipline and an absence of austerity which is not to be disproved by passages of vague application such as that in *Mahāsaccaka Sutta.* The latest available reference to Ājīvikas, that of Vaidyanātha Dīkṣita, the fifteenth century astrologer, confirms their reputation for voracity; the author states that the Ājīvika is devoted to food (*aśana-paro*) and loquacious (*jalpako*).[2]

If the Buddhist insisted on the hypocrisy of the Ājīvika in the matter of diet, the Jaina accused him of sexual laxity. The accusation is explicit in the dialogue between Gosāla and Adda in the *Sūtrakṛtāṅga*, wherein the former is made to declare that, according to his *dhamma*, the ascetic incurs no sin from women.[3] The same book also speaks of indifferent ascetics, the slaves of women, who maintain that there is no more sin in intercourse with women than in squeezing a boil.[4] These, however, are identified by Śīlâṅka not with the Ājīvikas but with the Buddhists or Śaivites. The *Sutṛakrtâṅga* again levels the same accusation at unnamed ascetics, whom Śīlâṅka identifies with the followers of Gosāla, and who appear to maintain the doctrine of *maṇḍala-mokṣa,* a characteristic feature of the creed of the Dravidian Ājīvikas.[5] "A wise man," states the *Sūtrakṛtâṅga,* "should consider that these (heretics) do not live a life of chastity."[6] The nature of the relations of Gosāla with his patron Hālāhalā the potter woman are nowhere explicitly stated, but it seems to be implied that they were not honest.

A possible Buddhist reference to Ājīvika sexual laxity occurs in the *Vinaya.*[7] At Sāvatthi a certain layman gave a building (*uddositaṃ*) to the community of *bhikkhunīs.* On his death his two sons divided the property, and the elder, an unscrupulous rogue, laid claim to the nunnery. After failing to obtain its return by legal means he tried to drive the *bhikkhunīs* out by threats.

[1] V. supra, p. 120, and infra, p. 136.
[2] *Jātakapārijāta* xv, 15. V. infra, p. 184.
[3] *Sū. kṛ.* ii, 6, 8, fol. 390. V. supra, pp. 53–54, 114, 121.
[4] *Jahā gaṇḍaṃ pilāgaṃ vā paripilejja muhuttagaṃ, Evaṃ vinnavaṇitthīsu doso tattha kao siā.* Ibid. i, 3, 4, 10, fol. 97.
[5] V. infra, pp. 257 ff.
[6] *Sū. kṛ.* i, 1, 3, 13, fol. 45. *Etāṇuvīti medhāvī bambhacere ṇa te vase.*
[7] *Vin.* iv, pp. 223 ff.

Their elder, Thullanandā, informed the officials (*mahāmattā*), who punished the young man. His final stratagem was to import a community of Ājīvika ascetics, to whom he gave a settlement (*Ājīvika-seyyam*) in the vicinity, with the instructions to entice the *bhikkhunīs* (*etā bhikkhuniyo accāvadatha*). The significance of the word *accāvadatha* is uncertain, and it is possible that the Ājīvikas were merely told to revile the nuns. This is the interpretation of Buddhaghosa.[1] But the *bhikkhunīs* had already been reviled to no effect, and it might be expected that a different stratagem would be tried in this case; therefore the alternative meaning of the word seems more appropriate here. With this uncertain exception the Buddhists do not depict the Ājīvikas as sexually lax, but only as devoted to useless and hypocritical fasts and penances.

Turning to later references we find but faint suggestions of Ājīvika licentiousness. The Ājīvika teacher in *Nīlakēci*, however, seems aware of the accusation, and tells his interlocutor not to be censorious because his community is addicted to *cuvai*, an ambiguous word which may mean sensual pleasure.[2] A Canarese poem, dated 1180, and inscribed near the doorway of the Gommateśvara temple at Śravaṇa Beḷgoḷā includes a verse on the "other guides who, while exhorting their ascetics against the evils of false penance, allow themselves to be closely associated with women".[3] The use of the word *āptar* to indicate the false guides, suggests that the Jaina author had the Ājīvikas in mind, since the term seems to have been a popular designation of Maṟkali among the Dravidian Ājīvikas.[4] The *Rājataraṅgiṇī* speaks of an ascetic, who may have been an Ājīvika, living in the hut of a prostitute.[5] These hints suggest that the small Ājīvika community retained some of its bad reputation; but as its influence waned the accusations seem to have been pressed home less fiercely, and in many cases to have been forgotten. With the exception of the doubtful phrase in *Nīlakēci*, the three chief Tamil sources make no mention of Ājīvika immorality.

[1] *Atikkamitvā vadatha akkosathā ti*. *Samantapāsādikā* iv, p. 906.

[2] *Cuvai-y ē-y uṭaiyamm eṉa nī-y ikaḻ al*. *Nīl*. 678. The commentary equates *cuvai* with *sarasam*, which is equally ambiguous.

[3] *Epi. Carn.* ii (2nd edn.), No. 234. The translation is that of Dr. Narasimhachar.

[4] V. supra, p. 79.

[5] V. infra, p. 209.

The long Jaina tradition that the Ājīvikas were not celibate cannot be wholly without foundation. It is clear that many ancient Indian ascetics, including the proto-Jainas who followed Pārśva,[1] took no vows of chastity. The legendary *ṛṣis* shared their austerities with their wives, and must have had later counterparts. Their own religious literature shows that the Jaina monks themselves were not always as strict in the maintenance of chastity as the founder of their order might have desired, and that occasional lapses were often looked upon as mere peccadilloes.[2] The dissolute religious mendicants of the farce *Mattavilāsa* are types of a class which must have been very widespread in Ancient India. We are not justified in believing, on the strength of Jaina evidence, that the Ājīvikas were necessarily as debauched and degenerate as the characters in that play however. That the Ājīvika order was capable of survival for two thousand years, that it produced scriptures, and a philosophy and logic of its own, is proof that some at least of its members were educated, thoughtful, and sincere. The references to stern Ājīvika austerities and to the Ājīvika practice of *ahiṃsā* in the texts which we have quoted, indicate that, however relaxed their discipline may have been in some respects, the Ājīvikas generally pursued their religious quest by the traditional Indian paths of pain, fasting, and gentleness.

Whether celibate or not, it would seem that the Ājīvika mendicant was by no means continuously engaged in austerities. Besides those describing his begging and ascetic practices, and the more reprehensible activities attributed to him, there are a number of references which show the Ājīvika monk playing a comparatively active part in everyday life. The *Majjhima*,[3] for instance, tells of Paṇḍuputta, the son of a wagon-maker,[4] an Ājīvika ascetic of Rājagaha. This man was seen by the *bhikkhu* Mahāmoggalāna, standing in a wagon-maker's shop, and intently watching the making of a felloe. When the wheelwright had finished his work the Ājīvika is said to have cried out

[1] Hoernle, *ERE*. i, p. 264, basing his view on *Uttarâdhyayana Sūtra* xxiii, 11 ff.

[2] *Sū. kṛ.* iv, 2, and Jain, *Life in Ancient India According to the Jaina Canon*, pp. 199–202.

[3] *Majjh.* i, p. 31.

[4] *Purāṇa-yānakāra-putta* suggests a repairer of old carts, perhaps a village wheelwright.

with joy at the excellence of the workmanship. His asceticism had by no means destroyed his interest in his hereditary trade, and he may be taken as a type of his fellow Ājīvikas.

The Ājīvika seems frequently to have been an astrologer or fortune-teller. *Nakkhatta Jātaka* [1] tells the story of an Ājīvika regularly dependent on a certain family for support (*kulūpaka*), who was consulted about the most propitious date for a wedding after the preliminary preparations had already been made, and who caused it to be postponed in his annoyance. A similar *kūlūpaga* Ājīvika was attached to the court of King Bindusāra, and correctly prophesied Aśoka's greatness.[2] The ascetics of both sexes who appear so frequently in later literature from the *Arthaśāstra* onwards as spies, confidential agents, matchmakers, and fortune-tellers, may have included Ājīvikas among their number.

The Final Penance

Whatever corruptions and laxities may have existed in the Ājīvika order, the *Bhagavatī Sūtra* clearly shows that the Ājīvika ascetic sometimes put an end to his own life by austerities of the extremest type.

It will be remembered that, after the magic duel between Mahāvīra and Gosāla, the former told his followers that the latter was mortally afflicted and was returning to Hālāhalā's pottery to die, but that before his death he would proclaim the eight finalities (*carimāiṃ*), the four drinks (*pāṇagāiṃ*), and the four substitutes for drink (*apāṇagāiṃ*).[3] These Mahāvīra described in cryptic language, which is only partially elucidated by the commentator Abhayadeva.[4] The eight finalities have already been enumerated [5] and seem to be portents of very rare occurrence. The four drinks and the four substitutes for drink, on the other hand, are apparently a series of rules regulating the final penance of the Ājīvika ascetic.

Mahāvīra, after describing the eight finalities, declared that Gosāla, to excuse his own unseemly conduct, would also institute

[1] *Jāt.* i, p. 257.
[2] *Mahāvaṃsa Comm.* i, p. 190. *Divyâvadāna* pp. 370 ff. V. infra, pp. 146–47.
[3] V. supra, p. 62.
[4] *Bh. Sū.* xv, *sū.* 554, fol. 679. Comm. fol. 684.
[5] V. supra, p. 68.

the new doctrine of the *pāṇagāiṃ* and *apāṇagāiṃ*. The former, which Abhayadeva defines as " kinds of liquid suitable to an ascetic ",[1] are :

1. *Goputthaë*, " that which has fallen from a cow's back." [2]
2. *Hattha-maddiyaë*, " that which is soiled by the hand, such as the water used in a pottery." [3]
3. *Āyavatattaë*, " that heated by the sun," and
4. *Silāpabbhatthaë*, " that fallen from a rock."

The substitutes for drink are :—

1. *Thāla-pāṇaë*, " taking a metal pot (*sthāla*), as though a drink to soothe fever—by implication holding an earthenware pot (*bhājana*) also." [4]
2. *Tayā-pāṇaë*, holding an unripe mango or other fruit in the mouth without drinking the juice.
3. *Simbali-pāṇaë*, holding unripe *simbali*-beans or certain other seeds in the mouth in the same way, and
4. *Suddha-pāṇaë*, the penance of the " pure drink ".

The last item of the second list is described in the text of the *Sūtra*. For six months the ascetic eats only pure food (*suddha-khāimāiṃ*) ; for two months he lies on the ground, for two on wood, and for two on *darbha* grass. On the last night of these six months two mighty gods, Punnabhadda and Māṇibhadda will appear, and with their cool hands will soothe his fevered body. " He who submits to (the caresses of) those gods will further the work of serpenthood. If he does not submit, a mass of fire arises in his body, and he burns up his body with his own heat. Then he is saved and makes an end. That is the pure drink." [5]

The six months' penance here described appears to have something in common with the fatal penance of the Jainas, and shows conclusively that the Ājīvika ascetic of greatest

[1] *Jalaviśeṣā vrati-yogyāḥ.*
[2] *Go-pṛṣṭhād yat patitaṃ.*
[3] *Hastena marddital̥ṃ mṛditaṃ malitam ity arthaḥ,* (sic) *yath' aitad ev' âtanyanik'-odakam.*
[4] *Sthālam traṭṭaṃ tat-pānakam iva dāh'-opaśama-hetutvāt sthāla-pānkam, upalakṣaṇatvād asya bhājanântara-graho 'pi dṛśyaḥ.*
[5] *Je ṇaṃ te deve sāijjati* (Comm. : *svadate, anumanyate*) *se ṇaṃ āsīvisattāë kammaṃ pakareti. Je ṇaṃ te deve no sāijjati, tassa ṇaṃ saṃsi sarīragaṃsi agaṇi-kāë sambhavati, se ṇaṃ saëṇaṃ teëṇaṃ sarīragaṃ jhāmeti. Taö pacchā sijjhati . . . antaṃ kareti. Se ttaṃ suddhapāṇaë. Bh. Sū.* xv, *sū.* 554, fol. 680.

sanctity, like the Jaina, and less regularly the Hindu, cheerfully died a lingering death for the sake of his spiritual welfare.

Of the eight items in the lists of *pāṇagāiṃ* and *apāṇagāiṃ* the last, the penance of the "pure drink", seems to include the other seven. Despite Abhayadeva's definition,[1] the four drinkables in the first list cannot have been the usual beverages of the Ājīvika, for in his argument with Adda Gosāla maintains that there is no sin for the ascetic in drinking cold water.[2] By this he must have implied water from any normal source of supply. In most respects Ājīvika dietary practice seems to have been less strict than that of the Jainas, and it cannot have included the insistence on the drinking of dirty or stale water only.

The *suddhapāṇaë* penance seems to have differed from the fatal penance of the Jainas in that it involved not death from starvation, but from thirst. The ascetic finding his physical powers waning would enter on the six months' course of austerities. At some stage in his penance he would refrain from all drinks but the four *pāṇagāiṃ*. At the final stage he would only allow himself the four *apāṇagāiṃ*. This interpretation is substantially that of Barua,[3] but we cannot wholly accept his explanation. "The practices of the four drinkables and four substitutes . . . appertain to three successive stages of religious suicide. . . . In the first stage the dying Ājīvika was permitted to drink something; . . . in the second stage he was permitted not to drink anything but to use some substitutes (*sic*) . . . while in the third he had to forego (*sic*) even that. . . . The Ājīvika had to lie down for six months, lying successively for two months at a time on the bare earth, on wooden planks, and on *darbha* grass. This indicates that the longest period for the penance was six months, each stage having been gone through in two months. . . ." Apparently Dr. Barua implies that the Ājīvika ascetic was capable of surviving for four months in a tropical climate without drinking. If this interpretation be correct it is surprising that a creed capable of imparting such superhuman endurance to its members should have become extinct.

In the text it is nowhere explicitly stated that the *pāṇagāiṃ* and *apāṇagāiṃ* are in any way connected with the first two

[1] V. supra, p. 128, n. 1. [2] V. supra, p. 121. [3] *JDL.* ii, p. 53.

stages of the *suddhapāṇaē* penance; in fact they are not said to be connected with it at all, except in so far as all eight were ordained by Gosāla in his last delirium. If, as seems probable, the first seven items of the lists are all linked with the *suddhapāṇaē*, the stage of the *apāṇāgāiṃ* can only have commenced within a few days of the end.

Dr. Barua further believes that Gosāla himself practised the penance. "Mahāvīra's prophecy," he writes, "that Gosāla . . . would die . . . in seven days . . . is in conflict with the statement that eight new practices of the Ājīvikas emerged from Gosāla's personal acts. Considering that the first seven practices . . . are traceable in his acts in the delirium of fever, a presumption is apt to arise that the eighth practice, called the Pure Drink, also arose from his personal example. . . . If the Ājīvikas observed this practice in blind imitation of their master, as I believe they did, Mahāvīra's prophecy can be reconciled with his statement about Gosāla's death only by the supposition that he did not actually die in seven days but survived the attack of fever for a period of six months, during which he practised the penance of Pure Drink in the manner above described." [1]

Dr. Barua's contention, on comparison with the text, seems to be based on inadequate premises. Gosāla is not explicitly stated to have practised any of the *pàṇagāiṃ* and *apāṇagāiṃ*. Of the four drinks in the former list the first, third, and fourth are not mentioned as having been used in any way by Gosāla. The second "water soiled by the hand, such as that used in a pottery", he did not drink, according to the letter of the text, but merely used to sprinkle his limbs.[2] Of the four substitutes for drink the only one suggested by Gosāla's delirious conduct is the second, holding an unripe mango in the mouth. The *Sūtra* states only that Gosāla held a mango stone in his hand,[3] and although the commentator suggests that he sucked it to allay his fever this is not expressly stated in the text, which makes no mention of Gosāla's lying on the ground, on wood, or on *darbha* grass. In fact the resemblances between the details of the Ājīvika fatal penance and those of Gosāla's last delirium are by

[1] *JDL.* ii, pp. 36–7.
[2] *Gāyāiṃ parisiñcemāṇe. Bh. Sū.* xv, *sū.* 553. fol. 679.
[3] V. supra, p. 61.

no means close. Perhaps, as the *Bhagavatī Sūtra* suggests, some features of the former were modelled on the latter. But that Gosāla himself died by this means cannot be demonstrated.

Certain elements in the penance are significant. The *goputṭhaë* (which both Hoernle and Barua interpret, perhaps unnecessarily, as "that which is excreted by the cow"[1]), occurs first in the list of the legitimate drinks of the dying ascetic; his last bed is the sacred *darbha* grass. These two features strongly indicate that the Ājīvika was by no means unaffected by orthodox ideas. We have already found one faint indication that some Ājīvikas may have been closer to the main current than their Buddhist and Jaina contemporaries,[2] and the inclusion of the cow and the *darbha* in the account of the Ājīvika fatal penance confirms our views. The strange divinities Punnabhadda and Māṇibhadda raise questions which are more appropriate to the second part of this work.[3] The fire which consumes the body of the emancipated ascetic, and the mysterious reference to "serpenthood", suggest a magical or tantric element in Ājīvikism, of which we have found traces elsewhere.[4]

Ājīvika Laymen

The early Ājīvika community, both religious and lay, was drawn from all sections of the population. Like Buddhism and Jainism, Ājīvikism seems to have made no stipulations about the status of its converts, and apparently did not encourage caste distinctions.

At the bottom of the scale of castes is Pāṇḍuputta, the son of a wagon-maker.[5] This trade, by the time of the Buddha, had lost the respect in which it was held in Ṛg-vedic times and had become a despised occupation.[6] Yet Pāṇḍuputta appears to have been a full member of the order, and well respected.

At the other extreme is the *kulūpaga* Ājīvika, Janasāna, the adviser to the chief queen of King Bindusāra, who, according to the *Mahāvaṃsa* commentary, came of brāhmaṇa stock.[7]

As an example of the numerous Ājīvikas who must have joined the Order from the military class we have a kinsman

[1] *ERE.* i, p. 263; *JDL.* ii, p. 53. [2] V. supra, p. 93. [3] V. infra, pp. 272–73.
[4] V. supra, pp. 112–13. [5] V. supra, pp. 126–27. [6] *CHI.* i, p. 207.
[7] V. supra, p. 127, and infra, pp. 146 ff.

(*ñāti sālohito*) of King Bimbisāra, who, even after becoming an Ājīvika monk, appears to have continued his friendly relations with the King.[1] The epic tradition of fatalism, of which the *Mahābhārata* presents many indications,[2] suggests that Ājīvikism made a special appeal to the warrior element of the population.

The greatest support for Ājīvikism seems to have come from the industrial and mercantile classes. The *Vinaya* mentions one unnamed *mahāmatta* who was an adherent of the Ājīvikas,[3] but with this and the other exceptions mentioned above all those Ājīvikas referred to in the Buddhist and Jaina texts whose caste affiliations are specified were of the trading classes.

Ājīvika layfolk seem to have been specially numerous at Sāvatthi, but there is evidence that they also existed elsewhere. Among the Sāvatthi Ājīvika lay-adherents were the faithful potter-women Hālāhalā, Gosāla's host for sixteen years[4]; Ayampula, the rich and earnest disciple who visited Gosāla by night during his last delirium[5]; and the wealthy *seṭṭhi* Migāra who, when he began to favour the Buddha, was besieged in his home by a body of ascetics who are called indiscriminately *naggasamaṇa*, *acelaka*, and *ājīvika*.[6] We have also a reference to a family of lay Ājīvikas visiting Sāvatthi from a village at some distance from the capital,[7] from which we may infer that the sect gained converts in the surrounding countryside.

At Polāsapura the Ājīvika community is said to have had its own meeting place at the time of Gosāla's visit,[8] so it may be inferred that the town was an early centre of the organized Ājīvika sect. The only local Ājīvika whose name is mentioned is Saddālaputta, who, like Hālāhalā, was a potter. He is described as being very wealthy, the owner of five hundred potters' workshops as well as a krore of hoarded gold and another krore lent out at interest.[9] Although these figures are no doubt exaggerated, and Saddālaputta himself may be a fictitious character, his story

[1] *Vin.* iv, p. 74. V. supra, p. 120, and infra, p. 136.
[2] V. supra, p. 7; and infra, p. 218.
[3] *Vin.* ii, p. 165. V. infra, p. 136.
[4] V. supra, p. 32, etc.
[5] V. supra, pp. 62–63.
[6] *Dhp. Comm.* i, pp. 390 ff. V. supra, p. 97; and infra, p. 138.
[7] V. infra, p. 135.
[8] V. supra, p. 115.
[9] *Uv. Das.* vii, 180 ff.

is significant both for the study of the economics of Ancient India and for that of the Ājīvikas.

Polāsapura, the town in which he lived, is of doubtful location. The only evidence of its whereabouts is given by the statement that its king was Jiyasattu, but this king's name occurs so frequently in the Jaina scriptures, and in so many and varied contexts, that it is impossible to attach it to any historical figure.[1]

Although the organized Ājīvika sect seems to have been strongest in Kosala, communities of Ājīvika laymen must have existed beyond the bounds of that kingdom at a very early period. The *Aṅguttara* mentions the conversion by the *bhikkhu* Ānanda of " a certain disciple of the Ājīvikas, a householder ",[2] at Kosambi, but no information of interest is given about this single witness to the presence of Ājīvikism in the kingdom of Vaṃsa. In Magadha we have evidence of the presence of early Ājīvikas of the pre-Makkhali loosely organized class, such as Upaka [3]; Pāṇḍuputta [4] is a further example of a Magadhan Ājīvika, whose relations with Makkhali Gosāla's order are uncertain. Barua [5] would include among wealthy Ājīvika supporters one Kuṇḍakoliya of Kampilla, a *seṭṭhi* even wealthier than Saddālaputta.[6] But this would appear to be an error, for throughout the relevant passage of the *Uvāsaga Dasāo* Kuṇḍakoliya is referred to as a " servant of the *Samaṇa* " (i.e. of Mahāvīra), and actually succeeds in converting the Ājīvika *deva* who tries to shake his faith in his master.

The above evidence indicates that at an early period communities of Ājīvika laymen were to be found in all the great cities of the Ganges basin. While they included members of all

[1] Hoernle (*Uv. Das.* vol. ii, p. 3, n. 4) suggested that Jiyasattu was Mahāvīra's maternal uncle Ceḍaga, the chieftain of Vesāli. This view is based on the statement of the text that Jiyasattu was king of Vāṇiyagāma, believed by Hoernle to be Vesāli. (*Uv. Das.* i, 3.) But the same text states that he was also king of Campā, Bāṇārasī, Ālabhiyā, Kampillapura, and Sāvatthī, and Ceḍaga can hardly have controlled these towns, most of which were in Kosala. Raychaudhuri (*PHAI.* p. 161) believes that the name was a title, held by a number of contemporary kings.

[2] *Aññataro Ājīvaka-sāvako gahapati. Aṅg.* i, p. 217.

[3] V. supra, pp. 94–95.

[4] V. supra, pp. 126–27.

[5] *JDL.* ii, p. 38.

[6] *Uv. Das.* vi, 163 ff.

classes the sect was especially patronized by members of the rising mercantile groups. That two potters, Hālāhalā and Saddālaputta should be included among the few names which are mentioned, that Gosāla should have used a potter's workshop at his headquarters, and that pots were employed in Ājīvika penances,[1] together suggest that the sect was in some way specially connected with the potter caste, and made a special appeal to its members.

There are few indications of the social status of Ājīvika laymen in later centuries. One intimation is, however, contained in the Tamil classic *Cilappatikāram.* Here the father of the heroine Kaṇṇaki, who, on her death, gave away all his wealth and entered the Ājīvika order,[2] is described as a *mānāykaṉ.*[3] This word Dikshitar translates as " sea-captain ",[4] but his translation may be questioned, and the word may here have the more usual meaning of "general". In either case the reference shows that the Dravidian Ājīvikas received the support of men of substance. The imposition of the Ājīvika tax in South India [5] indicates a certain degree of affluence among those subject to it.

The social status of the remnants of the Northern Ājīvika community seems to have fallen at an early date. By the time of the final composition of the *Vāyu Purāṇa,* which may perhaps be related to the Gupta period,[6] the Ājīvikas seem to have possessed the humble status of *śūdras,* or even of outcastes. They are described in the Purāṇa as being of mixed *varṇa,* a class of workmen, worshipping *piśācas* ; but they still seem to be comparatively wealthy, and employ much ill-gotten wealth on their religious ceremonies.[7]

Relations between Ājīvikas and Buddhists

The Pāli texts contain many strictures upon Ājīvika ascetics, and they are generally described as being foolish, repulsive, and hypocritical. In the *Majjhima* the Buddha is said to have told the wanderer Vacchagotta that no Ājīvika had ever " made

[1] V. supra, pp. 111–12.
[2] *Cilappatikāram* ed. Aiyar xxvii, 84–102.
[3] Ibid., i, 23.
[4] " *Śilappadikāram,*" p. 88
[5] V. infra, p. 195.
[6] Patil, *Cultural History from the Vāyu Purāṇa,* p. 16.
[7] *Vāyu,* 69, 285–6. V. infra, pp. 162 ff.

an end of sorrow" on his death, and that in the ninety-one *kalpas* of his previous births he remembered but one Ājīvika who had been reborn in heaven.[1] The latter was a believer in *karma* and in the efficiency of works, and therefore was not an orthodox follower of Makkhali Gosāla.

In the *Aṅguttara* the Buddha accuses the Ājīvikas, together with numerous other classes of ascetics, of committing all the five sins, and declares that they are all destined for the infernal regions.[2]

Ājīvika laymen are depicted as cruel and deceitful. The lay Ājīvikas from a distant village who bought the daughter of a Sāvatthi prostitute as a wife for their son, through the intervention of the *bhikkhu* Udāyi, are said to have treated her like a slave, and would allow neither her mother nor the matchmaker to see her.[3]

Two references in the *Vinaya* indicate the shame and annoyance felt by Buddhist monks at being mistaken for Ājīvikas. The first incident is said to have taken place when a group of *bhikkhus* was robbed of their robes on the road from Sāketa to Sāvatthi. Not being permitted to beg fresh robes of householders, they entered the city of Sāvatthi naked, and the citizens wondered at the handsome naked Ājīvikas whom they saw talking with the clothed *bhikkhus*.[4] The second incident also took place at Sāvatthi, at the Jetavana, when the Buddha allowed his monks to remove their robes and expose their bodies to a cooling shower of rain. At the time the pious laywoman Visākhā sent her maid to invite them to a meal, but when she saw the naked *bhikkhus* the girl returned to her mistress and declared that the *ārāma* was no longer occupied by Buddhist monks but by Ājīvikas.[5] As a result of both these incidents the Buddha amended the rules of the order, to avoid any danger of similar misapprehensions in future.

[1] *Ito kho so Vaccha ekanavuto kappo yam ahaṃ anussarāmi, n' âbhijānāmi kañci Ājīvakaṃ saggūpagaṃ aññatra ekena, so p' âsi kamma-vādī kiriya-vādī. Majjh.* i, p. 483.

[2] *Aṅg.* iii, p. 276. Buddhaghosa, however, is somewhat more lenient with the Ājīvikas. He states that their *niṭṭhā* or condition of perfection, is the heaven of Anantamānasa, and thus seems to imply that this heaven is attainable by Ājīvikas of the highest sanctity (*Papañca Sūdanī* to *Majjh.* 11, vol. ii, pp. 9–10. V. infra, p. 261).

[3] *Vin.* iii, pp. 135 ff. [4] Ibid. iii, pp. 212 ff. [5] Ibid. i, pp. 290 ff.

Yet the attitude of dislike and distrust indicated by these stories is only one side of the picture. There is evidence to show that, like Aśoka 250 years later, many laymen of the Buddha's time, while bestowing special favour on one sect, were the friends and patrons of all. We have seen that King Bimbisāra fed the Buddhist *saṅgha* and other religious communities, at the behest of one of his kinsmen who had become an Ājīvika ascetic.[1] A further *Vinaya* passage tells of a *mahāmatta* who was an Ājīvika disciple, and who also gave a meal to the Buddhist order, which was graced by the Buddha himself. On this occasion the Master is said to have reprimanded the *bhikkhu* Upananda for his impoliteness in coming late to the feast.[2] The *Vinaya* also mentions a Buddhist layman who visited a park in the company of a number of Ājīvikas [3]; and we have seen that the *bhikkhu* Udāyi was not too proud to act as matchmaker on behalf of Ājīvika laymen.[4]

A very significant indication of friendly relations between the two sects is the story of the announcement of the Buddha's *parinirvāṇa* to the elder Mahākassapa. At the head of a band of 500 *bhikkhus* he was resting by the roadside on the way from Pāvā to Kusinārā, when there passed by a certain Ājīvika, who came from Kusinārā holding a *mandārava* flower in his hand; this indicated that some great and auspicious event had taken place, for the *mandārava* grows in the worlds of the gods, and only rains upon earth on such occasions. The monks asked the Ājīvika if he knew their leader, and it was he who told them that Gotama had passed to *nirvāṇa* seven days previously.[5] In the *Vinaya* story the Ājīvika's words are very respectfully spoken. He addresses Mahākassapa by the title *āvuso*, and implicitly admits the greatness of the Buddha by referring to him as *parinibbuta* instead of *mata*.[6] He, too, is addressed by the courteous title *āvuso*.

Not only did Ājīvikas feed Buddhists, but on occasions Buddhists fed Ājīvikas. While at Vesāli the Buddha's followers

[1] Ibid. iv, p. 74. V. supra, pp. 120, 131–32.
[2] Ibid. ii, p. 165.
[3] Ibid. ii, p. 130. V. infra, p. 137.
[4] V. supra, p. 135.
[5] *Vin.* ii, p. 284.
[6] *Ām, āvuso, jānāmi. Ajja satt'-âha-parinibbuto samaṇo Gotamo. Tato me idaṃ mandārava-pupphaṃ gahitaṃ.*

PLATE III.

THE BUDDHA'S *PARINIRVĀṆA.*

(From Foucher, *L'Art Gréco-Bouddhique.*)

On the right an Ājīvika informs Mahākassapa of the Master's death.

found themselves with more food than they required, and gave their surplus to those ascetics who accepted leavings (*vighās'-âda*). An Ājīvika who had been thus fed by the *bhikkhus* was later overheard by one of them telling a fellow Ājīvika of the food which he had obtained from the "shaven-headed householder" (*muṇḍa-gahapatika*), Gotama. The *bhikkhus* reported the matter to their master, who forbade the distribution of surplus food to mendicants of other orders in future.[1]

This story may be the traditional explanation of a hardening and worsening of relations between the two sects, which perhaps took place in the Buddha's lifetime. Its implication is that the breach arose from the discourteous conduct of the Ājīvikas. Perhaps the latter, with their sterner discipline, began to ridicule the easy-going Buddhists, and the growth of mutual recriminations and of sarcastic attacks on both sides, led to the ostracism of the Ājīvikas by the Buddhist order. The incident of the Ājīvika who declared the Buddha to be a "shaven householder" is not the only such case recorded in Buddhist literature. The *Vinaya* also mentions a company of Ājīvika laymen who mocked a group of *bhikkhus* in an unnamed park, because the latter were carrying sunshades. The Ājīvikas are said to have derided the *bhikkhus* before the Buddhist laymen to whom they were talking, saying that they looked like officials of the treasury (*gaṇaka-mahāmattā*), and were "*bhikkhus* who were not *bhikkhus*" (*bhikkhū na bhikkhū*).[2]

It is clear from these examples that the Buddhists were very sensitive to these accusations of laxity in discipline. No doubt many of the simpler lay folk of the time were inclined to estimate the sanctity of a religious order by the severity of its discipline, and to bestow their alms accordingly. It may be inferred that the Ājīvikas were equally sensitive to the Buddhist accusations of hypocrisy. They are said to have expelled the repulsive Jambuka from their community for fear of the scandal that the Buddhist *saṅgha* would make of his conduct if it became known.[3]

With each sect attempting to win members from the others animosity must inevitably have arisen. The violence of the competition for supporters is evident from the story of Migāra,

[1] *Vin.* iv, p. 91. [2] Ibid. ii, pp. 130–1. [3] V. supra, p. 97.

the rich banker of Sāvatthi of whom we have heard before in more than one context.[1] Migāra first appears on the scene as an earnest devotee of the naked ascetics, but his loss of faith begins when his newly married daughter-in-law, the Buddhist laywoman Visākhā, refuses to pay reverence to the 500 mendicants whom he entertains, declaring that they are devoid of modesty and shame, and unworthy of respect. When Migāra agrees to entertain the Buddhist *saṅgha* the Ājīvikas besiege his home, in a frantic attempt to prevent their rivals from obtaining so wealthy and influential a convert.

That of Migāra is not the only example of conversions from Ājīvikism to Buddhism. The ascetics Upaka and Jambuka and the unnamed Ājīvika layman of Kosambi have already been mentioned.[2] The *kulūpaga* brāhmaṇa Ājīvika of the Mauryan court, Janasāna, is also said to have been converted to Buddhism.[3] The wanderer Sandaka, who seems to have owed loose allegiance to Makkhali Gosāla, is another case in point.[4] That strong animosity, aroused by rivalry in conversion, continued among the less tolerant members of both communities may be inferred from Aśoka's pleas for mutual forbearance and respect among the sects of his time.[5]

Relations between Ājīvikas and Jainas

That Ājīvikas and Jainas were originally on good terms and indeed closely related, is evident from the Jaina tradition of the early friendship and association of Gosāla and Mahāvīra.[6] The near relationship of the two sects is confirmed by the Buddhist tradition associating Makkhali Gosāla and Pūraṇa Kassapa, the two chief Ājīvika leaders, with Nigaṇṭha Nātaputta, or Mahāvīra, as members of the group of six heretics with whom the early Buddhists waged a continuous war of words. The frequent confusion of the terms *nirgrantha* and *ājīvika* in the Buddhist texts[7] also points in the same direction. That the confusion persisted in some Buddhist circles even as late as post-Mauryan times is shown by a story in the *Divyâvadāna*, in which

[1] *Dhp. Comm.* i, pp. 390 ff. V. supra, pp. 97, 132. [2] V. supra, pp. 94 f., 97, 133. [3] V. infra, pp. 146–47. [4] *Majjh.* i, p. 513. V. supra, pp. 18–19. [5] *CHI.* i, p. 504, etc. [6] V. supra, pp. 39 ff. [7] V. supra, pp. 96–97.

PLATE IV.

DISCOMFITURE OF A NAKED ASCETIC.

(From Foucher, *L'Art Gréco-Bouddhique.*)

This is believed by Foucher (op. cit., i, p. 532) to represent Visākhā defying a naked ascetic. The old man on the terrace is perhaps Migāra.

a *nirgrantha* layman is said to have defiled an image or picture (*pratimā*) of the Buddha, as a result of which desecration the Emperor Aśoka ordered the destruction of all the *ājīvikas* in the region.[1] Here the terms seem plainly intended to be taken synonymously, in striking contrast to Aśoka's own inscription, where the two sects are sharply distinguished.[2]

Our belief in the early and close relationship of the two sects is strengthened by similarities in practice and doctrine, such as in the custom of ascetic nudity, and by the Ājīvika *abhijātis*, or six classes of mankind.[3] The points in which these resemble and differ from the *leśyās* of the Jainas will be considered in our second part.[4] Meanwhile the classification is of interest for the intimations which it gives of the attitude of the early Ājīvikas to their rivals among the heterodox communities. The highest, or supremely white group (*parama-sukk'-âbhijāti*) contains only Nanda Vaccha, Kisa Saṅkicca, and Makkhali Gosāla. Below these is the white category (*sukk'-âbhijāti*), containing Ājīvikas and Ājīvinīs. Next comes the green (*halidda*), which holds " the householder clad in white robes, the disciple of the *acelakas* ", to which Buddhaghosa adds : " he (i.e. Makkhali) makes the *nigaṇṭha* (laymen), who give him his necessities, superior (to the *nigaṇṭha* ascetics of the red class)." [5] Fourth from the top is the red class (*lohita*), " *nigaṇṭhas* who wear a single garment " [6] ; while in the lowest place but one is the blue (*nīla*), " *bhikkhus* who live as thieves, and believers in *karma* and (the efficiency of) works." [7] Finally in the lowest and most debased and reprobate class, the black (*kaṇh'-âbhijāti*), are found thieves, hunters, and others who live by violence.

The classification of the *abhijātis* indicates that the Ājīvika regarded the Jaina as second to himself in sanctity. The Buddhist

[1] *Divyâvadāna*, p. 427. V. infra, pp. 147–48.

[2] V. infra, p. 148.

[3] *Aṅg.* iii, 383 ; *Sum. Vil.* i, p. 162. V. supra, pp. 20, 27, 109, and infra, pp. 243ff.

[4] V. infra, p. 245.

[5] *Gihī odāta-vasanā acelaka-sāvakā* (*Aṅg.* iii, 384). *Ayam attano paccaya-dāyake nigaṇṭhe hi pi jeṭṭhakatare karoti* (*Sum. Vil.* i, 162). Our interpretation of Buddhaghosa's obscure addition is admittedly tentative. It seems that in this case Buddhaghosa used the term *nigaṇṭha* very loosely.

[6] *Nigaṇṭhā eka-sāṭakā.* Hare (*Gradual Sayings* iii, p. 273) seems to accept an omitted *ca*. Hoernle gives a different interpretation (v. supra, p. 109).

[7] *Bhikkhū kaṇḍaka-vuttikā ye vā pan' aññe pi keci kamma-vādā kiriya-vādā* (*Aṅg.* iii, 383). Our interpretation differs from Hare's. V. infra, p. 243.

bhikkhu was but a poor third, and the orthodox brāhmaṇa was presumably included with the wretched *kurūra-kammanta* in the black category, although, as has been shown,[1] there are certain indications that early Ājīvika practice and doctrine were closer to orthodoxy in some particulars than were the practices and doctrines of Buddhism and Jainism.

The *Bhagavatī Sūtra's* account of Gosāla's death indicates that for most of the period of the ministry of the Ājīvika leader relations between Jaina and Ājīvika were not unfriendly. Āṇanda, Mahāvīra's disciple, to whom the long story of the merchants was told,[2] seems to have treated Gosāla with great respect before Mahāvīra forbade all association with him. Further evidence that Jaina strictures on Ājīvika morals did not always imply intolerant social relations is given by the story of Saddālaputta, wherein Gosāla is said to have praised Mahāvīra in the usual Jaina terms.[3] The *Bhagavatī Sūtra*[4] names twelve Ājīvika laymen, including one Ayampala or Ayambula, probably Ayampula of Sāvatthi,[5] who are held up to the Jainas as models of virtue and non-violence. They are surprisingly described as " worshippers of the *arhants* and the gods ", or " worshippers of the *arhants* as gods ",[6] although Abhayadeva the commentator states that the false *arhant* Gosāla is here meant. The Buddha declared that he knew of only one Ājīvika to reach heaven,[7] but the Jaina *Aupapātika Sūtra*[8] assures Ājīvika ascetics of various types[9] of a divinity of twelve *sāgarovamāiṃ* in duration in the heaven called *Accuakappa*. The promise is repeated in the *Bhagavatī Sūtra*.[10] The same rebirth was forecast for Gosāla by Mahāvīra, although in his case it was to be followed by a long succession of births in less pleasant conditions.[11]

Thus the early relations of the two sects seem to have been of a friendly and mutually respectful type, broken only from time to time by quarrels over doctrine and discipline. We have already suggested that relations between Ājīvikas and Buddhists worsened owing to strenuous competition in conversion. With the Jainas

1 V. supra, p. 131.
2 V. supra, p. 59.
3 V. supra, pp. 52–53.
4 *Bh. Sū.* viii, *sū.* 329, fol. 369. V. supra, p. 122.
5 V. supra, p. 62.
6 *Arihanta-devatā-gā.*
7 V. supra, pp. 134–35.
8 *Aupapātika Sūtra, sū.* 41, fol. 196.
9 V. supra, p. 111. Cf. infra, p. 261.
10 *Bh. Sū.* i, *sū.* 26.
11 Ibid. xv, *sū.* 559, fol. 687. V. infra, p. 142.

the same worsening may have taken place, and for the same reason. The *Uvāsaga Dasāo* speaks of two conversions from Ājīvikism, the first that of Saddālaputta by Mahāvīra,[1] and the second that of an unnamed Ājīvika *deva* by the Jaina layman Kuṇḍakoliya of Kampilla.[2] The *Bhagavatī* states that many of Gosāla's adherents deserted him after the magic duel at Sāvatthi. We have no mention of counter-conversions from Jainism and Buddhism to Ājīvikism, but if the lost Ājīvika scriptures were restored to us records of these too would doubtless be forthcoming. Dr. Barua has ingeniously suggested that the *Bhagavatī* account of the killing of the two Jaina disciples Savvâṇubhūti and Suṇakkhatta [3] conceals their defection from Jainism to the cause of Gosāla. In view of the clear statement of the text this must remain an unproved and unacceptable hypothesis. More probable is Barua's further suggestion, that Mahāvīra's ban on all contact between his followers and those of Gosāla may represent measures taken by the early Jaina community to counteract large-scale defections to the Ājīvikas.[4]

[1] *Uv. Das.* vii ; v. supra, p. 52.
[2] Ibid. vi ; v. supra, p. 133.
[3] V. supra, p. 66.
[4] *JDL.* ii, pp. 34–5. Barua's view that Suṇakkhatta of the *Bhagavatī* is identical with Sunakkhatta the Licchavi of *Majjh.* i, pp. 68 ff. is quite unprovable. The two characters have nothing in common except their names.

CHAPTER VIII

ĀJĪVIKAS IN THE NANDA AND MAURYA PERIODS

Mahāpadma

After the death of Gosāla, Mahāvīra is said to have prophesied his future births.[1] He forecast that the false prophet would ascend to the *Accua-kappa* heaven, and would there enjoy divinity for twelve *sāgarovamāiṃ* periods. Then he would be reborn on earth as Mahāpaüma, the son of King Sammuti and his queen Bhaddā, in the city of Sayaduvāra in the land of the Paṇḍas, which is situated at the foot of the Vindhyas in Bhāratavarṣa. On his accession the two *devas* Punnabhadda and Māṇibhadda would serve as his generals (*seṇā-kammaṃ kāhinti*), and he would ride through the city on a white elephant; hence he would obtain the titles Devaseṇa and Vimalavāhaṇa. He would become a violent persecutor of Jainas until, one day insulting the ascetic Sumaṅgala while the latter was engaged in meditation, he would be reduced by the magic power of the saint's asceticism to a heap of ashes.

The soul of Gosāla would then, according to Mahāvīra, continue to transmigrate through many births of all types, until at last the harvest of his evil deeds would be fully reaped, and he would become a Jaina ascetic Daḍhapaïnna in Mahāvideha. Remembering all his past lives he would die by slow starvation in the orthodox manner, and would thus make an end of all sorrow.[2]

Although Dr. Barua has tried to make a historical figure of Daḍhapaïnna,[3] the later rebirths as described in the *Bhagavatī*

[1] *Bh. Sū.* xv, fol. 687 ff.

[2] *Bh. Sū.* xv, *sū.* 560, fol. 694.

[3] " . . . Daḍhapaïnna, a wealthy citizen of the great Videha country, sought to bring about a reconciliation between the hostile sects by conferring with the Jainas " (*JDL.* ii, p. 54). " The Bhagavatī Sūtra refers to an Ājīviya committing religious suicide sometime after Gosāla's death " (ibid., p. 71). Barua backs both these statements by references not to the *Sūtra* but to Hoernle's paraphrase of its relevant chapter (*Uv. Das.*, vol. ii, app. i). Both the

seem to be of no value for the reconstruction of the story of the Ājīvikas. But it is possible that some significance is to be found in the account of Mahāpaüma, which seems to contain a veiled attack on a king who was a patron of the Ājīvikas and an opponent of the Jainas. If the king in question is not concealed by a false name the only historical figure whom the sovereign described in the *Bhagavatī* can represent is Mahāpadma Nanda. This conclusion has been tentatively accepted by Barua.[1]

The inference rests on very slight evidence. The great city of Sayaduvāra, with its hundred gates, suggests Pāṭaliputra; the inference that the author had Pāṭaliputra in mind is slightly strengthened by the alternative reading of the text, as used by Hoernle,[2] which locates the city in the land of the Puṇḍas, and beneath the Vaitāḍhya mountain.[3] The latter is a mountain of Jaina legendary geography which defies location, but which may represent the Himālayas. Puṇḍra, or Northern Bengal, was not far distant from Magadha and probably formed part of the Nanda dominions. The power and splendour of the Nanda are attested by various sources,[4] and in this respect also he resembles the Mahāpaüma of the *Bhagavatī*. The *Purāṇas* suggest that he was by no means orthodox.[5] Although the titles Devasena and Vimalavāhana are not elsewhere attributed to him he is referred to in the *Mahābodhi-vaṃsa* as Ugrasena.[6] Two kings named Devasena are mentioned in the legends of the *Kathā-sarit-sāgara*. Of these the first rules at Śrāvasti, and has nothing in common with Mahāpaüma of the *Bhagavatī*,[7] but the second has some points of similarity.[8] He rules in Puṇḍravardhana, thus agreeing with the Mahāpaüma of Hoernle's text of the *Bhagavatī Sūtra*. He compels brāhmaṇas and kṣattriyas

original and the paraphrase make it clear that Daḍhapaīnna is a Jaina ascetic of the normal type, who, by virtue of his spiritual perfection, remembers his past births and informs his disciples of his earlier birth as Gosāla. Barua's conclusion is quite unjustified.

[1] *JDL.* ii, p. 67.

[2] *Uv. Das.*, vol. ii, app. i, p. 11.

[3] The same forms occur in the *Sthānāṅga Sūtra* (ix, *sū.* 693, fol. 458), in the description of the capital of the great king Mahāpaüma, who will become the first *tīrthaṅkara* of the coming *Utsarpiṇī* age.

[4] *PHAI.*, pp. 187 ff.

[5] E.g. *Matsya Purāṇa*, 272, 18. *Sarva-kṣattr'-āntako nṛpaḥ.*

[6] *Mahābodhi-vaṃsa*, p. 98.

[7] *Kathā-sarit-Sāgara* iii, xv, pp. 200–1.

[8] Ibid. iii, xviii, pp. 268 ff.

to pass the night with his daughter, who is possessed by a *rākṣasa*, and thus encompasses their death ; this suggests the traditional antipathy of the historical Mahāpadma to the two higher castes. Finally he is reported to have said : " It is impossible to bar the course of fate, whose dispensations are wonderful."[1] We have here a further legend of a cruel king of Eastern India with a fatalist philosophy, but the link with the historical Mahāpadma is still very tenuous.

Evidence almost as strong can be found to suggest that the Mahāpaüma of the *Bhagavatī Sūtra* has no historical significance. No reference can be found to show that Mahāpadma's father was named Sammuti, for which name Hoernle quotes the variant Sumati ; the *Purāṇas* declare him to have been a baseborn son of his predecessor Mahānandin.[2] The only Nanda name which bears the faintest similarity to that of Mahāpaüma's father is that of the eldest of Mahāpadma's eight sons, called in the *Bhāgavata Purāṇa* Sumālya[3]; it is remotely possible that Sammuti is a corruption of this.

Doubts as to the historicity of the Mahāpaüma of the *Bhagavatī* are strengthened by the fact that there are several other figures of the same name and similar description in Jaina mythology.[4] The first *tīrthaṅkara* of the coming *Utsarpiṇī* will also be named Mahāpaüma, a reincarnation of the Magadhan king " Seṇiya Bhimbhisāra ", will be a prince of the same titles, kingdom, and parentage, and will only differ from the reincarnation of Gosāla in his later career. Other Mahāpaümas are the ninth *cakravartī* of the coming *Utsarpiṇī*, and the ninth of the current *Avasarpiṇī*. Furthermore, Jaina tradition, unlike that of the *Purāṇas*, is generally favourable to the Nandas ; Hemacandra's *Pariśiṣṭaparvan*[5] praises an unnamed Nanda king and repeats several favourable legends about him, none of which suggests that he was an enemy of Jainism.

Indeed it has even been suggested that Mahāpadma was himself a Jaina.[6] Arguments for this theory are based on the favourable

[1] *Gatiḥ śakyā paricchetuṃ na hy adbhuta-vidher vidheḥ.* Ibid. iii, 18, v. 267, p. 269.
[2] E.g. *Bhāgavata Purāṇa*, 12, 1, 8.
[3] Ibid., 12, 1, 11. *PHAI.*, p. 190, n. 1.
[4] *Abh. Rāj.*, s.v. *Mahāpaüma*.
[5] *Pariśiṣṭaparvan* vi, 231 ff.
[6] *CHI.* i, p. 164.

tone of the Jaina legends about him, and on the Hāthīgumphā inscription of Khāravela, which, according to one reading, records that Khāravela restored to Kaliṅga a statue of a *Jina*, taken by the Nanda.[1] The argument is not conclusive. If Mahāpadma had been an earnest Jaina it is unlikely that he would have outraged the Kaliṅgan Jaina community by robbing their temples of their ikons. It would seem more probable that he carried away the image as a trophy, obtained by harrying a sect to which he was opposed. The inscription is in very bad condition and the reading may be incorrect. Dr. Barua has suggested *janaṃ* for *jinaṃ*,[2] and the acceptance of this reading would seriously weaken the theory that Mahāpadma was a supporter of Jainism. Further, the Nanda mentioned in the Hāthīgumphā inscription may not have been Mahāpadma at all, but another Nanda king.

In favour of the view that Mahāpadma was a patron of Ājīvikism it may be argued that the Ājīvika community certainly existed in some strength in Magadha at the time, and received some patronage from the Mauryas, who were the successors of the Nandas. Whatever his sect, Mahāpadma seems to have been no friend of orthodox Hinduism, and it may therefore be inferred that he patronized heretical sects. The reference in the *Bhagavatī Sūtra* suggests that he may have given his special support to the Ājīvika *saṅgha*.

This view is slightly strengthened by a phrase in the *Mahāvaṃsa Commentary*, which states that the great Cāṇakya, after cursing the last Nanda, escaped from his clutches in the guise of a nude Ājīvika ascetic.[3] If any inference is to be derived from this late and unreliable tradition it is that Ājīvikas were numerous in Nanda times and not subject to persecution from the royal officers.

Ājīvikas in Maurya Times

It would seem that Ājīvikism spread fairly rapidly beyond the region of its origin. The *Mahāvaṃsa* records that, by the time of the Mauryas, it had found its way to Ceylon, where the

[1] *Epi. Ind.* xx, pp. 72 ff. *Nanda-rāja-nītaṃ ca Ka[li]ṅga-jinaṃ sanniveśa . . .*
[2] *IHQ.* xiv, pp. 261 ff.
[3] *Vaṃsattha-ppakāsinī*, vol. i, p. 183.

king Paṇḍukâbhaya, the grandfather of Aśoka's contemporary Devānampiya Tissa, built a "house of Ājīvikas" (*Ājīvikānaṃ gehaṃ*) at Anurādhapura.[1]

A passage in the *Petavatthu* tells of King Piṅgala of Suraṭṭha, who, two hundred years after the Buddha's *nirvāṇa*, left his kingdom in the service of the Mauryas (*Moriyānaṃ upaṭṭhānaṃ*).[2] As he was returning to his capital he was met by a *peta*, who told him that he was the disembodied soul of one who had formerly been a heretic of Suraṭṭha, who had held Ājīvika views. The passage indicates that Ājīvikism may have spread to Gujarāt by this period.

Evidence that Aśoka was a friend of the Ājīvika order, and that it flourished during his reign, rests on the very solid basis of his own inscriptions. Literary references also link him with the Ājīvikas. Both the *Divyâvadāna*[3] and the *Mahāvaṃsa Commentary*[4] tell of an Ājīvika mendicant attached to the court of King Bindusāra, Aśoka's father, who correctly prophesied the coming greatness of the Prince. In the first account he is called *Piṅgalavats'-âjīva*, a *parivrājaka*, and seems to have been a court prognosticator. At the invitation of Vindusāra he watches the princes at play, and by various omens he recognizes that Aśoka will become king. As Aśoka is not the favourite prince Piṅgalavatsa dares not tell the King of his prophecy, and when questioned refuses to give a definite answer. But he tells Aśoka's mother, Queen Subhadrâṅgī, of her son's coming greatness, and on her advice he leaves the kingdom, lest Vindusāra force an answer from him. On the death of Vindusāra he returns to the Magadhan court.

In the *Mahāvaṃsa Commentary's* version of the story the Ājīvika is a *kulūpaga*, or household ascetic, of the Queen. His name is given as Janasāna, of which there are the variants Jarasona and Jarasāna, and he is said to have been of brāhmaṇa family. The Commentary states that he was very wise, having been born as a python in the days of Buddha Kassapa, and in this form having overheard the discussions of *bhikkhus* well versed in philosophy. He correctly prophesies Aśoka's future greatness from the Queen's pregnancy longings; no reason is

[1] *Mahāvaṃsa* x, 101–2.
[2] *Petavatthu* iv, 3, p. 57.
[3] *Divyâvadāna*, pp. 370 ff.
[4] *Vaṃsattha-ppakāsinī* i, p. 190.

given for his quitting the court, but by the time of Aśoka's accession he appears to have abandoned his former patrons. The king is said on one occasion to have asked his mother whether any prophet had forecast his prosperity; the queen replied that Janasāna had done so, whereupon Aśoka sent a deputation with a carriage to bring the Ājīvika to the palace. Janasāna was then residing at an unnamed place a hundred *yojanas* distant from Pāṭaliputra; on the journey to the capital he met the elder Assagutta, by whom he was converted, and he entered the Buddhist order.

The two stories, while differing considerably in important details, including the name of the Ājīvika prophet, seem to have a basis of fact. The very discrepancies in the two accounts suggest that the authors drew their material independently from a widespread tradition which had developed with the passage of time. Such a story seems more probably dependent on a real occurrence than on a monkish fiction. We may therefore believe that Bindusāra kept at his court an Ājīvika fortune-teller who was *persona grata* to the chief queen. The *Divyâvadāna's* story of his flight is not altogether convincing; it fits too well into the framework of Vindusāra's hostility to Aśoka and the latter's usurpation of the throne of Magadha to give an impression of authenticity. The account of the conversion of Janasāna in the *Mahāvaṃsa Commentary*, with its strong flavour of pious edification, is even more suspect. But neither account is intrinsically impossible. Bindusāra's interest in unorthodox philosophy is strikingly attested by a classical reference.[1] We may conclude that, even before the introduction of Aśoka's policy of toleration, Ājīvikas were patronized by the court of Magadha.

The *Divyâvadāna* gives another much more questionable story of Aśoka's relations with the Ājīvikas.[2] Aśoka, hearing that a *nirgrantha* in Puṇḍravardhana had defiled a picture or statue of the Buddha, ordered the destruction of all Ājīvikas in the locality, as a result of which order 18,000 were massacred in a single day. The same crime was later committed by another *nirgrantha* layman in Pāṭaliputra, in punishment of which the king offered a reward of a *dīnāra* for the head of every

[1] Athenæus xiv, 67. Quoted *CII.* i, p. xxxv.
[2] *Divyâvadāna*, p. 427. V. supra, p. 139.

nirgrantha brought to him. This second wave of persecution led to the murder of the king's younger brother, Prince Vītâśoka.

The loose use of the terms *nirgrantha* and *ājīvika* in this story makes it uncertain whether they were intended to apply to the order of Mahāvīra or to that of Makkhali ; it may indeed have been intended to refer to both sects indiscriminately. As it stands, the story is quite incredible, in that it makes the apostle of toleration a monster of quite un-Buddhist fanaticism. If it has any significance it is to indicate a tradition of hostility to Ājīvikas and Jainas, which may have occasionally flared up under other monarchs into open persecution. The story suggests that Ājīvikism was specially prevalent at the time in Puṇḍra, a suggestion also conveyed by the Jaina story of Mahāpaüma.[1] The trampling on the image, with its indication of iconoclasm on the part of the anti-Buddhist *nirgrantha-ājīvikas*, is a theme which recurs at a much later date in Kashmīr, in connection with the mysterious naked ascetics employed by King Harṣa.[2]

The inscriptions of Aśoka give us references which for the first time are completely reliable records of the contemporary influence of the Ājīvika sect. These occur in the Seventh Pillar Edict, and in the dedicatory inscriptions in the Barābar and Nagārjunī caves.

The Seventh Pillar Edict[3] is found in only one version, on the Delhi-Topra pillar. It was issued in the twenty-seventh year of Aśoka's consecration, or 237 B.C., according to Hultzsch's computation. It describes the imperial policy for the propagation of *dharma*, and especially the duties of the officers of public morals (*dharma-mahāmātra*), who, in Hultzsch's translation, "were ordered . . . to busy themselves with the affairs of the *saṃgha* ; likewise others were ordered . . . to busy themselves also with the Brāhmaṇas (and) Ājīvikas ; others were ordered . . . to busy themselves also with the Nirgranthas ; others were ordered . . . to busy themselves also with various (other) sects ; (thus) different Mahāmātras (are busying themselves) specially with different (congregations)."[4]

[1] V supra, pp. 142 ff. [2] V. infra, pp. 206 ff. [3] *CII.* i, pp. 131 ff.

[4] . . . *saṃghaṭhasi pi me kaṭe ime viyāpaṭā hohaṃti ti, hemeva bābhanesu ā[j]īvikesu pi me kaṭe ime viyāpaṭā hohaṃti nigaṃthesu pi me kaṭe ime viyāpaṭā hohaṃti nānā-pāsaṃḍesu pi me [ka]ṭe ime viyāpaṭā hohaṃti ti paṭivisiṭhaṃ paṭīvisiṭhaṃ tesu tesu [te] . . . mātā.* Ibid., p. 136, ii, 15–16.

The absence of any conjunction linking the words *bābhaṇesu* and *ājīvikesu* has led Bühler to interpret the former as an adjective governing the latter . . . " likewise I have arranged it that they will be occupied with the Brāhmaṇical Ājīvikas ".[1] Following Kern, he expresses his belief that the Ājīvikas were Vaiṣṇavas.[2] The theory of Kern and Bühler has been attacked by Hoernle [3] and D. R. Bhandarkar,[4] and few would now accept it. In the Seventh Pillar Edict the word *bābhanesu* seems certainly to be a noun. The absence of a copulative conjunction presents a difficulty, but no doubt other examples can be found wherein a *ca* seems to be omitted. But, even granting all these provisos, there may be a modicum of truth in the old theory of Kern and Bühler. A close connection between the Brāhmaṇa and the Ājīvika is indicated by Asoka's classification of the sects. The bodies among which the *mahāmātras* were active seem to be divided into four sections, to each of which is given a clause in the inscription, the clauses each concluding with the verb *hohaṃti*. The four classes are (1) the Buddhist *saṅgha*, (2) Brāhmaṇas and Ājīvikas, (3) *Nirgranthas* or Jainas, and (4) various heretics. Even if we admit that Aśoka intended to make a distinction between Brāhmaṇas and Ājīvikas, it is evident that he considered the Ājīvikas to be more closely related to the orthodox brāhmaṇas than were the Jainas, since Brāhmaṇa and Ājīvika are included in the same clause. We have already found references which point to the fact that the Ājīvikas were nearer to the orthodox ascetic orders in their conduct than were either of the other great heretical communities.[5] Aśoka seems to have recognized this fact. It will also be remembered that Jarasāna, the Ājīvika fortune-teller at his father's court, came of a brāhmaṇa family.[6] Even before Aśoka's day it is possible that some of the Northern Ājīvikas had begun to draw very close to the parent stock.

The Seventh Pillar Edict also gives some indication of the influence of the Ājīvikas at the time. The Ājīvika *saṅgha* appears as a fully developed religious community. on an equal footing with the two other non-brāhmaṇic systems, and is not relegated to the last category of the " various heretics ". It may be suggested

[1] *Epi. Ind.* ii, p. 272.
[2] *IA.* xx, p. 362.
[3] *ERE.* i, p. 267.
[4] *IA.* xli, pp. 286–290.
[5] V. supra, p. 131.
[6] V. supra, p. 146.

that, since Aśoka mentions the Ājīvikas before the *Nirgranthas*, or Jainas, the former sect seemed to the king to be either more influential or more worthy of support than the latter.

THE BARĀBAR AND NĀGÂRJUNĪ CAVES

Even more convincing evidence of the continued influence of the Ājīvikas in Magadha are the dedicatory inscriptions of Aśoka in the artificial caves of the Barābar Hill,[1] fifteen miles north of Gayā. These caves are four in number, three of which contain Aśokan inscriptions. The nearby hill of Nāgârjunī contains three similar caves, which were dedicated to the Ājīvikas by Aśoka's successor Daśaratha.[2]

Of the three Barābar caves with dedicatory inscriptions (Plate V), the first two, according to Hultzsch's restoration of the texts,[3] were given to the Ājīvikas in the twelfth year of Aśoka's consecration. The first cave is named in the inscription *Nigoha* (Skt. *Nyagrodha*) (Plate V, i), and the second is referred to merely as a cave in the Khalatika Mountain (Plate V, ii). Little doubt can exist about the interpretation of these two inscriptions, but the third (Plate V, iii) has been badly defaced, and is in parts illegible. Hultzsch reconstructs the text as :—

Lājā Piyadasī ekunavī-
sati-vasā [*bh*] *isi* [*t*]*e ja* [*lagh*] *o*
[*sāgamā*] *thāta* [*me*] *iyaṃ kubhā*
su[*p*]*i*[*y*]*e kha* . . . . [*di*]
nā.

"When King Priyadarśin had been anointed nineteen years, this cave in the very pleasant Kha [latika mountain] was given by me for (shelter during) the rainy season." [4] The inscription is followed by the auspicious symbols of swastika and dagger.

Senart, basing his view on the reproduction in the first edition of *Corpus Inscriptionum Indicarum*, read in the third line the word *caṃdamasūliyaṃ*, and translated, on the analogy of the Daśaratha inscriptions: "[*Ceci est fait*] *pour aussi longtemps*

[1] *CII.* i, pp. 181 ff. V. Plate V.
[2] *IA.* xx, pp. 361 ff. V. Plate VI.
[3] *CII.* i, p. 181.
[4] Ibid., p. 182.

PLATE V.

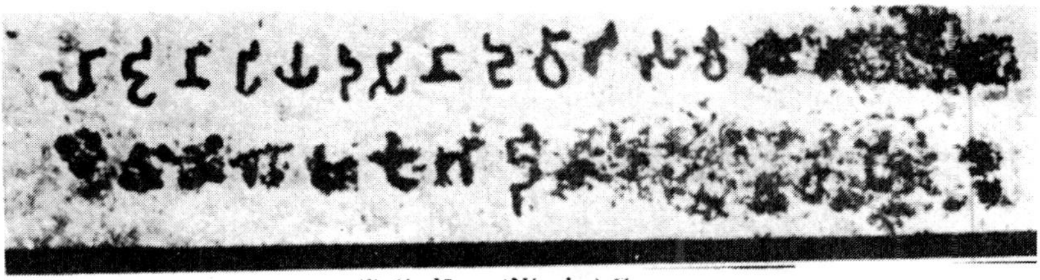

(i) Sudāma (Nigoha) Cave.

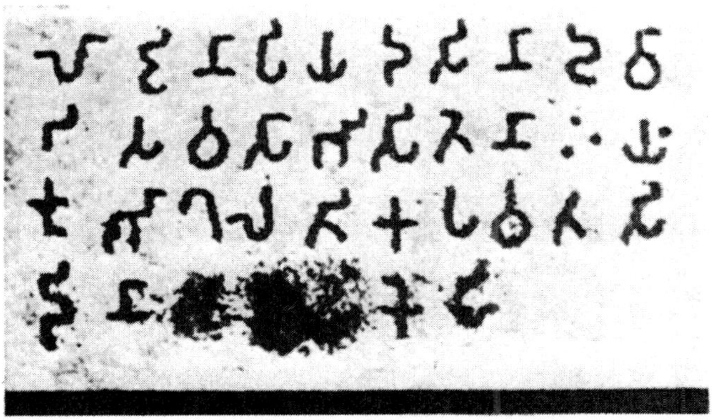

(ii) Viśvâmitra Cave.

(iii) Karṇa Chopār Cave.

BARĀBAR CAVE INSCRIPTIONS.
(From *CII*, i.)
Scale : one-fifth approx.

que dureront la lune et le soleil."[1] Bühler cautiously avoided any attempt at a transcription of the doubtful letters.[2] Senart's translation will not stand in the light of the more recent reproduction employed by Hultzsch, whose interpretation is not inconsistent with the remains of the text. It might be expected that some reference to the Ājīvikas would occur in the third inscription on the analogy of the first and second, but this does not seem to be the case; no trace of the relevant *akṣaras* can be found in its defaced portions. It seems quite reasonable to believe, however, that the Ājīvikas occupied the third cave, as they did the other two.

One question not absolutely certain is whether the donor of the caves was in fact Aśoka. This uncertainty has been recognized by Hultzsch,[3] who admits that they may have been given by another member of the Maurya dynasty. But he points out that "two of the caves . . . were dedicated . . . when the donor had been 'anointed twelve years' . . . This happens to be the regnal year in which the author of the rock- and pillar-edicts commenced to issue 'rescripts of morality'". If the Piyadasi of the Barābar Hill inscriptions was not Aśoka then we must assume that he was Candragupta, Bindusāra, or one of the shadowy successors of Daśaratha, for the latter has left dedicatory inscriptions in the caves of the nearby Nāgârjunī Hill in which he has used his personal name, and we may assume that, had he been the donor of the Barābar caves, he would have recorded his name in these also. No other king has the same strong inherent probability of being the donor of the Barābar caves as has Aśoka. We have no evidence that the custom of incising inscriptions upon rock was practised before his reign, and there are no epigraphic records whatever of the successors of Daśaratha.

The Daśaratha inscriptions of the Nāgârjunī Hill caves (Plate VI) are in better condition than those of Barābar. The formula used in the dedication differs from that of Aśoka: "The Vahiyakā cave has been given by Dasalatha, dear to the gods, to the venerable Ājīvikas, immediately on his accession, to be a place of abode during the rainy season as long as moon and sun (shall

[1] *Les Inscriptions de Piyadasi*, vol. ii, p. 212.
[2] *IA.* xx, p. 364.
[3] *CII.* i, p. xxix.

endure)"[1] (Plate VI, i). The other two caves, called Gopikā and Vaḍathikā, bear similar inscriptions, the only significant alterations being in their names (Plates VI, ii and iii).

The caves themselves are impressive monuments to the patience and skill of Mauryan craftsmen and to the honour in which the Ājīvikas were held at the time. The hills in which they are located must have been especially popular with hermits, for they seem to be covered with the traces of religious occupants, both Buddhist and Hindu.[2] In the time of Cunningham the caves were visited by thousands of pilgrims annually,[3] and presumably are still so visited. When Cunningham inspected them the floors were strewn to a depth of three feet with broken pottery and brick, among which were mixed fragments of stone pillars, indicating that at one time the caves had had porticos or cloisters of some sort.

Of the caves on Barābar Hill, that now called Karṇa Chopār (Plate VII, i), which contains the third Aśokan inscription, measures 33 ft. 6½ in. by 14 ft. by 10 ft. 9 in.[4] The roof is vaulted, and the whole surface of the granite walls of the cave is polished. The interior is of a plain rectangular shape, and contains a small platform, raised 1 ft. 3 in. from the floor level, and measuring 7 ft. 6 in. by 2 ft. 6 in. On the doorway of the cave are inscriptions in Gupta characters: "*Bodhimūla*" and "*Daridrakāntāra*" which suggest that at some time the cave was taken over by Buddhists. Other Gupta inscriptions appear to be the autographs of visitors.

The cave now called Sudāma (Plate VII, ii), in the inscription referred to as the Nigoha cave, consists of two apartments. The outer one, entered by a small recessed doorway at the side, measures 32 ft. 9 in. in length by 19 ft. 6 in. in breadth, and has an arched roof rising from a height of 6 ft. 9 in. at the walls to 12 ft. 3 in. at the centre. The inner chamber is approximately circular, of 19 ft. 11 in.–19 ft. diameter; its outer wall, facing

1 *Vahiyak[ā] kubhā Daṣalathena Devānaṃpiyenā*
ānaṃtaliyaṃ abhisitenā [Ājīvikehi]
bhadaṃtehi vāṣa-niṣidiyāye niṣiṭhe
ā-caṃdama-sūliyaṃ. Bühler, *IA.* xx, p. 364. The interpretation of *vāṣa-niṣidiyāye* is that of Fleet (*JRAS.* 1906, p. 404).

2 Cunningham, *Four Reports* . . . Vol. i, p. 41.

3 Ibid., p. 43.

4 Ibid., p. 45.

PLATE VI.

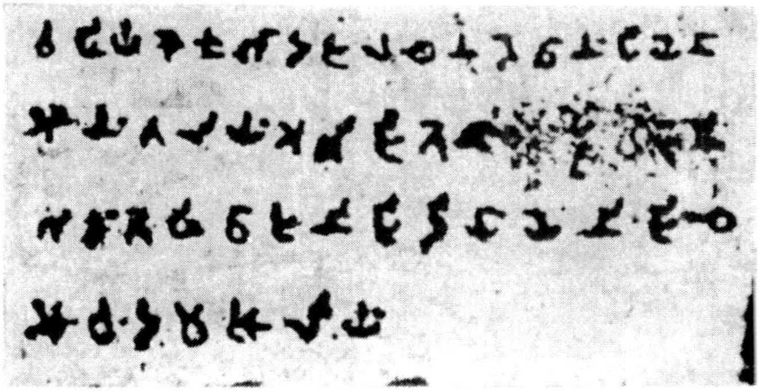

(i) Vahiyakā Cave.

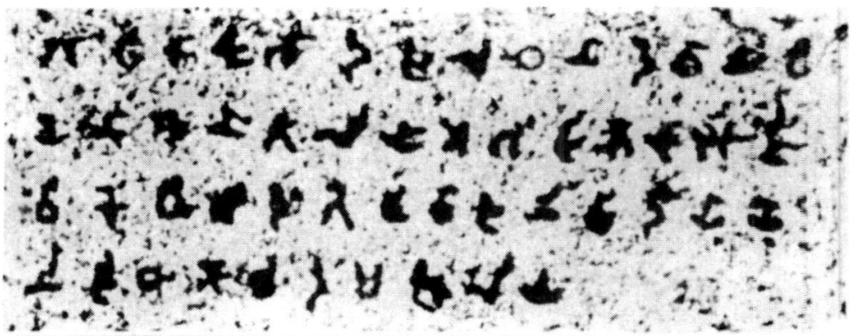

(ii) Gopikā Cave.

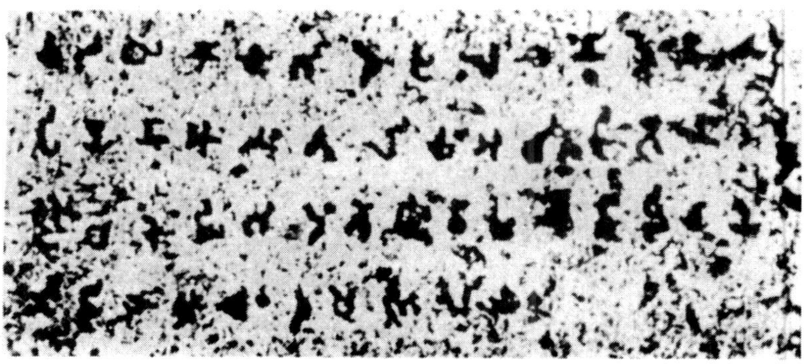

(iii) Vaḍathikā Cave.

NAGÂRJUNÎ CAVE INSCRIPTIONS.
(From *IA*, xx.)
Scale : one-fourth approx.

on the rectangular outer chamber, is undercut " to represent thatch with its overhanging eaves ".[1] The whole structure is of the same high polish as the others.

The cave of the second inscription, called in modern times the Viśvâmitra cave (Plate VII, iv), is of similar design, with a circular inner chamber of about 11 feet in diameter, somewhat smaller than that of the Sudāma, which is unpolished, and apparenty incomplete. The outer chamber is cut straight back from the rock face, and the entrance, according to Cunningham's diagram, extends to the full height and breadth of the chamber. Its length is 14 feet and its breadth 8 ft. 4 in. The Aśokan inscription is engraved on the right-hand wall near the entrance. The floor of the cave contains four socket-holes, which apparently held timber framing.[2]

The fourth cave of the Barābar group (Plate VII, iii) contains no Aśokan inscription. This is the Lomas Ṛṣi, the structure and dimensions of which are very similar to those of the Sudāma cave. The outer chamber is polished, but the inner chamber is rough-hewn. Cunningham suggests that the work was abandoned on reaching a deep fissure, which forms one of the natural lines of cleavage of the rock. The similarity of interior workmanship and design convinced Cunningham that the Sudāma and Lomas Ṛṣi caves had been excavated at the same time and for the same religious purpose, and that an Aśokan inscription originally existed in the porch, and was removed when the latter was enlarged.[3] The carved porch of the Lomas Ṛṣi cave is its most outstanding feature. This highly finished entrance, with its frieze of elephants, was thought by Cunningham to have been constructed in the Gupta period, since an epigraph of Anantavarman Maukhari is to be found inscribed above it. This view was supported by Fleet,[4] but few would now subscribe to it. The arch is carved in slavish imitation of timber construction, and this, and other details of its workmanship and design, indicate a much earlier date.[5] Fergusson recognized that the façade was of approximately the same period as the cave itself.[6] The row of elephants above the entrance emerges from two

[1] Ibid., p. 46. [2] Ibid., pp. 47–8. [3] Ibid., p. 47. [4] *CII.* iii, p. 222.
[5] Brown, *Indian Architecture*, p. 13.
[6] *History of Indian . . . Architecture*, 1910 edn., vol. i, p. 131.

crocodile-like *makaras* at either side, and appears to be worshipping three *caityas*. Whether these elephants are specifically Ājīvika symbols cannot be decided with certainty. The "Last Sprinkling Elephant" was one of the eight finalities (*carimāiṃ*) of the Ājīvikas,[1] and King Harṣa of Kashmir, who may have been a patron of the sect, introduced an elephant motif on his coins[2]; but these feeble indications are very inconclusive. From the *Bhagavatī Sūtra* it would seem that the Ājīvikas, like their rivals, respected *caityas*,[3] which were probably sacred sites in pre-Āryan times. It is not therefore impossible that the façade of the Lomas Ṛṣi cave was added by a later patron of the Ājīvikas, not long after the death of Aśoka.

The Lomas Ṛṣi cave bears on the door-jamb the short inscriptions *Bodhimūla* and *Kleśa-kāntāra*, in Gupta characters of two different sizes and hands. This indicates its later occupation by Buddhists. Above the porch is a longer inscription of Anantavarman Maukhari,[4] in which he records that he placed in the cave an image of Kṛṣṇa. Anantavarman apparently visited the Hill before his accession to the throne, for the inscription refers to his father Śārdūlavarman in the present tense, and gives the son no royal titles.[5] It must therefore have been engraved shortly before *c.* A.D. 450,[6] and the caves cannot have been evacuated by the Ājīvikas at a later date than this.

Of the three Nāgârjunī caves the Gopikā (Plate VII, v) is a single rectangular chamber, its length parallel to the rock-face, entered by a passage in the middle of its length. Its dimensions are 46 ft. 5 in. by 19 ft. 2 in., and its ends are semicircular. The vaulted roof is 6 ft. 6 in. high at the walls, rising to 10 ft. 6 in. at the centre. The interior, like those of the Barābar caves, is highly polished. As well as the dedicatory inscription of Daśaratha it bears an inscription of Anantavarman, which records that the Prince caused an image of Kātyāyanī to be placed in the cave, and gave a village, the name of which is illegible, to the support of the goddess Bhavānī, of whom Kātyāyanī appears to be an epithet.[7] A hundred years ago the cave was occupied by a Muslim holy man, but it was empty when surveyed by Cunningham.[8]

[1] V. supra, p. 68. [2] V. infra, p. 205. [3] V. supra, pp. 31–32.
[4] *CII.* iii, pp. 221–3. [5] Pires, *The Maukharis*, p. 52.
[6] Ibid., chart opposite p. 156. [7] *CII.* iii, pp. 226–8.
[8] Cunningham, op. cit., pp. 48–9.

PLATE VII.

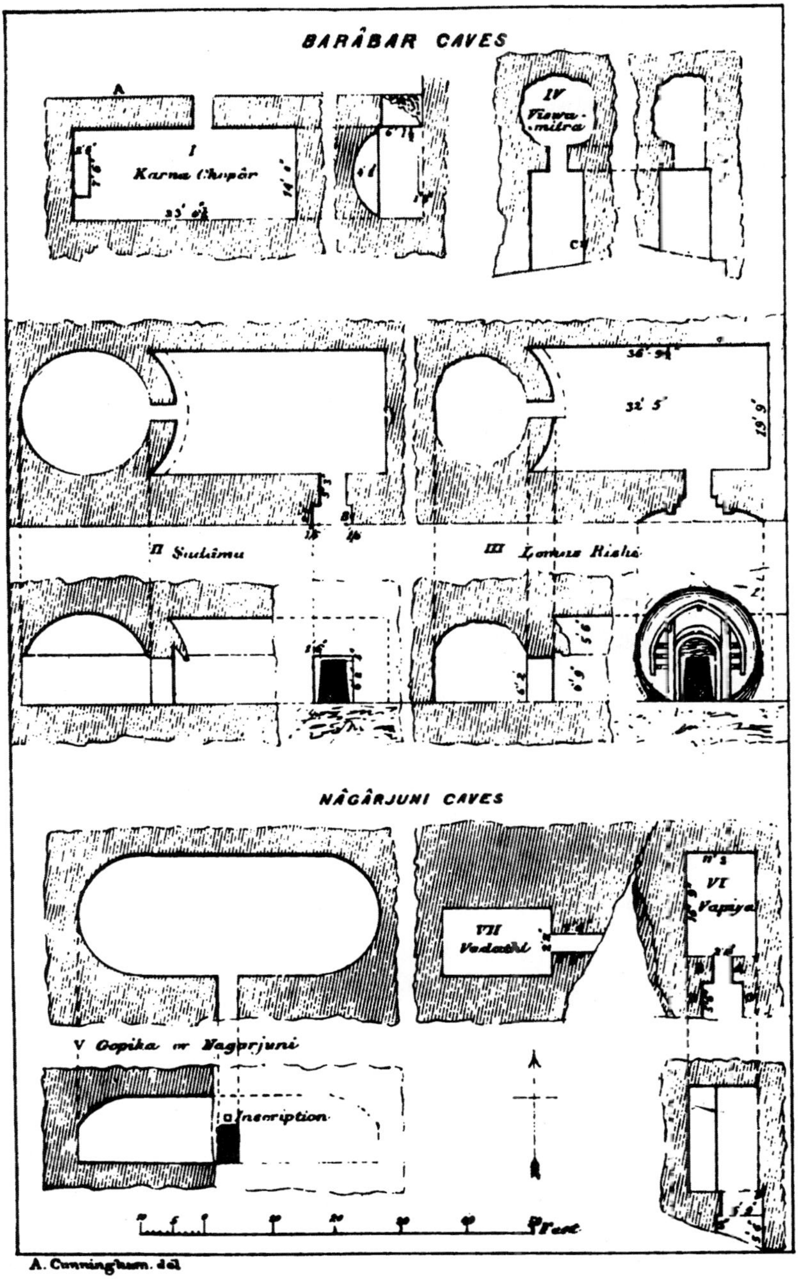

A. Cunningham. del.

Plans of the

BARĀBAR AND NĀGÂRJUNĪ CAVES.

(From Cunningham, *Four Reports*, vol. i.)

The Vahiyakā cave (Plate VII, vi) consists of a single rectangular chamber measuring 16 ft. 9 in. by 11 ft. 3 in., entered by a small porch and a narrow doorway. The vaulted roof is 10 ft. 6 in. at its highest point. Like those of the other caves, the whole interior is highly polished. Near its entrance is a well 23 feet deep, from which fact Cunningham interpreted the inscription of Daśaratha to read *Vapīyakā-kubhā* ("the Well Cave").[1] It bears no Maukhari inscription, but one in characters of a somewhat later style records that "Ācārya Śrī Yogânanda does reverence to Śiva".[2] Like the two other Nāgârjunī caves, this was later occupied by Muslim hermits.

The third cave, the Vaḍathikā, (Pl. VII, vii) is entered by a very narrow passage, 7 ft. 2 in. long by only 2 ft. 10 in. wide, which was originally closed by a wooden door, the socket-holes of which remain. It is smaller and less imposing than the other two Nāgârjunī caves, the chamber being only 16 ft. 4 in. long. Cunningham gives its breadth as 4 ft. 3 in., but this seems to be a misprint; his small diagram suggests a breadth of about 10 feet. The cave has been divided into two by a rude brick wall of which "the only opening to the inner room appears to be too small for the passage of any grown-up man, and could only have been used by the occupant for the reception of food". Cunningham does not state how he managed to pass through this small opening to survey the whole room; presumably the wall was partly broken down when he visited the caves.[3] He gives no estimate of the date of the construction of this interior partition, but there seems no special reason to believe that it had any connection with the cave's first Ājīvika occupants. It is known, however, that the Ājīvikas sometimes performed penances in large jars,[4] and it may be that even the earliest occupants of the caves also practised self-immurement. This cave also contains an inscription of Anantavarman Maukhari, recording that he installed in it an image of Bhūtapati and Devī, probably an *Ardhanārīśvara* figure of Śiva.[5]

[1] Ibid., p. 50.

[2] *Ācārya śrī Yogânanda praṇamati Siddheśvara.* Cunningham, op. cit., pl. xx, no. viii. In Cunningham's eye copy there seems to be no trace of *visarga* or *anusvāra*. The Ācārya's name is also recorded in the Gopikā Cave.

[3] Cunningham, op. cit., pp. 50–1.

[4] V. supra, p. 111.

[5] *CII.* iii, pp. 223–5.

The large cave chambers of Nāgârjunī were excavated, as the inscriptions proclaim, as shelters for Ājīvika ascetics during the rainy season. The caves of Lomas Ṛṣi, Sudāma, and Viśvâmitra, of the Barābar group, apparently served a different purpose, for all possess a circular inner chamber, which seems to have been a sanctuary of some sort. This inner chamber is in the spot which, in Buddhist cave temples, is occupied by the *stūpa*, or symbolic mound, hewn out of the living rock.[1] Only two caves of the Lomas Ṛṣi type are known, other than those of Barābar. Of these one, at Guntupaḷḷi in the Kistna District of Madras Province, which contains a *stūpa*, is thought to be a little later in date than those of Barābar.[2]

This cave is not far distant from the region where Ājīvikas are known to have persisted in comparative strength until the Middle Ages.[3] In the tenth century a village called Ācuvulapaṟṟu, the name of which may contain the Tamil inscriptional form of the word Ājīvika, existed in the same neighbourhood.[4] It is therefore not impossible that the Guntupaḷḷi cave was also once an Ājīvika hermitage.

The second cave, at Kondīvte near Bombay, is Buddhist. It is of later construction, but it retains the circular inner chamber with a *stūpa*.[5] It is possible that the Barābar caves originally also contained *stūpas*, not hewn from the rock, but artificially erected and since removed.

In the designs of the Lomas Ṛṣi and Sudāma caves we probably have a representation in stone of the earliest Ājīvika meeting-place—a rectangular courtyard, at one end of which was a circular thatched hut, perhaps containing some sacred symbol. This, no doubt, was the *Ājīviya-sabhā* of the *Uvāsaga Dasāo*.[6]

The fact that these caves are the earliest surviving religious edifices in India suggests that the Ājīvikas were the first community to use material more solid than wood for religious purposes. That Aśoka should have gone to so much expense and

1 Fergusson, *History of Indian . . . Architecture*, p. 131.
2 Brown, *Indian Architecture*, p. 19.
3 V. infra, pp. 187 ff.
4 V. infra, p. 187.
5 Brown, loc. cit. Fergusson, *Cave Temples of India*, pp. 360–1.
6 V. supra, pp. 115–16.

PLATE VIII.

FAÇADE OF THE LOMAS ṚṢI CAVE.
(From *JBORS*, xii.)

trouble to provide the community with hermitages is indicative of his support of the sect, and of its influence in Magadha at the time. That Daśaratha, Aśoka's grandson, should have recorded that he dedicated the Nāgârjunī caves immediately after his consecration strongly indicates that he bestowed his special favour on the sect. The fact that his name is omitted from the king-lists both of the Buddhists and of the Jainas suggests that he was looked on with disfavour by both sects, perhaps on account of his patronage of the Ājīvikas.[1]

But the prosperity of the Ājīvikas, and their enjoyment of the patronage of the Kings of Magadha, may not have been long-lasting. The inscriptions of Aśoka and Dasaratha have been mutilated or defaced, most of them in such a manner as to indicate that the original inhabitants of the caves were evicted in favour of their religious opponents. Of the three Aśokan inscriptions of the Barābar caves that of the Karṇa Chopār (Pl. V, iii) has been so badly defaced as to be almost illegible; the Sudāma inscription has the word *s'âbhisitenā* in the first line and *ājīvikehi* in the second effaced (Pl. V, i); while of the Viśvâmitra cave inscription (Pl. V, ii) the *akṣaras ā, jī,* and *vi* only are effaced, while the rest of the inscription is remarkably clear and legible. Of the three Daśaratha inscriptions of the Nāgârjunī caves, that in the Vahiyakā (Pl. VI, i) has the whole word *Ājīvikehi* obliterated; the Gopikā cave inscription shows no signs of deliberate defacement, although some *akṣaras* are badly worn (Pl. VI, ii); while the Vaḍathikā cave inscription (Pl. VI, iii) is defaced in two letters—the *Ā* and *jī* of *Ājīvikehi.*

The selective nature of most of these defacements indicates that they were carried out by the religious rivals of the Ājīvikas, who made use of the caves after them, and did not wish to be reminded of the former occupants. The evidence of later inscriptions, and of the other remains in the vicinity, shows that, after the Ājīvikas, the caves were occupied by Buddhist, Hindu, and Muslim in turn. Of these, it is improbable that the Muslims were responsible for the defacement of the inscriptions, for it appears that, by the time of the Muslim invasion, the Brahmī alphabet was illegible even to the most learned Brāhmaṇas.[2]

[1] De la Vallée Poussin, *L'Inde aux Temps des Mauryas,* pp. 165–6.
[2] Ishwari Prasad, *History of Mediaeval India,* p. 290.

Hultzsch has suggested that the inscriptions were defaced at the time of the installation of the Hindu images by Anantavarman.[1] There is little to be said in favour of this view, which rests on a very slender basis, and is disproved by the fact that the only cave inscription in which the word *Ājīvikehi* remains quite intact, that of the Gopikā cave on Nāgârjunī Hill, is one of the three in which Anantavarman placed a Hindu ikon.[2] If the defacement had been the work of the carvers of the Maukhari inscriptions they would surely have taken special care to obliterate all record of the Ājīvikas in those caves which their master had dedicated to Hindu deities.

A very clever suggestion has been put forward by Dr. A. Banerji Sastri.[3] The Hill of Barābar, called Khalatika in the Aśokan inscriptions, was known in the time of Anantavarman as Pravaragiri. It also had another name, which is incised in the rock in Brahmī characters, in two forms, Gorathagiri and Goradhagiri.[4] The *Mahābhārata* refers to a hill of the same name as situated not far from Rājagṛha.[5] According to Jayaswal's reading of the Hāthīgumphā inscription of Khāravela, that king occupied Gorathagiri in the eighth year of his reign, in the course of his Magadhan campaign. A clause in the 7th–8th line of the inscription is read by Jayaswal as: "*Aṭhame ca vase mahati senāya maha*[*ta-bhitti*]*-Goradhagiriṃ ghātāpayitā Rājagahaṃ upapīḍāpayati.*"[6] This Jayaswal translates: "In the eighth year he (Khāravela) having got stormed (*sic*) the Gorathagiri (fortress) of great enclosure (lit. 'wall', 'barrier') by a great army causes pressure around Rājagṛha."[7] The word *Goradhagiri*, supposed by Jayaswal to exist at the end of the seventh line of the inscription, is not definitely legible in the reproduction to which he refers,[8] but his reading is apparently supported by Konow[9] and also by other competent authorities,[10] and does not seem to be questioned in this particular. Banerji Sastri[11] suggests that Khāravela, known to be an earnest Jaina, was responsible for the expulsion of the Ājīvikas from the caves, the mutilation

1 *CII.* i, p. xxviii.
2 V. supra, p. 134.
3 *JBORS.* xii, pp. 53–62.
4 Jackson, *JBORS.* i, pp. 159–172.
5 *Mbh. Sabhā* xviii, 30 (Poona edn.).
6 *JBORS.* iv, p. 399.
7 Ibid., pp. 378–9.
8 *JBORS.* iii, opp. p. 472.
9 *Acta Orientalia* i, pp. 12–42.
10 *PHAI.*, p. 348. Sircar, *Select Inscriptions*, vol. i, p. 208.
11 *JBORS.* xii, pp. 60–1.

of the inscriptions of Aśoka and Daśaratha, and the carving of the façade of the Lomas Ṛṣi cave. He believes that the façade shows resemblances to those of the Jaina caves of Udayagiri, in one of which Khāravela's inscription is found; he admits that these resemblances are not striking, but points specially to the monsters at the corners of the frieze of the Lomas Ṛṣi cave, which are very similar in design to those at Udayagiri, where the elephants are replaced by lotuses or lions.

This argument is not convincing, but is a mere expression of possibility. It seems more plausible if we adopt Jayaswal's date, and place Khāravela in the first half of the second century B.C.[1] But few recent authorities would admit that he reigned so early; the latter half of the first century B.C. is the date now usually favoured for the Khāravela inscription, which must thus have been inscribed a century or more after those of Daśaratha.[2] The Lomas Ṛṣi façade seems to be either Mauryan or immediately post-Mauryan—the very primitive imitation of woodwork in the design,[3] and the early form of the crocodile-like creatures to the right and left of the frieze,[4] point to an early date for its construction.

Even though Khāravela may not have caused the carving of the entrance to the Lomas Ṛṣi cave it is still possible that he was responsible for the eviction of the Ājīvikas and for the defacement of the Mauryan inscriptions. But the evidence is quite inconclusive. On the basis of a barely legible inscription Khāravela is said to have occupied the hill, and he is known to have been a Jaina; these are the only facts on which the argument is based. Any local Magadhan ruler between the Maurya and Gupta periods is an equally possible persecutor of the Ājīvikas.

The Ājīvikas must have lost possession of the caves and the inscriptions must have been defaced at some time before the fifth century A.D., and probably before the commencement of the Gupta era, at a period when the Brahmī alphabet was still widely understood. Whether the Ājīvikas voluntarily abandoned the caves or were forcibly evicted, it is evident that their influence

[1] *JBORS.* iv, p. 369.
[2] Sircar, *Select Inscriptions*, vol. i, p. 206, n. 1.
[3] Fergusson, *Cave Temples of India*, p. 38.
[4] Vogel, *Revue des Arts Asiatiques*, vi, p. 138.

waned rapidly in Magadha from the end of the Maurya period onwards. We find no later material or epigraphic remains of them in Northern India, and although references to them occur in Sanskrit literature for over a thousand years after the deaths of their Maurya patrons, these are brief and few. It is doubtful if they were again a significant factor in North Indian culture.

CHAPTER IX

ĀJĪVIKAS IN LATER TIMES

REFERENCES IN SANSKRIT LITERATURE

After the Mauryas the Ājīvikas, although occasionally mentioned in Sanskrit literature, never again appear in Northern India as serious rivals to the greater sects. The passages from the early Buddhist and Jaina scriptures may indeed have taken final shape at a comparatively late period, but the flourishing Ājīvika community referred to therein seems to be a recollection of Maurya and pre-Maurya times, rather than a picture of conditions in the fourth and fifth centuries A.D.

In the *Arthaśāstra* the Ājīvikas are mentioned once. The householder who feeds *Śākyas*, Ājīvikas, or other base mendicants at sacrificial or commemorative ceremonies is to be fined a hundred (*paṇas*).[1] The Ājīvika is mentioned with the Buddhist as the leading representative of the heretical orders. He is still a significant force in the community, for he, and not the *Nirgrantha*, comes second in the list. The latter is presumably included in the general group of base mendicants of other sects. It will be remembered that Aśoka, in the Seventh Pillar Edict, gave the Ājīvika precedence over the *Nirgrantha*,[2] and the absence of reference to the latter by name in this passage suggests an early date for at least this regulation of the *Arthaśāstra*. Had it been composed as late as the third century A.D., as Keith supposes,[3] surely the *Nirgrantha* would have been mentioned in preference to the Ājīvika as a typical representative of heterodoxy. By this time there is ample archæological evidence to show that

[1] *Śāky-ājīvak'-ādīn vṛṣala-pravrajitān devapitṛ-kāryeṣu bhojayataś śatyo daṇḍaḥ. Arthaśāstra* iii, 20, p. 199.

[2] V. supra, p. 150.

[3] *Asutosh Mookerji Commemoration Volume*, pt. i, pp. 8–22.

Jainism was widespread, while similar evidence of Ājīvikism is non-existent.

The *Mahābhārata*, with its many strata, cannot well be attributed to any century. No doubt it was in process of receiving final shape during the period between the Maurya and the Gupta dynasties, and its contents may be taken as indicative of the climate of thought and of social conditions in Western India during that period. It contains no reference to the Ājīvikas—indeed it appears to contain no specific references to the greater heterodox orders of Buddhism and Jainism; but, besides the strange story of Maṅki,[1] it has a number of passages very similar in content to the doctrine of Makkhali Gosāla as outlined in the *Sāmañña-phala Sutta*. This perhaps indicates that Gosāla's teachings were by no means uninfluential. We have already suggested that he did but systematize an attitude to life which must have existed long before the emergence of the sect, and which may even have been found among Āryan warriors before their entry into India.[2] The Ājīvika sect must have acted as a stimulus to such an attitude, which is explicitly expressed in several *Mahābhārata* references.[3]

Though the Ājīvika doctrine of fate may have found its supporters the sect itself continued to decline. A reference in the *Vāyu Purāṇa* seems to depict the Ājīvikas struggling for survival, as a sort of secret society. The relevant passage follows a description of the goblins (*piśācā*), who lurk at twilight among ruined houses, at crossroads, and at other places of doubtful omen. "Roads, rivers, fords, *caitya*-trees, highways—*piśācas* have entered all these places. Those unrighteous people the Ājīvas, as ordained by the gods, are the confusers of *varṇa* and *āśrama*, a people of workmen and craftsmen. Goblins are the divinities in their sacrifices, which they perform with wealth (stolen) from beings who resemble the immortals (i.e. brāhmaṇas) and (gained by acting as) police spies, and with much other ill-gotten wealth, and with honey, meat, broth, ghee, sesamum, powder, wine, spirits, incense, greens, *kṛśara* (boiled sesamum and rice), oil, fragrant grass (? *bhadra*), treacle, and porridge. The Lord Brahma likewise appointed black garments, incense,

[1] V. supra, pp. 38–39. [2] V. supra, p. 7. [3] V. infra, p. 218.

and flowers to be the oblations of the goblins at the quarters of the moon." [1]

The equivalence of the Ājīva here mentioned and the Ājīvika is attested by the lexicographers.[2] The *Vāyu*, which is mentioned by Bāṇa and refers to the Guptas, is probably an early specimen of its class.[3] In it the habits of the Ājīvikas seem to have changed very considerably since the days of Makkhali Gosāla. The sect has developed a magical and sacrificial cult, and its members are typified not as naked ascetics but as workmen and craftsmen. We may conclude that this description represents the Ājīvikas at a later stage than do any of the Buddhist or Jaina references so far considered. It is perhaps a picture of the degenerate remnant of the Ājīvika lay community in North India during the Gupta period.

The same text gives a description of *nagna* ascetics, who should not under any circumstances be allowed to be present at *śrāddha* ceremonies. "Formerly brāhmaṇas, kṣattriyas, vaiśyas, and śūdras were perverted into heretics by the *Asuras*, defeated in the battle of gods and demons. This (perversion) is not the creation of the Self-existent. Since the *nirgranthas* who perform no *śrāddha* and the ragged (beggars) live by force, they who do not live righteously are the naked (ascetics) and other peoples. The twice-born man with vainly matted locks, vainly tonsured, vainly naked, (performing) vain fasts, muttering vain (*mantras*)—he is of the naked (ascetics) and other (heretical) peoples, base-born men, outcastes, the destroyers of prosperity. Although they do not perish as a result of the deeds which they commit,

[1] *Patho nadyo 'tha tīrthāni caitya-vṛkṣān mahāpathān*
Piśācā viniviṣṭā vai sthāneṣv eteṣu sarvaśaḥ. 284.
Adharmikā janās te vai Ājīvā vihitāḥ suraiḥ
Varṇâśramāḥ saṅkarikāḥ kāru-śilpi-janās tathā. 285.
Amṛtôpama-sāttvānāṃ cauraviśvāsa-ghātinām
Etair anyaiś ca bahubhir anyāy'-ôpārjitair dhanair,
Ārabhante kriyā yās tu, piśācās tatra devatāḥ, 286.
Madhu-māṃs'-audanair dadhnā tila-cūrṇa-sur'-âsavaiḥ
Dhūpair hāridra-kṛśarais taila-bhadra-guḍ'-âudanaiḥ. 287.
Kṛṣṇāni c' aiva vāsāṃsi dhūpāḥ sumanasas tathā
Evaṃ yuktāḥ subalayas teṣāṃ vai parva-sandhiṣu
Piśācānām anujñāya Brahmā so 'dhipatir dadau. 288.

Vāyu, 69. The text is obscure and corrupt. On the second line of v. 285 I have translated *Varṇâsramāḥ saṅkarikāḥ* as though a single compound adjective. My rendering of the first line of v. 286 is very tentative.

[2] V. infra, pp. 182–84.

[3] Winternitz, *Geschichte der indischen Literatur*, i, p. 463.

they are well known as men of evil courses. In vain does the conceited man go to a *śrāddha* ceremony or to (a sacrifice) performed by them." [1]

This passage, as well as that previously quoted, seems to be very corrupt, and has a number of variant readings. Among these an alternative for the second half of verse 30 may be of significance. As well as the reading *śaktyā jīvanti karpaṭāḥ* there is the variant *Śākyā puṣṭi-kalaṃśakāḥ*.[2] The word *puṣṭi-kalaṃśakāḥ* here seems to be out of place, since it occurs again at the end of verse 32, where it is probably a corruption of *puṣṭi-vināśakāḥ*. On comparing these two versions, both of which are probably corrupt, we are tempted to offer the tentative reconstruction: *Ye viśrāddhaka-nirgranthāḥ Śāky'-Ājīvika-karpaṭāḥ*. This, with the first half of the following verse, might be translated: "The *nirgranthas*, who perform no *śrāddha*, the Buddhist (*Śākya*) and Ājīvika ragged mendicants (and) they who do not live according to *dharma* are the *nagna* people etc."

In the first *Vāyu Purāṇa* reference we read of the Ājīvas, apparently prosperous craftsmen and artisans, who devote their ill-earned wealth to the worship of the goblins who haunt the sacred groves, with ceremonies suggestive of later tantrism.[3] In the second passage we have a group of false ascetics, naked and otherwise (*nagn'-âdi*), who, like the Ājīvas, are the objects of the scorn and opprobrium of the orthodox. Whatever reading we accept for the crucial second half of the 30th verse of the

[1] *Brāhmaṇāḥ kṣattriyā vaiśyā vṛṣalāś c'aiva sarvaśaḥ*
Purā devâsure yuddhe nirjitair asurais tadā 29.
Pāṣaṇḍa-vaikṛtās tāta, n' aiṣā sṛṣṭiḥ Svayaṃbhuvaḥ.
Yad viśrāddhaka-nirgranthāḥ śaktyā jīvanti karpaṭāḥ. 30.
Ye dharmaṃ n' ânuvartante, te vai nagn'-âdayo janāḥ.
Vṛthā-jaṭī vṛthā-muṇḍī vṛthā-nagnaś ca yo dvijaḥ 31.
Vṛthā-vratī vṛthā-jāpī te vai nagn'-âdayo janāḥ
Kul'-âdhamā Niṣādāś ca tathā puṣṭi-vināśakāḥ. 32.
Kṛta-karm'-âkṣitās tv ete kupathāḥ parikīrtitāḥ,
Ebhir nirvṛttaṃ vā śrāddhaṃ vṛthā gacchati mānavān. 33.
Vāyu, 78. In the Poona text the second half of v. 32 reads: *Kulandhamā nikāśāś ca tathā puṣṭi-kalaṃśakāḥ*. For this I have substituted a variant reading (p. 291, n. 21); and I have altered *kulandhamā* to *kulâdhamā*. Otherwise the text seems almost unintelligible.

[2] *Vāyu* (Poona edn.), p. 291, n. This reading is accepted by the Calcutta text (vol. i, p. 191).

[3] An alternative interpretation might be offered that the goblins receive, by decree of Brahma, the offerings intended by the Ājīvas for other divinities.

second passage, it is clear that the group *nagn'-âdi* must include the ascetic leaders of the Ājīvas of the first passage; unless indeed the author of the first passage has confused ascetics and goblins, and the *piśācas* who lurk in the twilight in ruined buildings, in groves, and at crossroads actually represent the Ājīvika ascetics, who, like the Bodhisatta Ājīvika of the *Jātaka*,[1] fled at the sight of men, no doubt in this case owing to rising popular antagonism.

This puzzling reference in the *Vāyu Purāṇa* leaves many questions unsettled, but at least it indicates that there survived in North India in Gupta times an Ājīvika community, which had by now become corrupt and was probably rapidly declining.

Mahāyāna Buddhist literature refers to Ājīvikas in connection with its legends of the Buddha, but otherwise takes little note of them. The *Lalita Vistara* mentions them briefly in a list of ascetics which includes *carakas*, *parivrājakas*, *vṛddhaśrāvakas*, *gautamas*, and *nirgranthas*.[2] They are included in a similar list in the *Saddharma-Puṇḍarīka*,[3] where it is stated that a Bodhisattva does not associate with them.

More significant is a reference in Kumāradāsa's *Jānakīharaṇa*. Here Rāvaṇa, planning the rape of Sītā, approaches Rāma's hermitage in the guise of "a *maskarin*, a false Ājīvika, his head adorned with piled and matted locks".[4] Here the word *maskarin* is employed with *Ājīvika*, but in other references it would seem to refer to ascetics of a different type[5]; we have already suggested that the term included any mendicant bearing a staff.[6] The matted locks of this false Ājīvika are not altogether consistent with the description of Ājīvikas in earlier sources, where they are said to have pulled out their hair by the roots.[7] We cannot decide whether the author was using the term loosely, whether he was ill-informed as to the habits of Ājīvikas, or whether he had in mind a sub-sect of the Ājīvika order which had abandoned the custom of tonsure.

[1] V. supra, p. 110.
[2] *Lalita-Vistara*, ed. Lefmann, vol. i, p. 380, l. 12.
[3] xiii, Kern edn., pp. 275–6.
[4] *Dambh'-âjīvikam uttuṅga-jaṭā-maṇḍita-mastakam*
Kañcin maskariṇaṃ Sītā dadarś' âśramam āgatam. x, 76.
[5] V. supra, pp. 99–100.
[6] V. supra, p. 100.
[7] V. supra, p. 106.

The *Jānakī-haraṇa*, the authorship of which is attributed to a King of Ceylon, is thought to have a southern or Sinhalese provenance.[1] The *Bhaṭṭi-kāvya*, written on the same theme and at about the same time, but probably originating from Valabhī,[2] describes the ascetic guise of Rāvaṇa in terms which leave no doubt that the author has in mind a Śaivite ascetic; like Kumāradāsa's ascetic his hair is piled upon the top of his head (*śikhī*); he holds an earthen pot; he has a skull in place of the usual begging bowl; he wears two garments died with lac; and he bears a staff.[3] Mallinātha's commentary states that he must have been a *tridaṇḍin*, or Śaivite ascetic, for he is said to have a topknot, whereas the *ekadaṇḍins* or Vaiṣṇavite ascetics, with whom Ājīvikas were sometimes included, did not wear topknots.[4] The ascetic is further described as a knower of the soul (*ātma-vid*), and as maintaining the vow of a *maskarin* (*dhārayan maskari-vratam*).

In both references the ascetic is a *maskarin*, but in the former he is referred to as an Ājīvika, while in the latter he is clearly orthodox. It will be remembered that Ājīvikas survived in South India, the home of the *Jānakī-haraṇa*, while in the north they seem to have been almost forgotten. It is perhaps significant that the Southern poem at least employs the term Ājīvika, even though the sectarian affiliations of its owner may be in some doubt.

Professor D. R. Bhandarkar, however, is of the opinion that the authors of both poems were describing Ājīvikas. " Rāvaṇa . . . approaches Sītā in a disguised form (and) is called both Ājīvika and Maskarin, which must therefore be taken to be synonymous terms. In the Bhattikāvya also Rāvaṇa is represented . . . in the garb of a maskarin. Among . . . various characteristics . . . that of his being a *śikhin* is specified. From this the commentator Mallinātha argues that he was a Tridaṇḍin, and not an Ekadaṇḍin as the latter have no matted hair. But this does not agree with what Utpala says, for . . . he gives Ekadaṇḍin as a synonym of Ājīvika. The word *śikhin*

[1] Keith, *History of Sanskrit Literature*, p. 119.

[2] Ibid., p. 116.

[3] *Bhaṭṭikāvya*, v, 61–3.

[4] *D a ṇ ḍ a v ā n tridaṇḍ' îty arthaḥ. Ata eva śikh' îty uktam, ekadaṇḍinaḥ śikh'-âbhāvāt.*

of the Bhaṭṭikāvya . . . agrees with the *uttuṅga-jaṭā* of the Jānakī-haraṇa, and as the latter calls an Ājīvika a Maskarin it appears that an Ājīvika was really a Tridaṇḍin and not an Ekadaṇḍin as Utpala supposes." [1]

This argument falls to the ground when it is recognized that the terms *ājīvika* and *maskarin* are not, as Bhandarkar assumes, synonymous.[2] In its wide connotation the latter term might be applied to the Vaiṣṇavite beggar with his single staff, to the Śaivite with his triple staff, to the staff-bearing Ājīvika, perhaps even to the Digambara Jaina, who also carried a staff, and no doubt to many nondescript religious mendicants who habitually carried staves. It seems, however, that the term *maskarin* was most frequently applied to the Śaivite ascetic. For example the *Harṣacarita* introduces a *maskarin* who comes as a messenger from the great Śaivite ascetic Bhairavâcārya to the court of Harṣa's ancestor Puṣyabhūti. His figure is graphically described by Bāṇa, and has few characteristics in common with the Ājīvika. He wears a ragged robe, which is stained red ; he has a skull, which he uses as a begging bowl and stores in a box of *kharjūra* wood ; and he possesses various other articles which hang from a pole over his shoulder. He is evidently a Śaivite like his master.[3]

In the same text we find that " renowned *maskarins*, who had correctly learnt the truths of the soul ",[4] attended the court of Harṣa's father, Prabhākaravardhana. These are evidently orthodox ascetics. The lexicographers also show that the *maskarin* and the Ājīvika were, from the doctrinal point of view, in different categories.[5]

Dr. Barua [6] cites references from the *Pañcatantra* and the *Mudrārākṣasa* to *kṣapaṇakas* whose characters and descriptions " combine the Jaina with the Ājīvika ". Those in the former reference do honour to Jinendra.[7] In the latter [8] one of the spies of Cāṇakya, the great minister of Candragupta, is a tonsured

[1] *IA*. xli, p. 290.
[2] V. supra, pp. 99–100.
[3] Ed. Führer, pp. 152–3.
[4] *Yathāvad-adhigat'-âdhyātma-tattvās . . . saṃstutā maskariṇaḥ*. *Harṣacarita*, ed. Führer, p. 239.
[5] V. infra, p. 182.
[6] *JDL*. ii, pp. 62 ff.
[7] *Pañcatantra* v, 1. Bühler edn., vol. iii, pp. 38–41.
[8] The character called simply *Kṣapaṇaka*, in *Mudrārākṣasa*, act iv.

ascetic who respects the teaching of the *Arhants*, foretells the future, and uses the slogan: "There is no sin for the true believers" (*N' atthi pāvaṃ sāvagāṇaṃ*). The *kṣapaṇakas* in the former reference seem to be Jainas, and the ascetic of the latter also suggests a Jaina in most particulars. We can draw no inferences from the fact that he was a fortune-teller, for fortune-telling was the trade not only of Ājīvikas, but of ascetics of all orders, as Barua himself admits. The only hint of Ājīvikism in this figure is the antinomianism of his slogan, which suggests the doctrine ascribed by the Buddhists to Pūraṇa Kassapa and Pakudha Kaccāyana.[1] It is therefore possible that Viśākhadatta did introduce an Ājīvika trait into the character of his ascetic.

Another doubtful case is to be found in the *Harṣacarita*. Prince Harṣa, following his brother Rājyavardhana against the Hūṇas, hears of the illness of his father, Prabhākaravardhana, while somewhere to the north of the capital Sthānvīśvara. On his way back to his dying father he meets an evil omen in the form of a naked ascetic (*nagn'-âṭaka*), his body covered with many days' accumulation of dirt, and "marked with a peacock's plume".[2] This dirty and repulsive character suggests a Digambara Jaina monk, with his peacock-feather brush. On the other hand mysterious naked ascetics, also called *nagn'-âṭakas*, appear in Kashmīr in the eleventh century.[3] These seem not to have been Jainas, and may have been Ājīvikas. In South India we find Digambaras and Ājīvikas living in the same districts, and the same may have happened in North-Western India, where Jainism seems to have found a home at an early date. The ascetic met by Harṣa may therefore have been an Ājīvika, although it is perhaps more probable that he was a Digambara, whose sect still survives in the same region.[4]

Varāhamihira and Utpala

The astrologer Varāhamihira, writing a century earlier than Bāṇa, seems to have known of Ājīvikas, whom he mentions in

[1] V. supra, pp. 13, 16.
[2] *Śikhi-piccha-lañcana*. *Harṣacarita*, ed. Führer, p. 213.
[3] V. infra, pp. 205 ff.
[4] Jacobi, *ERE*. vii, p. 472.

a catalogue of ascetics. His tenth century commentator, Utpala or Bhaṭṭôtpala, apparently confused them with Vaiṣṇavites, quoting in support the Jaina writer Kālakâcārya, of the fifth century. The passages have been variously explained, and are worthy of close scrutiny.

The relevant verse in Varāhamihira's *Bṛhajjātaka* states that ascetics of various orders are born under the influence of four or more powerful planets occupying a single astrological house. According to the dominant planet of the group, so will the child become an ascetic of one or other order.[1] Varāhamihira mentions seven types of ascetic, with the heavenly bodies under whose influence they are born; seven categories are further defined by Utpala, as follows :—

1. *Śākyas*, defined by Utpala as *Raktapaṭa* (Red-robed), born under the dominant influence of Mars (*Māheya*).
2. *Ājīvikas*, called by Utpala *Ekadaṇḍins*, born under Mercury (*Jña* or *Budha*).
3. *Bhikṣus*, called by Utpala *Sannyāsīs*, born under Jupiter.
4. *Vṛddhas*, called by Utpala *Vṛddhaśrāvakas* or *Kapālīs* (skull-bearing Śaivite ascetics), born under the Moon.
5. *Carakas*, called by Utpala *Cakradharas*, born under Venus (*Sita* or *Śukra*).
6. *Nirgranthas*, the member of whom is described by Utpala as a " naked ascetic without a robe, etc. ",[2] born under Saturn (*Prābhākarī* or *Saura*); and
7. *Vanyâśanas* who, according to Utpala, are eaters of what is to be found in forests—hermits eating roots and fruits. These are born under the Sun (*Ina*).

Having described each type of ascetic in turn, Utpala continues with the definitions of Kālakâcārya. These are as follows :—

Tapasvī	born under		the Sun;
Kapālika	,,	,,	the Moon;
Raktapaṭa	,,	,,	Mars;
Ekadaṇḍin	,,	,,	Mercury;

[1] *Ekasthaiś caturādibhir balayutair jātāḥ pṛthagvīryagaiḥ*
Śāky'-âjīvika-bhikṣu-vṛddha-carakā nirgrantha-vanyâśanāḥ
Māheya-jña-guru-kṣapākara-sita-prābhākar'-înaiḥ kramāt
Pravrajyā balibhiḥ samāḥ parajitais tat-svāmibhiḥ pracyutiḥ.
Bṛhajjātaka xv, 1.

[2] *Nagnaḥ kṣapaṇakaḥ prāvaraṇ'-âdi-rahitaḥ.*

Yati born under Jupiter;
Caraka ,, ,, Venus; and
Kṣapaṇaka ,, ,, Saturn.

After this quotation Utpala further defines some of the terms used by Varāhamihira. "Here the word *Vṛddhaśrāvaka* implies ascetics who serve Maheśvara, and the word *Ājīvika* those who serve Nārāyaṇa."[1]

This remarkable passage was noted by Kern,[2] who inferred from it that the Ājīvikas were orthodox Vaiṣṇava ascetics. His view was supported by Bühler.[3] The passage was studied by Hoernle,[4] who commented on it fully. "Bhaṭṭotpala (states) . . . that the Ekadaṇḍins or Ājīvikas are devotees of Nārāyaṇa, that is Viṣṇu. On the other hand Śīlâṅka, speaking of the Ekadaṇḍins in another connection, declares them to be devotees of Śiva.[5] It is clear that what these two commentators had in their mind was the class of ascetics who are still known as Daṇḍins . . . . These ascetics are usually classed as belonging to the Śaivite division of Hindus: but they are rather eclectics in that they invoke not only Śiva but also Viṣṇu as Nārāyaṇa." Hoernle then continues with a description of these ascetics, taken from the *Bombay Gazetteer*.[6] After further discussion he concludes: "Ekadaṇḍin is a general term for a class of ascetics which includes two subdivisions, the orthodox Śaivite Daṇḍins and the heterodox Jain Ājīvikas or Digambaras. (Here Hoernle refers to his own theory, considered below,[7] that the Ājīvikas merged with the Digambara Jainas.) The Jain writer Kālakâcārya, of course, meant to indicate the latter by the word ekadaṇḍin; and Varāhamihira therefore, to preclude misunderstanding, substituted the more definite term Ājīvika. The orthodox commentator, Bhaṭṭotpala, misunderstanding the

[1] *Atra vṛddhaśrāvaka-grahaṇaṃ Maheśvar'-âśritānāṃ pravrajyānām upalakṣaṇam, Ājīvika-grahaṇaṃ ca Nārāyaṇ'-âśritānām.*

[2] *Der Buddhismus und seine Geschichte in Indien*, vol. i, p. 17.

[3] *IA.* xx, p. 362.

[4] *ERE.* i, pp. 236–7.

[5] Hoernle gives no reference for this statement. Sīlâṅka's comment on *Sū. Kṛ.* ii, 6, in one place refers to *ekadaṇḍins* as performing *Vrateśvara-yāga* (fol. 401), but a few lines later he speaks of them as having undertaken the restraints and rules of the *Pāñcarātra*, which was certainly a Vaiṣṇavite sect (fol. 402).

[6] *A Gazetteer of the Bombay Presidency*, vol. ix, pt. i, p. 542.

[7] V. infra, pp. 175 ff.

position, confused the heterodox Ājīvika with the orthodox Daṇḍin." We agree with Hoernle's conclusion that the term *ekadaṇḍin*, like *maskarin*, was a word which embraced a large class of mendicants. But he is perhaps too intuitive in recognizing Kālakâcārya's intention, and Varāhamihira's wish " to preclude misunderstanding ", which was apparently ineffectual in the case of Utpala, who " misunderstood the position ".

Even in the fifth century, when Kālakâcārya wrote, the Ājīvika must have been much rarer than most other types of staff-bearing mendicant. We believe that Kālaka intended by the term *ekadaṇḍin* not the Ājīvika, as Hoernle believes, but the whole class of ascetics bearing single staves. For astrological purposes both Vaiṣṇava *ekadaṇḍins* and Ājīvikas would be classed together on the strength of this common characteristic. In compiling the *Bṛhajjātaka* Varāhamihira probably used the term Ājīvika in preference to *ekadaṇḍin* for the simple reason that the latter term would not fit well into the metrical scheme of the *Śārdūla-vikrīḍita* stanza, with the handling of which he seems to have experienced some difficulty.

Utpala's position may be made clear by a further quotation from Kālakâcārya, occurring in the former's long commentary to the crucial verse of Varāhamihira : " The planets *Sūrya*, etc., in order are to be known as the presiding influences (*nāha*) of consecrations into the systems (*maggesu*) of Fire (*Jalaṇa*), Hara, Sugata, Keśava, Śruti, Brahman, and the Naked." [1] To this Utpala adds : " The Keśava-devotee means the Bhāgavata." [2] After the Sun and Moon Kālaka plainly intended the five planets to be read in their traditional Indian order ; Mars, Mercury, Jupiter, Venus, and Saturn. Thus Mercury, said by Varāhamihira to dominate the Ājīvika, would occur fourth on the list, and, according to Kālakâcārya's second classification would become the presiding planet of the devotee of Keśava, or Viṣṇu. When commenting on Varāhamihira Utpala must have had before him the two lists of Kālakâcārya, whom he seems to have respected highly. Kālaka declared that the ascetic born under Mercury was a devotee of Viṣṇu and an

[1] *Jalaṇa-hara-sugaä-kesava-suï-bramha-ṇagga-maggesu*
Dikkāṇaṃ ṇāävvā surāï gahā kameṇa nāha-gaūṇ.

[2] *Keśava-bhaktaḥ. Bhāgavata ity arthaḥ.*

ekadaṇḍin; Varāhamihira stated that he was an Ājīvika; both were great astrologers and worthy of Utpala's confidence; therefore the term Ājīvika implied the devotee of Nārāyaṇa.

It is, however, by no means certain that Utpala's misunderstanding was as grave as Hoernle supposed. It will be shown in the second part of this work [1] that by the time of Utpala the Southern Ājīvikas had adopted several theistic beliefs, for instance devotion to the divine Maṟkali and a theory of *avatāras*. On the other hand the Pāñcarātra Vaiṣṇavites held a theory of *niyati*, which perhaps owed something to Ājīvikism.[2] The heresy of Buddhism gradually drew nearer to the main stream from which it had deviated, and Jainism and Sikhism have done likewise. It would be surprising if at least some members of the small Ājīvika sect had not by the time of Utpala absorbed elements of the doctrines of the rising schools of theism.

Before leaving this crucial passage of Utpala's commentary we must consider the interpretation of Professor D. R. Bhandarkar,[3] which is supported by Barua.[4] According to Bhandarkar the phrases: *Atra vṛddhaśrāvaka-grahaṇaṃ Maheśvar'-āśritānāṃ pravrajyānām upalakṣaṇam, Ājīvika-grahaṇaṃ ca Nārāyaṇ'-āśritānām*, have been completely misunderstood by Kern and Bühler, because they concentrated their attention upon the second phrase without giving due consideration to the first. The true rendering of the second phase should not be; "And the use of (the term) Ājīvika refers to those who have taken refuge in Nārāyaṇa," but ". . . used as a mark to denote the monastic orders seeking refuge with Nārāyaṇa". "The point which Kern lost sight of," continues Bhandarkar, "was the word *upalakṣaṇa*, 'a mark indicative of something that the word itself does not actually express.' Sanskrit commentators often employ the word *upalakṣaṇa* when they want a certain word or expression in the original to denote things, not, truly speaking, signified by that word or expression. . . . Thus according to Utpala, Ājīvika does not signify *Nārāyaṇ-āśrita* . . . but simply indicates it. . . . The theory propounded by Professor Kern . . . has, therefore, no grounds to stand on."

[1] V. infra, pp. 275 ff.
[2] V. infra, p. 281.
[3] *IA.* xli, pp. 287–8.
[4] *JDL.* ii, p. 73.

Dr. Barua expresses gratitude to Professor Bhandarkar for his discovery of the true meaning of this passage, and gives a rather imaginative paraphrase of it. " Professor Bhandarkar," he writes, " has rendered a great service by rectifying a fatal error in the interpretation of Utpala's commentary, which led such veteran Sanskritists as Professors Kern and Bühler to suppose that the Ājīvikas were the worshippers of Nārāyaṇa, i.e. Bhāgavatas. But now thanks to Professor Bhandarkar no one doubts that Utpala's meaning was just the contrary. The Ājīvikas and the Bhāgavatas furnished him with a typical instance whereby he could illustrate *upalakṣaṇa*, a figure of Rhetoric used in characterizing what a word does not denote. ' Ājīvikagrahanaṃ ca Nārāyaṇâśritānām,' i.e. to accept one as an Ājīvika is not to denote a worshipper of Nārāyaṇa."

In fact the term *grahaṇa* in this context means simply " a word mentioned ",[1] and not, as Barua implies, " the acceptance " of one as belonging to the class denoted by the word. *Upalakṣaṇa* means " implying something that has not been expressed ",[2] the connotation of the word, as distinct from its denotation. Thus *vṛddhaśrāvaka* literally means " an elderly disciple ", but its secondary meaning or *upalakṣaṇa* is, according to Utpala, " a devotee of Śiva." Similarly *Ājīvika* means, according to the usual interpretation, " a professional ascetic " [3]; but Utpala declares that it further means " a devotee of Nārāyaṇa " by *upalakṣaṇa*.

The futility of Bhandarkar's attempt to escape this conclusion is evident without long comment. The term Ājīvika, on his interpretation of Utpala, does not " refer " to worshippers of Nārāyaṇa, but " is used as a mark to denote " them. It does not " signify " them, but " simply indicates " them. For all these hair-splitting distinctions without difference Professor Bhandarkar cannot show that Utpala's phrase means any more than : " The word Ājīvika connotes a worshipper of Nārāyaṇa."

On Dr. Barua's interpretation of Professor Bhandarkar's explanation of this passage any comment is unnecessary.

As with so many other references to the Ājīvikas, we cannot

[1] Monier Williams, *Sanskrit–English Dictionary*, s.v.
[2] Ibid., s.v. *upalakṣaṇa*.
[3] V. supra, pp. 101–2.

draw final conclusions from this quotation from Utpala. Certainly he believed that the Ājīvikas were Vaiṣṇavites. This conclusion may have been reached after the rule of thumb equation of Varāhamihira's Ājīvika with Kālaka's *ekadaṇḍin*, but it is possible that Utpala had heard something, perhaps at third or fourth hand, of the Dravidian Ājīvikas, some of whom had by this time become theistic in their outlook. From the space which Utpala devoted to the explanation of the term, it would seem that it was by now little known in North India. Thus this crucial reference provides, if nothing more, yet another indication of the lingering death which Ājīvikism was dying.

Śīlâṅka and the Trairāśikas

Like Utpala, Śīlâṅka, the ninth century [1] commentator to the *Sūtrakṛtâṅga*, seems to have been in some confusion about the Ājīvikas. He had a sound understanding of *niyativāda*,[2] a cardinal doctrine of the Ājīvikas, which was attributed by the later Jaina commentator Guṇaratna to Pūraṇa,[3] who was remembered as a prophet by the Southern Ājīvikas.[4] On the other hand Śīlâṅka does not associate the *Niyati* doctrine with Gosāla, with Pūraṇa, or with Ājīvikism. He recognizes one significant teaching of later Ājīvikism, the doctrine of *maṇḍala-mokṣa*,[5] which he correctly attributes to the followers of Gosāla ; but besides this he states in another context that the Ājīvikas believe in the doctrine of salvation by good conduct (*vinayavāda*), and he associates them with the Digambara Jainas and with the lesser Jaina schism of the Trairāśikas.

The relevant references in Śīlâṅka's commentary are quoted below :—

1. The text refers to Mahāvīra as having understood the doctrines of the *Kriyāvādins*, *Akriyāvādins*, *Vainayikas*, and *Ajñānavādins*. On the third of these schools Śīlâṅka comments : " Saying ' Salvation comes only from good conduct ', the followers of the doctrine of Gośālaka walk in the path of good conduct, and are hence termed Vainayikas." [6]

[1] Glasenapp, *Der Jainismus*, p. 107. [2] V. infra, pp. 230 ff.
[3] V. supra, p. 81. [4] V. supra, p. 80. [5] V. infra, p. 259.
[6] *Vinayād eva mokṣa ity evaṃ Gośālaka-mat'-ânusāriṇo vinayena carant' îti Vainayikā vyavasthitāḥ.* To *Sū. kṛ.* i, 6, 27, fol. 152.

2. On another passage, which describes certain ascetics who revile the monk leading a righteous life, Śīlâṅka comments with an ambiguous phrase which has formed the basis of an important theory of Hoernle's : " They are the Ājīvikas who follow the doctrine of Gośāla, or Digambaras." [1]

3. He uses a similar phrase when commenting on a verse describing the best means of converting the heretical opponents of Jainism : " They are the Ājīvikas, etc., who follow the doctrine of Gośāla, or Boṭikas (i.e. Digambaras)." [2]

4. On the theory that the soul freed from *karma* may yet become defiled and return to *saṃsāra*, Śīlâṅka states that the view is held by " the Trairāśikas, who follow the doctrine of Gośāla, and who have twenty-one *sūtras*, arranged according to the order of the Trairāśika *sūtras* in the *Pūrvas* ".[3]

The second and fourth of these references have been used by Hoernle to further his theory that the later Ājīvikas merged with the Digambara Jainas. He writes : " Śīlâṅka states that the reference is to the Ājīvikas or Digambaras. Seeing that, in his comment on another passage of the same work, he identifies . . . the Ājīvikas with the Terāsiyas (Sanskr. Trairāśikas), it follows that in Śīlâṅka's view the followers of Gosāla, the Ājīvikas, the Terāsiyas, and the Digambaras were the same class of religious mendicants." [4]

We do not believe that these references are more conclusive as proofs of the merging of the Ājīvikas and the Digambaras than is the dubious statement of Utpala as proof of the merging of the Ājīvikas and the Vaiṣṇavites. Hoernle notes only two of the references ; on a careful examination of all of them it may be necessary to modify his theory.

In the second phrase, Hoernle has interpreted the conjunction *vā* in the sense of " i.e." It is doubtful if the particle was ever used in Sanskrit, as is " or " in English, in this sense, to denote the synonymity of two or more words or phrases. We admit that Śīlâṅka, by the use of the word *vā*, indicated

[1] *Te ca Gośālaka-mat'-ânusāriṇa Ājīvikā Digambarā vā.* Ibid., to i, 3, 3, 8, fol. 90.

[2] *Te Gośālaka-mat'-âṇusāriṇa Ājīvik'-âdayaḥ* (sic) *Boṭikā vā.* Ibid., to i, 3, 3, 14, fol. 92.

[3] *Trairāśikā Gośālaka-mat'-ânusāriṇo, yeṣām ekaviṃśati sūtrāṇi Pūrva-gata-trairāśika-sūtra-paripātyā vyavasthitāni.* To *Sū. kṛ.* i, 1, 3, 11, fol. 45.

[4] *ERE.* i, p. 262.

that the Ājīvikas were " of the same class of religious mendicants as the Digambaras ". But the text of the *Sūtrakṛtâṅga* plainly shows that the class implied by Śīlâṅka was a very wide one, comprising all those who revile the righteous Śvetâmbara monk. The third phrase makes the position clearer. Here Śīlâṅka makes separate mention of the Boṭikas or Digambaras, who are not included among the miscellaneous ascetics represented by the word *ādayaḥ*, appended to *Ājīvika*. The adjective *Gośālaka-mat'-ânusāriṇa* may apply only to the first, or to both, of the two nouns, but in view of the word *ādayaḥ*, it would seem that Śīlâṅka intended it to apply to the first ; otherwise he would have added this word to *Boṭika-* instead of to *Ājīvika-*. Thus it appears that he did not look on the Boṭika as a follower of Gosāla, and made a clear distinction between the two sects. If any doubts remain they are removed by a fifth phrase of Śīlâṅka, on a verse condemning the dietary habits of non-Jaina ascetics, which, he states, is " a description of the evil conduct of Ājīvikas, etc., followers of other doctrines, *and* Digambaras ".[1] In this phrase, not noticed by Hoernle, the conjunction *ca* is used in place of the ambiguous *vā*.

His use of the word *ādayaḥ* indicates that Śīlâṅka knew of more than one sect of followers of Gosāla, and that the term Ājīvika was not regularly used by all his followers. We shall see in our second part that differences of doctrine developed within the Ājīvika community, small though it was.[2] Is it possible that the Vainayikas, called by Śīlâṅka followers of Gosāla,[3] but not referred to as Ājīvikas, were one such schism ? Śīlâṅka declares in another context that the Vainayikas seek a rebirth in heaven (not complete salvation or *mokṣa*, as in the first reference quoted above), by fourfold good conduct, in mind, word, body, and in giving towards gods, kings, ascetics, kinsfolk, elders, inferiors, mother, and father—a total of thirty-two categories.[4] The same statement concerning the Vinayavādins is made by the later commentator Guṇaratna, but he includes among their

[1] *Ājīvikâdīnāṃ paratīrthikānāṃ Digambarāṇāṃ c' âsadācāra-nirūpaṇāya.* Śīlâṅka to *Sū. kṛ.* i, 3, 3, 12, fol. 91.

[2] V. infra, pp. 279–80.

[3] V. supra, p. 174.

[4] *Vainayikānāṃ vinayād eva kevalāt paralokam ap' îcchatāṃ dvātriṃśad anena prakrameṇa yojyāḥ : tad yathā sura-nṛpati-yati-jñāti-sthavir'-âdhama-mātṛ-pitṛṣu manasā vācā kāyena dānena ca caturvidho vinayo vidheyaḥ.* To *Sū. kṛ.* i, 12 *niryukti*, fol. 209. Cf. infra, p. 261, n. 2.

teachers such famous names as Vasiṣṭha, Vālmīki, and Vyāsa,[1] as well as Parāśara, who is elsewhere said by Guṇaratna to have taught a doctrine of natural evolution[2]; and he nowhere connects them with Gosāla or with the Ājīvikas. The doctrines of Gosāla are often obscure; it is true that the Ājīvikas were frequently accused by their opponents of antinomianism and immorality, but perhaps their ethics were not in most respects less strict than those of other sects of the time; yet, even after making the utmost allowance for the *odium theologicum* of their opponents, it seems unlikely that the average follower of Gosāla's doctrines placed so strong an emphasis on ethics as Śīlâṅka suggests. Unless Śīlâṅka was mistaken we can only explain this puzzling reference by suggesting that the Vinayavādins or Vainayikas were a later sect, which perhaps arose as a schism of the Ājīvikas, and which, while maintaining very different doctrines, yet remembered Gosāla with respect. If it be admitted, on the strength of Utpala's statement and of other less definite suggestions, that some of the Ājīvikas drifted towards unorthodox Vaiṣṇavism, we may tentatively identify these with the Vinayavādins, and thus also account for the statement of Guṇaratna that the latter revered the saints of Purāṇic legend. Thus we may also account for the difficult *-ādayaḥ* in the third phrase of Śīlâṅka quoted above.

In Śīlâṅka's fourth phrase the false prophet is said to be the leader of the Trairāśikas. A sect of Trairāśikas, a schism of the Jaina community, is well known in early Jaina literature, and is said to have been founded in the city of Antariñjikā by the monk Rohagupta, in the 544th year of Mahāvīra's *nirvāṇa*,[3] or in A.D. 18, according to the traditional reckoning. The Trairāśikas held unorthodox views, resembling those of the Vaiśeṣika school of philosophy, on the fundamental categories of Indian metaphysics, and they admitted only three principles of predication, *sat*, *asat*, and *sadasat* as against the seven of Jaina logic.

[1] To *Ṣaddarśana-samuccaya*, p. 19.

[2] V. supra, pp. 81–82.

[3] *Niryukti* to *Āvaśyaka Sūtra* 2451, quoted *Abh. Rāj.*, s.v. *Terāsiya*. V. also Guérinot, *La Religion Djaïna*, pp. 47–8. The *Kalpa Sūtra* (*Sthavirāvalī*, 6, ed. Jacobi, p. 80) makes Rohagupta a pupil of Mahāgiri, the eighth *sthavira*, and second after Bhadrabāhu. This tradition would date the origin of the Trairāśikas over 200 years earlier than would that of the *Āvaśyaka Sūtra*.

In the *Samavāyâṅga* Commentary[1] it is stated that the Ājīvikas were also called Trairāśikas, and held the three-category system of logic. It is nowhere stated that they maintained the Vaiśeṣika categories of the Rohagupta Trairāśikas. It is unlikely that a paṇḍit of the calibre of Śīlâṅka could have confused the latter with the Ājīvikas, although they too had a *trairāśika* system of logic, and perhaps other points of doctrine in common with the Trairāśikas of Rohagupta. The fact that the two sects were well known to have been founded by different teachers, living in periods five hundred years apart, should be sufficient to show that they were not, as Professor Hoernle believed, identical.

In this connection the passage in the *Samavāya*,[2] commented on by Abhayadeva, is important. Both the text and the commentary are repeated almost verbatim in the *Nandi Sūtra*,[3] with its commentary by Haribhadra. This passage purports to describe the *Dṛṣṭivāda*, the lost twelfth *aṅga* of the Jaina canon. That book appears to have been a comparison, in parallel passages, of the doctrines of orthodox Jainism with those of three heresies, the Ājīvika, the Catuṣkanayika, and the Trairāśika. The first part of this text was a description of the *parikammāiṃ*, which the scholiasts define as the preparations necessary to grasp the meaning of the *sūtras* correctly. These *parikammas* were divided into seven groups, which were in turn divided into subsections. Their names are given as *siddha-seṇiyā-parikamme*, *maṇussa-*, *puṭṭha-*, *ogahaṇa-*, *uvasampajja-*, *vippajaha-*, and *cuyâcuya-seṇiyā-parikamme*. The commentators seem to have had little knowledge of the true nature of these *parikammas*, and they need not detain us. Significant for our purpose is a passage in the text: "Six (of these *parikammas*) are orthodox, seven are Ājīvika, six are Catuṣkanayika, seven are Trairāśika."[4] The Ājīvikas and the Trairāśikas are said to maintain the *cuyâcuya-seṇiyā-parikamma*, which was not recognized by the orthodox Jainas, nor by the Catuṣkanayikas.

[1] To *sū*. 147, fol. 130. V. infra, p. 179.

[2] *Samavāya*, *sū*. 147, fol. 128 ff.

[3] *Nandi*, *sū*. 56, fol. 107 ff.

[4] *Cha sasamaïyāiṃ, satta ājīviyāiṃ, cha caükkaṇaïyāiṃ, satta terāsiyāiṃ*. *Samavāya*, fol. 128. The Bombay text has *satta . . . sasamaïyāiṃ*, which is certainly a misprint, since it does not agree with the commentary, nor with Weber's paraphrase (*IS*. xvi, p. 364). The *Nandi* (fol. 108) mentions only the last two, *cha caükkaṇaïāiṃ, satta terāsiāiṃ*.

The sect of the Catuṣkanayikas seems to have differed from orthodox Jainism mainly in the fact that it compressed the orthodox seven *nayas* into four, omitting the first Jaina *naya* (*naigama*), and including it with the second or third (*saṅgraha* and *vyavahāra*), according to its reference to generals or particulars ; and throwing the last three Jaina *nayas* (*sāmprata*, *samabhirūḍha*, and *evambhūta*) together, as being all three concerned with words. The four *nayas* or standpoints of the sect thus become :—

1. *Saṅgraha*, predication from the general properties of a thing ;
2. *Vyavahāra*, from its individual aspect ;
3. *Ṛjusūtra*, from its momentary condition ; and
4. *Śabdâdi*, from the implication of the words used to designate it.[1]

It thus seems that the Catuṣkanayikas were a small subsect of the Jainas, with a somewhat unorthodox epistemology.

In describing the three heresies the commentaries refer to the Ājīvika system as that propagated by Gosāla[2]; later, after dealing with the Catuṣkanayikas, it is stated that " the Ājīvikas are also called Trairāśikas ".[3]

The summary of the *Dṛṣṭivāda* continues with a description of the contents of its second part, *suttāiṃ*. It is stated that the doctrines of all four sects are contained therein, and are repeated in the form of *sūtras* in both orthodox and heretical recensions. Each of the four sects has twenty-two *sūtras*, of which those of the orthodox are in the form of separate aphorisms (*chinnacheanaīāiṃ*), while the Ājīvika *sūtras* are combined, and the *sūtras* of the Trairāśikas and the Catuṣkanayikas are arranged with reference to the three or four *nayas* of the respective sects.[4] Here the Ājīvikas are again referred to as followers of Gosāla's doctrines, and the Trairāśikas also are said to be called Ājīvikas.[5]

It is not made clear whether these four parts of the *sūtra*

[1] *Nandi* Comm., fol. 113. *Samavāya* Comm., fol. 129.

[2] *Gośālaka-pravarttit'-âjīvika-pākhaṇḍika-siddhānta.* *Samavāya*, Comm., loc. cit.

[3] *Tā eva c' Ājīvikās Trairāśikā bhaṇitāḥ.*

[4] *Samavāya* Comm., fol. 130. *Nandi* Comm., fol. 108. The Nandi declares that the Catuṣkanayika *sūtras* are in accordance with orthodox usage.

[5] *Trairāśikāś c' Ājīvikā ev' ôcyante.*

section of the *Dṛṣṭivāda* were written from the orthodox angle, as mere statements of the doctrines of the heresies, or whether they contained passages from authentic scriptures of the sects; the former alternative seems more probable. In either case the lost *Dṛṣṭivāda* must represent a stage in the history of Jainism when sectarian animosity was by no means as strong as it later became. Reasons for the regrettable disappearance of the work may be readily suggested.

But although the four sects were akin they are nowhere said to have been identical. None of the statements contained in the *Samavāya* or the *Nandi*, or in their commentaries, justifies Hoernle's view that the Ājīvikas and the Trairāśikas of Rohagupta were the same sect. We interpret them to mean that the Ājīvikas were sometimes also called Trairāśikas, because they maintained the doctrine of the three *nayas*. From one of the statements [1] it would appear that the Trairāśikas were also occasionally called Ājīvikas. The Rohagupta Trairāśikas, who had some points in common with the Ājīvikas and some with the Vaiśeṣikas, were probably in other respects much closer to Jaina orthodoxy than were the Ājīvikas of Gosāla's sect. That the commentaries to the *Nandi* and *Samavāya* use the words "founded by Gosāla" only in respect of the Ājīvikas, and never of the Trairāśikas, also strongly suggests that the two were separate though in some respects similar. The Trairāśika sect of the Jaina church was founded by Rohagupta; but the Ājīvikas, who were also *trairāśikas* were founded by Gosāla. In using the phrase *Gośālaka-pravartita* the commentators seem to have been consciously trying to avoid any cause of confusion between the two communities.

We are now in a position to understand a little better the fourth statement of Śīlâṅka quoted above,[2] which declares that the belief in return from *mokṣa* is held by the Trairāśika followers of Gosāla, who have twenty-one *sūtras* arranged according to the order of the Trairāśika *sūtras* in the *Pūrvas*. The last word probably refers to the fourteen *Pūrvas* of the original Jaina canon, which have long been lost. According to the *Samavāya* and the *Nandi* [3] these were summarized in the third part of the *Dṛṣṭivāda*, called *Pūrvagatam*. Śīlâṅka seems to

[1] V. supra, p. 179, n. 5. [2] V. supra, p. 175. [3] Loc. cit.

have confused this part with the second, which contained the *sūtras* of the four sects, unless indeed he looked upon the *Dṛṣṭivāda* as itself a *Pūrva*. He seems to have known of the *Dṛṣṭivāda*, but he disagrees with the *Samavāya* and the *Nandi* in attributing twenty-one *sūtras* to the Trairāśikas in place of twenty-two in the *Samavāya* and *Nandi* lists. Either Śīlâṅka did not know of these lists, or he was quoting from a defective memory. The best interpretation of his obscure phrase that we can offer is: "The Trairāśikas who follow Gosāla (i.e. the Ājīvikas, not the Rohagupta Trairāśikas) have *sūtras* arranged in the same way as are those of the Trairāśikas (i.e. the Rohagupta Trairāśikas) in the *Pūrvas* (i.e. the *Dṛṣṭivāda*)."

Nemicandra on the Ājīvikas

The non-canonical Jaina work *Pravacana-sār'-ôddhāra*, composed by Nemicandra in the twelfth century,[1] contains interesting verses in which all ascetics are classified in five categories: *Nirgranthas* (Jainas), *Śākyas* (Buddhists), *Tāpasas* (*Jaṭilas*, or brāhmaṇical ascetics with matted locks), *Gairukas* (ascetics who bear a triple staff, and whose clothes are stained with red ochre), and *Ājīvas* (the followers of Gosāla).[2]

Since Nemicandra was a Jaina philosopher, and his own sect occurs first on the list, it seems that the author intended his five groups of ascetics to be read in declining order of excellence. If so it is plain that he viewed the Ājīvikas with disfavour. Moreover, since Nemicandra was a Jaina of the Digambara sect,[3] his reference to the Ājīvikas further disproves Hoernle's contention that they and the Digambaras were the same.

1 *Abh. Rāj.* iv, p. 2158, s.v. *Nemicanda*.

2 *Niggantha-Sakka-Tāvasa-Geruya-Ājīvā pañcahā samaṇā,*
Tammi nigganthā te je Jiṇa-sāsaṇa-bhavā muṇiṇo, 731.
Sakkā ya Sugaya-sīsā, je jaḍilā te u Tāvasā gīyā,
Je dhāū-rattā-vatthā tidaṇḍiṇo Geruyā te u, 732.
Je Gosālaga-mayam aṇusaranti bhannanti te u Ājīvā.
Samaṇattaṇeṇa bhuvaṇe pañcavi pattā pasiddhim ime, 733.
Pravacanasāróddhāra i, sect. 94, fol. 212. A Berlin MS. of this text (Weber, *Verzeichniss*, no. 1939), reads *samaṇatteṇaṃ* in the last line of v. 733.

3 Guérinot, *La Religion Djaïna*, p. 82.

Lexicographical References

Several lexicographers of the tenth to the twelfth centuries mention the Ājīvikas in the company of a motley collection of ascetics. Their citations are significant in that they indicate that the name was not forgotten, but can be accepted as evidence of the continued existence of Ājīvikas only in South India, for which much stronger evidence may be found elsewhere. Halâyudha and Yādava were southerners,[1] and had no doubt come into contact with the Tamil Ājīvikas, whom we consider in the next chapter. For Hemacandra and Ajayapāla, who wrote in Gujarāt,[2] we cannot suggest personal knowledge of the Ājīvikas; they probably included the word in their lists by borrowing from the Southern dictionaries, or because of its presence in Jaina literature.

The earliest surviving lexicographer, Amara, does not mention the word Ājīvika, although *maskarin* occurs in his *Kośa*,[3] with the names of a few other ascetics both orthodox and heretical.

Halâyudha gives two lists of unorthodox ascetics in separate verses,[4] the first of which, including such words as *muni*, *yati*, *śvetavāsāḥ*, and *sitâmbara*, contains clothed heretical ascetics, and the second members of the naked category:—

Nagnâṭo digvāsāḥ kṣapaṇaḥ śramaṇaś ca jīvako jainaḥ
Ājīvo maladhārī nirgranthaḥ kathyate sadbhiḥ.

"By the educated a naked wanderer is called *digvāsāḥ*, etc."

Maskarin is included by Halâyudha among a further group of holy men, which contains such orthodox types as *pārāśarin* and *tapasvin*.[5]

Hemacandra's *Abhidhāna-cintāmaṇi* does not mention the Ājīvika, but *maskarin* is included in two verses containing the names of mendicants of more or less orthodox types.[6] The same author's *Anekârtha-saṅgraha* gives *kṣapaṇa* as one of the several possible meanings of *Ājīvaka*.[7]

[1] Keith, *History of Sanskrit Literature*, pp. 133, 478.
[2] Keith, op. cit., pp. 133, 478.
[3] *Amarakośa* ii, 41.
[4] *Abhidhāna-ratnamālā* ii, 189–190.
[5] Ibid., ii, 254.
[6] *Abhidhāna-cintāmaṇi* vv, 809–810.
[7] *Anekârtha-saṅgraha*, ed. Zachariae, 3, 41.

Vaijayantī gives the following names of naked

paṇa-śramaṇau nagno nagnâṭaś ca digambaraḥ
vo jīvako jaino nirgrantho malavāry api.[1]

Ajayapāla, probably following Hemacandra, quotes as one possible meaning of *jīvaka.*[2]

ıese lexicographical references Hoernle notes only one, Halâyudha, who " enumerates a large number of names ..ıe two Jain divisions, the Śvetâmbaras . . . and the Digambaras. . . . The latter, he says, are also known as the Ājīva, which is only a shorter form of Ājīvika. . . . It is evident now, from what has been said, that the terms Nigganṭha and Ājīvika denote the two Jaina orders which are known to us as Śvetâmbaras and Digambaras ".[3]

This appears to be an over-simplification. The verse which, according to Hoernle, enumerates the titles of Śvetâmbaras, actually includes such broad general terms as *tapasvin*, *śānta*, *muni*, and even *liṅgin*, which probably refers to a Śaivite ascetic bearing a *liṅgam*. On the other hand the next verse, giving names of naked ascetics, contains the word *śramaṇa*, a term certainly used by the Śvetâmbaras and Buddhists as well as the Digambaras, and also *nirgrantha*, which term, on Hoernle's theory, specifically denoted the Śvetâmbara, as opposed to the Ājīvika or Digambara.

We can only conclude that these verses do not contain exactly synonymous terms, but the names of various types, clothed and otherwise, who were not attached to any orthodox Hindu order, and had various characteristics in common. That the Ājīvikas shared many characteristics with the Jainas cannot reasonably be denied, but that at the time of Halâyudha they had wholly merged with the Digambaras is not established. Hoernle's theory rests on a very dubious interpretation of the relevant reference, and is quite untenable against much contrary evidence, such as that provided by the Southern Digambara sources found by K. B. Pathak,[4] which show that, at about the same time as the

[1] *Vaijayantī*, ed. Oppert, p. 202, v. 16.
[2] *Nānârtha-saṅgraha*, ed. Cintamani, p. 39, v. 3.
[3] *ERE.* i, pp. 266–7.
[4] *IA.* xli, pp. 88–90. V. infra, pp. 203–4.

lexicographers were, according to Hoernle, identify Ājīvikas with the Digambaras, the latter sect was co... them with the Buddhists.

Hoernle's further suggestion, that the term *nirgrantha* imp... only a Śvetâmbara Jaina, is quite unfounded. The evidence ... Halâyudha [1] and Yādava,[2] both of whom include the *nirgranth...* in the same category as the *nagnâṭa*, should be adequate to disprove the theory. The term was obviously used for a Jaina of any type.

The Last References to Ājīvikas

The Jaina commentator Malliṣeṇa, whose *Syādvāda-mañjarī* was written as late as A.D. 1292,[3] knew of the Ājīvikas. They are referred to by him as though still in existence; he understands an important point of their doctrine, and he even quotes what appears to be a verse from an Ājīvika religious poem.[4] It is probable that he was in touch with the Ājīvikas of the Tamil country, who were still active at the time.

The last reference known to us in Sanskrit literature occurs in the *Jātaka-pārijāta*, the work of the astrologer Vaidyanātha Dīkṣita, who was probably born *c.* 1425–50.[5] He declares that the *Jīvaka*, according to the lexicographers a legitimate synonym of Ājīvika,[6] is born in the same astrological conditions as those stated by Varāhamihira,[7] under the influence of four or five planets, with that of Mercury dominant.[8] Like Varāhamihira he gives a catalogue of seven types of ascetic: the *Vānaprastha*, an ascetic dwelling in forests and mountains; the *Vivāsas*, habitually naked; the *Bhikṣu*, an *ekadaṇḍin* and a great soul wise in Upaniṣadic lore; the *Caraka*, one who wanders to many lands; the *Śākya*, a *yogī* of evil habits; the *Guru*, honoured and of royal fortune; and the *Jīvaka*, fond of food and talkative.[9]

[1] V. supra, p. 182. [2] V. supra, p. 183.
[3] Keith, *History of Sanskrit Literature*, p. 497.
[4] *Syādvāda-mañjarī*, Bombay edn., p. 3. V. infra, p. 222.
[5] *Jātaka-pārijāta*, ed. V. S. Sastri, vol. i, introduction, p. vi.
[6] V. supra, pp. 182–83. [7] V. supra, p. 169. [8] *Jātaka-pārijāta*, xv, 15.
[9] *Vānaprasthas tapasvī vana-giri-nilayo, nagna-śīlo Vivāsā,*
Bhikṣuḥ syād ekadaṇḍī satatam upaniṣat-tattva-niṣṭho mahâtmā,
Nānā-deśa-pravāsī Caraka-pativaraḥ, Śākya-yogī kuśīlo,
Rāja-śrīmān yaśasvī Gurur, aśana-paro jalpako Jīvakaḥ syāt.
Jātaka-pārijāta xv, 16.

Vaidyanātha, unlike Utpala, does not identify the Ājīvika with the *ekadaṇḍin*, nor with the naked *Vivāsas*. His use of the word "talkative" (*jalpako*) suggests that he had some personal knowledge of the sect, for no such word is elsewhere to be found applied to the Ājīvikas. Chattering ascetics are certainly referred to in the Buddhist texts,[1] but the Ājīvikas are nowhere accused of being more loquacious than their rivals.

At about the same time, or perhaps a little earlier,[2] Guṇaratna, the Jaina commentator of Haribhadra's *Ṣaḍdarśana-samuccaya*, although not using the term Ājīvika, shows a sound knowledge of the doctrines of the *niyativādins*, and names one of their founders, Pūraṇa.[3] It is probable that he too obtained his knowledge from Dravidian sources.

The decline of the Ājīvikas is indicated by the *Sarva-darśana-saṅgraha*, which, despite its claim to completeness, makes no mention of them whatever, although it contains a chapter on such an obscure sect as the *Raseśvara-darśana*, which taught that the use of mercury was necessary to salvation.[4]

This chain of fleeting references, dating from Gupta times to the fifteenth century, is sufficient to indicate that the Ājīvikas survived over that period. In the Dravidian South, as will be shown in our next chapter, they maintained themselves against discriminatory taxation until the fourteenth century. There, with Hindu, Jaina, and Buddhist, they were a definite factor in the religious situation of Colamaṇḍalam, and their system was important enough to warrant detailed refutations from their chief rivals. In the North, on the other hand, Ājīvikism may have become insignificant even as early as the Śuṅga period; but the references leave little doubt that occasional Ājīvika mendicants were to be found there at a much later date. In Kashmīr they may even have risen for a short while to a position of great influence, under the mad king Harṣadeva, when strange naked ascetics destroyed the orthodox ikons of the capital.[5]

No doubt the surviving Ājīvikas compromised with the doctrines and customs of the more popular faiths around them; as

1 E.g. *Sandaka Sutta*, *Majjh.* i, pp. 513 ff.
2 Glasenapp, *Der Jainismus*, p. 108.
3 V. supra, pp. 81–82.
4 *Sarva-darśana-saṅgraha*, pp. 202–9.
5 V. infra, pp. 205 ff.

a little known minor community they would often be confused with the greater sects; thus Utpala declares that they were *ekadaṇḍin* Vaiṣṇavites[1]; the commentator to the *Ācārasāra* believes them to be Buddhists[2]; and in the Jaina Tamil work *Nīlakēci* the Ājīvika leader declares that his followers are not Digambaras, although they might be mistaken for them.[3]

We may suggest that the small Ājīvika communities of ascetics and laymen, most common in the region of the Palar River, above Kāñcī, slowly approached more and more closely to the more popular and influential faiths in their districts. An Ājīvika theism developed in the later period,[4] and some Ājīvikas may, as Utpala suggests, have drifted towards Vaiṣṇavism. Magical ceremonies were not unknown to the Ājīvikas,[5] and some Ājīvika communities may gradually have merged with the left-hand or tantric sects. While Hoernle's theory as formulated is certainly incorrect, there is no doubt that it contains a partial truth. The latest surviving description of Ājīvika doctrine, that in the *Civañāṉa-cittiyār*,[6] shows us a system not far removed from Jainism. The Ājīvikas rose side by side with the Jainas and some groups must ultimately have merged with them. We may conclude that the work of the great popular religious reformers of the late Middle Ages completely annihilated the scattered and degenerate remnants of what was once a vigorous and independent sect, enjoying the patronage of the greatest of India's rulers.

[1] V. supra, pp. 169–70. [2] V. infra, pp. 203–4. [3] V. infra, p. 202.
[4] V. infra, p. 276. [5] V. supra, pp. 112–13, 162 ff. [6] V. infra, p. 203.

Yādava's *Vaijayantī* gives the following names of naked heretics :—

> *Kṣapaṇa-śramaṇau nagno nagnâṭaś ca digambaraḥ*
> *Ājīvo jīvako jaino nirgrantho malavāry api.*[1]

Finally Ajayapāla, probably following Hemacandra, quotes *kṣapaṇa* as one possible meaning of *jīvaka.*[2]

Of these lexicographical references Hoernle notes only one, that of Halâyudha, who " enumerates a large number of names of the two Jain divisions, the Śvetâmbaras . . . and the Digambaras. . . . The latter, he says, are also known as the Ājīva, which is only a shorter form of Ājīvika. . . . It is evident now, from what has been said, that the terms Niggantha and Ājīvika denote the two Jaina orders which are known to us as Śvetâmbaras and Digambaras ".[3]

This appears to be an over-simplification. The verse which, according to Hoernle, enumerates the titles of Śvetâmbaras, actually includes such broad general terms as *tapasvin*, *śānta*, *muni*, and even *liṅgin*, which probably refers to a Śaivite ascetic bearing a *liṅgam*. On the other hand the next verse, giving names of naked ascetics, contains the word *śramaṇa*, a term certainly used by the Śvetâmbaras and Buddhists as well as the Digambaras, and also *nirgrantha*, which term, on Hoernle's theory, specifically denoted the Śvetâmbara, as opposed to the Ājīvika or Digambara.

We can only conclude that these verses do not contain exactly synonymous terms, but the names of various types, clothed and otherwise, who were not attached to any orthodox Hindu order, and had various characteristics in common. That the Ājīvikas shared many characteristics with the Jainas cannot reasonably be denied, but that at the time of Halâyudha they had wholly merged with the Digambaras is not established. Hoernle's theory rests on a very dubious interpretation of the relevant reference, and is quite untenable against much contrary evidence, such as that provided by the Southern Digambara sources found by K. B. Pathak,[4] which show that, at about the same time as the

[1] *Vaijayantī*, ed. Oppert, p. 202, v. 16.
[2] *Nānârtha-saṅgraha*, ed. Cintamani, p. 39, v. 3.
[3] *ERE.* i, pp. 266–7.
[4] *IA.* xli, pp. 88–90. V. infra, pp. 203–4.

lexicographers were, according to Hoernle, identifying the Ājīvikas with the Digambaras, the latter sect was confusing them with the Buddhists.

Hoernle's further suggestion, that the term *nirgrantha* implied only a Śvetâmbara Jaina, is quite unfounded. The evidence of Halâyudha [1] and Yādava,[2] both of whom include the *nirgrantha* in the same category as the *nagnâṭa*, should be adequate to disprove the theory. The term was obviously used for a Jaina of any type.

The Last References to Ājīvikas

The Jaina commentator Malliṣeṇa, whose *Syādvāda-mañjarī* was written as late as A.D. 1292,[3] knew of the Ājīvikas. They are referred to by him as though still in existence; he understands an important point of their doctrine, and he even quotes what appears to be a verse from an Ājīvika religious poem.[4] It is probable that he was in touch with the Ājīvikas of the Tamil country, who were still active at the time.

The last reference known to us in Sanskrit literature occurs in the *Jātaka-pārijāta*, the work of the astrologer Vaidyanātha Dīkṣita, who was probably born *c.* 1425–50.[5] He declares that the *Jīvaka*, according to the lexicographers a legitimate synonym of Ājīvika,[6] is born in the same astrological conditions as those stated by Varāhamihira,[7] under the influence of four or five planets, with that of Mercury dominant.[8] Like Varāhamihira he gives a catalogue of seven types of ascetic: the *Vānaprastha*, an ascetic dwelling in forests and mountains; the *Vivāsas*, habitually naked; the *Bhikṣu*, an *ekadaṇḍin* and a great soul wise in Upaniṣadic lore; the *Caraka*, one who wanders to many lands; the *Śākya*, a *yogī* of evil habits; the *Guru*, honoured and of royal fortune; and the *Jīvaka*, fond of food and talkative.[9]

[1] V. supra, p. 182.
[2] V. supra, p. 183.
[3] Keith, *History of Sanskrit Literature*, p. 497.
[4] *Syādvāda-mañjarī*, Bombay edn., p. 3. V. infra, p. 222.
[5] *Jātaka-pārijāta*, ed. V. S. Sastri, vol. i, introduction, p. vi.
[6] V. supra, pp. 182–83.
[7] V. supra, p. 169.
[8] *Jātaka-pārijāta*, xv, 15.
[9] *Vānaprasthas tapasvī vana-giri-nilayo, nagna-śīlo Vivāsā,*
Bhikṣuḥ syād ekadaṇḍī satatam upaniṣat-tattva-niṣṭho mahâtmā,
Nānā-deśa-pravāsī Caraka-pativaraḥ, Śākya-yogī kuśīlo,
Rāja-śrīmān yaśasvī Gurur, aśana-paro jalpako Jīvakaḥ syāt.
Jātaka-pārijāta xv, 16.

CHAPTER X

THE SOUTHERN ĀJĪVIKAS

The Ājīvikas maintained themselves in the Dravidian-speaking part of India in a more flourishing condition than in the North, and survived in the Tamil country until at least the fourteenth century. This fact may be established on very solid evidence: firstly by a number of inscriptions mentioning the Ājīvikas, and covering a period of nearly a millennium; secondly by the three Tamil religious texts, *Maṇimēkalai*, *Nīlakēci*, and *Civañāṉa-cittiyār*, of widely differing date, each of which gives an outline of Ājīvika doctrine from the Buddhist, Jaina, and Śaivite standpoints respectively; and thirdly by a number of shorter references in other Tamil and Canarese works.

THE INSCRIPTIONS

The epigraphic references to the Ājīvikas may be classified chronologically as follows:—

1. Siṃhavarman Pallava's grant of the village of Vilavaṭṭi to the Brāhmaṇa Viṣṇuśarman.[1] The village is identified by Dr. Kṛṣṇamacarlu with Viḍavalūru, in the Nellore District of Madras. The grant is dated in the tenth year of the King's reign, or A.D. 446. Among the numerous local taxes mentioned are those on iron, leather shops, clothworkers, cloak makers, ropeworks, and Ājīvikas.[2]

2. A grant of the Eastern Cālukya Ammarāja II (945–970) of the four adjacent villages of Tāṇḍikoṇḍa, Ammalapūṇḍi, Gollapūṇḍi, and Ācuvulaparṟu to the temple of Samastabhu-vanâśraya at Vijayavāṭī.[3] Of these villages only the first can be traced, but they were all in the District of Guntūr. The component

[1] *Epi. Ind.* xxiv, pp. 296–303.
[2] *Loha-carmmakārâpaṇa-paṭṭakāra-prāvārañcara-rajju-pratihārâpaṇ'-Ājīvika-karāṇi.* Ibid., p. 303.
[3] *Epi. Ind.* xxiii, pp. 161–170.

Ācuvula in the name of the fourth village is probably equivalent to *Ācuva*, the usual form of Ājīvika in the Tamil inscriptions, and the name therefore means "the village of the Ājīvikas".

3. An inscription of Kaṉṉaradeva or Kṛṣṇa III Rāṣṭrakūṭa (mid tenth century) on the walls of the Kailāsanathasvāmin temple at Kāvanūr, in the North Arcot District of Madras.[1] This lays down that seller and purchaser or mortgager and mortgagee must belong to the same community (*jāti*) . . . in the case of land being gifts to Gods, physicians, or Ājīvikas.[2]

4. An inscription of Rājendra Coladeva at Āvaṇi, Kolar District, Mysore,[3] dated in the King's third year (A.D. 1072). In it the inhabitants of the *viṣaya* declare a list of local taxes, and decide that the *Ācuvi-makkaḷ* are to pay one *kācu* each for the minor tolls, and that if they fail to do so they are to pay a further *kācu*. . . . Except for the house of the schoolmaster, the temple-manager, and the village watchman, and the houses which have paid the minor tolls, one-quarter *kācu* is levied on every house.[4]

5. An inscription assigning local taxes to the Virattaneśvara temple, Kīlūr, South Arcot District, Madras, dated the 33rd year of the reign of Kulottuṅga Coladeva (A.D. 1103).[5] Among the taxes is the *Ācuvi-kācu*.

6. An inscription of Rājarāja III's seventh year (c. A.D. 1223) at Tiruvoṟṟiyūr,[6] decreeing the levying of new taxes on this and other villages which had hitherto been exempt. Among the taxes is "the *kācu* paid by the people of the Ājīvikas", or

[1] *AR.*, No. 159 of 1921.

[2] Sastri, *The Colas*, vol. i, p. 445. The text of the inscription has been supplied by the Government Epigraphist for India.

[3] *Epi. Carn.* vol. x, Mulbagal 49 (*a*).

[4] *Ciṟucuṅkattukku Ācuvi-makkaḷ Ācuvam uṇṇum pērāl orukāciṭuvatākavum . ṟaiyāviṭṭāl orukāciṟippatākavum . . . ṉṟu . . . . uvāttivīṭum tiru-kkōyil-uṭaiyāṉ vīṭum taḷaṟar-vīṭum ciṟucuṅkattukku iṟutta vīṭu tavira nīkki niṉṟa vīṭukaḷukku vīṭṭāl kāl kācu koḷvatākavum.* Rice's transliteration is modified in accordance with the system of the Madras University *Tamil Lexicon*. The obscure words *Ācuvam uṇṇum* in the inscription cannot be interpreted unless we accept the suggestion that *unnum* is a misreading or a scribe's error for *eṉṉum*. In this case we would translate the phrase: "The people of the Ājīvikas, called the *Ācuvam* should pay one *kācu* per head." *Ācuvam* was probably a collective name for the whole Ājīvika community.

[5] *AR.*, no. 283 of 1902. *SII.* vii, 912. Professor Sastri believes that this inscription is of Kulottunga III Parakesarī, in which case its date would be c. A.D. 1211 (*The Colas*, vol. ii, p. 709).

[6] *AR.*, no. 199 of 1912.

"the Ājīvika poll-tax" (*Ācuvikaḷ-pērāṟ-kācu*), which is followed by the tax on the *Uvaiccas* (*Uvaiccar-pērāṟ-kuṭi-k-kācum*).[1]

7. An inscription of Rājarāja III's 22nd year, Śaka 1160, or A.D. 1238, at the Perumal Temple, Poygai, near Viriñcipuram,[2] recording the gift of the village of Kumāramaṅgalam to the temple. Among the taxes there levied was the *Āciva*(*ka*)-*kācu*.

8. An inscription of Rājarāja III's 24th year, Śaka 1161 (A.D. 1239–1240), in the same location.[3] This records the gift to the temple of the village of Puttūr, where the *Ācuva-k-kaṭamai* was levied.

9. An inscription of Rājarāja III's 28th year (A.D. 1243–4), in the same location.[4] This records the gift of the village of Aṭṭiyūr to the temple, with all taxes and rights, including the *Ācuva-k-kaṭamai*.

10. A fragmentary inscription of one Rājagambhīra-Śambhuvarāyaṉ, dated in the year following Śaka 1180 (A.D. 1259), at the Ammaiappeśvara temple, Paḍaveḍu.[5] The donor gave a village, the name of which is lost, to the temple; among the taxes there levied were the *Uvaccaṉ-per-k-kaṭamai* and the *Ācuvikaṉ-per-k-kaṭamai*. The tax on the Uvaccas, which occurs in the list immediately before that on the Ājīvikas, and which is also found in the Tiruvoṟṟiyūr inscription (No. 6 above), is of some significance, and is considered below.[6]

11. An inscription at Channakēśava Temple, Maḍivāḷa, Kolar District, Mysore,[7] dated in the 37th year of a king whose name is illegible, but who was probably the Hoysala Rāmanātha Deva, in which case the date of the inscription would be c. A.D. 1291. Various village taxes, including the *Ācuva-k-kaṭamai* are devoted to the maintenance of a perpetual lamp in the temple for the victory of the King.

12. An inscription at Kalluhaḷḷi, Kolar District, Mysore, dated Śaka 1215 (A.D. 1294)[8] A minister of Rāmanātha Deva

[1] Sastri, *The Colas*, vol. ii, p. 334, n. The text of this inscription has been supplied by the Government Epigraphist for India.
[2] *SII*. i, no. 59.
[3] *SII*. i, no. 61. No. 62 is a duplicate of this inscription.
[4] *SII*. i, no. 64.
[5] *SII*. i, no. 78.
[6] V. infra, pp. 192–93.
[7] *Epi. Carn*. x, Kolar, no. 28.
[8] *Epi. Carn*. x, Kolar, no. 18.

makes a religious donation of village taxes, including the *Ācuva-k-kaṭamai*.

13. An inscription at Kaivāra, Kolar District, Mysore, dated in the 40th year of the Hoysala Rāmanātha Deva (A.D. 1294).[1] Lands are donated to establish an annual festival on the King's birthday. The *Ācuva-k-kaṭamai* occurs among the numerous taxes mentioned.

14. An inscription at Maḍivāḷa, Bowringpet taluq, Kolar District, Mysore, dated Śaka 1251 (A.D. 1339).[2] Village taxes, including the *Ācuvam aulambalam*, are dedicated to the local temple.

15. An inscription at Haḷepāḷya, Kolar District, Mysore, dated Śaka 1268 (A.D. 1346).[3] A grant to one Komuppaṉ of the village of Mātaraicaṉ-paḷḷi, with the right to receive all taxes, including the *Ācuvam taṟi-iṟai*.

16. A further inscription at Kaivāra (v. No. 13, above), remitting certain taxes to the temple of Bhīmeśvara, including the *Ācuva-k-kaṭamai*.[4] The grant is dated Śaka 1267 (A.D. 1346).

17. An inscription at Guḍihaḷḷi, Kolar District, Mysore, dated Śaka 1268 (A.D. 1346).[5] Certain inhabitants of the *nāṭu*, including the *sāmantâdhipati* Aṅkaya-nāyakkar, make a grant to the temple at Ceṅkai. Among the taxes mentioned is the *Ācuvam avalambalam*.

The presence of the word Ājīvika in certain South Indian inscriptions was known to Hoernle,[6] who, following Hultzsch,[7] identified the Ājīvikas there mentioned with the Jainas. Barua also noted the recurrence of the name.[8] But neither authority appears to have been aware of the full range of inscriptions, their knowledge being based on those at Poygai. We have here evidence that the Ājīvikas existed not only around one small centre during the first half of the thirteenth century, but that they were present in what are now the Arcot and Nellore districts of

[1] *Epi. Carn.* x, Chintamani, no. 88.
[2] *Epi. Carn.* x, Bowringpet, no. 28. This is not the same village as that of no. 11 above, which is in Kolar taluq.
[3] *Epi. Carn.* x, Malur, no. 39.
[4] *Epi. Carn.* x, Chintamani, no. 90.
[5] *Epi. Carn.* x, Sidhlaghatta, no. 67.
[6] *ERE.* i, p. 266.
[7] *SII.* i, p. 88, n. 5.
[8] *JDL.* ii, p. 78.

Madras Province, and in the Kolar District of Mysore, for at least nine hundred years, from A.D. 446, the date of the inscription of Siṃhavarman Pallava, until A.D. 1346, the date of the Guḍihaḷḷi inscription. The evidence of the astrologer Vaidyanātha Dīkṣita,[1] indicates that they survived into the following century.

Few authorities seem to have devoted much thought to these inscriptions. Professor Nilakanta Sastri has noted the Ājīvika references in two at present unpublished[2] without pausing to consider their significance from the point of view of religious history, while Professor B. A. Saletore has remarked on the implications of the Āvaṇi inscription, and has correctly interpreted the nature of the Ājīvika tax there levied.[3]

A further brief contribution on these inscriptions has been provided by Professor A. Chakravarti, who quotes and considers the Poygai inscriptions in his introduction to *Nīlakēci*,[4] and arrives at original conclusions. " It is evident," he writes, " that Dr. Hultzch (*sic*) makes an unfortunate mistake in translating *Ācuvakkaṭamai* as the tax on Ajivikâs (*sic*). *A priori* it is absurd to suggest that any minister would propose levying a tax on wandering mendicants who have to beg for their daily food. . . . Further, from the context it is clear that the term refers to some kind of professional tax since it occurs in the midst of words relating to professional tax, ' the tax on looms, the tax on shops, the tax on gold-smiths (*sic*), and the tax on oil mills, and *Ācuvakkaṭamai* translated as the tax on Ajivikâs (*sic*).' Probably the term *Ācuvakkaṭamai* refers to the tax laid on Bronzesmiths (*sic*) who made moulds for casting vessels and other objects of bell-metals. The Tamil term *ācu* is generally used synonymously with mould. Hence it can only mean a tax on moulding and casting. It is not for us to determine exactly what it means. It is enough for our purpose to state that it does not and cannot mean tax on Ajivikās (*sic*) and the rendering given by Dr. Hultzch (*sic*) is evidently wrong." [5]

Professor Chakravarti is right to refuse to accept the equivalence of *Ācuva* and *Ājīvika* without question; but we cannot admit his two objections. The first is quickly answered.

[1] V. supra, p. 184.
[2] Nos. 3 and 6 above.
[3] *Mediæval Jainism*, pp. 223–4.
[4] " *Neelakesi* ", pp. 251–261.
[5] Op. cit., p. 261.

The tax was levied not on Ājīvika mendicants, but on their patrons, the Ājīvika laymen. Chakravarti's second objection is more serious. The tax is usually listed among many trade taxes of various kinds. The usual form of the word as it occurs in the inscriptions is *Ācuva*, a possible Dravidian corruption of *Ājīva* or *Ājīvika*, but a word which might be based, as Chakravarti suggests, upon a Tamil word *ācu*. One of the Poygai inscriptions, however, gives a form much closer to the correct Sanskrit—*Ācivi(ka)*,[1] and any doubts should finally be set at rest by the earliest of our inscriptions, that of Siṃhavarman Pallava.[2] This is in Sanskrit, and the *Ājīvika-kara* is there mentioned in its correct Sanskrit form.

Professor Krishnaswami Aiyangar, controverting the earlier view of Sewell, that the tax was levied " on everyone who professed the Jaina religion ",[3] remarks that : " There is nothing to warrant that it (i.e. the tax) was taken from them (i.e. the Ājīvikas) as it is included among other general taxes. It is likely that it was intended for feeding and otherwise providing for these mendicants by the community." [4] He suggests that the tax was not a special tax on Ājīvikas, but a tax on the village communities for the benefit of the Ājīvika ascetics. The general disfavour in which the Ājīvikas were held makes this theory intrinsically improbable ; it is completely disproved by reference to the Āvaṇi inscription,[5] where the word *Ācuvimakkaḷ* is obviously in the nominative, and where it is plainly shown that the Ājīvikas were taxed at a higher rate than the rest of the villagers. Several other inscriptions would be very difficult to understand, on Professor Aiyangar's hypothesis.

As Chakravarti has noticed, the Ājīvika tax is usually mentioned together with a number of trade taxes, including those on the low-caste leather-workers and oil-pressers. Moreover, the Tiruvoṟṟiyūr and Paḍaveḍu inscriptions [6] mention the tax with that on the *Uvaccas*. The latter term is sometimes used in Tamil for Muslim settlers, and it was interpreted in this sense by

[1] No. 7 above.
[2] No. 1 above.
[3] *Historical Inscriptions of South India*, p. 137. Sewell apparently accepted the general theory that the Ājīvikas were Digambara Jainas.
[4] Ibid., p. 137, n. 1.
[5] No. 4 above. V. infra, pp. 194–95.
[6] Nos. 6 and 10 above.

Hultzsch.[1] It may also mean the low-caste temple-drummers of the sect of Kālī.[2] In either sense the term indicates unorthodoxy, and that the Ājīvika should have been placed beside the Uvacca indicates that both were looked upon as unorthodox. The juxtaposition of the Ājīvika, the leather-worker, the oil-presser, and the weaver in other inscriptions is also significant, and perhaps indicates that the Ājīvikas were treated as a caste, following one dominant occupation. The close connection in earlier times between Ājīvikas and potters and their wares [3] suggests that pottery was their traditional craft, and it is perhaps significant that the relevant inscriptions do not elsewhere mention taxes on potters. On the other hand the considerable fund of taxable wealth which they must have possessed, and the dislike which seems to have been felt for them, suggest that they may have been moneylenders or money-changers.[4]

The Siṃhavarman grant proves that, by the middle of the fifth century A.D., the Ājīvikas were well established in the district, for the tax was not then newly imposed upon them, but its proceeds were merely transferred by the King to the recipient of the grant. The legends of the Jainas, with whom the Ājīvikas seem to have been originally associated, ascribe the first important penetration of Jainism into South India to the Maurya epoch, when the pontiff Bhadrabāhu led a band of ascetics, including the ex-Emperor Candragupta himself, to Śravaṇa Beḷgoḷā.[5] Aśoka sent Buddhist missionaries to the Tamil country, and his political influence extended as far as North Mysore.[6] The Maurya period seems to have been one in which all unorthodox sects flourished and expanded. Probably Ājīvika ascetics found their way to the Tamil country during this period, when they were patronized by Mauryan kings, and perhaps exercised considerable influence.

At this time it is unlikely that Brāhmaṇical Hinduism had made any important impression on the indigenous population, whose religious practices seem to have centred round

[1] *SII*. i, p. 82, n. 4.
[2] Madras University *Tamil Lexicon*, s.v. *Uvacca*.
[3] V. supra, p. 134.
[4] I am indebted to Dr. L. D. Barnett for this suggestion.
[5] *PHAI*., pp. 241–2.
[6] Ibid., pp. 256–7.

wild nature deities, propitiated by village witch-doctors with ceremonies which involved religious hysteria and the shedding of blood.[1] Dancing, probably ecstatic,[2] and bloody magical ceremonies [3] seem to have been practised by the early Ājīvikas. Thus the unkempt Ājīvika ascetic might make a greater immediate impression upon the early Dravidians than did the grave Buddhist *bhikkhu.* Although Ājīvikism never gained so strong a hold as did its rivals, we may suggest that it survived longer in the Dravidian South than in the North because it was more in keeping with Dravidian character and tradition.

We may surmise that, with the growing influence of Hindu Buddhist and Jaina missionaries, the status of the Ājīvikas in the South fell. Village communes levied a special tax upon them, which was maintained under the orthodox Pallavas, Colas, and Hoysalas.

This tax is referred to as *kara*, *kācu*, *kaṭamai*, *avalampalam*, and *taṟi-iṟai.* The Āvaṇi inscription [4] indicates that the term *Ācuvi-kācu* was, at least sometimes, taken in its literal sense, as the gold coin of that name, weighing about 28 grains.[5] The same inscription points to the fact that the *Ācuvi-kācu* was a poll-tax. The Ājīvika community paid it "per person" (*pēṟāl*), while the quarter *kācu* levied in respect of the minor tolls upon the rest of the village community was paid "per house" (*vīṭṭāl*). From this we infer that the Ājīvika household might pay as much as twenty or thirty times the tax of the orthodox ; and the tax was doubled if payment fell into arrears.

The word *pēṟāl*, here used in respect of the Ājīvika tax, recalls the phrases *Acuvikaḷ-pēṟāṟ-kācu* and *Ācuvikaṉ-per-k-kaṭamai*, in other inscriptions.[6] It seems that in both these cases *pēr* or *per* must be read in the sense of a person or individual. This is the view taken by Saletore.[7] An alternative suggestion,[8] that *pēṟāl* means "in the name of" the Ājīvikas, does not seem probable. The contrast between *pēṟāl* and *vīṭṭāl*

[1] Iyengar, *History of the Tamils to* 600 A.D., pp. 74 ff.
[2] V. supra, p. 117.
[3] V. supra, pp. 112–13.
[4] No. 4 above.
[5] Madras University *Tamil Lexicon*, s.v. *kācu*.
[6] Nos. 6 and 10 above.
[7] *Mediæval Jainism*, pp. 223–4.
[8] Offered by Dr. S. Vithiananthan.

in the Āvaṇi inscription, and the use of the words *pēr* and *per* in the two other inscriptions mentioned, provide convincing evidence that the Ājīvika tax was, in these cases at least, a poll-tax, in contrast to the house-taxes paid by most other members of the village community. But even on the alternative interpretation of the Āvaṇi inscription, it seems that the Ājīvikas paid much heavier taxes than did other classes of the community. Probably they were considerably richer than the average peasant of the time, for the assembly of the *viṣaya* would hardly have imposed this oppressive tax if it had not considered its victims capable of paying it. The tax at Āvaṇi is a measure of the unpopularity of the Ājīvikas, and shows that they were under a disability which marked them as a class apart from the rest of the population.

In considering the Ājīvikas in South India we must not disregard the many inscriptions in which no reference to them occurs. It is by no means certain that the examples given above exhaust the inscriptional references to Ājīvikism, for the full text of many inscriptions is not available. But it is certain that there are many inscriptions from the region where Ājīvikas are known to have existed, which make no mention either of the sect or of a tax upon it. One significant inscription of this type is to be found at Kaivāra,[1] where the Ājīvika tax was levied in A.D. 1294.[2] This inscription, which is dated A.D. 1375, lists a number of village taxes, but not that on the Ājīvikas. We may infer that by this time they had ceased to exist in the village. That the tax was rescinded by the village commune is *a priori* less likely. Similar evidence of the period of the disappearance of the Ājīvikas in other villages is unfortunately lacking.

The absence of the tax in villages other than those mentioned may either be due to the fact that no Ājīvikas resided therein, or that they were not specially taxed. The latter alternative is more probable, since literary evidence indicates that Ājīvikas existed further south than the villages mentioned in the inscriptions, in Madurā and Malabar,[3] and it is hardly likely that the Ājīvikas in the extreme south came by sea. We have no reason to believe that an Ājīvika tax was imposed there ;

[1] *Epi. Carn.* x, Chintamani, 94. [2] V. supra, no. 13.

[3] V. infra, pp. 197 ff.

but there is evidence that Jainism was sometimes severely persecuted by Pāṇḍyan kings,[1] and it is not impossible that the Ājīvikas further south suffered more severely at the hands of orthodoxy than did those of the Arcot and Kolar districts.

Ājīvikas in Tamil Literature

There appears to be no definite reference to Ājīvikas in the earliest Tamil literature, the only possible exception being the unidentified quotation by Naccinārkkiniyar in his commentary to the *Tolkāppiyam*, which we have already mentioned.[2] In the anthologies of erotic and martial poems, which form the most striking monument of ancient Dravidian culture, the *antaṇar* or brāhmaṇas are already present, although the Āryan way of life has only partially imposed itself.[3] Yet the voluminous literature of the anthologies seems to contain no certain reference to any of the unorthodox sects. The famous *Tirukkuṟaḷ*, somewhat later than the anthologies, admittedly contains ten verses on fate (*ūḻ*).[4] But all can be interpreted as applying to the orthodox *karma*, and although it is possible to suggest that they were in part inspired by Ājīvika ideas this cannot be finally established.

In view of the Jaina tradition of the migration under Bhadrabāhu, and of the claim of Aśoka to have sent Buddhist missionaries to the Dravidian lands, we cannot accept the negative evidence of the anthologies as proof of a late penetration of heterodoxy into the Tamil country. The Bhaṭṭiprolu Casket, of the end of the second century B.C.,[5] indicates that Buddhists existed in the Āndhra country at this date, and it would be rash to claim that there were none further south. As we have already suggested, it is probable that the heterodox sects began their southward expansion during the Maurya period. But at the time of the composition of the anthologies it may be assumed that they had made little impression upon the lives of the people in the districts south of the Kāviri, where most of the earliest Tamil literature was written.

[1] Smith, *Early History of India*, pp. 474–5.
[2] V. *supra*, p. 111.
[3] *CHI.* i, p. 596.
[4] *Tirukkuṟaḷ*, 371–380.
[5] Sircar, *Select Inscriptions* i, p. 215, n. 1.

Although Tamil authorities of the older school claimed a much greater antiquity for their early literature, we may tentatively attribute the oldest and most important of the anthologies, the *Puṟanāṉūṟu* and the *Akanāṉūṟu*, to the early centuries of the Christian era.[1] Somewhat later come the so-called "epics", two of which contain definite evidence of the presence of Ājīvikas in the extreme south.

The translator of *Maṇimēkalai*, Dr. Krishnaswami Aiyangar, has claimed that the Buddhist logic propounded in the work is earlier than that of Diṅnāga, and has suggested the fourth century A.D. for the composition of the text.[2] Rather the evident similarity of the two systems suggests the reverse. It is not probable that the great Buddhist logician borrowed his system almost intact from an obscure Tamil poet, or even from an unknown third source to which both he and Cāttaṉ of Madurā may have been indebted. More probably the author of *Maṇimēkalai* was himself versed in Diṅnāga's logic. Therefore we must posit a somewhat later date for the composition of *Maṇimēkalai* than Dr. Aiyangar would admit, and suggest that it and the kindred "epic" *Cilappatikāram* represent conditions as they existed in South India in the sixth or seventh centuries of the Christian era.

As already noticed,[3] *Cilappatikāram* gives evidence of the existence of a community of Ājīvika ascetics at Madurā, whose order the father of the heroine Kaṇṇaki entered on the death of his daughter. They are described as "saints with the mien of gods, Ājīvikas (performing) severe penances".[4] This indicates that Ājīvikas were at least occasionally respected and it gives no suggestion of slackness or hypocrisy among their monks.

The reference in *Maṇimēkalai* is longer and more important. The poem treats of the religious quest of the heroine Maṇimēkalai, who, after many adventures of a magical and mystical type, arrives at Vañji, where she finds many religious teachers of different sects, and listens to their doctrines. Already a convinced

[1] De la Vallée Poussin, *Dynasties et Histoire* . . ., pp. 315–19.

[2] *Maṇimekhalai in its Historical Setting*, pp. 78 ff.

[3] V. supra, p. 134.

[4] *Kaṭavular-kōlatt'-aṇṇalar perun-tavatt'-Ācīvakar*. *Cilappatikāram* xxvii, 98–9.

Buddhist, she decides that no other sect has any profound knowledge of the truth, and becomes a nun. The text is an example of a class of philosophic literature which, stripped of its fictional trappings, resulted in such works as *Civañāṉa-cittiyār*, and the *Sarva-darśana-saṅgraha*. The doctrines of the opposing sects are stated in *Maṇimēkalai* briefly, with an attempt at objectivity. Among the teachers of Vañji is "The Elder, knowing the book of the Ājīvikas",[1] who delivers a lecture which is of great importance for the elucidation of Ājīvika doctrine and which will be considered in our second part. The author to whom the work is attributed, Cāttaṉ of Madurā, seems to have looked upon Vañji, the ancient capital of the Kerala kingdom, as a centre in which representatives of many religions and sects rubbed shoulders. His testimony suggests that Ājīvikism had by this time penetrated to Malabar. Some doubt exists as to the exact location of the ancient Vañji, which was probably at what is now Tiru-karur, near Cochin.[2]

The most valuable reference to Ājīvikas in Tamil literature is that contained in the anonymous Jaina poem *Nīlakēci*. This seems to have been written by an author who had read the Buddhist *Maṇimēkalai*, and wished to provide a Jaina counterpart to that work. But the poem is a step nearer to the fully developed study of various philosophical systems than *Maṇimēkalai*, wherein the philosophy is subordinate to the story.

From the literary point of view the narrative of *Nīlakēci* is of little importance, but serves merely as a framework for the substance of the poem, the exposition of various philosophical systems, and the detailed refutation of all but that of the Jainas. The story has, however, some significance for the light it throws on the date of the work, and for its reference to the Ājīvika teacher, Pūraṇa. The animal sacrifices at the temple of Kālī in Puṇḍra-vardhana are interrupted through the preaching of a Jaina ascetic, Municandra. The goddess summons from the South one of her underlings, the demi-goddess Nīlakēci, to shake Municandra's resolution and thus destroy his power. Nīlakēci, after tempting the ascetic in various ways reminiscent of those used by Māra against the Buddha, admits herself beaten, and is initiated by the *muni* into the Jaina faith with a long discourse on Jaina

[1] *Ācīvaka-nūl-aṟinta-purāṇaṉ*. *Maṇi*. xxvii, 108.

[2] *CHI*. i, p. 595.

cosmology and the doctrine of *karma*. On her conversion Nīlakēci makes good use of her power of flight by passing rapidly from one city to another, challenging the greatest non-Jaina teachers to debate, and invariably defeating them, with arguments often of considerable subtlety. It will be seen that this narrative is a mere vehicle for a dissertation on Jainism and the refutation of opposing theories.

The list of teachers whom Nīlakēci is said to have defeated in debate, and the cities in which they are said to have taught, is of some interest. Despite the Śaktic narrative framework the main enemy of the author of this poem is evidently Buddhism, the doctrines of which are the first to be refuted and to which are devoted four chapters, while the other sects receive only one each.

The names of Nīlakēci's opponents, in their Sanskrit forms, are :—

1. The Buddhist nun Kuṇḍalakeśī at Kāmpilya ; she describes the greatness of the Buddha and the five *skandhas* of Buddhism ;
2. Arkacandra, at Ujjain ; he is a Buddhist preacher specially interested in ethics ;
3. Maudgalyāyana (Tamil, Mokkala) at Padmapura, who rather attacks Jaina doctrines than defends his own ;
4. Buddha himself, at Kapilapura, which is said to be by the seashore ; he discusses the five *skandhas*, the four noble truths, the doctine of emptiness (*śūnyavāda*), and that of momentariness (*kṣaṇikavāda*) ; he finally abandons his doctrine of soullessness (*anātma*) as a result of Nīlakēci's subtle arguments ;
5. Pūraṇa the Ājīvika, at Kukkuṭanagara ;
6. Parāśara the Sāṅkhya, at Hastināpura ; his doctrine, while recognizing twenty-five *tattvas*, is monistic, and describes Puruṣa as free from all activity, without *guṇas*, always an enjoyer, not undergoing modifications, not bound by *karma*, eternal, all-pervading, all-perceiving, all-enjoying existence ;
7. Lokajit, a Vaiśeṣika teacher, at a place unspecified ;
8. Bhūtika, a teacher of the Veda, at the town of Kākanti [1] ; his doctrine is that of the eternal and self-existent Vedas ; and finally

[1] Kākan, Monghyr District (Jain, *Life in Ancient India*, p. 291).

9. Piśācaka, a materialist (*bhūtavādī*), at the court of a king named Madanajit, the location of whose capital is not stated.

The presence of such figures as Maudgalyāyana, Buddha, and Parāśara suggests that the anonymous author intended his poem to be historically plausible. He appears to have considered Pūraṇa, whom he thought of as the contemporary of Buddha, to be the founder of Ājīvikism. Thus we have independent confirmation of the historicity of Pūraṇa Kassapa of the Pāli canon.

The doctrines propounded by the teachers give some indication of the date of the composition of the work. The author seems to have known *Maṇimēkalai*, and consciously to have modelled his poem on the philosophical part of that work. His language is somewhat later than that of *Maṇimēkalai*. We may therefore suggest the seventh century A.D. as the earliest possible date of the poem's composition. The work must have been in existence by the end of the thirteenth century, if, according to Professor Chakravarti's theory, Vāmanamuni, the commentator to *Nīlakēci*, lived at that time.[1] It is probable, however, that the poem antedates its commentator by several centuries on the evidence of the doctrines of the nine teachers. *Nīlakēci* must have been written when it was still possible for a Dravidian Jaina to look on Buddhism as his sect's most dangerous rival. The author has nothing to say about the Vedânta school of Śaṅkara or the Viśiṣṭâdvaita of Rāmânuja, so we may assume that he wrote before the influence of these philosophers was much felt in South India. Moreover he does not mention devotional Śaivism. It therefore seems that *Nīlakēci* was written before any of these sects became very influential in the Tamil country. We may suggest the ninth century as the latest date at which it could have been written.

Professor Chakravarti does not agree with this conclusion. The absence of references to the Ājīvikas in the Tamil devotional anthologies convinces him that they were extinct when the hymns were composed.[2] He overlooks the reference to them in the *Civañāṉa-cittiyār*, of the fourteenth century. The author of *Nīlakēci* states that he learnt Jaina doctrine from one Tēvar,

[1] Chakravarti, "*Neelakesi*," p. 11.
[2] "*Neelakesi*," p. 8.

whom Chakravarti identifies with the author of the *Tirukkuṟaḷ*.[1] Hence he believes that the poem was written as early as the first century A.D. Overlooking any other objections to this very early date, the identification proposed by Chakravarti cannot be proved. Chakravarti gives the name in its honorific plural form, "Thevar," which title is sometimes used to mean Tiruvaḷḷuvar.[2] But the text gives the name in the singular form, *Tēvaṉ*, which is not so used, but may be applied to the Jaina *Arhant*.[3] We must therefore reject Cakravarti's conclusion that *Nīlakēci* was written at so early a date, and assign the work to the eighth or ninth century.

Most of the information about the Ājīvikas given by the poem concerns their philosophy, and will be considered in the second part of this work. It does, however, shed a little light on the general character of Dravidian Ājīvikism at the period.

In the poem Nīlakēci is said to have "gone to the great city of Kukkuṭa, and entered Camataṇṭa",[4] where she found Pūraṇa's monastery. Vāmanamuni, the commentator, gives no information about Camataṇṭa, other than that it is the name of a town (*ūr*). The former place he ignores. In a footnote Professor Chakravarti states that Kukkuṭa- or Kōḻi-nagar is a name of Uraiyūr or Trichinopoly, but he gives no basis for this doubtful statement. The scenes of Nīlakēci's other philosophical debates are all in Northern India, and we may infer that the author thought of Kukkuṭanagara as also situated in the north. The *Dhammapada Commentary* mentions a town called Kukkuṭavatī,[5] elsewhere referred to as Kukkuṭa, somewhere in the Himālayan region, at a distance of 120 leagues from Sāvatthi. Perhaps Kukkuṭanagara was the town remembered by the Ājīvikas as the birthplace of Pūraṇa, since the Buddha is represented in the poem as meeting Nīlakēci in Kapilapura or Kapilavastu, the city of his birth. Camataṇṭa, or Samadaṇḍa, may have been a near-by suburb or village.

A second possibility is that the Tamil author imagined the events as taking place in Samataṭa, the Delta region of Bengal.

[1] Ibid., p. 10. Reference to *Nīl.* v, 5.
[2] Madras University, *Tamil Lexicon*, s.v. *tēvar*.
[3] Ibid., s.v. *tēvaṉ*.
[4] *Kukkuṭa mā nakar niṉṟu . . . pōy c-Camataṇṭam pukkāḷ.* *Nīl.* 666.
[5] *Dhp. Comm.* ii, pp. 116 ff., teste *DPPN.* s.v. *Kukkuṭavatī*.

The near-by region to the west of the Delta was sometimes called Daṇḍabhukti,[1] and Samadaṇḍa may be a corruption of the two names Daṇḍabhukti and Samataṭa. If so the name Kukkuṭanagara ("City of the Cock") may be explained by the similarity of the words *Tāmralipti*, the chief river-port of the area, and *tāmracūḍa* ("the copper-crested"), a common literary epithet for the cock. That the author of *Nīlakēci* had but a poor knowledge of North Indian geography is proved by his placing Kapilapura on the sea coast, and in such an author confusion is not impossible. If this alternative be accepted it may indicate that the Dravidian Ājīvikas looked upon Bengal as the original home of their faith.

The Ājīvika hermitage is described as adorned with fragrant flowers,[2] and thus gives the impression of being a pleasant and comfortable place. Here the teacher rules with great respect and dignity, and expounds the Ājīvika scriptures (*āraṇam*) to visitors. He is "the Great Mind, the great one than whom none is greater, Pūraṇaṉ the Lord, the Most Learned".[3] He is careful to stress that his followers are not Jainas, as though the two sects might easily be confused.[4] From this it might be inferred that the Southern Ājīvikas practised nudity, and that the confusion was thus likey to arise, but Vāmanamuni in his commentary took the phrase to mean that the Ājīvikas, like the Jainas, maintained an *anekântavāda* system of epistemology,[5] and that misunderstanding might thus occur. The Ājīvika monks are described as *mā-tavar*, or ascetics performing extreme penances. Yet the teacher concludes his speech by urging his visitor not to condemn them because of their addiction to *cuvai*, which, as we have seen,[6] may mean sensual pleasure. The chapter on the Ājīvikas in *Nīlakēci* yields no other information about the history and development of the Ājīvika sect in the South.

Civañāṉa-cittiyār, one of the most famous Tamiḻ Śaivite

[1] *History of Bengal*, vol. i, ed. Majumdar, p. 23 and map opp.
[2] *Kaṭi-malar-pūm-paḷḷi. Nīl.* 667.
[3] *Pēruṇar-veytipperitum-periyavaṉ Pūraṇaṉ eṉpāṉ peruvaṟakkaṟṟavaṉ. Nīl.* 668.
[4] *Ayaliyar tām alla v Ācīvakarkaḷ. Nīl.* 669.
[5] *Tikamparatvam oppiṉum anēkāntavātikaḷ ākiya nirkkiranta-v-allar Ājīvakar.*
[6] V. supra, p. 125.

texts, is the third important source for Dravidian Ājīvikism. Its author, Aruṇandi Śivâcārya, lived in the thirteenth century,[1] and we therefore see in his work Ājīvikas in their final phase. The text is in two parts, the *Parapakṣam* and the *Supakṣam*. The former outlines the chief opposing systems of the time, including Materialism, Buddhism, Jainism, and the orthodox sects, each of which is refuted. The second part is an exposition of Śaivite doctrine and philosophy, and is of no importance for our study.

In the *Parapakṣam* the Ājīvikas are discussed immediately after the Jainas. The latter are described as naked ascetics,[2] thus showing that the author had the Digambara sect in mind. Even at this late date, therefore, the Ājīvikas were distinct from the Digambaras. But Aruṇandi appears to have considered the Ājīvikas akin to the Jainas, for they are referred to in his poem as *Ācīvakaṉ amaṇarkaḷ*[3] (Skt. *śramaṇa*), the usual Tamil word for Jaina ascetics.

Aruṇandi says little about the customs of the Ājīvikas. They practise severe penances, and pull the hairs from their heads. Their doctrine is one of atomism; *Niyati* the principle of determinism, which looms so large in the Pāli accounts of Makkhali Gosāla's system, is scarcely mentioned; and something like the usual doctrine of *karma* is maintained. Apparently Aruṇandi had met Ājīvikas who had moved far in the direction of Jainism, without completely losing their identity.

Certain references of Canarese provenance, collected by Dr. K. B. Pathak[4] must here be mentioned. The first of these is in the *Ācārasāra* of Vīranandi, a Digambara work in Sanskrit, of the twelfth century. This states that the mendicant (*parivrāṭ*) who practises extreme penance will reach the heaven of Brahmakalpa, lower than that destined for the Ājīvika, who, ignorant of the true doctrine though he be, will attain the higher heaven of Sahasrāra-kalpa.[5] The commentary adds that the

[1] V. Nallaswami Pillai, "*Śivajñāna Siddhiyār*," pp. xlv–vi.
[2] *CÑC.*, p. 213.
[3] *CÑC.*, p. 255, v. 1.
[4] *The Ājīvikas a Sect of Buddhist Bhikkhus*, *IA.* xli, pp. 88–9.
[5] *Parivrāḍ brahmakalpântaṃ yāty ugrâcāravān api Ājīvakaḥ Sahasrāra-kalp'-ântaṃ darśan'-ôjjhitaḥ. Ācārasāra* xi, 127 (as quoted by Pathak, loc. cit.). In Bombay edn. xi, 128.

Ājīvika is a kind of Buddhist *bhikṣu*, subsisting upon rice-gruel (*kāñji*).[1] *Vaṭṭakera's Mūlâcāra*, not quoted by Pathak, contains a similar verse, followed by one which states that non-Jaina ascetics can rise no higher than Sahasrāra.[2]

Dr. Pathak also quotes a commentary to Nemicandra's *Trilokasāra* by Mādhavacandra, another Southern Digambara, who disagrees with Vīranandi and Vaṭṭakera, and, like the *Aupapātika Sūtra*,[3] forecasts an even more exalted destiny for Ājīvika ascetics. Ājīvika ascetics, who eat *kāñji*, etc., will reach Acyutakalpa, the last stage before *nirvāṇa*, but will go no further, while the naked *carakas*, and the *parivrājakas* with one or three staves, will be reborn in the lower heaven of Brahmakalpa.[4] This statement is confirmed by the Canarese commentator, Padmaprabha Traividya.[5]

These passages show that the Ājīvika, although by one commentator believed to be a sort of Buddhist, was *persona grata* to the Digambara Jaina. He is promised a very high place in the Jaina heavens, rising far above the orthodox *caraka*, *ekadaṇḍin*, and *tridaṇḍin*. This surely indicates that the Jaina theologians recognized him as akin to themselves, and paid him qualified respect. It is evident from these quotations and from the *Civañāṉa-cittiyār*, that some Ājīvikas were being absorbed into Jainism during the Middle Ages. As we shall show, other Ājīvikas developed theistic tendencies, and may have found a place in the growing devotional Vaiṣṇavism of the time.

[1] *Ājīvakaḥ : Bauddha-bhedam appa kāṃji bhikṣu.* Quoted Pathak, loc. cit.

[2] xii, 132–3. Bombay edn., vol. ii, p. 264.

[3] V. supra, p. 140.

[4] *Nagn'-âṇḍa-lakṣaṇāś carakā ekadaṇḍi-tridaṇḍi-lakṣaṇāḥ parivrājakā Brahmakalpa-paryantaṃ gacchanti, na tata upari. Kāñjik'-âdi-bhojina Ājīvā Acyutakalpa-paryantaṃ gacchanti, na ṭata upari.* Mādhavacandra to *Trilokasāra*, 545. Quoted Pathak, loc. cit.

[5] *Ājīvā ambila kūḷan umbaru Acyuta̤-pad-otti Acyuta-kalpa-paryyaṃta(m) puṭṭuvaru.* Quoted Pathak, loc. cit.

APPENDIX TO PART I

THE ICONOCLAST ASCETICS OF KASHMĪR [1]

Kalhaṇa's *Rājataraṅgiṇī* states that ascetics, in many respects resembling the Ājīvikas, appeared in Kashmīr in considerable numbers during the reign of the tyrannical and ill-fated King Harṣa or Harṣadeva (1089–1101).

The chronicler relates that this king was, from his youth, strongly influenced by the customs of Southern India. He was the contemporary of the Cālukya Vikramâditya VI Tribhuvanamalla, whose court poet was Bilhaṇa the Kashmīrī,[2] and who is mentioned in the chronicle by his *biruda* Parmāḍi or Parmāṇḍi. Harṣa is said to have fallen deeply in love with Candalā, the queen of Parmāḍi, and to have vowed to win her by force; it appears that he actually contemplated an expedition against the Cālukya for this purpose.[3] One of his youthful friends was a southerner, Keśin the Karṇāṭa, who was killed in a fruitless *coup d'état* against Harṣa's father, King Kalaśa.[4] The poet further states that Harṣa favoured southern fashions, and introduced coin-types from Kārṇāṭaka.[5]

The latter statement is strikingly confirmed by the coins themselves. For at least two centuries Harṣa's predecessors had issued only a bronze coinage, bearing on the obverse a seated goddess, and on the reverse a standing king.[6] Harṣa's bronze coins, probably issued early in the reign, bear the same devices, but he also issued a plentiful gold and silver coinage, which generally bears new types. The first of these, in gold only, has the device of a horseman, which was probably borrowed from the Śāhi dynasty of Gandhāra; while the second type, both in gold and silver, bears on the obverse a standing elephant

[1] The substance of this appendix has appeared in *BSOAS*. xii, pp. 688 ff.

[2] *Rājataraṅgiṇī*, ed. Stein, vii, 935–7.

[3] Ibid., vii, 1119–1127.

[4] Ibid., vii, 675.

[5] *Dakṣiṇāty' âbhavad bhaṅgiḥ priyā tasya vilāsinaḥ,*
Karṇāṭ'-ânuguṇaṣ ṭaṅkas tatas tena pravartitaḥ. Ibid., vii, 926.

[6] Cunningham, *Coins of Mediæval India*, p. 45.

and on the reverse the inscription only.[1] The latter type, according to Rapson, was borrowed from the coinage of Koṅgudeśa.[2]

The chronicler tells the source of the precious metals from which Harṣa minted this abundant new coinage. When the king was short of money his evil counsellor Loṣṭadhara, grandson of Haladhara, advised him to restore his fortunes by looting the treasure of the temples and melting down the images of the gods. He is also said to have advised the confiscation of the *agrahāras* belonging to the Kalaśeśvara temple at Śrīnagara, and even its demolition to provide materials for bridge-building.[3] The king was at first dissuaded by his righteous counsellor Prayāga, but ultimately he accepted Loṣṭadhara's advice, and methodically looted first the temple treasures, and then the sacred ikons themselves. The policy of iconoclasm was so thorough that one Udayarāja was specially appointed as " superintendent of the destruction of the gods " (*dev'-ôtpāṭana-nāyaka*).[4] Of the larger images in the kingdom only four, two Hindu and two Buddhist, were spared.[5] This was followed by the inevitable palace revolution, and the assassination of the king. Harṣa's tragic end, graphically described by Kalhaṇa, took place in the hut of a base ascetic (*kṣudra-tapasvin*) Guṇa, whither the king had been led by his faithful attendant Mukta. The ascetic betrayed his hiding-place to the usurper Uccala, the hut was surrounded, and the king and his good friend Prayāga were slain on the spot by Uccala's troops.[6]

As minor characters in this tragic story there appear strange naked ascetics, employed by Harṣa to remove the images from the temples. They are described as " naked wanderers with wasted noses, feet, and hands ",[7] and as " broken (i.e. crippled) naked wanderers ".[8] They were not satisfied with the mere removal of the images, but, acting on Harṣa's instructions, they deliberately defiled them. " On their faces he had ordure and urine, etc., thrown by naked wanderers . . . in

[1] Cunningham, loc. cit.
[2] *Indian Coins*, p. 32.
[3] *Rājataraṅgiṇī* vii, 1075–8.
[4] Ibid., vii, 1089–1091.
[5] Ibid., 1096–8.
[6] Ibid., vii, 1635 ff.
[7] *Nagn'-âṭaiḥ śīrṇa-ghrāṇ'-âṅghri-pāṇibhiḥ.* Ibid., vii, 1092.
[8] *Rugṇa-nagn'-âṭakāḥ.* Ibid., vii, 1094.

order to ruin the images of the gods. The forms of the gods, made of gold, silver, and other (metals), rolled like bundles of firewood in the dung-covered roads. Crippled and naked ascetics and others dragged the images of the gods, covered with spittle, by ropes tied to their ankles." [1]

Harṣa's deliberate pollution of the images was obviously inspired by some motive other than poverty. Stein, in a footnote to his translation of this passage,[2] suggests that the king was influenced by Islām, and draws attention to two other verses in the poem in support. These are : " There was no temple in town or city which was not deprived of its images by Harṣarāja the Turk (*turuṣka*) " [3] ; and " He continually maintained with his wealth Turkish (*turuṣka*) captains of hundreds (and yet) the fool ate (the flesh of) village pigs until his death ".[4]

These two references, only one of which refers to Harṣa as a *Turuṣka*, are inconclusive. The first verse employs the word metaphorically. It must be remembered that Kalhaṇa wrote when the memory of Mahmūd's pillage of Hindu and Buddhist temples was still fresh. The second verse merely states that Harṣa was not affected by Islām, at least in diet, despite his Turkish mercenary officers. The naked ascetics described in the *Rājataraṅgiṇī* cannot have been Muslims, who have never held that nudity is necessary for salvation. It is hardly likely that they were Jainas, who have never shown marked hostility to the Hindu gods, or (except in the case of the much later sect of the Sthānakavāsīs) to the use of ikons in religious ceremonies.

These ascetics, whoever they were, clearly objected to the graphic or plastic representation of supernatural beings. We have no definite evidence that the Ājīvikas held such views, but the *Divyâvadāna*'s account of the Ājīvika or Nirgrantha who defiled a picture of the Buddha faintly suggests it.[5] The

1 . . . . *Vadaneṣu sa nagn'-âṭaiḥ*
Mūrti-nāśāya devānāṃ śakṛn-mūtr'-ady apātayat. 1092.
Svarṇa-rūpy'-âdi-ghaṭitā gīrvāṇ'-âkṛtayo 'luṭhan
Adhvasv indhana-gaṇḍālya iva śâvaskareṣv api. 1093.
Vibudha-pratimāś cakrur ākṛṣṭā gulpha-dāmabhiḥ
Thūtkāra-kusuma-cchannā rugṇa-nagn'-âṭak'-âdayaḥ. 1094. Ibid., vii.

2 *Kalhaṇa's Chronicle of the Kings of Kashmīr*, vol. i, p. 353.

3 *Rājataraṅgiṇī*, vii, 1095.

4 Ibid., vii, 1149.

5 V. supra, p. 147.

story of Gosāla's giving away his picture-board,[1] on abandoning the career of a *maṅkha*, may be a trace of an incident in the founder's life which led to iconoclastic tendencies in the sect. If these feeble indications that the Ājīvikas opposed the use of religious images were the only argument in favour of their identity with Harṣa's *nagn'-âṭakas* the evidence would be very weak indeed. There are, however, a number of other faint indications and resemblances which, if taken together, strengthen the probability.

We have already seen that Ājīvikas were to be found in Southern India, and Harṣa's personal interest in the South is well established. Travellers from the Deccan were frequent in the north. The *Rājataraṅgiṇī* quotes a song, said to have been sung at Harṣa's court, in which a traveller from the Deccan is told of the King's desperate love for Candalā.[2] It is said that the fame of Harṣa's liberality reached the court of Parmāṇḍi, where the poet Bilhaṇa, hearing of it, longed to return to his native country.[3] A few years after Harṣa's death we find the Gāhaḍavāla King Govindacandra patronizing a Buddhist monk Vāgīśvararakṣita, who came from the Cola country.[4] Legends state that Rāmânuja visited Kashmīr.[5] Much evidence may be found to indicate close cultural and religious contacts between Kashmīr and the Deccan at this period.

In such circumstances it is not impossible that a group of Ājīvika ascetics found its way to Kashmīr from the Deccan and obtained the confidence of the king, who was always ready to patronize the purveyors of novelties, and seems to have had a taste for the bizarre. On the other hand Bāṇa indicates the presence of *nagn'-âṭas* of some sort in Northern Panjāb or Kashmīr some 450 years earlier,[6] and the ascetics may have been an indigenous and previously insignificant group of Ājīvikas who rose to prominence as a result of Harṣa's patronage.

The phrase *rugṇa-nagn'-âṭaka* used by Kalhaṇa may be compared to the phrases *nagna-bhagna* and *nagga-bhogga*, to

[1] V. supra, p. 40.
[2] *Rājataraṅgiṇī* vii, 1123.
[3] Ibid., vii, 935–7.
[4] *Epi. Ind.* xi, pp. 20–6.
[5] De la Vallée Poussin, *Dynasties . . .*, p. 325.
[6] V. supra, p. 168.

which reference has already been made.[1] Unless these ascetics suffered from a disease such as leprosy they must have been ritually mutilated in some way. This suggests the Ājīvika initiation referred to in the *Jātaka*,[2] in which the novice had to grasp a heated lump of metal. Such an ordeal, if sufficiently protracted, might well fit the ascetic for Kalhaṇa's epithet *śīrṇa- . . . pāṇi*. The same ceremony may also be connected with the name of Harṣa's evil genius, Loṣṭadhara. From the name of his grandfather, Haladhara, he appears to have come from an orthodox Vaiṣṇavite family, but his own name (" Lump-holder ") is very unusual, if not unique. Was this name connected with an initiatory ordeal, and adopted by its owner to mark his adherence to Ājīvikism ?

On his gold and silver currency, probably minted after the looting of the temples, Harṣa did not use traditional Kashmīr coin device of the seated goddess. The disappearance of the goddess is itself significant, and may be connected with the iconoclasm of the *nagn'-âṭas*. It is just possible that the elephant which replaced the goddess was an Ājīvika religious symbol. The elephant is, of course, the attendant of Lakṣmī, and has some symbolic significance in Buddhism ; but it may well also have been an Ājīvika emblem. We recall the elephants of the façade of the Lomas Ṛṣi Cave,[3] and the " Last Sprinkling Scent Elephant ", one of the eight *carimāīṃ* of the Ājīvikas.[4]

Finally the " base ascetic " with whom Harṣa took refuge from the troops of Uccala has some Ājīvika characteristics. He lives with a prostitute, Bhiśca,[5] and thus lays himself open to the same sort of accusations as were levelled at Makkhali Gosāla and his followers.[6] His hut is near a charnel-ground (*pitṛvana*), where a necromancer (*siddha*) named Somânanda worshipped certain divinities called Someśvaras.[7] We have already seen that the Ājīvikas appear to have performed tantric ceremonies,[8]

[1] V. supra, p. 105.
[2] V. supra, p. 104.
[3] V. supra, pp. 153–54.
[4] V. supra, pp. 68–69.
[5] *Rājataraṅgiṇī* vii, 1637.
[6] V. supra, pp. 124 ff.
[7] *Somânand'-âbhidhānasya pūjyāḥ siddhasya devatāḥ*
Someśvar'-âbhidhāḥ santi kāścit pitṛvan'-ântare. Rājataraṅgiṇī, vii, 1635.
[8] V. supra, pp. 112–13, 162 ff.

and are said by one source to have worshipped *piśācas*.[1] The sorcerer seems to have been in some way connected with the ascetic, whose hut has " a courtyard marked by him (i.e. by Somânanda or perhaps by them, the Someśvara gods), its site hidden by high trees ".[2] This suggests the design on which the Ājīvika caves of Barābar were based, the round hut in the rectangular courtyard.[3] Finally the name of the ascetic, Guṇa, is the same as that of a famous *acelaka* or Ājīvika teacher of the *Jātaka*,[4] who propounds a fatalist atomism entirely consistent with the doctrines of the Ājīvikas.

We cannot claim that these resemblances finally prove the identity of Harṣa's *nagn'-âṭas* and the Ājīvikas, but we may well ask : If they were not Ājīvikas, what were they ?

1 V. supra, pp. 162 ff.
2 *Tal-lāñcit'-âṅganā tuṅga-taru-pracchanna-vāṭikā*
Abhūd Guṇ'-âbhidhānasya kuṭī kṣudra-tapasvinaḥ. *Rājataraṅgiṇī*, vii, 1636.
3 V. supra, p. 156.
4 V. supra, pp. 20, 104–5.

PART TWO

DOCTRINES OF THE ĀJĪVIKAS

CHAPTER XI

ĀJĪVIKA SCRIPTURES

THE *MAHĀṆIMITTAS*, THE *MAGGAS*, AND THE *OṆPATU-KATIR*

The contempt in which the Ājīvikas were held by their opponents does not conceal the fact that the sect possessed a fully elaborated system of belief, and that it produced its own philosophers and logicians, uninspired though they may have been, whose works and names are unfortunately lost to us. Moreover, it seems that Ājīvika doctrine, like that of Hinduism and Buddhism, did not remain static during the two millennia of the sect's existence, but developed by a process comparable to that by which the Mahāyāna system emerged from early Buddhism.

That the Ājīvikas had a canon of sacred texts in which their doctrines were codified, is clear from several passages cited in the Pāli and Prākrit texts of Buddhism and Jainism, or by the Jaina commentators, which give the impression of being adaptations or actual quotations from these scriptures.

The Jaina version of the origin of the Ājīvika canon is given in the *Bhagavatī Sūtra*,[1] where it is said that the six *disācaras* "extracted the eightfold *Mahāṇimitta* in the *Puvvas*, with the *Maggas* making the total up to ten, after examining hundreds of opinions", and that this was approved by Gosāla Maṅkhaliputta after brief consideration. Abhayadeva gives the names of the eight *aṅgas* of the *Mahāṇimitta* as follows :—

1. *Divyam*, "of the Divine."
2. *Autpātam*, "of portents."
3. *Āntarikṣam*, "of the sky."
4. *Bhaumam*, "of the earth."
5. *Āṅgam*, "of the body."
6. *Svāram*, "of sound."
7. *Lākṣaṇam*, "of characteristics"; and
8. *Vyāñjanam*, "of indications."

[1] *Bh. Sū.* xv, *sū.* 539, fol. 658–9. V. supra, pp. 56 ff.

These eight *Mahāṇimittas* are listed in the *Sthānâṅga Sūtra*,[1] with the variation *Suviṇe* (dreams) for *Divyam*; here the commentator Abhayadeva makes it quite clear that they are systems of prognostication. The *Uttarâdhyayana Sūtra*[2] gives a similar list, and adds that the Jaina *bhikkhu* should not live by such means. The Jaina saint Kālaya, or Kālaka is said to have learnt the *Mahāṇimittas* from the Ājīvikas.[3] We have seen that the Ājīvika mendicant often acted as an astrologer or reader of omens,[4] and it may be that the early scriptures of the Ājīvikas did contain considerable sections on these topics.

That the Jainas, despite the veto of the *Uttarâdhyayana*, also employed the eightfold *Mahāṇimitta* is shown by Kālaka's knowledge of it, and by an inscription at Śravaṇa Beḷgoḷā, which states that the pontiff Bhadrabāhu "knowing the eightfold *Mahāṇimitta*, seeing past, present, and future, foretold in Ujjayinī a calamity of twelve years' duration".[5]

The two *Maggas* are said by Abhayadeva to have been those of song and dance.[6] This statement, although disbelieved by Barua, may be based on accurate information, and the *Maggas* may represent texts containing Ājīvika religious songs and directions for ritual dances respectively.

These ten scriptures are said to have been plagiarized from the *Puvvas*. By the *Puvvas* it seems that the author of the *Bhagavatī* meant the Jaina *Pūrvas*, the earliest scriptures of the sect, which are now lost. The accusation of plagiarism, whether correct or not, is a further indication of the close connection of Ājīvikism and Jainism in origin. Hoernle makes this point strongly in his article on the Ājīvikas.[7] Barua, on the other hand, interprets the word *puvva* in the text not in the specialized Jaina sense, but merely as "past traditions".[8] The commentator Abhayadeva is himself vague, and defines the *puvvas* as "certain scriptures called *Pūrvas*".[9] Barua's view is perhaps strengthened

[1] *Sthānâṅga*, viii, 608.
[2] *Uttarâdhyayana*, xv, 7.
[3] *Pañcakalpa Cūrṇī*, *teste* Jain, *Life in Ancient India* . . ., p. 208.
[4] V. supra, p. 127.
[5] *Epi. Carn.* ii, no. 1.
[6] V. supra, pp. 116–17.
[7] *ERE*. i, p. 261.
[8] *JDL*. ii, p. 41.
[9] *Pūrv'-âbhidhāna-śruta-viśeṣa*. *Bh. Sū.*, fol. 659.

by the fact that the eightfold *Mahāṇimitta* of the Ājīvikas bears no resemblance to the titles of the fourteen lost *Pūrvas* of the Jaina tradition.[1] The whole passage defies definitive interpretation. It indicates, however, that the Ājīvikas had scriptures at an early period, that the latter included considerable sections on divination, and that they may have had something in common with the earliest scriptures of the Jainas.

The Tamil sources make it clear that the Dravidian Ājīvikas also had scriptures, which they prized very highly. The Ājīvika sage in *Maṇimēkalai* is " the knower of the Book of the Ājīvikas ",[2] and his lecture is said to contain the essence of the teaching of this text, which is also called " the Book of Maṟkali ".[3] Apparently this is no mere fortune-teller's manual, but a dissertation on the nature of the universe and the means of salvation. The Ājīvika teacher in *Nīlakēci* further gives the name of the scripture as *Oṉpatu-katir* (" The Nine Rays ").[4] It is said in the text to describe the atomic structure of the universe,[5] and is one of the four cardinal points of the Ājīvika faith, the other three being the Lord (*Aṇṇal*), the Elements (*Poruḷ*), and their modifications (*Nikaḻvu*).[6] Around the Ājīvika *nūl* a mythology seems to have grown. The scripture was delivered by the divine Maṟkali,[7] who is otherwise characterized by his perfect silence. Very reasonably the Jaina interlocutor asks how, if the God is silent, he could have declared the scriptures.[8] Besides Maṟkali two divinities, Okkali and Ōkali, are mentioned as being responsible for the diffusion of the text among men.[9] They were probably thought to have acted as intermediaries between Maṟkali and his worshippers; in the words of the commentator Vāmanamuni, they instructed in the scriptures.[10]

The accounts of the Ājīvika scriptures in the Jaina *Sūtra*

[1] *Uppāya, Aggeṇīya, Vīriya, Athiṇatthippavāya, Nāṇappavāya, Saccappavāya, Āyappavāya, Kammappavāya, Paccakkhāṇappavāya, Vijjāṇuppavāya, Avañjha, Pāṇāū, Kiriyāvisāla*, and *Logabindusāra. Samavāya, sū.* 147, fol. 128.

[2] *Ācīvaka-nūl-aṟinta. Maṇi.* xxvii, 108.

[3] *Maṟkali-nūl.* Ibid., xxvii, 163.

[4] *Nīl.*, 671.

[5] Ibid., 674.

[6] Ibid., 679. Vāmanamuni gives the Sanskrit equivalents of the four as *Āpta, Āgama, Padârtha*, and *Pravṛtti.*

[7] Ibid., 680.

[8] Ibid , loc. cit.

[9] Ibid., 681. V. infra, pp. 272–73.

[10] *Ākam'-ōpatēcañ ceyyum.*

and the Tamil poems differ considerably. In place of the eightfolk *Mahāṇimitta* and the two *Maggas* of the former the latter gives us the *Maṟkali-nūl* or the *Oṉpatu-katir*. It is possible that the Southern Ājīvikas produced new scriptures in the same manner as did the Mahāyāna Buddhists.

Pāli and Prākrit Quotations

Buddhist and Jaina texts and commentaries contain fragments in verse and prose which appear to be adaptations or quotations from Ājīvika sources and may indeed be paraphrases of the scriptures of the sect. The very important passage in the *Sāmañña-phala Sutta*,[1] already quoted, with its Māgadhisms and its impressive simile of the ball of thread, may well be authentic. Another such passage may be the story of the merchants in the *Bhagavatī Sūtra*,[2] which Gosāla is said to have told to the monk Āṇanda, and which may have been borrowed by the Jaina author from an Ājīvika collection of *jātakas* or cautionary tales.

The Pāli scriptures contain a number of verse passages praising the heretic teachers or propounding unorthodox doctrines, which may also have been taken, perhaps with some alteration, from Ājīvika sources. Thus the *Saṃyutta Nikāya* [3] contains verses in praise of the heretics, said to have been sung by various *devaputtas* in the presence of the Buddha.

The verse sung in praise of Pūraṇa Kassapa closely follows the doctrine ascribed to him in the *Sāmañña-phala Sutta*,[4] and may be the concoction of an early Buddhist poet:

"Kassapa sees neither sin nor merit for the self in this world in maiming, slaying, striking, or violence. Since he has declared our faith, the Master is worthy of honour." [5]

The verse praising Makkhali Gosāla, on the other hand, ascribes to him qualities which elsewhere in the Pāli canon

[1] V. supra, pp. 13-14.
[2] V. supra, p. 59.
[3] *Saṃ.* i, pp. 66 ff.
[4] V. supra, p. 13.
[5] *Idha chindita-mārite hatajānisu Kassapo*
Pāpaṃ na pan' upassati puññaṃ vā pana attano.
Sa ce vissāsam ācikkhi satthā arahati mānanam. *Saṃ.* i, p. 66.

he is not said to possess, and may be a genuine Ājīvika composition :

" Self-restrained, with penance and aversion (from things of the senses), abandoning speech (and) quarrelling with mankind, equable, abstaining from things to be avoided, truthful—now surely such a man commits no sin ! " [1]

Finally, after a verse in praise of Nigaṇṭha Nātaputta, occurs one in which four heretics are praised together :

" Pakudhaka Kātiyāna, Nigaṇṭha, and these two Makkhali and Pūraṇa, leaders of a school, versed in asceticism—surely now they are not far removed from the righteous ! " [2]

This verse, as we have seen,[3] looks back to a period when the non-Buddhist heterodox sects were not sharply differentiated.

The *Mahānāradakassapa Jātaka* [4] also contains a number of verses expressing heterodox views, which may have been taken from authentic sources. These are put into the mouth of the ascetic teacher Guṇa, who is called indiscriminately *acelaka* and *ājīvika*, and are verse paraphrases of some of the doctrines assigned in the *Sāmañña-phala Sutta* to Makkhali, Pūraṇa, and Pakudha. Similar passages may be found in *Mahābodhi Jātaka*,[5] and in the *Petavatthu*.[6] These verses, and the similar prose passages in the *Sāmañña-phala Sutta* seem to have had a common source, whether in prose or verse, in an authentic Ājīvika work.

Comparison between the expressions of Ājīvika views in Buddhist and Jaina texts shows notable similarities. Thus the *Sāmañña-phala Sutta's* version of Makkhali's doctrine contains the phrases : *N'atthi attakāre, n'atthi parakāre, n'atthi purisakāre, n'atthi balaṃ, n'atthi viriyaṃ, n'atthi purisa-thāmo, n'atthi purisa-parakkamo . . . Sabbe satta niyati-saṅgati-bhāva-pariṇatā . . .*

[1] *Tapo-jigucchāya susaṃvuttatto,*
Vācaṃ pahāya kalahaṃ janena,
Samo, savajjā-virato, saccavādi,
Na hi nūna tādisaṃ karoti pāpam. Saṃ., loc. cit.

[2] *Pakudhako Kātiyāno, Nigaṇṭho,*
Ye ca p' ime Makkhali-Pūraṇāse,
Gaṇassa satthāro, sāmañña-pattā,
Na hi nūna te sappurisehi dūre. Saṃ., loc. cit.

[3] V. supra, p. 80.

[4] *Jāt.* vi, pp. 219 ff.

[5] *Jāt.* v, pp. 227 ff. V. supra, p. 18.

[6] *Petavatthu*, iv, 3, p. 57 f. V. supra, pp. 20, 146, and infra, pp. 271–72.

sukha-dukkhaṃ paṭisaṃvedenti.[1] With this we may compare the words of the Ājīvika *deva*, addressed to the Jaina layman Kuṇḍakoliya in the *Uvāsaga Dasao* : *N'atthi uṭṭhāṇe i vā kamme i vā bale i vā vīrie i vā purisakkāra-parakkame i vā. Niyayā savvabhāvā.*[2] (" There is no effort nor deed (*karma*), nor strength, nor courage, nor human action, nor prowess. All beings are determined.")

The *Praśnavyākaraṇa Sūtra* [3] contains a passage which also suggests the text of the *Sāmañña-phala Sutta.* This purports to describe the doctrines of *nāstikas*, but some parts of it are perhaps derived from the same sources as Makkhali Gosāla's doctrine in the *Sutta*. Thus, the first phase, *n'atthi jīvo, na jāī iha pare vā loe*, suggests the slogan of the materialist Ajita Kesakambalī, *n'atthi ayaṃ loko, n'atthi paro loko.*[4] But the terms in which the *Praśnavyākaraṇa* speaks of the view that no merit accrues from religious activities, *dāṇa-vaya-posahāṇaṃ tava-sañjama-bambhacera-kallāṇaṃ āiyāṇaṃ n'atthi phalaṃ*, resemble Makkhali Gosāla's *na . . . sīlena vā vatena vā tapena vā brahmacariyeṇa vā* in the *Sāmañña-phala Sutta.*[5] The phrase in the *Praśnavyākaraṇa*, *ammā-piyaro n'atthi na vi atthi purisakāro* seems to look back to the sources which provided *n'atthi mātā, n'atthi pitā* [4] in Ajita's creed, and *n'atthi purisakāre* [5] in that of Makkhali. The dialectical peculiarities of the two passages have already been noticed.[6]

A further recollection of Ājīvika sources may be contained in the *Mahābhārata*, wherein the fatalist Maṅki declares *haṭhe n'aiva pauruṣam*, " there is no valour in force." [7] Similar complaints of the uselessness of courage and human effort (*pauruṣa* or *puruṣakāra*) may be found in the epic, for instance, in the words of Bhīma to the python in whose coils he struggles ; " Who can conquer Fate by human effort (*puruṣakāreṇa*). I consider fate to be supreme, but human effort (*pauruṣam*) useless." [8]

An impressive parallel to Makkhali Gosāla's description of the cosmic process in the *Sāmañña-phala Sutta* is to be found in

[1] V. supra, pp. 13-14.
[2] *Uv. Das.* vi, 166. V. supra, p. 133.
[3] *Praśnavyākaraṇa*, *sū.* 7, fols. 26-8.
[4] V. supra, p. 4, n. 15.
[5] V. supra, p. 3, n. 14.
[6] V. supra, pp. 24 ff.
[7] *Śānti*, 176, 12. (Kumbhakonam edn.). V. supra, pp. 38–39.
[8] *Vana*, 176, 27. (Poona edn.). Numerous verses of similar import are to be found in the *Mbh.*, e.g. *Udyoga*, 40, 30 ; *Bhīṣma*, 58, 1. (Poona edn.).

the *Bhagavatī*. Here Gosāla, after declaring his seven *pauṭṭa-parihāras* [1] states that all those who had reached or were reaching or would reach salvation must "finish in order 8,400,000 *mahā-kappas*, seven divine births, seven groups, seven sentient births, seven 'abandonments of transmigration' (*paüṭṭa-parihāra*), 500,000 *kammas*, and 60,000 and 600 and the three parts of *kamma*. Then, being saved, awakened, set free, and reaching *nirvāṇa* they have made or are making or will make an end of all sorrow." [2] The phrase *caürāsītiṃ mahākappa-saya-sahassāiṃ* in this passage corresponds to the *Sāmañña-phala Sutta's cull' âsīti mahākappuno sata-sahassāni*.[3] The seven "divine births" (*divve*) are perhaps represented by the *satta devā* of the Pāli, and the seven sentient births (*sanni-gabbhe* in Prākrit and *saññi-gabbhā* in Pāli) occur in both texts. The totals of *kammas* differ, but in the *Bhagavatī's* enumeration of the *kammas* and the *Sāmañña-phala Sutta's* total of chief uterine births (*yoni-pamukha*) the formulas are similar. The former has *pañca kammāni saya-sahassāiṃ, saṭṭhiṃ ca sahassāiṃ chac ca sae, tinni ya kammaṃse*, while the latter has *cuddasa kho pan' imāni yoni-pamukha-sata-sahassāni, saṭṭhiñ ca satāni, cha ca satāni, pañca ca kammuno satāni, pañca ca kammāni, tīṇi ca kammāni, kamme ca aḍḍha kamme ca*.[3] The close similarity shows that both passages are garbled borrowings from a common source.

Barua has recognized that the passages from the Jaina scriptures quoted above resemble that in the *Sāmañña-phala Sutta*, and on this and other evidence has declared that there existed an "Ājīvika language", in which Ājīvika texts were recited and written.[4] As examples of this Ājīvika language he quotes :—

1. The genitive singular form *mahākappuno* in the *Sāmañña-phala Sutta's* account of Makkhali's doctrine,[5] which seems to

[1] V. supra, pp. 31–32.

[2] *Savve te caürāsītiṃ mahākappa-saya-sahassāiṃ, satta divve, satta sañjūhe, satta sannigabbhe satta paüṭṭa-parihāre, pañca kammāṇi saya-sahassāiṃ saṭṭhiṃ ca sahassāiṃ chac ca sae, tinni ya kammaṃse aṇupuvveṇaṃ khavaïttā, tao pacchā sijjhanti bujjhanti muccanti parinivvāïnti savvadukkhāṇam antaṃ kareṃsu vā karenti vā karissanti vā. Bh. Sū.* xv, *sū.* 550, fol. 673. I accept Hoernle's reading of *kammāṇi* for *kammaṇi* in the text (*Uv. Das.*, vol. ii, app. ii, p. 19, n. 5). India Office MS. 7447 has *kammāiṃ*.

[3] V. supra, p. 14, n. 3.

[4] *JDL.* ii, pp. 46 ff.

[5] V. supra, p. 14, n. 3.

stand in place of the genitive plural and which represents the regular Pāli *mahākappassa* ;

2. The word *supina*, interpreted by Buddhaghosa as "a dream". This Barua equates with the Ardha-māgadhī *suviṇa* which, he says, means "a bird" (Sanskrit *suparṇa*). Actually this word has the same normal meaning as *supina* in Pāli [1] ;

3. The form *hupeyya*, as used in the words of the Ājīvika Upaka, "*hupeyya āvuso*",[2] which he believes was specifically an Ājīvika expression. In one version of the story the phrase occurs as *huveyya pāvuso*,[3] from which Barua concludes that "the sounds *p* and *v* were interchangeable in the Ājīvika language" ; and

4. The regular use of the present tense with future meaning. This Barua deduces from a single phrase placed in the mouth of Upaka in the commentary to the *Sutta Nipāta*, *sace Chāvaṃ labhāmi jivāmi, no ce marāmi* [4] (If I win Chāvā I shall live, if not I shall die).

We do not believe that these four references are sufficient to indicate that there was a special "Ājīvika language". The language of the *Sāmañña-phala Sutta* passage attributed to Makkhali is, however, sufficient to indicate that some of the earliest Ājīvika religious literature, whether verbal or written, was composed in a Māgadhī dialect probably very like the language of the Jainas.[5]

Quotations by the Commentators

Whatever the language of early Ājīvikism, it is probable that, like the Jainas and the Buddhists, the Ājīvikas in later times adopted Sanskrit for their religious writings. Several Sanskrit verses, quoted by Jaina commentators with reference to Ājīvikism or *niyativāda* seem to be borrowed from such Ājīvika literature. One such verse, indeed, seems to have been specially popular with the commentators as a brief statement of the fundamental doctrine of *niyativāda*, for it is quoted by no less than three of them, Śīlâṅka, Jñānavimala, and Abhayadeva :

[1] V. infra, p. 252. [2] *Vin.* i, p. 8. V. supra, p. 94. [3] *Majjh.* i, p. 171.
[4] *Paramatthajotikā II*, vol. i, p.259. [5] V. supra, pp. 24 ff.

" Whatever thing, fortunate or unfortunate, is to be obtained for men will come of necessity by recourse to the power of destiny. Though beings make great effort, that which is not to be will not be, nor does that which is to be perish." [1]

In his commentary to the *Praśnavyākaraṇa Sūtra* Jñānavimala quotes further verses :—

" Some babble that the universe is produced by Fate, saying ' Destiny is everywhere the stronger ', (as in) such (verses) as :—

" ' For what reason does a man obtain that thing which he must obtain ? Inevitable Fate ! Therefore I do not grieve or despair. That (destiny) which is ours is not that of others.

" ' Fate suddenly, bringing what is desired even from another continent, even from the midst of ocean, even from the end of (the world in any) direction, makes (it appear) before one's face.

" ' According to one's destiny so is one's intellect successful, so is one's resolution, so are one's companions.' " [2]

The *niyativādins*, to whom these verses are referred by the commentator, are stated by Guṇaratna to be followers of Pūraṇa,[3] the prophet of the Southern Ājīvikas ; it may therefore be assumed that the verses refer to the Ājīvikas, whose doctrines they well express. Jñānavimala furnishes his commentary with many authentic quotations from orthodox Hindu sources, thus strengthening the probability that he borrowed also from actual Ājīvika works.

A further verse is given by Abhayadeva in his commentary

[1] *Prāptavyo niyati-bal'-âśrayeṇa yo 'rthaḥ*
So 'vaśyaṃ bhavati nṛṇāṃ śubho 'śubho vā.
Bhūtānāṃ mahati kṛte 'pi hi prayatne
N' âbhāvyaṃ bhavati na bhāvino 'sti nāśaḥ. Śīlâṅka to *Sū. kṛ*, i, 1, 2, 2, and ii, 1, 29 ; Jñānavimala to *Praśnavyākaraṇa*, 7 ; Abhayadeva to *Uv. Das.* vi, 165.

[2] *Kecin " niyati-bhāvitaṃ jagad " iti jalpanti, " bhavitavyat' aiva sarvatra balīyas' " iti, yathā :*
" *Prāptavyam arthaṃ labhate manuṣyaḥ. Kiṃ kāraṇaṃ ? Daivam alaṅghanīyam.*
Tasmān na śocāmi na vismayāmi. Yad asmadīyaṃ na hi tat pareṣām.
" *Dvīpād anyasmād api, madhyād api jalanidher, diśo' py antāt,*
Ānīya jhaṭ iti ghaṭayati vidhir abhimatam abhimukhībhūtam.
" *Sā sā sampadyate buddhir, vyavasāyaś ca tādṛśaḥ,*
Sāhāyās tādṛśā jñeyā yādṛsī bhavitavyatā."
Jñānavimala to *Praśnavyākaraṇa, sū.* 7.

[3] V. supra, pp. 81–82.

to the *Uvāsaga Dasāo*, following that quoted above. The verse is cited with reference to the story of Kuṇḍakoliya and the Ājīvika *deva* [1] :—

"That which is not to be comes not, that which is to be comes without effort; but it perishes, even in the palm of the hand, of one for whom it is not destined." [2]

Guṇaratna, the commentator to Haribhadra's *Ṣaddarśana-samuccaya*, quotes further verses which he attributes to the *niyativādins* :—

"Since all things come about in determined form, they are produced by Destiny, conformably to its nature.

"An object, the time of its existence, its origin, and its duration [3] come about in determined order. Who is able to resist it (i.e. Destiny)?" [4]

Finally, Malliṣeṇa quotes a remarkable verse in his *Syādvāda-mañjarī* :—

"And thus say those who follow the Ājīvika school :—

"'The knowers, the founders of the faith, having gone to the highest state, return again to existence, when the faith suffers injury.'" [5]

This quotation states an important point of later Ājīvika doctrine, which is confirmed by other sources.[6]

These verses indicate that, besides their early literature in Prākrit, and the Tamil scripture *Oṉpatu-kaṭir*, the Ājīvikas

[1] V. supra, p. 133.

[2] *Nā hi bhavati yan na bhāvyaṃ, bhavati ca bhāvyaṃ vinâ 'pi yatnena.*
Karatala-gatam api naśyati yasya tu bhavitavyatā nâsti. Abhayadeva to *Uv. Das.* vi, 165.

With the above cf. *Hitôpadeśa* i, 29 :
Yad abhāvi na tad bhāvi, bhāvi cen na tad anyathā,
Iti cintā-viṣa-ghno 'yam agadaḥ kiṃ na pīyate ?

[3] This seems to be the purport of the Sanskrit, which defies literal translation.

[4] *Niyaten' aiva rūpeṇa sarve bhāvā bhavanti yat*
Tato niyati-jā hy ete tat-svarūp'-ânuvedhataḥ.
Yad yad' aiva yato yāvat tat tad' aiva tatas tathā
Niyataṃ jāyate nyāyāt. Ka enāṃ bādhituṃ kṣamaḥ? Guṇaratna to *Ṣaddarśana-samuccaya*, p. 12.

[5] *Tathā c' âhur Ājīvika-nay'-ânusāriṇaḥ :*
"*Jñānino, dharma-tīrthasya kartāraḥ, paramaṃ padaṃ*
Gatv', âgacchanti bhūyo 'pi bhavaṃ tīrtha-nikārataḥ."
Syādvāda-mañjarī, ed. Dhruva, p. 3.

[6] V. infra, p. 260.

possessed a later literature in Sanskrit, containing much philosophical poetry. It might be suggested that these verses were composed by the commentators themselves, to illustrate the views they were discussing. Yet here are eight verses, quoted by different commentators in different centuries, and all attributed to Ājīvikas or *niyativādins*. It is more probable that some at least are genuine, than that all are spurious.

CHAPTER XII

NIYATI

The fundamental principle of Ājīvika philosophy was Fate, usually called *Niyati*. Buddhist and Jaina sources agree that Gosāla was a rigid determinist, who exalted *Niyati* to the status of the motive factor of the universe and the sole agent of all phenomenal change. This is quite clear in our *locus classicus*, the *Sāmañña-phala Sutta*.[1] Sin and suffering, attributed by other sects to the laws of *karma*, the result of evil committed in previous lives or in the present one, were declared by Gosāla to be without cause or basis,[2] other, presumably, than the force of destiny. Similarly, the escape from evil, the working off of accumulated evil *karma*, was likewise without cause or basis.[3]

Fatalism proper finds no place in orthodox Hinduism, Buddhism, or Jainism. A man's fortune, his social status, and his happiness or grief, are all ultimately due to his own free will. The Indian doctrine of *karma*, as it is usually interpreted, provides a rigid framework within which the individual is able to move freely and to act on his own decision. His present condition is determined not by any immutable principle, but by his own actions performed either in this life or in his past lives. By freely choosing the right course and following it he may improve his lot and ultimately win salvation either by his own unassisted efforts, or, if he is a member of a devotional sect, with the aid of a personal deity.

This doctrine Gosāla opposed. For him belief in free will was a vulgar error. The strong, the forceful, and the courageous, like the weakling, the idler, and the coward, were all completely subject to the one principle which determined all things.[4] "Just

[1] V. supra, pp. 13-14.

[2] *N' atthi hetu, . . . n' atthi paccayo sattānaṃ saṃkilesāya.* *Dīgha* i, 53.

[3] *Ahetu-apaccayā sattā visujjhanti.* Ibid.

[4] *N' atthi purisakāre, n'atthi balaṃ, n'atthi viriyaṃ, n'atthi purisa-parakkamo. Sabbe sattā . . . avasā abalā aviriyā niyati-saṅgati-bhāva-pariṇatā.* Ibid.

as a ball of thread when thrown will unwind to its full length, so fool and wise alike will take their course, and make an end of sorrow." [1]

This absolute determinism did not preclude a belief in *karma*, but for Makkhali Gosāla the doctrine had lost its moral force. *Karma* was unaffected by virtuous conduct, by vows, by penances, or by chastity, but it was not denied.[2] The path of transmigration was rigidly laid out, and every soul was fated to run the same course through a period of 8,400,000 *mahākalpas*. This figure is corroborated by independent testimony,[3] and is a measure of the gigantic and weary universe of the Ājīvika cosmologists.

The process of regular and automatic transmigration seems to have been thought of on the analogy of the development and ripening of a plant. All beings were " developed by Destiny (*Niyati*), chance (*saṅgati*), and nature (*bhāva*) ".[4] This ripening process was completely predetermined, thus differing from the *pariṇāma* of the Sāṅkhya, wherein " evolution follows a definite law which cannot be overstepped (*pariṇāma-krama-niyama*), or in other words there are some natural barriers which cannot be removed, and thus the evolutionary course has to take a path to the exclusion of those lines where barriers could not be removed." [5] Sāṇkhya accepts the proposition that progress and change are rigidly limited by natural law. Ājīvikism goes further and declares that they are completely controlled.

The term *niyati-saṅgati-bhāva-pariṇatā* in the *Sāmañña-phala Sutta* is ambiguous and obscure. It may be translated " ripened by the nature of the lot of (i.e. decreed by) Destiny ", or " brought about by the existence of union with Destiny ". But we prefer to follow Buddhaghosa and to take the three first elements of the compound as in *dvandva* relationship, translating the phrase as above.

[1] *Seyyathā pi nāma sutta-guḷe khitte nibbeṭhiyamānam eva phaleti, evam eva bāle ca paṇḍite ca sandhāvitvā saṃsaritvā dukkhass' antaṃ karissanti.* Ibid.

[2] *Tattha n'atthi : imin' âhaṃ sīlena vā vatena vā tapena vā brahmacariyeṇa vā aparipakkaṃ vā kammaṃ paripācessami paripakkaṃ vā kammaṃ phussa-phussa-vyanti karissāmî ti. H'evaṃ n' atthi.* Ibid.

[3] V. supra, p. 219.

[4] *Niyati-saṅgati-bhāva-pariṇatā.* *Dīgha* i, p. 53. Buddhaghosa interprets *pariṇatā* as " differentiated " (*nāna-ppakāratam pattā*). *Sum. Vil.* i, p. 160.

[5] Das Gupta, *Indian Philosophy*, vol. i, p. 256.

The terms *bhāva* and *saṅgati* appear to represent categories in the Ājīvika metaphysical system which are subordinate to *Niyati*. *Bhāva* seems in this context to be synonymous with *svabhāva*, inherent character or nature. It suggests, below the fundamental category of *Niyati*, sets of conditions and characteristics in each entity, which, acting as factors subordinate to the great principle, control growth, development, and rebirth. Some heretics exalted *Svabhāva* to the status of *Niyati* in the regular Ājīvika system. Their doctrines are mentioned by the Jaina commentators, though not in such detail as those of the *niyativādins* or Ājīvikas. Thus Jñānavimala writes: "Some believe that the universe was produced by *Svabhāva*, and that everything comes about by *Svabhāva* only."[1] Guṇaratna quotes a verse which he attributes to the supporters of this doctrine: "What makes the sharpness of thorns and the varied nature of beasts and birds? All this comes about by *Svabhāva*. There is nothing which acts at will. What is the use of effort?"[2] Hence it appears that the *svabhāvavādins* agreed with the *niyativādins* on the futility of human efforts. They were classed in the group of *akriyāvādins*, or those who did not believe in the utility or effectiveness of *puruṣakāra*. It would seem that the *svabhāvavādin* differed from the *niyativādin* in that, while the latter viewed the individual as determined by forces exterior to himself, for the former he was rigidly self-determined by his own somatic and psychic nature. These ideas have much in common and we suggest therefore that *svabhāvavāda* was a small sub-sect of Ājīvikism.

Saṅgati, interpreted by Hoernle, on the basis of Buddhaghosa, as "environment",[3] we would translate as "lot" or "chance". It seems to represent the principle of *Niyati* as manifested in action. The term is known to Jaina writers, and is connected by them also with the *niyativādins* or the Ājīvikas. Thus, the *Sūtrakṛtâṅga*, quoting the opinions of foolish philosophers,

[1] *Kecit svabhāva-bhāvitaṃ jagad manyante, svabhāven' aiva sarvaḥ sampadyate.* To *Praśnavyākaraṇa* 7, fol. 29. V. also Sīlâṅka to *Sū. kṛ.* i, 1, 2, 2, fol. 30.

[2] *Kaḥ kaṇṭakānāṃ prakaroti taikṣṇyaṃ,*
Vicitra-bhāvaṃ mṛga-pakṣiṇāṃ ca?
Svabhāvataḥ sarvam idaṃ pravṛttam.
Na kāmacāro 'sti. Kutaḥ prayatnaḥ? *Tarka-rahasya-dīpikā* to *Ṣaḍdarśana-samuccaya*, p. 13. V. also *Abh. Rāj.* s.v.

[3] *ERE.* i, p. 261. *Uv. Das.* vol. ii, app. 2, pp. 16–17.

declares one of their doctrines to be that pleasure and pain are not caused by oneself or others, but are the work of chance.[1] On this Śīlâṅka comments: "Now the *niyativādin* declares his attitude. (The word) *saṅgaïyaṃ* (in the text) implies transmigration wholly by inner development. Experience of all joy and sorrow whatever is fortuitous. Therein *Niyati* is its (i.e. chance's) essential nature as fortuity. They say that since joy and sorrow, etc., are not produced by human action and so on, therefore for all beings they are caused by Destiny and are fortuitous."[2]

The above verse and its commentary explain both the phrases *n'atthi hetu* in the *Sāmañña-phala-Sutta* passage and *niyati-saṅgati-bhāva-pariṇatā*. For the *niyativādin* causation was illusory. The European doctrine of causation conceived the universe as determined by an immense number of causes, going back to a first cause, which might or might not be expressed in theological terms. The Ājīvika theory was evidently very different from this. The universe seems to have been thought of as a continuous process, which was recognized by some later Ājīvikas to be on ultimate analysis illusory.[3] The only effective cause was *Niyati*, which was not merely a first cause, but, in its aspects as *saṅgati* and *bhāva*, or chance and inner character, was also the efficient cause of all phenomena. *Saṅgati* and *bhāva*, the manifestations of *Niyati* in individuals, were only apparent and illusory modifications of the one principle, and did not in fact introduce new causal factors into the universal process. Thus, the Ājīvika was sometimes called a believer in the doctrine of causelessness (*ahetukavādin*).[4] Since all human activities were ineffectual he was also an *akriyāvādin*, a disbeliever in the efficiency of works.

The Ājīvika process of salvation is sometimes in the Pāli texts

[1] *Na taṃ sayaṃ kaḍaṃ dukkhaṃ, kao annakaḍaṃ ca ṇaṃ?*
Suhaṃ vā jaï vā dukkhaṃ, sehiyaṃ vā asehiyaṃ.
Sayaṃ kaḍaṃ na aṇṇehiṃ, vedayanti puḍho jiyā.
Saṅgaïṃ taṃ tahā tesiṃ, iham egesi āhiaṃ. *Sū. kṛ.* i, 1, 2, 2–3, fol. 30.

[2] *Niyativādī svâbhiprāyam āviṣkaroti. Saṅgaïyaṃ ti samyak svapariṇāmena gatiḥ. Yasya yadā yatra yat sukha-duḥkh'-ânubhavanaṃ sā saṅgatiḥ. Niyatis tasyāṃ bhavaṃ saṅgatikam. Yataś c' aivaṃ na puruṣakār'-âdi-kṛtaṃ sukha-duḥkh'-âdi, atas tat teṣāṃ prāṇināṃ niyati-kṛtaṃ saṅgatikam ity ucyate.* Śīlâṅka to *Sū. kṛ.*, loc. cit.

[3] V. infra, pp. 235 ff.

[4] E.g. *Jāt.* v, p. 228.

called *saṃsāra-suddhi*, or salvation by transmigration, a very apt definition of the doctrine. "There is no short cut (lit. door) to bliss, Bījaka. Wait on Destiny. Whether (a man has) joy or sorrow, it is obtained through Destiny. All beings are purified through transmigration, (so) do not be eager for that which is to come."[1]

Niyativāda Dialectic

The usual Buddhist criticism of the Ājīvika *Niyati* doctrine was pragmatic. Thus, the *Sandaka Sutta* of the *Majjhima Nikāya*[2] condemns the four "antitheses to the higher life" (*abrahmacariya-vāsā*), which include the doctrines elsewhere ascribed to Makkhali, Pūraṇa, Pakudha, and Ajita. The fatalism of Makkhali entails the antinomianism of Pūraṇa. Since there is no possibility of modifying one's destiny by good works, self-control, or asceticism, all such activity is wasted. The Ājīvika doctrines are, in fact, conducive to luxury and licentiousness. This practical criticism of the Ājīvika philosophy might have been easily countered by the Ājīvikas with the claim that ascetics performed penances and led righteous lives under the compulsion of the same all-embracing principle as determined the lives of sinners, and that they were ascetics because *Niyati* so directed it. This very obvious argument occurs nowhere in the Buddhist scriptures, though it was known to the Jaina commentator Śīlâṅka,[3] who quoted it as one of the arguments used by *niyativādins*.

Although orthodox Hindu literature rarely mentions the Ājīvikas, we have some evidence that Hinduism was not wholly unaware of them. The doctrine of *Niyati* is mentioned in the compendium of Suśruta, among a number of other theories on the nature and origin of the universe.[4] The *Śvetâśvatara Upaniṣad* gives a list of first causes according to the

[1] *N' atthi dvāraṃ sugatiyā. Niyatiṃ kaṃkha, Bījaka.*
Sukhaṃ vā yadi vā dukkhaṃ, Niyatiyā kira labbhati.
Saṃsāra-suddhi sabbesaṃ, mā turittho anāgate. *Jāt.* vi, p. 229. Cf. *Ime sattā saṃsāra-suddhikā.* *Jāt.* v, p. 228.

[2] *Majjh.* i, pp. 513 ff. V. supra, pp. 18-19.

[3] V. infra, p. 233.

[4] *Suśruta Saṃhitā* iii, 1.

unorthodox systems, which includes most of the hypothetical entities referred to with disapproval by the Jaina commentators—time, nature, destiny, chance, the elements, and the Sāṅkhya category of Puruṣa.[1] Commenting on this passage Śaṅkara ascribes belief in *Niyati* to the Mīmāṃsakas, no doubt erroneously, and describes it as "*karma* characterized by the equal (reward) of good and evil". He briefly dismisses the theory by stating that Destiny is variable (in its operation).[2]

Jaina criticisms of Ājīvika determinism are based both on logic and common sense. Of the triter sort is the argument of the *Uvāsaga Dasāo*, attributed to the Jaina layman Kuṇḍakoliya in his debate with the Ājīvika *deva*.[3] The latter praises Gosāla's determinist theory and disparages Mahāvīra's doctrine of qualified free-will. Whereupon Kuṇḍakoliya asks the *deva* whether he attained his own divine status by any efforts on his part. He replies that he obtained heavenly bliss without effort (*anuṭṭhāṇeṇaṃ*). "Why then," asks Kuṇḍakoliya, "are not those other living beings in whom there is no effort . . . also *devas*?"[4] This argument, though blatantly illogical, is sufficient to convince the *deva* of the wrongness of his views, but we may be sure that the early Ājīvikas had their rejoinders to such feeble attacks.

Another amusing argument of a similar nature is ascribed to Mahāvīra himself, in the account of his conversion of the Ājīvika potter, Saddālaputta.[5] Mahāvīra asks whether the potter's ware is made by dint of exertion or not, to which the Ājīvika replies that it is made without exertion. Mahāvīra then asks what Saddālaputta would do if one of his workmen stole or broke his pots, or made overtures to his wife. To this the potter indignantly replies that he would berate and strike the culprit, or even kill him. But such actions, Mahāvīra retorts, would

[1] *Kālaḥ, svabhāvo, niyatir, yadṛcchā,*
bhūtāni, yoniḥ, puruṣ', (sic) *êti cintyāḥ.*
Saṃyoga eṣāṃ nanu ātma-bhāvād.
Ātm' âpy anīśaḥ sukha-duḥkha-hetoḥ. *Śvetâśvatara*, i, 2.

[2] *Niyatir aviṣama-puṇya-pāpa-lakṣaṇaṃ karma. Niyatir iti Mīmāṃsakāḥ. Niyater api anaikântatvād dūṣitam etan matam.* Śaṅkara to *Śvetâśvatara*, loc. cit.

[3] *Uv. Das.* vi, 166–8. V. supra, p. 133.

[4] *Je . . . ṇaṃ jīvāṇaṃ n' aṭṭhi uṭṭhāṇe . . . te kiṃ na devā? Uv. Das.* vi, 168.

[5] Ibid., vii, 198–9. V. supra, pp. 52, 132.

be quite inconsistent with the doctrine of *Niyati* and of no exertion. If all things are unalterably fixed (*niyayā savvabhāvā*) and there is no exertion, no man can steal or break the pots, and the potter cannot revile or strike or kill the culprit. Yet such things do happen in everyday life, and so the claim that there is no exertion and that all things are determined is false. No doubt the Ājīvika had his answer to this appeal to common sense, which reminds us of Dr. Johnson's famous refutation of Berkeleyan idealism. We may surmise that the *niyativādin* explained the apparent existence of freedom of choice by the postulate of a double standard of truth. In other and more exalted Indian philosophical systems such a double standard of practical and empirical (*vyāvahārika*) and absolute (*pāramârthika*) truth existed, and its adoption by the Ājīvikas would solve the apparent antinomy of a postulated determinism and an inner conviction of free-will. In everyday life, and for all practical purposes, free-will existed, and the Ājīvika layman like Saddālaputta acted on that assumption. But ultimately free-will was illusory—*Niyati* was the only determining factor, and human power and effort were completely ineffectual.

The Jaina commentators give us a better impression than do the Buddhist and Jaina Prākrit texts of the *niyativādin's* powers of logical argument. Thus Śīlâṅka in his commentary to the *Sūtrakṛtâṅga*, quotes the arguments of the *niyativādins*, who, although not expressly identified with them, must surely have been Ājīvikas. "If happiness is experienced as a result of human activity there should be no difference in the reward (of equal exertion), nor should there be lack of reward when equal effort is exerted, whether by servants, merchants, or, peasants etc. Yet it is often seen that even when no means of livelihood such as service, etc., is followed, rich reward is obtained. So nothing is achieved by human effort." [1] This is another example of the argument used by Mahāvīra against Saddālaputta, the argument from human experience ; but here it is employed by the Ājīvika against his opponents. The successes and failures of men of equal ability prove that their happiness

[1] *Yadi puruṣakāra-kṛtaṃ sukhâdy anubhūyeta tataḥ sevaka-vaṇik-karṣak'-âdīnāṃ samāne puruṣakāre sati phala-prāpti-vaisadṛśyaṃ phal'-âprāptiś ca na bhavet. Kasya cit tu sev'-âdi-vyāpār'-âbhāve 'pi viśiṣṭa-phal'-âvāptir dṛśyata iti. Ato na puruṣakārāt kiñcid āsādyate.* Śīlâṅka to *Sū. kṛ.* i, 1, 2, 2, fol. 30.

does not depend on their own powers. Man is not an effective factor in the universal process.

Continuing his discussion of *niyativāda* Śīlâṅka, with commendable impartiality, temporarily adopts the determinist attitude, and considers possible causes of the manifest inequalities of the world. " What then (is the cause) ? Only Destiny. . . . Time is not the agent, for the variety of results (of effort) in the world is inconsistent with the uniformity of time. Variation in the effect arises from variation in the cause, not from uniformity." [1]

After thus dismissing Time as a possible prime mover, Śīlâṅka considers the theistic explanation from the Ājīvika point of view. " Likewise happiness and grief do not come about through the agency of God. (If they do,) is God formed or formless ? If he has form he has no more the capacity to create all things than has the ordinary man (who also has form). If he is formless, his inactivity must be greater than that of empty space (which is also formless). Moreover, if he be subject to passion and other (emotions), since he is not superior to us (mortals), etc., he is not the maker of the universe. And if he were devoid of passion the variety of good and evil fortune, of lord and poor man, which he has caused in the world, would not come about. Therefore God is not the creator." [2] The logic of this passage seems to be that, as all beings, who are subject to passions, are created and ineffectual, so God, if also subject to passions, must also be created and share the ineffectuality of the creature. On the other hand, if he were devoid of passions he could not be responsible for the inequalities and injustices in the world.

[1] *Kiṃ tarhi? Niyater ev' eti . . . . N' âpi kālaḥ kartā, tasy' aikarūpatvāj jagati phala-vaicitry'-ânupapatteḥ. Kāraṇa-bhede hi kārya-bhedo bhavati, n'âbhede.* Śīlâṅka, loc. cit. The commentator continues very tersely : *Tathā hi ; ayam eva hi bhedo bheda-hetur vā ghaṭate yad uta viruddha-dharm'-âdhyāsaḥ kāraṇa-bhedaś ca.* This obscure passage seems to imply that variations do in fact occur, and that they must have a cause. Thus the *kālavādin* has committed the fallacy of ascribing contrary qualities to Time, since the cause must itself be variable. He simultaneously asserts the uniformity of Time and the variety of its effects.

[2] *Tath' êśvara-kārtṛke 'pi sukha-duḥkhe na bhavataḥ. Yato 'sāv Īśvaro mūrto 'mūrto vā? Yadi mūrtas, tataḥ prākṛta-puruṣasy' eva sarva-kārtṛtv'-âbhāvaḥ. Ath' âmūrtas? Tathā saty ākāśasy' eva sutarāṃ niṣkriyatvam. Api ca yady asau rāgâdimāṃs, tato 'smad-ādy-avyatirekād viśvasy' âkart' aiva. Ath' âsau vigata-rāgas tatas tatkṛtaṃ subhaga-durbhag'-êśvara-daridr'-âdi-jagad-vaicitryaṃ na ghaṭāṃ prāñcati. Tato n' Êśvaraḥ kart' êti.* Śīlâṅka, loc. cit.

Śīlâṅka, still writing as a *niyativādin*, next dismisses the *svabhāvavādin*, who, as we have seen, held a doctrine very similar to that of the Ājīvika: " Moreover the causing of joy and sorrow cannot be ascribed to inherent character (*svabhāva*). For is this different from a man or the same as he? If it is different it is not capable of causing the joy and sorrow which befall him, on account of that difference. Nor (if it is) the same (as he). For, if it were, it would be a mere man, and it has been shown that man cannot be an effective agent." [1]

Karma, the favourite Indian scapegoat for all human misfortune and inequality, is disposed of similarly. " Nor is *karma* a possible cause of joy, sorrow, etc. For is a man's *karma* different from the man or the same (as he)? If the same, *karma* is mere man, and the flaw (in this argument) has already been stated. If it is different, then is it conscious or unconscious? If conscious, there are two consciousnesses in one body. If unconscious, how can it be an effective agent in the production of joy and sorrow, when it is as devoid of freedom as is a mere block of stone." [2] After thus exhausting the possible causes of man's joy and sorrow Śīlâṅka states the *niyativādin's* view, that these are caused by chance or one's lot (*saṅgati*) of which *Niyati* is the essential nature (*bhāvaṃ*). This passage we have paraphrased above.[3]

An even more important passage on the arguments of the *niyativādins* is contained in the same text. A chapter in the second part of the *Sūtrakṛtâṅga* deals with four schools of false teaching, the *Lokāyata* or materialist, the atomist, the theist, and the determinist. The chief argument of the last is paraphrased by Śīlâṅka at the outset in terms similar to those of the earlier passage. " Of those who put forth equal effort only one has material success, through the force of Fate. Hence only

[1] *Tathā svabhāvasy' âpi sukha-duḥkh'-âdi-kartṛtv'-ânupapattiḥ. Yato 'sau svabhāvaḥ puruṣād bhinno 'bhinno vā? Yadi bhinno na puruṣ'-âśrite sukha-duḥkhe kartum alaṃ tasmād bhinnatvād iti. N' âpy abhinnaḥ. Abhede puruṣa eva syāt, tasya c' âkartṛtvam uktam eva.* Śīlâṅka, loc. cit.

[2] *N' âpi karmaṇaḥ sukha-duḥkhaṃ prati kartṛtvaṃ ghaṭate. Yatas tat karma puruṣād bhinnam abhinnaṃ vā bhavet? Abhinnaṃ cet, puruṣa-mātrat'-âpattiḥ karmaṇaḥ, tatra c' ôkto doṣaḥ. Atha bhinnaṃ. Tat kiṃ sacetanam acetanaṃ vā? Yadi sacetanam, ekasmin kāye caitanya-dvay'-âpattiḥ. Ath' âcetanam. Tathā sati kutas tasya pāṣāṇa-khaṇḍasy' êva' âsvatantrasya sukha-duḥkh'-ôtpādanaṃ prati kartṛtvam iti?* Śīlâṅka, loc. cit.

[3] V. supra, p. 227.

Fate is the cause." [1] He then quotes one of the verses paraphrased above.[2]

The text of the *Sūtrakṛtâṅga* then states the thesis of the *niyativādin*. "Here are two men. One maintains (the efficiency of) action, the other does not. . . . Both equally and alike are affected by (a single) cause.[3] To this Śīlâṅka adds : ". . . One of them maintains (the efficiency of) action, saying that action, such as going from one country to another, is (characteristic) of a man, not of something compelled by time, or by God, etc. But (actually it pertains to) one driven by Fate. And likewise with inaction. If they, not being free, follow the doctrines of action and inaction (respectively), both (may be) equal (in fortune), owing to their subservience to Fate. But if they were free, then, owing to the difference between action and inaction, they would not be equal (in fortune). Hence, being alike dependent on a single cause, by the force of Fate they have taken to the doctrines of determinism and free-will respectively." [4] This argument is a repetition of the previous one. The man who exerts himself and the passive believer in Destiny may both enjoy equal fortune. But if their efforts were really effective the energetic man would be more fortunate than the other. Both are, in fact, dependent on Destiny, and their very belief or disbelief in the Ājīvika doctrine of *Niyati* is also dependent on that principle.

The *Sūtrakṛtâṅga* continues that the fool imagines that he is responsible for his own sorrow, as others are responsible for that which befalls them. But the wise man recognizes that he is not the cause of his own grief.[5] Śīlâṅka expands this passage : "By

[1] *Samāna-kriyāṇāṃ kasya cid eva Niyati-balād artha-siddhiḥ. Ato Niyatir eva kāraṇam.* Śīlâṅka, loc. cit.

[2] V. supra, p. 221.

[3] *Iha khalu duve purisā bhavanti. Ege purise kiriyam āikkhaï, ege . . . ṇo kiriyaṃ . . . Dovi te purisā tullā egaṭṭhā kāraṇaṃ āvannā. Sū. kṛ.* ii, 1, 12, fol. 287.

[4] *. . . Ekaḥ kriyām ākhyāti. "Kriyā hi deśād deśântar'-âvapti-lakṣaṇā puruṣasya bhavati, na kāl'-êśvar'-âdinā coditasya bhavati." Api tu Niyati-preritasya. Evam akriyā 'pi. Yadi tāv asvatantrau kriyāvādam akriyāvādaṃ ca samāśritau, tau dvāv api Niyaty-adhīnatvāt tulyau. Yadi punas tau svatantrau bhavatas tataḥ kriy'-âkriyā-bhedān na tulyau syātām iti. Ata ekârthāv eka-kāraṇ'-âpannatvād iti Niyati-vaśen' aiva tau niyati-vādam aniyati-vādaṃ c' âśritāv iti bhāvaḥ.* Śīlâṅka to above, fol. 288.

[5] *Mehāvī puṇa evaṃ vippaḍivedenti* (sic) . . . "*aham aṃsi dukkhāmi vā soyāmi vā . . . ṇo ahaṃ evam akāsi*". *Sū. kṛ.*, loc. cit.

Destiny, though against his will, he is so made that he suffers a series of sorrows. . . . So the determinist, rejecting the visible human action and having recourse to the doctrine of invisible destiny, is ironically called a wise man." [1] This last sentence is another appeal to common sense, of the sort used by Mahāvīra in his argument with Saddālaputta.[2] But Śīlâṅka continues with his exposition of the Ājīvika standpoint. "In this world (*atra*) grief does not arise for a man, even though he delight in evil courses, while for another virtuous man it does. Therefore only Destiny is the cause. . Thus, with the doctrine of Destiny established, in order to show everything else to be subject to Destiny, he maintains that, so determined, all beings . . . have union with new bodies ; a (new) body is not obtained by anything else such as *karma*, etc. So they experience under the compulsion of Destiny (*niyatitā*) the varied stages of life from childhood to old age. Under the compulsion of Destiny they are separated from their bodies. And under the compulsion of Destiny they experience various repulsive conditions, such as being hump-backed, one-eyed, . . . a dwarf, . . . death disease, and sorrow." [3] The text of this section of the *Sūtrakṛtâṅga* concludes with a passage which is repeated for all four types of heretic, accusing them of ignorance and licentiousness.

Śīlâṅka then proceeds to demolish the *niyativādin's* arguments. Is *Niyati* determined by its own nature or by another *niyati* ? If by its own nature, why are not all other entities so determined ? If by a higher *niyati*, that too must be determined similarly, and so on in an infinite regression.[4] Again, owing to the character

[1] *Niyaty' aiv' âsāv anicchann api tat kāryate yena duhkha-paramparā-bhāg bhavati . . . Pare' py evam eva yojanīyam . . . Sa kila niyativādī dṛṣṭaṃ puruṣākāraṃ parityajy' âdṛṣṭa-niyati-vād'-âśrayeṇa mahāvivek' îty evam ullaṇṭhyate.* Śīlâṅka to above, fol. 288.

[2] V. supra, pp. 229–30.

[3] *Atr' aikasy' âsad-anuṣṭhāna-ratasy' âpi na duḥkham utpadyate, parasya tu sad-anuṣṭhāyino tad bhavat' îty ato Niyatir eva kartr' îti. Tad evaṃ niyativāde sthite param api yat kiñcit tat sarvaṃ Niyaty-adhīnam iti darśayitum āha . . . ye ke ca na . . . prāṇinas te sarve 'py evaṃ niyatitā eva . . . śarīra-sambandham āgacchanti ; n' ânyena kena cit karm'-âdinā śarīraṃ grāhyate. Tathā bāla- . . . vṛddh'-âvasth'-âdikaṃ vividha-paryāyaṃ niyatitā ev' ânubhavanti ; tathā niyatitā eva . . . śarīrāt pṛthagbhāvam anubhavanti ; tathā niyatitā eva vividham . . . avasthā-viśeṣaṃ kubja-kāṇa- . . . vāmana- . . . maraṇa-roga-śok'-âdikaṃ bībhatsam āgacchanti.* Śīlâṅka, op. cit., fols. 288–9.

[4] *Asau Niyatiḥ kiṃ svata eva niyati-svabhāvā ; ut' ânyayā niyatyā niyamyate ? . . . Tatra yady asau svayam eva tathā-svabhāvā sarva-padārthānāṃ eva tathā-svabhāvatvaṃ kiṃ na kalpyate ? . . . Ath' ânyayā niyatyā tathā*

of *Niyati* as inherent nature (*Niyater svabhāvatvāt*), things must come about through it (*Niyati*) with its determined nature, and not through (a *Niyati* possessing) various inherent natures. But, since *Niyati* itself is single that which it causes should be uniform, in which case there should be no variety in the world. This, however, is not borne out by experience.[1]

Śīlâṅka dismisses the Ājīvika argument for determinism from the fact of human inequality by recourse to the doctrine of *karma*. The man who is prosperous and fortunate is enjoying the fruits of virtuous conduct in past lives.

A similar but shorter discussion of *Niyativāda* occurs in Guṇaratna's commentary to the *Ṣaḍdarśana-samuccaya*, where a further argument for determinism is put forward, based on the uniformity and regularity of natural processes. *Niyati*, declares Guṇaratna, taking the determinist point of view, is the principle by which all things are manifested in determined form. Everything whatever is found to exist in a determined form. Otherwise, in the absence of a controlling agent, there would be no laws of cause and effect, and no fixed form of anything. What man skilled in logic can deny *Niyati*, the existence of which is proved by the determinate nature of the effects (of like causes)? [2]

The Development of the *Niyati* Doctrine

For the early Ājīvikas *Niyati* is the ruling principle of the cosmic process. This concept of process, of the slow evolution of all entities along rigidly determined lines, is clearly stated in the Pāli and Ardha-māgadhī sources. The universe is, in fact, a dynamic one. But the Tamil texts which treat of Ājīvikism show that other views existed.

niyamyate. S' âpy anyayā, s' apy anyay' êty evam anavasthā. Śīlâṅka, op. cit., fol. 289.

1 *Tathā Niyateḥ svabhāvatvān niyata-svabhāvay' ânayā bhavitavyaṃ, na nānā-svabhāvay' êti. Ekatvāc ca Niyates tat-kāryeṇ' âpy ekâkāreṇ' aiva bhavitavyaṃ. Tathā ca sati jagad-vaicitry'-âbhāvaḥ, Na c' aitad dṛṣṭam iṣṭaṃ vā.* Ibid.

2 *Niyatir nāma tattv'-ântaram asti yad-vaśād ete bhavāḥ sarve 'pi niyaten' aiva rūpeṇa prādur-bhāvam aśnuvate, n'ânyathā . . . . Yad yadā yato bhavati tat tadā tata eva niyaten' aiva rūpeṇa bhavad upalabhyate. Anyathā kārya-kāraṇa-vyavasthā. Tata evaṃ kārya-naiyatyataḥ pratīyamānām enāṃ Niyatiṃ ko nāma pramāṇa-patha-kuśalo bādhituṃ kṣamate.* Op. cit., p. 12.

We have seen that the atomic doctrines ascribed in the *Sāmañña-phala Sutta* to Pakudha Kaccāyana, which certainly had their effect on Southern Ājīvikism,[1] maintained that the elementary categories were as firm as mountains, neither moving nor developing nor in any way affecting one another.[2] The author of this passage conceives a static, not a dynamic universe. Similarly, Mahāvīra tried to convince Saddālaputta that his action in punishing a careless or immoral workman would be a real action, and not a mere illusion.[3] Hoernle translates the phrase *niyayā savvabhāvā* not, as might be expected, as "all things are determined", but as "all things are unalterably fixed",[4] which makes better sense of Mahāvīra's argument. Here are the germs of the static view of the universe ascribed to the Ājīvikas in *Nīlakēci*.

We have no information as to the process of thought which led to the emergence of the new doctrine of *Avicalita-nityatvam*, or a completely static universe. It was probably imported into the Ājīvika system by the school of Pakudha, which seems to have played a significant part in the formation of the doctrines of the Southern Ājīvikas. The doctrine could easily be harmonized with the determinism of Makkhali Gosāla, and is, in fact, a logical development of the latter. We conceive the train of thought which led the Ājīvika teachers of the South to accept the doctrine to have been as follows: If all future occurrences are rigidly determined and there is no room for novelty in the universe, coming events may in some sense be said to exist already. The future exists in the present, and both exist in the past. Time is thus on ultimate analysis illusory, and if so all motion and change, which take place in time, must be illusory also. Thus, we have almost arrived at the system of Parmenides.

This is the doctrine of the Ājīvika teacher in *Nīlakēci*. "Though we may speak of moments," he declares, "there is (really) no time at all." [5] This sentence clearly shows that the Ājīvikas were well versed in the doctrine of the two orders of reality, which we have already suggested as the Ājīvika

[1] V. supra, p. 91. [2] V. supra, p. 16. [3] V. supra, p. 230.
[4] *Uv. Das.*, vol. ii, p. 132.
[5] *Kaṇam ē-y eṉiṉ umm oru kālam ilai. Nīl.* 677.

solution to the paradoxes of the *Niyati* theory.[1] In his sermon, however, the theory of the static universe is not explicitly stated. Such a theory is, however, criticized at length by his interlocutor, and commented on by Vāmanamuni, so it seems certain that it was held.

From this passage we obtain a clear idea of the theory, called by the commentator *Avicalita-nityatvam*, or unchanging permanence, which, for the Ājīvika, is said to obscure all knowledge of the truth.[2] Every phase of a process is always present. Just as the stars still exist after the sun has risen, so in a soul which has attained salvation its earthly births are still present.[3] Nothing is destroyed, and nothing is produced.[4] Events are rigidly fixed.[5] The doctrine of *Niyati* had developed far from that of Makkhali Gosāla in the Pāli scriptures. Not only are all things determined, but their change and development is a cosmic illusion.

This static view of the universe is countered by several arguments from human experience and common sense. If souls in a state of salvation retain their old incarnations in latent form the saint must from time to time show characteristics of the boar, and eat filth.[6] If the passage of time is illusory the food we eat must already be excreta.[7] The pragmatic argument is also used. The doctrine of unchanging permanency destroys all moral sanctions—the ascetic is still a householder, and may behave as such.[8] The obvious unreality of the doctrine is illustrated by a number of homely examples. If it be true, ghee is on fire, and the child has already conceived. If all change is illusory, how can the elements rise and fall, as the Ājīvika doctrine itself claims ? [9] According to *Avicalita-nityatvam* a horse trots while still in its stable.[10] How can the ripening of fruit be explained ? [11] How can boats be hollowed from logs, or bowls be beaten from sheets of metal ? [12] Even words undergo grammatical change.[13] Causation must exist, for the child will not grow unless its growth is

[1] V. supra, p. 230.

[2] *Avicalita-nityatvam keṭum ādaliṉ, uṉakku-t tattuvañāṉam illai-y ām.* To *Nīl.* 694.

[3] *Nīl.* v, 695.

[4] *Tāṉ keṭā-v-illaṉa-v-un toṉṟā-v eṉṟ' oppiyā tum illatu.* Ibid., 696.

[5] *Niyatan nikaḻcci.* Ibid., 711.

[6] Ibid., comm. to 695.

[7] Ibid., 696.

[8] Ibid., 697.

[9] Ibid., 698.

[10] Ibid., 699.

[11] Ibid., 700.

[12] Ibid., 701.

[13] Ibid., 703.

caused by adequate nourishment and care.[1] These examples show conclusively that the school of Ājīvikism treated by this text had a metaphysic very similar to that of the Eleatics.

The other Tamil sources do not mention the doctrine of unchanging permanence. But the length at which it is treated in *Nīlakēci*, and the reliability of that work, together with the traces of such a theory to be found in Northern works, are sufficient evidence that it was held by some Ājīvikas at least. Vāmana, the 13th–14th century commentator on the work,[2] seems to have understood the doctrine, and greatly expands and elucidates the elliptical verses of the text. From this we may infer that the static world view was held by some Ājīvikas until the sect lost its independent existence. It was probably conceived and elaborated by the ascetic leaders of Ājīvikism, and had little influence upon the laymen.

Maṇimēkalai and *Civañāṉa-cittiyār* stress the Ājīvikas' atomic doctrines rather than their determinism. Indeed the Ājīvika teacher in *Maṇimēkalai* is scarcely aware of the doctrine of *Niyati*, and merely states in a single line that Fate (*ūḻi*) is responsible for existence.[3] *Civañāṉa-cittiyār* understands the doctrine, but here it is referred to in only one of the ten verses in which Ājīvika teaching is propounded, and in the six verses of refutation determinism is not explicitly mentioned. The text states that wealth and poverty, pain and pleasure, living in one country and travelling to another, are ordained beforehand in the womb, and that the world moves subject to a sure Fate.[4] The reference to the womb in this verse suggests that with the school of Ājīvikas represented by this text, which is almost the latest of our sources, the orthodox Hindu and Jaina view was in process of replacing the traditional Ājīvika doctrine of *Niyati*. By this time the distinction between *Niyati* and *karma* had almost gone. In fact one verse of the *Civañāṉa-cittiyār* states that *kaṉma* is the cause of the incarnation of the soul.[5] Ājīvika doctrine never wholly excluded *karma*, but insisted that it operated in an automatic and determinate manner.[6] It seems that the status

[1] Ibid., 710.

[2] V. supra, p. 200.

[3] *Munnuḷa-v ūḻ' ē piṉṉum uru-v ippatu.* *Maṇi.*, xxvii, 164.

[4] *Tēṟiya-v ūḻir paṭṭu-c celvat' ivv ulakam.* *CÑC.*, p. 265, v. 9.

[5] *Caṉittant' ak-kaṉmattāl ē naṇṇiṭum urukkaḷ āki.* Ibid., p. 261, v. 6.

[6] V. supra, p. 225.

of *karma* rose as that of *Niyati* fell. This is strongly indicated by the commentary of Tattuvappirakācar to *Civañāṉa-cittiyār*, which interprets *ūḻi* (Fate, Sanskrit *Niyati*) as *viṉai* (action, Sanskrit *karma*).

It seems that within the later Ājīvika sect at least two schools emerged. With the first, typified by the Ājīvika teacher in *Maṇimēkalai*, *Niyati* was pushed more and more into the background. With the second school, whose doctrines are discussed in *Nīlakēci*, the *Niyati* doctrine developed into *Avicalita-nityatvam*, and new features emerged, which will be discussed in the following chapters.

Just as the simpler Buddhists must have found the Theravāda teachings unpalatable and difficult to understand and developed for themselves a more emotional approach to their religion, taking some of their logicians and metaphysicians with them, so with the Southern Ājīvikas the sterile doctrines of *Niyati* and *Avicalita-nityatvam* seem to have been put on one side by some branches of the sect and replaced by more attractive and more intelligible teachings.

With the decline of *Niyati* in importance the idea of the futility of human effort probably slipped into the background also. Nīlakeci seems aware of the doctrine, and counteracts it with the usual argument, that it leads to antinomianism.[1] But *Maṇimēkalai* states that those who do not wish for destruction (*aḻiyal vēṇṭār*) will obtain the supremely white birth, and salvation.[2] This suggests not a mere acquiescence in Destiny, but a definite effort of will on the part of the believer. Indeed it is probable that the rigid determinism of Ājīvika theory never greatly affected Ājīvika practice, and that its influence on day-to-day life was negligible.

[1] *Nīl.* 697. [2] *Maṇi.* xxvii, 156.

CHAPTER XIII

ĀJĪVIKA COSMOLOGY

THE CATEGORIES OF THE *SĀMAÑÑA-PHALA SUTTA*

We have shown that for the early Ājīvika all the processes of nature, including the actions of human beings, were rigidly fixed by *Niyati*. According to the inherent character of that impersonal principle the universe retained its shape and size, and new entities replaced those which passed away in rigidly determined order. The total of the contents of the universe was always absolutely the same. That this was the Ājīvika view even before the emergence of the later doctrine of *Avicalita-nityatvam* is evident from the long list of categories in the *Sāmañña-phala Sutta*.[1]

The full significance of this remarkable list is by no means clear, but from the last sentence of the relevant passage of the *Sutta* it would appear that it is no mere catalogue of the contents of the cosmos, but a list of conditions and states, the whole range of which must be passed through before emancipation. It seems that Buddhaghosa [2] often did not understand the text upon which he was commenting, but merely guessed at its meaning. The accuracy of the list itself cannot be relied on, for before being written it must have been passed down by word of mouth by several generations of Buddhists who did not understand its full significance and were often careless of the accuracy of what was to them an unimportant passage. That later copyists introduced further errors seems probable, in view of the large number of variant readings quoted in the PTS. edition of the text. Nevertheless the partial accuracy of the *Sāmañña-phala Sutta's* catalogue is confirmed by Jaina sources.[3] As it is, it gives us the best available picture of the fantastic universe conceived by the early Ājīvikas. We consider the items of the list, in the order in which they are given in the *Sutta*.

[1] V. supra, p. 14. [2] *Sum. Vil.* i, pp. 161–4. [3] V. supra, pp. 218–19.

Y o n i - p a m u k h a. Chief sorts of womb, or birth. Of these there are 1,400,000 and 6,000 and 600, or 1,406,600 in all. This figure probably applies to the total number of species of living beings in the universe, and the final phrase of the list (" through which fool and wise alike will take their course ")[1] implies that each transmigrating soul must be reborn in each state in the course of its *saṃsāra.*

K a m m a. The classification of the *kammas* is very obscure, and the significance of the term in this context is not absolutely certain. We have seen that the place of *karma* in early Ājīvikism was taken by *Niyati.*[2] Yet on the lower level of truth the transmigratory chain of cause and effect does not seem to have been categorically denied. Possibly the numerous *karmas* are the ways in which an individual's behaviour can, on the *vyāvahārika* plane only, affect his future condition. On the *pāramârthika* level of truth, of course, the only effective agent is *Niyati.*

The *kammas* are divided into groups. There are five hundred, five, three, one, and one-half a *kamma.* On the first group of five hundred Buddhaghosa comments: " By mere sophistry he explains a useless heresy."[3] The five are interpreted by Buddhaghosa as actions connected with the five senses, although he seems to prefer the alternative theory that the five are an appendage to the five hundred.[4] The three, he states, are act, speech, and thought; the one is either act or word; and the half is thought. This interpretation is far from complete or satisfactory, but Buddhaghosa's explanation of the *aḍḍha-kamma* is supported by a passage in Yaśomitra's commentary to the *Abhidharma Kośa.*[5] This implies that the Ājīvika disagrees with the Buddhist view of *kāma* as the covetous imaginings of the mind, and maintains that passions only arise from sensuous perceptions, and not from thought alone. With the Ājīvikas *kāma* was external to the man, with the Buddhists it was

[1] *Yāni bāle ca paṇḍite ca sandhāvitvā saṃsaritvā dukkhass' antaṃ karissanti.* V. supra, p. 14, n. 3.

[2] V. supra, p. 224.

[3] *Takka-mattakena niratthakaṃ diṭṭhiṃ dīpeti. Sum. Vil.*, loc. cit.

[4] *Ādisu pi es' eva nayo. Keci pan' āhu pañca kammān' iti pañc'-indriya-vasena bhaṇati.* Ibid.

[5] *Abhidharmakośa-vyākhyā*, ed. Wogihara, vol. i, pp. 257–8. V. also De la Vallée Poussin, *L'Abhidharma-kośa de Vasubandhu*, vol. iii, pp. 7–8.

internal. On the Ājīvika theory, even the Buddha was liable to *kāma* with all its consequences, on looking at sense-objects. Thus thought could not be productive of such strong karmic effects as physical activity or the operation of the senses. This may account for the Ājīvika conception of the inactivity and silence of the Lord Maṟkali,[1] and for the practice of penance in large jars,[2] perhaps to avoid the use of the senses, and hence the development of *kāma*.

The *Bhagavatī Sūtra* gives different figures for the totals of *kammas*, but it confirms the Pāli source in showing that the Ājīvikas believed in a large number of these, which were divided into groups. In the *Bhagavatī* there are 500,000 *kammas*, 60,000 and 600, together with three parts of *kamma*,[3] which must be worked out in order before the process of salvation is completed. Here the figures 60,000 and 600 suggest the totals of the *yoni-pamukha* in the Pāli text, and the *kamm'-aṃse*, or parts of a *kamma*, perhaps correspond to the act, speech, and thought of Buddhaghosa. Although our translation of *tinni ya kamm'-aṃse* is based on the commentator Abhayadeva,[4] it seems possible that a second *ya* is to be understood at the end of the phrase, in which case it should be translated as three (*kammas*) and a part of a *kamma*. Thus the *kamm'-aṃse* of the *Bhagavatī* would represent the *aḍḍha-kamma* of the *Sāmañña-phala Sutta*.

The *Sūtra* shows that, whatever the correct total of the *kammas* according to Ājīvika doctrine, they were types of action affecting the individual soul in its transmigration, which each must perform in regular order (*aṇupuvveṇaṃ khavaïttā*). On the higher level of truth they were not causal factors, but from the relative viewpoint they had to be taken into account.

Paṭipadā. "Paths." These are sixty-two in number and are unexplained by Buddhaghosa. Rhys Davids renders the word as "modes of conduct". Perhaps it should be taken in its pregnant Buddhist sense, and signifies religious systems of conduct, of which the *majjhimā paṭipadā* of Buddhism was one. We may infer that the transmigrating soul must pass through each in the course of its pilgrimage.

[1] V. infra, p. 276.
[2] V. supra, p. 111.
[3] *Bh. Sū.* xv, *sū.* 550, fol. 673. V. supra, p. 14, n. 3.
[4] *Trīṃś ca karma-bhedān.* Op. cit., fol. 675.

Antara-kappa. Lesser periods within the *kappa* or aeon. Buddhaghosa points out that there are actually sixty-four *antarakappas* to each *kappa*, whereas Makkhali allowed only sixty-two. Either Ājīvika chronometry differed in this particular from that of the Buddhists, or an error crept into the text at an early date.

Abhijāti. Classes of men. These we have already discussed in another context.[1] The Ājīvika sixfold classification is given in full in the *Aṅguttara*, where it is ascribed to Pūraṇa Kassapa.[2] The *Aṅguttara* passage is borrowed, with few alterations, by Buddhaghosa.[3] That the Ājīvikas divided humanity into six groups, classified according to their psychic colour, is confirmed by Tamil sources.

The classification of the Pāli text is as follows :—

1. Black (*kaṇha*) includes all who live by slaughter and cruelty, such as hunters, fowlers, fishermen, thieves, gaolers, and others.

2. Blue (*nīla*), contains, according to the *Aṅguttara*, " monks who live as thieves " (*kaṇḍaka-vuttikā*), together with other believers in the efficiency of works. Hare [4] translates this phrase as " who live as though with a thorn in their side ", on the strength of Buddhaghosa, who apparently interprets *kaṇḍaka* or *kaṇṭaka* as " thorn ", gives it the secondary sense of " impediment ", and states in a very obscure manner that the four *paccayas* of the Buddhist *bhikkhu* are implied.[5]

3. Red (*lohita*), *nigaṇṭhas*, who wear a single garment. The exact significance of this apparently simple phrase is far from clear, as we have already shown.[6] It probably applies to all monks of a Jaina type.

4. Green (*haliddā*) are the lay disciples of the *acelakas*. This passage also has its obscurities,[7] but seems to refer to Ājīvika laymen, who are promoted above the ascetics of other communities.

5. White (*sukka*). *Ājīvikas* and *Ājīvinīs* (the latter called in the *Aṅguttara Ājīvakiniyo*). Ājīvika ascetics of both sexes.

[1] V. supra, p. 139. [2] *Aṅg.* iii, p. 383 f. [3] *Sum. Vil.* i, p. 162.

[4] *Gradual Sayings*, iii, p. 273. V. supra, p. 139, n. 7.

[5] *Te Kira catusu paccayesu kaṇṭkake pakkhipitvā khādanti. Bhikkhū ca kaṇṭaka-vuttikā ti ayaṃ hi 'ssa pāli yeva. Sum. Vil.* i, 162.

[6] V. supra, p. 139, with n. 6, and p. 109.

[7] V. supra, p. 139, with n. 5.

6. Supremely White (*parama-sukka*). According to the texts, this class contains three names only, those of Nanda Vaccha, Kisa Saṅkicca, and Makkhali Gosāla.[1] We cannot believe that the class was such a small one, and suggest that it contained all the *arhants*, *tīrthaṅkaras*, or *āptas* of Ājīvika mythology.[2]

The omission of the non-Ājīvika layfolk, who did not live by killing man or beast, suggests that the list of categories is incomplete. No system could ignore such people in its classification.

The Ājīvika use of the term *abhijāti* is confirmed by the *Bhagavatī Sūtra* ; here, when Gosāla declares that his body is now inhabited by the soul of Udāī,[3] he states that the soul of the original Gosāla was of the white class (*sukk-âbhijāīe*).

That the Ājīvikas classified humanity according to its spiritual colour is confirmed by *Maṇimēkalai* and *Civañāṉa-cittiyār*. The former text [4] quotes the colours of the births (*piṟappu*, equivalent to Sanskrit *abhijāti*) as follows : (1) Black (*karu*), (2) dark blue (*karu-nīla*) ; (3) green (*pacu*) ; (4) red (*cem*) ; (5) golden (*poṉ*), and (6), white (*veṇ*). It is further stated that those in the pure white (*kaḻi-veṉ*) category reach salvation.[5] It may be suggested that the *poṉ* category in this list corresponds to the *sukka* of the Pāli, and the *veṇ* to *parama-sukka*. The text, however, also mentions a pure white category, the colour of salvation, and this is confirmed by the *Civañāṉa-cittiyār*, which includes " supremely white " as one of the six colours, stating that it only exists in those who are saved from *saṃsāra* (*vīṭṭiṉ*), while the others are to be found on earth.[6] It will be noted that in the *Maṇimēkalai* list green is lower in the scale than red. If we attribute the colours to the same classes as those in the Pāli list, this would place the *nirgranthas* above the Ājīvika laymen, and is not wholly impossible. The *Maṇimēkalai* order is that of the Jaina *leśyās*, to which the Ājīvika *abhijātis* are closely akin.

The list of colours given in *Civañāṉa-cittiyār* seems to be without order : white (*veṇmai*), golden (*poṉmai*), red (*cemmai*), blue (*nīl*), pure white (*kaḻi-veṇmai*), and green (*paccai*).[7] The black

[1] V. supra, pp. 27 ff.

[2] V. infra, p. 275.

[3] *Bh. Sū.* xv, *sū* 550, fol. 673. V. supra, p. 31.

[4] *Maṇi.* xxvii, 150–5.

[5] *Kaḻi-ven piṟappiṟ kalantu vīḷ-aṇaikuvar.*

[6] *CÑC.*, p. 263, v. 8.

[7] Ibid.

of the other two lists is omitted. The disorderly arrangement of the colours seems to indicate that the author of *Civañāṉa-cittiyār* was unaware of their full significance; apparently at this late stage of Ājīvikism the doctrine of *abhijāti* was becoming confused.

The *abhijātis* have much in common with the Jaina *leśyās*. According to this classification the six colours are: (1) black (*kaṇha*), (2) blue (*nīla*), (3) grey (*kāü*), (4) red (*teu*), (5) yellow (*paṃha*), and (6) white (*sukka*).[1] All have characteristic psychic tastes and smells, and give characteristic sensations of touch. In the black class is the man of blood and violence; in the blue among others, are the envious, the deceitful, and the luxurious; in the grey are the heretic and the thief; these three are evil *leśyās*. The three latter *leśyās* contain men of good *karmic* character; in the red category are the well-disciplined and studious; in the yellow those men who are calm, attentive, and subdued; while in the white are men who meditate on the law and the truth with their minds at ease, and are self-controlled, even though they may not be wholly free from passion. The *leśyās* are conceived as substances, which may adhere to the soul for a longer or shorter time, and all living beings are subject to them,[2] although men only are quoted as examples.

The Ājīvika system of spiritual colours is a general classification of humanity according to creed or occupation, while that of the Jainas classifies man's psychic development and virtue. There can be no doubt that, as Hoernle has suggested,[3] the two doctrines are connected. But it cannot be shown that their similarity indicates the dependence of Ājīvikism on Jainism, or the reverse. It seems more probable that the two systems of colour classification are derived from a common body of ideas which were widespread among ascetic groups in the days of the Buddha. Of the two the precisely defined Ājīvika *abhijātis* are less sophisticated and therefore probably earlier than the Jaina *leśyās*, the differences of which are mainly of degree, and the dependence of which on moral characteristics is more strongly stressed.

It may be concluded that the Ājīvika believed that the soul must transmigrate through all the *abhijātis* before its release

[1] *Uttarâdhyāyana*, xxxiv. [2] Ibid., verse 47. [3] *ERE.* i, p. 262.

from *saṃsāra*. Even the most highly developed soul must have spent part of its long existence among the basest and wickedest of mankind.

Purisa-bhūmi. Stages of human existence. These are said by Buddhaghosa to be eight, namely:—

1. *Manda-bhūmi* (stupid stage), the condition of the new-born infant;
2. *Khiddā-* (pleasure), the older infant who laughs and weeps without self-control;
3. *Vīmaṃsā-* (investigation), the stage at which the child begins to walk, holding his parents' hands;
4. *Ujugata-* (upright walking), when the child is capable of walking without help;
5. *Sekha-* (learning), when he learns arts and crafts;
6. *Samaṇa-* (monkhood);
7. *Jina-* (enlightenment), at the end of his service at the feet of a spiritual instructor; and
8. *Pañña-bhūmi,* the stage of highest cognition, when he does not speak at all.

It is doubtful whether Buddhaghosa's interpretation of the eight stages of man is wholly correct, especially as it disregards the stage of the householder, and applies therefore only to those ascetics who abandon their homes in their youth, unless the layman is looked upon as never passing the stage of *sekha-bhūmi*. Another surprising feature of the list is the inclusion of a stage above that of *jina*, which does not here seem to connote the same degree of spiritual excellence as elsewhere. It is possible that Buddhaghosa has reversed the order of the seventh and eighth stages; but it will be remembered that other sources speak of the silence of Makkhali,[1] and the final stage of human development may have been introduced in order to establish his superiority over other leaders of the sect.

If Buddhaghosa had not specified the eight *purisa-bhūmiyo* it would have been logical to interpret them in its literal sense as "worlds of men", fewer in number than the purgatories and serpent-realms also mentioned in the list, through which the transmigrating soul must pass. We cannot avoid the suspicion that the eight stages of men were devised by Buddhaghosa

[1] V. supra, p. 52.

himself, since there is no confirmation from other sources of this Ājīvika classification of the stages of life.

Ājīva. This is translated by Rhys Davids, on the basis of Buddhaghosa, as "professions", of which there are 4,900. The scholiast's brief comment (*ājīva-vutti*) does not completely convince us that the term is thus used here. The Siamese version of the text gives it as *Ājīvaka*,[1] and *Ājīva* itself is a legitimate form of the word *Ājīvika*,[2] in the sense of an ascetic. If we accept Buddhaghosa's interpretation, the phrase must imply that the soul in its rebirths takes up 4,900 different means of earning a living; otherwise it could imply that it is born 4,900 times as an Ājīvika. The latter interpretation is supported by the Tibetan version of the text, which, according to Rockhill, gives this item as "4,900 *akelakas*" (sic).[3] Barua [4] accepts this interpretation.

Paribbājaka. Wandering mendicants, also to the number of 4,900. We do not believe that this means "sorts of mendicant", as Rhys Davids translates it, but rather that the soul will be reborn as a wandering ascetic 4,900 times in the course of its transmigration.

Nāgâvāsa. Of these there are again 4,900. They must be, in Buddhaghosa's words *nāga-maṇḍala*, or regions of serpents. The evidence of the Jaina sources indicates that the Ājīvikas were interested in the *nāgas* of popular religion, who played a significant part in their mythology. Thus Gosāla compares himself to a gigantic serpent, destroying those who attack him.[5] On the last night of the Ājīvika six months' fatal penance those ascetics who yield to the ministrations of the two gods, Punnabhadda and Māṇibhadda, will not be emancipated but will "do the work of serpenthood".[6] This cryptic phrase probably means that they will be reborn as serpents in one of the *nāgâvāsas*.

Indriya. Of these there are 2,000. Buddhaghosa gives no elucidation of the word, which Rhys Davids translates

[1] *Teste* Rhys Davids, *Dialogues of the Buddha*, i, p. 72, n.
[2] V. supra, pp. 163, n. 1, 181–83.
[3] *The Life of the Buddha*, p. 103.
[4] *ABORI*. viii, p. 185, and n. 16.
[5] V. supra, p. 59.
[6] *Āsīvisattāe kammaṃ pakareti.* V supra, p. 128, and infra, pp. 257 ff.

"faculties".[1] The 2,000 must include not only the human senses, but many supernatural ones, of which the transmigrating soul was thought to make use in the course of its long pilgrimage.

Niraya. These, 3,000 in number, are certainly purgatories.

Rajo-dhātu. Of these there are only thirty-six. They are interpreted by Buddhaghosa as "places covered with dust, such as shelves and foot-rests",[2] an explanation accepted by Rhys Davids for want of a better. Barua translates as "celestial, mundane, or passionate grades",[3] without comment or explanation. Franke suggests the possibility of some connection between this phrase and the *rajo guṇa* of Sāṅkhya philosophy.[4] The Vedic meaning of the word *rajas,* "atmosphere," must not be forgotten as a possible interpretation. The most probable meaning of the phrase seems to us to be "elements of impurity", or perhaps "of passion".

The three following categories, of each of which there are seven members only, are best considered together. They are :—

Saññi-gabbha, according to Buddhaghosa types of sentient birth, such as camels, oxen, etc. ;

Asaññi-gabbha, types of unconscious birth, such as rice, barley, wheat, etc. ; and

Nigaṇṭhi-gabbha, types of birth from knots, as examples of which Buddhaghosa gives the sugar-cane, the bamboo, and the reed.[5]

We can feel no confidence in Buddhaghosa's explanation of these three items. First in the catalogue of Ājīvika categories occurs the item, "1,406,000 *yoni-pamukha,*" which seem to be chief sorts of birth. On this interpretation the twenty-one classes of birth above are but a drop in the ocean of the *yoni-pamukha,* and seem quite unworthy of being placed in a category of their own. To this it might be objected that the *yoni-pamukha* represent species, while the seven members of each of the three above classes are genera. The three categories are followed by those of *deva, mānusa,* and *pesāca,* and it is there-

[1] *Dialogues of the Buddha,* i, p. 72.
[2] *Raja-okiṇṇa-ṭṭhānāni hatthapīṭha-pādapīṭh'-ādīni. Sum. Vil.* i, p. 163.
[3] *Pre-Buddhistic Indian Philosophy,* p. 306.
[4] *Dīgha Nikāya in Auswahl Übersetzt,* p. 57.
[5] *Ganṭhimhi jāta-gabbhā ucchu-veḷu-nāl'-ādayo. Sum. Vil.,* loc. cit.

fore not impossible that this section of the list is an enumeration of the chief types of each category of living being, all of which are included in the *yoni-pamukha* at the head of the list. Thus the seven *saññi-gabbha* might well be divided in some such way as human, mammal, bird, reptile, fish, insect, and worm, and the seven *asaññi-gabbha* in a similar way. But Buddhaghosa must surely have been mistaken in his interpretation of the *niganṭhi-gabbhā*; we cannot believe that the larger grasses played so great a part in the Ājīvika scheme that they required a category to themselves. We would tentatively suggest that the *niganṭhi-gabbhā* were "those not bound", not in this case members of the *Nirgrantha* sect, but beings not so closely tied to gross matter as are mortals.[1] Thus the category of *niganṭhi-gabbhā* would link with the *devā* who follow, and correspond to the *satta sañjūhe* of the *Bhagavatī Sūtra* list, which we consider in the following paragraph. We believe that the *niganṭhi-gabbhā* were seven types of demigod, *yakṣa*, *apsaras*, etc.

The *Bhagavatī Sūtra* throws some further light on these obscure categories, and must modify our interpretation. Here Gosāla is said to have maintained that before its final release the soul must pass through seven divine (births), seven *sañjūhe*, and seven conscious births, using for the latter the same phrase as the Pāli text, *sanni-gabbhe*.[2] The first group of seven is interpreted by the commentator Abhayadeva as existences as a god, the second as existences in the seven *saṃyūthas* or groups (of demigod), and the third as human existences. These lives, as Gosāla himself explains later in the *Sūtra*, will all be lived at intervals by the soul nearing salvation.[3]

These groups of seven births occur at the end of the soul's long cosmic journey of 8,400,000 *mahākappas*' duration. The text of the *Bhagavatī Sūtra* gives a list of the last fourteen births, as follows :—

[1] This interpretation is partially confirmed by the Tibetan version, which gives "seven modes of existence as *asuras*" in place of the *niganṭhi-gabbhā* of the Pāli, which appears as "49,000 of the nirgrantha species (of mendicant)". Rockhill, op. cit., pp. 103–4.

[2] *Satta divve, satta sañjūhe, satta sannigabbhe. Bh. Sū.* xv, *sū.* 550, fol. 673.

[3] *Sapta divyān, devabhāvān; . . . sapta saṃyūthān, nikāyaviśeṣān; . . . (sapta) sañjñi-garbhān, manuṣya-garbha-vasatīḥ; ete ca tan-matena mokṣa-gāminām sapta-sāntarā bhavanti, vakṣyati c' aiv' aitān svayam eva.* Abhayadeva to *Bh. Sū.*, fol. 675.

1. In the *Uvarille Māṇase* or upper Māṇasa heaven, as a god ;
2. The first conscious birth (*sanni-gabbhe*) ;
3. In the middle (*Majjhile*) Māṇasa ;
4. Second conscious birth ;
5. In the lower (*Heṭṭhile*) Māṇasa ;
6. Third conscious birth ;
7. In the upper Superior Māṇusa (*Māṇusuttare*) ;
8. Fourth conscious birth ;
9. In the middle Māṇusuttara ;
10. Fifth conscious birth ;
11. In the lower Māṇusuttara ;
12. Sixth conscious birth ;
13. In the heaven of Bambhaloga, or of Brahma, where the soul resides for the duration of ten divine *sāgarovama* periods ; and finally
14. The seventh and last conscious birth, at the end of which the soul performs the seven reanimations (*paüṭṭa-parihāra*),[1] and finally passes to *nirvāṇa* after the penance of the " Pure Drink ".[2]

It will be seen that the names of the Ājīvika heavens are not the same as those of the Jainas,[3] except for Bambhaloga. The difference in the names of the three higher heavens and those of the lower, *Māṇusuttara* and *Māṇasa*, is unexpected, and is probably the result of the error of an early scribe.[4]

It seems probable that the seven *saññi-gabbhā* of the Pāli list are the same as those of the *Bhagavatī* ; on the analogy of the latter text's account of the heavenly births it is also probable that each of the " sentient births " was in a different state or condition. The *Bhagavatī* list makes no mention of the *asaññi-gabbhā* of the Pāli, but it is possible that the latter's *nigaṇṭhi-gabbhā* represent the *Bhagavatī's* seven *sañjūhe*. The latter term is also used with each of the Māṇasas and Māṇusuttaras in the second *Bhagavatī* list,[5] and in this context is interpreted by Abhayadeva

[1] V. supra, pp. 30 ff.
[2] V. supra, pp. 127 ff.
[3] Saudharma, Īśāna, Sanatkumāra, Māhendra, Brahmaloka, Lāntaka, Mahāśukra, Sahasrāra, Ānata, Prāṇata, Āraṇa, and Acyuta, in rising order of excellence. Guérinot, *La Religion Djaïna*, p. 184.
[4] This is confirmed by Abhayadeva, who reads *Māṇas'-ottara*. *Bh. Sū.* comm., fol. 676.
[5] *Uvarille Māṇase Sañjūhe deve uvavajjati*, etc. *Bh. Sū.*, loc. cit.

as "a god of a special class".[1] The wording of the first list (*satta divve, satta sañjūhe, satta sannigabbhe*), however, indicates that the seven *sañjūhe* were thought of as distinct from the *divve*, or divine births in the Māṇasas and Māṇusuttaras.

D e v a, of which there are seven. Buddhaghosa takes this term as meaning gods, and naïvely states that there is in fact a very large number of gods, thus stressing the Ājīvika's ignorance. The word should surely be interpreted adjectivally, as equivalent to the Sanskrit *daiva*, corresponding to the *satta divve* of the *Bhagavatī* list. These are the seven divine births in the Māṇasa and Māṇusuttara heavens.

M ā n u s a. These are also seven. Buddhaghosa accepted this word literally, and noted that the total number of men was not seven, but infinite. Were it not for the equivalence of the *Bhagavatī's sanni-gabbhe* and of the *saññi-gabbhā* of the Pāli, it might be suggested that the seven *mānusa* were the last seven human births of the soul. It is also possible that they are connected with the *paüṭṭa-parihāras*, and represent the seven human bodies which the soul reanimates in its last existence, but these are better represented by the *paṭuvā* below. We have already seen that, according to the *Bhagavatī Sūtra* the Ājīvika heavens were called *māṇasa* and *māṇusuttara*. It is possible that *mānusa* in the Pāli list is an error, and that the term should be *mānasa*, the seven heavens which the soul inhabits in its last seven divine births. It will be recalled that the confusion of *māṇasa* and *māṇusa* occurs in the Prākrit text itself.

P e s ā c a. Again seven. Both the readings *pisāca* and *pesāca*[2] occur, of which Buddhaghosa accepts the former, and contents himself with stating that the total of goblins is in fact very large. We believe that the word is adjectival, and refers to seven births as *piśācas* or goblins, which the soul must experience before its release from *saṃsāra*.

S a r a. Interpreted by Buddhaghosa as "great lakes" (*mahā-sarā*) of which he gives the names: Kaṇṇamuṇḍa, Rathakāra, Anotatta, Sīhappapāta, Tiyaggaḷa, Mucalinda, and Kuṇāladaha. It will be noted that the term used for the Ājīvika heavens, *mānasa*, may also mean "a lake", and that the

[1] *Nikāya-viśeṣe deve.* Abhayadeva to above, fol. 676.
[2] *Sum. Vil.* i, p. 164, n. 4. *Dīgha* i, p. 54, n. 2.

Ājīvika system of chronometry also knew a period called a *sara*, of which 300,000 constituted a *mahākappa*.[1] But possibly Buddhaghosa's explanation is correct, and these are seven great lakes, in each of which the soul becomes a denizen before the end of its journey. The names given by Buddhaghosa are those of the seven lakes of Himavant according to Buddhist geography.[2] It is not impossible that the Ājīvikas had a similar classification.

P a ṭ u v ā. Of these, according to the *Sutta*, there are seven and seven hundred. The word is not translated by Rhys Davids, who admits that he does not know its meaning. While it is given in this form in the *Dīgha*, Buddhaghosa reads *pacuṭā*,[3] and there are several variants, such as *pamuṭā*, *pamucā*, and *papuṭā*.[4] Buddhaghosa equates the word with *ganṭhika*, a knot or block, a very improbable meaning. The text of the *Sutta* gives the total of the *paṭuvās*, like those of the two following categories, as seven and seven hundred. In the case of the two latter, Buddhaghosa interpreted the seven as being of major and the seven hundred of minor rank, but his commentary makes no reference to seven hundred *pacuṭā*. We therefore conclude that the text on which he worked gave the total of these as seven only, on the analogy of the previous categories. We believe that the *paṭuvā* actually represent the seven *paüṭṭa-parihāra* of the *Bhagavatī*.[5] Succeeding generations of scribes, ignorant of the true meaning of the term, might easily corrupt the first element of the Prākrit term into the forms given above.

P a p ā t a. Precipices, seven and seven hundred in number. Perhaps these are falls from a higher to a lower state of being.

S u p i n a. This word Barua has identified with the Sanskrit *suparṇa*, a divine bird,[6] but we cannot agree. *Supina*, in Pāli, like *suviṇa* in Ardha-māgadhī, must be equivalent to the Sanskrit *svapna*, and mean dream. We can only suggest that the seven and seven hundred *supinā* are dreams of great psychic significance, supposed to occur just before the final emancipation of the soul.

M a h ā k a p p a. Great aeons, of which the number is 8,400,000. Through these, and all the preceding categories, fool

[1] V. infra, p. 253. [2] *PTS. Dictionary*, s.v. *sara*. [3] *Sum. Vil.* i, p. 164.
[4] *Sum. Vil.* i, p. 164, n. 7. [5] V. supra, p. 31. [6] V. supra, p. 220.

and wise alike must travel before they " make an end of sorrow ". The same total of *mahākappas* is given in the *Bhagavatī Sūtra*, where it is stated that they and the other categories must all be duly passed before release from transmigration, when the souls accomplish their journey (*sijjhanti*), are enlightened (*bujjhanti*) set free (*muccanti*), and finally emancipated (*parinivvāinti*), making an end of all sorrows.[1] These terms may give us some idea of the Ājīvika conception of final bliss, but it must be noted that with some later Ājīvikas even the state of *nirvāṇa* does not seem to have been looked upon as final.[2]

The verb in the final clause of the above passage in the *Bhagavatī* is quoted in its past, present, and future forms.[3] This indicates that the Ājīvika cosmos contained many more *mahākappas* even than the enormous figure quoted, and that at any time a soul might complete its 8,400,000 aeons of *saṃsāra* and attain *nirvāṇa*. These *mahākappas* are not the total of universal time, but merely the aeons through which each soul must pass in order to gain salvation.

The *Bhagavatī Sūtra* gives an estimate of the duration of a *mahākappa*, which shows that Ājīvika chronometric speculations were even wider in conception and more awe inspiring than were those of other Indian schools, all of which seemed to delight in imagining fantastically long periods of time. After expounding his doctrine of transmigration Gosāla is purported to have said that according to his system the bed of the Ganges was 250 *yojanas* in length, half a *yojana* in width and 500 *dhanus* in depth. Seven *gaṅgās* equal one *mahāgaṅgā*; seven *mahāgaṅgās* equal one *sādīṇagaṅgā*; seven *sādīṇagaṅgās*, one *maccugaṅgā*; seven *maccugaṅgās*, one *lohiyagaṅgā*; seven *lohiyagaṅgās*, one *āvatīgaṅgā*; and seven *āvatīgaṅgās* equal one *paramāvatī*. The latter therefore equals seven to the seventh power or 117,649 *gaṅgās*. If one grain of sand were removed every hundred years from the bed of this imaginary river the total time required for the removal of all the sand would be one *sara*. 300,000 *saras* of this duration equal one *mahākappa*, and even here Ājīvika chronometry does not stop. Gosāla concludes by

[1] *Bh. Sū.* xv, *sū.* 550, fol. 673.

[2] V. infra, pp. 257 ff.

[3] *Savva-dukkhass' antaṃ kareṃsu vā karenti vā karissanti vā. Bh. Sū.*, loc. cit.

stating that 8,400,000 *mahākappas*, the period of the transmigration of a soul, are called one *mahāmāṇasa*.[1]

Buddhaghosa gives another account of the *mahākappa*, according to which its duration seems comparatively modest; a *mahākappa* is the time taken to exhaust a great lake seven times, by removing one drop of water every hundred years.[2] This definition agrees with that of the *Bhagavatī* in so far as it introduces a lake (*sara*) into the calculations. But here the *mahākappa* consists of only seven *sara*, in place of the 300,000 of the *Bhagavatī*.

Beside the system of *Mahākalpas*, the *Bhagavatī Sūtra* also indicates that the Ājīvikas maintained a doctrine of cosmic progress and decay, similar to that of the Jainas, since Gosāla is referred to as the twenty-fourth *tīrthaṅkara* of the Avarsarpiṇī age, or aeon of decline.[3] As his status would thus correspond exactly with that of Mahāvīra in Jainism, the suspicion cannot be avoided that the passage is a Jaina interpolation, although, in view of the close connection between the two sects, it is not impossible that it represents authentic Ājīvika teaching.

The Eight Last Things

A few further categories are mentioned in the *Bhagavatī Sūtra*, but do not occur in the Buddhist texts. These include the four *pāṇagāiṃ* and the four *apāṇagāiṃ*, the eight *carimāiṃ*, and the six *anaïkkamaṇijjāiṃ*. The two former are rules governing the conduct of the ascetic in his last penance, and have already

[1] *Bh. Sū.*, loc. cit. The text used by Hoernle seems to have differed somewhat in its terminology from the Bombay edition. The commentator Abhayadeva appears to have confused the *sara* with the *māṇasa* heaven, and the *mahāmāṇasa* period with the heaven called *māṇusuttara* (v. supra, p. 250). He believed that the soul would spend *sara* and *mahāmāṇasa* periods in the *māṇasas* and *māṇusuttaras* respectively (to *Bh. Sū.*, fol. 676). The text of the *Bhagavatī* may thus be interpreted (v. supra, p. 219, n. 2). But if the last births are excluded from the total of the *mahākappas* the *kammas* must also be excluded, and the soul must be thought of as performing these 560,600 types of deed outside the period of 8,400,000 *mahākappas*. This does not seem the intention of the text. The *Samañña-phala Sutta* reference clearly shows that the categories are of different orders, and include actions, types of being, and their cosmic locations, all within the framework of the 8,400,000 *mahākappas*.

[2] *Sum. Vil.* i, p. 164.

[3] V. supra, p. 68.

been dealt with.[1] The eight *carimāiṃ* have also been treated in another context,[2] and require little further attention.

The ultimates or finalities are stated by the *Bhagavatī* to be connected with the last life on earth of the migrant soul, and to herald its final release.[3] As Hoernle realized, they are based on the actions of Gosāla in his delirium and on events which occurred at about the time of his death. The *Sūtra* declares that they were laid down by Gosāla to excuse his own objectionable conduct, to which Abhayadeva adds that he declared that there was no sin in these actions since they were inevitable at the death of a *jina*.[4] The first four items of the list, the last drink, song, dance, and greeting, are evidently related to the behaviour of the dying *tīrthaṅkara*; the following three, the storm cloud, the sprinkling elephant, and the battle with large stones, are portentous events which herald his *nirvāṇa*; while the eighth and last is the *tīrthaṅkara* himself. No information about these eight finalities, as part of the Ājīvika creed, occurs in other sources. They have no philosophical value, but are probably a mere list of omens, borrowed from the popular traditions of the less instructed members of the Ājīvika sect.

THE SIX INEVITABLES

Another Ājīvika doctrine of little apparent importance, and naïve in its simplicity and triteness, is that of the six inevitables (*anaïkkamaṇijjāïṃ*). These six factors, inevitably accompanying all existence, are said to have been declared by Gosāla immediately after he and the six *disācaras* had codified the Ājīvika scriptures,[5] and, if we accept the *Bhagavatī Sūtra's* definition of them, say little for the profundity of those works. The six are: gain (*lābhaṃ*), loss (*alābhaṃ*), joy (*suhaṃ*), sorrow (*dukkhaṃ*), life (*jīviyaṃ*), and death (*maraṇaṃ*).

It does not seem likely that these six were very important. Some of the Dravidian Ājīvikas, following the doctrine ascribed in

[1] V. supra, pp. 127 ff.

[2] V. supra, p. 68.

[3] *Bh. Sū.* xv, *sū.* 554, fol. 679.

[4] *Etāni ca kila nirvāṇa-kālè jinasy' âvaśyam-bhavīn' îti n' âsty eteṣu dosaḥ*, fol. 684.

[5] V. supra, p. 56.

the *Dīgha* to Pakudha Kaccāyana, certainly classed joy, sorrow, and life as atomic, together with the four material atoms.[1] We read nothing of a sixfold classification elsewhere. The nearest approach to such a classification occurs in the *Civāñāṉa-cittiyār*, wherein Fate (*ūḻi*) is said to produce wealth (*pēṟu*), poverty (*iḻavu*), obstacles (i.e. misfortunes, *iṭaiyūṟu*), joy (*iṉpam*), separation (*pirivu*), dwelling in one place (*irukkai*), travel (*vēṟ' oru nāṭṭiṟ cēṟal*), old age (*mūppu*), and death (*cātal*).[2] These categories resemble those of the *Bhagavatī Sūtra*, but contain additions. We may infer that they derive from the same source as the *anatikramaṇīyas* of the Prākrit text; this may have been an Ājīvika hymn or popular poem, for the *anatikramaṇīyas* seem to possess no profound metaphysical significance.

Other Ājīvika Categories

The Tibetan version of the *Sāmañña-phala Sutta* categories, according to Rockhill's translation,[3] differs somewhat from the Pāli. The list contains seven senses (*sañjña*), seven modes of existence as *asuras*, seven and seven hundred " kinds of writing ", seven and seven hundred " proofs ", 49,000 " of the *garuḍa* species ", ten " kinds of ranks ", and eight *mahāpuruṣas*. Of these the *asura* existences replace the *nigaṇṭhi-gabbhā* of the Pāli, which in Rockhill's version become 49,000 of the *nirgrantha* species. It is possible that the obscure *paṭuvā* of the Pāli list are represented by the Tibetan " kinds of writing " or " proofs ", but neither of these is helpful in the elucidation of the Pāli term. The *mahāpuruṣas* evidently represent the *purisa-bhūmiyo* of the Pāli, which do not occur in the Tibetan list. The Tibetan totals sometimes differ from the Pāli, as does the order in which the items occur. The list seems to be even more corrupt than the Pāli version, and throws little fresh light upon it.

A probable recollection of the Ājīvika list of categories is contained in Jiṇapaha Sūri's *Vihimaggapavā*.[4] After the passage already quoted,[5] mentioning Ājīvika begging practices, the text reads : " (According to) Gosāla's instructions there are forty-nine

[1] V. infra, pp. 262 ff.
[2] *CÑC.*, p. 265, v. 9.
[3] *The Life of the Buddha*, pp. 103–4.
[4] Weber, *Verzeichniss*, vol. ii, p. 870.
[5] V. supra, p. 54, n. 4.

times (*kālā*), beside which they declare 2,600 further (times), time by time." [1] This fleeting reference appears to recall some of the contents of the original Ājīvika list, but *kālas* are not included in any versions known to us; *Nīlakēci* explicitly states that the Ājīvika does not recognize the category of time.[2] But the figure forty-nine occurs in the Pāli list, and the enumeration of the times is also suggestive of it. We can only conclude that Jiṇapaha Sūri had obtained a very fragmentary and garbled knowledge of the Ājīvika's fantastic system of cosmological classification.

MAṆḌALA-MOKṢA

Time for the Ājīvika seems to have been infinite, containing an incalculable number of *mahāmāṇasa* periods. But the time spent by the soul during its passage through *saṃsāra* was finite, and limited to one *mahāmāṇasa*, or 8,400,000 *mahākappas*. "*Saṃsāra* is measured as with a bushel, with its joy and sorrow and its appointed end." [3] The soul passes through *saṃsāra*, and, after being reborn in many forms and conditions, and in various regions of the universe in regular and rigidly unalterable order; after passing seven times from one human body to another without dying; and after performing the suicidal penance of six months' duration, it may reach the state of bliss beyond *saṃsāra*. It would seem, from an obscure passage in the *Bhagavatī*, that souls were sometimes fated by *Niyati* to reach the very threshold of the blessed state, only to fall and resume their wanderings through the cosmos. In the description of the final penance it is stated that on the last night of the ascetic's life the gods Punnabhadda and Māṇibhadda descend and caress his limbs with their cool hands; if he resists or ignores their attentions he will be released from *saṃsāra*, his body consumed by spontaneous combustion; if he submits to them, he will "further the work of serpenthood" (*āsīvisattāe kammaṃ pakareti*).[4]

On the subjective and everyday level of truth this ordeal is

[1] *Gosāl'-āṇunnaṃ . . . egūnavannāsā kālā havanti; tad uvari sesāṇi chavvīsaṃ sayāṇi ekkekkeṇa kāleṇa vaccanti.*

[2] V. supra, p. 236.

[3] V. supra, p. 14.

[4] *Bh. Sū.* xv, *sū.* 554, fol. 680. V. supra, p. 128.

the last test of the ascetic's resolution. On the brink of death from thirst and starvation he must resist the divine ministrants, and still maintain his stern self-control. Otherwise his life of penance and asceticism will have been fruitless, and he will be reborn in one of the 4,900 worlds of *nāgas*. This is the only interpretation which we can place upon the strange phrase of the *Sūtra*.

From the ultimate and absolute point of view the decision whether or not to resist the caresses of the *devas* is not in the ascetic's hands. His rebirth as a serpent, or his salvation, are determined by *Niyati*. The passage suggests that, within the period of 8,400,000 *mahākappas* during which it passed through *saṃsāra*, the soul was thought to be destined to perform several cycles in regular order, passing through the rigidly fixed series of births, only at the last moment to yield to the *devas*, fall back, and repeat the dreary process. At the very end of its destined span it would resist, and be freed from birth and death.

Thus by the dispensation of *Niyati* the ultimate salvation of all souls was assured, and thus the gloomy reaches of Gosāla's cosmos were lighted by a faint gleam of optimism. This has been stressed by Barua, anxious to present his "Pre-Buddhistic Indian Philosophers" in the most favourable light possible.[1] But the doctrine that all beings reach ultimate and inevitable perfection raises certain awkward questions, which must have occurred both to the friends and the opponents of Ājīvika fatalism. If all souls are ultimately removed from the material universe of *saṃsāra* what becomes of that universe? Either it remains uninhabited, or it is absorbed in some sort of *pralaya*, or new souls must be continually coming into being to replace those entering *nirvāṇa*. Again, if the period of the soul's existence in the universe is 8,400,000 *mahākappas*, a time unconscionably long, but certainly not infinite, the soul's existence must have had a beginning. Either at the beginning of its course in the cosmos it was created out of absolute nothingness, or it was in some way injected into the universe from the ground or substratum underlying space and time, to which it returns on its *nirvāṇa*.

Such problems as these were tackled by Hindu, Buddhist,

[1] *Pre-Buddhistic Indian Philosophy*, pp. 316–17.

and Jaina theologians, and, we may infer, by the Ājīvikas also. While we have little direct evidence that such questions were ever posed by the Ājīvikas, a new doctrine indicates that they did arise in the Ājīvika community, and were solved to the sect's satisfaction. The new doctrine is that called in *Nīlakēci Maṇḍala-mokṣa*, or cyclic salvation. It appears to have emerged some time after the death of Gosāla, and to have been held especially by the Dravidian Ājīvikas.

It is first mentioned in the *Sūtrakṛtâṅga* : " It is said by some that the sinless soul is pure, but will again become sinful through pleasure and hatred. He who here has been a restrained monk afterwards becomes sinless. As pure water free from defilement becomes again defiled (so does he again become sinful)." [1]

On these verses Śīlâṅka comments that the Trairāśika followers of Gosāla are meant.[2] He interprets the verses as meaning that the blessed souls in a state of *mokṣa* are still conscious of the affairs of the world. They are liable to feel triumph and joy at the victories of the faith, and anger and hatred when it is in danger. Hence they again fall back into *saṃsāra*.[3] Hoernle believed that the verses referred to the Jaina *arhants* from the Ājīvika point of view.[4] This seems certainly to be a false interpretation, for other sources explicitly state a doctrine of *maṇḍala-mokṣa*, to which this verse and Śīlâṅka's commentary closely correspond.

It is thus clear that for some Ājīvika schools at any rate, *nirvāṇa* was not the end. Sin penetrated even beyond the bounds of the universe, and was still liable to drag back the emancipated soul for another round of 8,400,000 *mahākappas* in *saṃsāra*.

This doctrine is not elsewhere mentioned in the Pāli or Jaina Prākrit texts, and seems not to have loomed large in the minds of the earlier Ājīvikas. But it became an important feature of the doctrines of the Dravidian sect, and is referred to by two of our three main Tamil sources.

[1] *Suddhe apāvae āyā ihaṃ egesiṃ āhiyaṃ*
Puṇo kiḍḍā padoseṇaṃ so tattha avarajjhaï.
Iha saṃvuḍe muṇī jāe pacchā hoï apāvae,
Viyaḍ-ambu jahā bhujjo nīrayaṃ sarayaṃ tahā.
Sū. kṛ. i, 1, 3, 11–12, fol. 45.

[2] V. supra, pp. 175 ff.

[3] *Svaśāsana-pūjām upalabhy', ânya-śāsana-parābhavaṃ c' ôpalabhya . . . pramodaḥ sañjāyate, svaśāsana-nyakkāra-darśanāc ca dveṣaḥ.* Śīlâṅka, to *Sū. Kṛ.*, loc. cit.

[4] *ERE.* i, p. 264.

Nīlakēci states explicitly that the doctrine of *maṇḍala*, the return of souls from the highest bliss, was devised in face of the objections we have suggested above to the older Ājīvika cosmic theories. In a given place there is a limited number (of souls), and so by devising (the doctrine of) *maṇḍala* the Ājīvikas remove objections, bringing back (the saved souls).[1] The elliptical verse is much expanded by the commentator Vāmanamuni, who makes it clear that the Ājīvikas postulated the doctrine to allow for the continuity of the universe. But for that purpose, he continues, it is quite unnecessary, for the number of *jīvas* or living souls in the universe is infinitely infinite (*anantânantam*), and no subtraction from the total can make it less than infinity. The Jaina commentator's logic is sound, but we have no confirmation that the Ājīvikas did actually believe that the number of souls in the universe was infinite. The sharply defined and classified nature of the Ājīvika cosmos, and the Ājīvika predilection for very high numbers, suggest that the total number of souls in the universe was considered to be finite, as the Jaina commentator's insistence on the infinity of souls also indicates.

Civañāṉa-cittiyār contains what seems to be a further refinement of the same doctrine. There are two classes of *arhant*, called *maṇṭalar* (Skt. *maṇḍala*) and *cempōtakar* (Skt. *sambodhaka*), of whom the former return to earth and reveal the scriptures.[2] This theory would seem to be that mentioned in the verse quoted by Malliṣeṇa, in which the Ājīvika *tīrthaṅkaras* are said to return to earth when the religion is in danger.[3] The doctrine may be that implied in Buddhaghosa's classification of the seventh and eighth of the stages of man, wherein the *jina-bhūmi* is below the *pañña-bhūmi*, whose occupants do not speak at all.[4]

Thus the Ājīvikas seem to have developed from the doctrine of *maṇḍala-mokṣa* the tenet that the great teachers of the faith performed from time to time an *avatāra* in order to restore the true scriptures and the pure doctrine. The Ājīvika *nirvāṇa* seems to have been far less rarefied than that of the other sects. Here too *Niyati* held sway, and would from time to time drive

[1] *Eṉ taṉai-y ākki-y iṭavakai-y uṭ poruḷ īṟu colli maṇṭalam ākki maṟuttuṅ koṇarum. Nīl.* v. 716.

[2] *Iru-pāṉmaiyar ivar, maṇṭalar cempōtakar eṉṟē; varu-pāṉmaiyar ivar maṇṭalar, maṇ mēl varu nūlum taru-pāṉmaiyar eṉi nī . . . CÑC.*, p. 269, v. 2.

[3] V. supra, p. 222. [4] V. supra, p. 246.

souls back to the universe in order to restore the prescribed total of souls in *saṃsāra*. But according to *Civañāṉa-cittiyār* some of the liberated souls had somehow become free of the liability to return. They were the *sambodhaka*, beings completely outside the universe, whose status in this respect resembles that of the Jaina *tīrthaṅkaras*. The *maṇḍalar*, on the other hand, remind us of the Vaiṣṇavite *avatāras*, and the Mahāyāna Buddhist *bodhisattvas*.

Our picture is by no means complete, but it shows that the Ājīvika *nirvāṇa* differed from that conceived by more orthodox sects. The supreme state of bliss did not entirely transcend the affairs of the world, and was still subject to *Niyati*. It was in fact little different from the other sects' conception of the highest heaven. This fact may throw light on the surprising statement of Śīlâṅka, who, writing surely with full knowledge of the Jaina attacks on Ājīvika antinomianism and immorality, states in his commentary to the *Sūtrakṛtâṅga* that the followers of Gosāla are called Vainayikas [1]; these, he declares elsewhere, desire the attainment of salvation in h e a v e n, from good conduct alone.[2] The phrase *svarga-mokṣa* perhaps indicates that the Jaina looked on the Ājīvika *nirvāṇa* as comparable to his own heaven. It will be remembered that both the *Aupapātika Sūtra* and the Jaina commentator Mādhavacandra promise the Ājīvika ascetic an abode in the highest Jaina heaven of Acyuta-kalpa.[3] This seems to indicate that the Jaina metaphysicians believed that the state which the Ājīvikas fondly imagined to be the highest was actually a lower and less rarefied paradise. The same view appears to have been held by Buddhaghosa, who states that brāhmaṇas, *tāpasas*, *paribbājakas*, and Ājīvikas held the heavens of Brahma-loka, Abhassarā, Subhakiṇhā, and Anantamānasa respectively to be the highest state (*niṭṭhā*). Buddhaghosa adds that all these ascetics believed to be complete emancipation what in fact was only *arahat*-ship.[4]

[1] V. supra, pp. 174 ff.

[2] *Vainayikā vinayād eva kevalāt svarga-mokṣ'-âvāptim abhilaṣanto mithyā-dṛṣṭayo.* Introduction to *Sū. kṛ.* i, 12, fol. 208.

[3] V. supra, pp. 140, 204.

[4] *Brāhmaṇānaṃ hi Brahmaloko niṭṭhā, tāpasānaṃ Abhassarā, paribbājakānaṃ Subhakiṇhā, Ājīvikānaṃ Anantamānaso . . . . Sabbe vā c'ete arahattam eva niṭṭhā ti vadanti. Papañca Sūdanī*, to *Majjh.* ii, vol. ii, pp. 9–10.

CHAPTER XIV

OTHER DOCTRINES OF THE ĀJĪVIKAS

THE ELEMENTS

That the Ājīvikas of South India had a theory of elemental atoms is made clear by all the three chief Tamil sources. This atomic theory does not seem to be connected in origin with the doctrine of *Niyati* ascribed in the *Sāmañña-phala Sutta* to Makkhali Gosāla, but was probably derived from the primitive Eleatic atomism of Pakudha Kaccāyana in the same text. Pakudha must therefore be included with Makkhali Gosāla and Pūraṇa Kassapa among the founders of the community. We have already quoted the relevant passage,[1] which states that there exist seven elemental categories (*kāyā*), namely earth (*paṭhavi-kāya*), water (*āpo-k.*), fire (*tejo-k.*), and air (*vāyo-k.*), with joy (*sukha*), sorrow (*dukkha*), and life (*jīva*) as the seventh. Although all seven are described as *kāyā*, in their enumeration this word is not suffixed to the last three ; this perhaps indicates that the three latter elements were thought of as different and less solid than the others. Linguistic evidence points to the possibility that they are an addition to the theory by another hand.[2]

The seven elements are described as unmanufactured (*akaṭā*) ; they are barren (*vañjhā*), which must imply that they do not multiply as do living beings ; and they are as firm as mountains and as stable as pillars.[3] They do not move nor develop nor affect one another.[4] As a corollary all change is illusion—No man slays nor causes to slay.[5] Thus Pakudha's theory of the seven stable elements leads to the later Ājīvika doctrine of *avicalita-nityatvam*.

[1] V. supra, p. 16.

[2] V. supra, p. 25.

[3] *Kūṭaṭṭhā, esika-ṭṭhāyi-ṭṭhitā. Dīgha* i, p. 56.

[4] *Na iñjanti na vipariṇamanti, na aññamaññaṃ vyābādhenti, n'âlam aññamaññassa sukhāya vā dukkhāya vā sukhadukkhāya vā.* Ibid.

[5] *N' atthi hantā vā ghātetā.* Ibid.

In none of the Pāli texts is this theory associated with Makkhali Gosāla, so perhaps it was not his. Yet it is often to be found connected with parts of Makkhali's teaching, when these are ascribed to some other philosopher. Thus the doctrine of the ancient teacher Guṇa, in *Mahānāradakassapa Jātaka*,[1] contains first a statement of the ineffectuality of all effort, whether human or divine, followed by an enumeration of the seven *kāyā* which are indivisible and do not injure one another (*acchejjā avikopino*), and concludes by a statement of Makkhali's doctrine of automatic salvation in a period of 8,400,000 *mahākappas* through the power of *Niyati*. This teaching is falsely called in the text *ucchedavāda* or annihilationism, but is obviously Ājīvikism, and Guṇa himself is referred to as an Ājīvika.

These elemental theories seem gradually to have gained in importance at the expense of the doctrine of *Niyati*, which, as we have seen, plays a lesser part in the Tamil than in the Pāli and Prākrit texts.

The earliest of the three chief Tamil sources, *Maṇimēkalai*, states that the atoms are the chief subject of discussion in the Ājīvika scripture called "the Book of Maṟkali".[2] They are described as "atoms of four types, together with life".[3] Thus it is evident that the atom of life is thought to be somewhat different from the four material elements. It is later stated that this element has the special characteristic of perceiving all the other four atoms in their combinations.[4] The other two categories of Pakudha are included almost as an afterthought in the penultimate line of the Ājīvika elder's sermon—"Joy and sorrow, even these are atoms".[5] The atoms are said to be neither destroyed nor created, and one atom cannot penetrate another. An atom will not split, nor multiply by fission, nor will it expand or grow.[6]

Unlike the bodies (*kāyā*) of Pakudha Kaccāyana the atoms in *Maṇimēkalai* do move and combine, at least on the lower level of truth. They may come together densely to form a diamond,

[1] *Jāt.* vi, pp. 219 ff. Cf. *Petavatthu* iv, 3, pp. 57–61. V. infra, p. 271.
[2] *Nūṟ-poruḷkaḷ.* *Maṇi.* xxvii, 112.
[3] *Uyir ōṭ' oru nāl-vakai aṇu.* Ibid., xxvii, 113.
[4] *Av vakai-y aṟivat' uyir eṉpa paṭum ē.* Ibid., 119.
[5] *Iṉpam un tuṉpam um ivai-y um aṇu-v eṉa.* Ibid., 163.
[6] *Citaivatu ceyyā putitāy-piṟant' oṉṟ' oṉṟiṟ pukutā. . . . Oṉṟ' iraṇṭ' āki-p piḷappatuñ ceyya-v aṉṟi-yum avaṟ poṟ parappatuñ ceyyā.* Ibid., 127–131.

or loosely, as in a hollow bamboo.[1] These combinations seem to have been thought of as mere juxtapositions of atoms of various types,[2] and not as the mingling of one atom with another.[3] Thus the character of the atoms of Pakudha is in one particular maintained in *Maṇimēkalai*, although the latter text does not confirm their immobility.

The combination of atoms occurs in fixed ratios of " one, three-quarters, half, and one-quarter—according to their combinations in this ratio so do they receive their names ".[4] This passage may be elucidated by a comparison with a similar passage in *Civañāṉa-cittiyār*. This text states that the atoms will only combine in fixed proportions, into a sort of molecule, that of earth containing four atoms of earth, three of water, two of fire, and one of air.[5] These proportions, 4 : 3 : 2 : 1, are the same as those of *Maṇimēkalai*, $1 : \frac{3}{4} : \frac{1}{2} : \frac{1}{4}$, and it seems probable that both refer to the same doctrine. Buddhist atomic theory allows no molecule of one element only, but teaches that all gross matter is to some extent adulterated by the presence of atoms of other elements.[6] We may believe that the Ājīvikas held similar views. The molecule of earth was constituted in the above proportions, and no doubt the molecules of the other elements were similarly constituted, but with the relative preponderance appropriately changed. To this doctrine of molecular combination *Maṇimēkalai* adds that the atoms cannot be seen in their pure state, but only when they form aggregates as *bhūtas* or objects.[7]

It is nowhere in the text stated whether all atoms of one class were thought of as being identical, or whether it was considered that special differences existed within each genus of atom, to account for the great differences in the material contents of the world. It would seem, however, that the macroscopic differences

[1] *Vayiram āy-c ceṟintu vaṟpam um ām vēy āy-t tuḷai paṭum.* Ibid., 133–6.
[2] *Ceṟintu.* Ibid., 135.
[3] *Oṉṟ' oṉṟiṟ pukutā.* Ibid., 128.
[4] *Oṉṟu muk-kāl arai kāl āy uṟun tuṉṟum ik-kataṉāṟ peyar cola-p paṭum ē.* Ibid., xxvii, 140–1.
[5] *Kūṭu-neṟi nila' nāṅku, nīr mūṉṟ' iṉṟ', iraṇṭ' aḷal, kāl oṉṟ' āy.* *CÑC.*, p. 262, v. 7. I am much indebted to Mr. M. S. H. Thompson for valuable advice on this point.
[6] V. infra, p. 269.
[7] *Pūtatt' iraṭci-y uḷ.* *Maṇi.* xxvii, 1, 147.

in the structure and texture of matter were thought of as caused by the variation of the densities of the microscopic *aṇus* which composed it.[1] The diminutive size of the atom is clearly stated. A single atom can only be detected by a divine eye,[2] but a large aggregate of atoms may be seen, just as a single hair is invisible in the twilight, while a number of hairs together may be perceived.[3]

The four material elements are said to have characteristic properties and tendencies. Earth is hard, and has a downward tendency ; water is cold, and has a similar tendency to descend and find its level upon earth ; fire burns and moves upwards ; while air has the attribute of motion in a horizontal direction.[4]

Nīlakēci confirms most of the statements of *Maṇimēkalai*. Here, however, the elements are only five in number, and joy and sorrow are nowhere mentioned as being atomic in nature. Their characteristics are expressed somewhat differently. Here earth has all sense qualities except sound[5] ; water, coolness (*taṇmai*) ; fire, burning (*eṟittal*), wind, blowing and howling (*ceṟitta virai-y oṭ'*) ; and life, instructing and knowing (*aṟittal aṟital*).[6] The elements are not said to combine in regular ratios, as in *Maṇimēkalai*. They are without *guṇa*,[7] which the commentator Vāmanamuni translates as *iyalpu*, quality or characteristic. The sensual qualities of the elements thus do not appear to have been thought of as present in the individual atoms, but were latent in them, emerging only on their combination. Atoms could not interpenetrate.[8]

Civañāṉa-cittiyār repeats the doctrine of *Maṇimēkalai*, with few significant variations. The atoms are the usual five, to which virtue and vice are added, apparently as an afterthought, in the final verse of the ten which expound Ājīvika doctrine.[9]

[1] V. supra, p. 264, n. 1.

[2] *Ōr aṇu-t teyva-k-kaṇṇōr uṇarkuvar.* *Maṇi.* xxvii, 1, 146.

[3] *Mālai-p-pōtil oru mayir aṟiyār, cālatt' iraṇ-mayir tōṟṟutal cālum.* *Maṇi.* xxvii, 148–9.

[4] *Vaṟpam āki-y uṟu nilan tāḻntu coṟ paṭu ; cītatt' oṭu cuvai-y uṭaittāy iḻiṉ eṉa nilañ cērnt' āḻvatu nīr ; tī-t teṟutal u' mēṟ cēr iyalpum uṭaittāṅ ; kāṟṟu v ilaṅki-y acaittal kaṭaṉ.* Ibid., 120–4.

[5] *Pulam āk oli-y oṉṟ' oḻiya mutark' āñ.* *Nīl.* 675.

[6] Ibid., 676.

[7] *Kuṟitta poruḷiṉ kuṇam āl ivai-y ē.* Ibid.

[8] Ibid., v. 677.

[9] *Puṇṇiya pāvam eṉṉum iraṇṭiṉ um porunt' avaittē.* *CÑC.* p. 265, v. 10.

The change from the "joy and sorrow" of Pakudha and *Maṇimēkalai* to "virtue and vice" indicates a movement towards orthodoxy, and brings the Ājīvika classification of the elements nearer to the six Jaina categories of soul, matter, space, time, *dharma*, and *adharma*. We have already pointed out that Aruṇandi, the author of *Civañāṉa-cittiyār*, seemed to look upon the Ājīvikas as an unorthodox branch of Jainism,[1] and the alteration in the names of the two last categories seems to be a further indication of the direction in which the sect was moving. The characteristics of the atoms, as described in this text, are substantially the same as those mentioned in *Maṇimēkalai*.

The two later texts, *Nīlakēci* and *Civañāṉa-cittiyār*, put forward arguments to refute the atomic theories of the Ājīvikas. Nīlakēci attacks Ājīvika atomism, as she does the theory of *Niyati*, with appeals to experience and common sense. The arguments of *Civañāṉa-cittiyār* are somewhat subtler. If atoms have tendencies to move in different directions [2] they must be mutually repulsive, and cannot hold together. If they do not join or interpenetrate, interstices must exist between them, and therefore they should fall apart.[3] The Ājīvika apparently had his answers to these two objections; the elements, including the atom of life, are held together by wind or air (*vaḷi*), whose atoms move horizontally, and thus tend to counteract the upward tendency of fire and the downward tendencies of earth and water; the elements are united by "eternal action" (*nīṭa-viṉai*), which seems to be a synonym of *Niyati*.[4] This term *viṉai* (Skt. *karma*) is used in the commentary to refer to what is called *ūḻi* (Skt. *Niyati*) in the statement of doctrine,[5] thus giving yet another indication of the gradual merging of the Ājīvika *Niyati* theory with the orthodox doctrine of *karma*.

In *Civañāṉa-cittiyār* the Śaivite has the last word in the argument. Neither air nor eternal action can unite body and soul, for both lack intelligence. "So seek ye the one Lord. He is the creator." [6]

[1] V. supra, p. 203.
[2] V. supra, p. 265.
[3] *CÑC.*, pp. 272–3, vv. 4–5.
[4] Ibid., p. 274, v. 6.
[5] V. supra, p. 238.
[6] *Tēṭāy Oruvaṉai nī-y, ivai Ceyvāṉ uḷaṉ.* *CÑC.*, loc. cit.

Ājīvika Atomism in Relation to other Indian Atomic Doctrines

If we compare Ājīvika atomism with other Indian atomic theories we find significant agreements and differences. With the Jainas the atom (*paramâṇu*) is not differentiated according to elements; it is permanent and unchanging in its substance, but liable to change in its qualities. Atoms are susceptible to taste, smell, colour, and touch, and combine into aggregates or molecules (*skandha*). The atom is the minutest separable portion of the ultimate undifferentiated matter (*pudgala*), of which the universe is formed, and its classification by elements is not fundamental.[1] While differing from Ājīvika atomism in this very important respect, Jaina theory agrees in its tendency to conceive categories as material which by other sects are thought of as abstract or spiritual. Thus both *dharma* and *karma* are looked on by the Jainas as atomic.[2] But with the Jainas *jīva*, the soul, is not *paudgalika*, or material, and thus Ājīvikism goes further than Jainism in its materialism. For the Jaina *jīva* is *amūrta* and *arūpa* [3]; the Ājīvikas of the sect described in *Nīlakēci* certainly thought otherwise,[4] and the inclusion of *jīva* as one of the elements in both Pakudha's doctrine in the *Sāmañña-phala Sutta* and in all three Tamil sources indicates that it was generally looked on as material by all Ājīvikas.

The atomism of the orthodox Vaiśeṣika school differs from both that of the Ājīvikas and that of the Jainas. The claim of the Jainas to have first formulated an Indian atomic theory may be found in their attribution of the foundation of Vaiśeṣika physics to the schismatic Rohagupta, the leader of the Trairāśika school, with which the Ājīvikas held their logic in common.[5] This claim is not made until the late *Āvaśyaka Sūtra*, and while the doctrine there attributed to Rohagupta contains the nine substances, seventeen qualities, five forms of motion, and other

[1] Jacobi, in *ERE*. ii, pp. 199–200. Schubring, *Die Lehre der Jainas*, pp. 88 ff.

[2] *ERE*. ii, loc. cit. Schubring, op. cit., pp. 112–13. Guérinot, *La Religion Djaïna*, pp. 142–5.

[3] Guérinot, op. cit., p. 117.

[4] V. infra, pp. 270 ff.

[5] *Āvaśyaka Sūtra*, *niryukti*, 2490 ff., quoted *Abh. Rāj.* s.v. *Terāsiya*. V. supra, pp. 174 ff.

elements of Vaiśeṣika theory,[1] it is nowhere stated that the *aṇus* are divided into categories according to the elements. From the point of view of the text the atom of Rohagupta is still the undifferentiated atom of the Jainas, and not that of the Vaiśeṣika.

The Vaiśeṣika atoms have specific qualities according to the elemental categories to which they belong,[2] and in this respect they resemble those of the Ājīvikas. The Vaiśeṣika classification is more complete and thorough than that of the Ājīvikas. The attributes of the four material elements are distributed as follows: earth possesses odour, savour, colour, touch or temperature, gravity, velocity, and fluidity; in water odour is replaced by viscosity; fire has temperature, colour, fluidity, and velocity; and air, touch and velocity.[3] This classification is much more detailed than that of the Ājīvikas; but it is to be noted that *Nīlakēci's* version of the Ājīvika atomic theory states that "earth has all sense qualities except sound"[4]; this gives promise of a detailed classification such as that of the Vaiśeṣika, with an immaterial *ākāśa* to be the vehicle of sound, but the promise is not fulfilled, and the remaining elements are in no way related to the senses. Vaiśeṣika agrees with Ājīvikism in stating that the qualities of the atoms can only be discerned in aggregates; in the isolated atom qualities and characteristics are potential, only emerging on juxtaposition.[5]

A third Indian atomic theory is that of the Sarvâstivādin school of Buddhism. In this the four elements are given qualities and functions on principles rather different from those of the Vaiśeṣika:—

	Attribute.	*Function.*
Earth . . .	Solidity	Supporting
Water . .	Moisture	Cohesion
Fire . . .	Heat	Ripening
Air . . .	Motion	Expansion[6]

[1] V. Keith, *Indian Logic and Atomism*, p. 14. Jacobi, Introduction to *SBE*. xlv, p. xxxv f.
[2] Keith, op. cit., p. 212.
[3] Ibid., p. 220.
[4] V. supra, p. 265.
[5] Keith, op. cit., p. 220.
[6] McGovern, *Manual of Buddhist Philosophy*, vol. i, p. 115.

The atom of Buddhism is not eternal, as in the other three systems, since Buddhism dogmatically asserts the impermanence of all things. It is conceived as " flashing into being ; its essential feature is action or function and therefore it may be compared to a focus of energy ".[1] The atoms constitute molecules (*saṃghāṭa, paramâṇu, kalāpa*), which must include at least one atom of all four elements, and which acquire their characteristics according to the atoms predominantly composing them. As well as atoms of the four elements, the molecules also contain atoms of a special type related to the five senses, which are responsible for their perception by the sense organs. They cohere by virtue of the atoms of water in each.[2]

It will be seen that the qualities of atoms in Buddhism are more like those of the Ājīvika atomic system than those of the Vaiśeṣika and closely correspond to the system described in *Maṇimēkalai*, which is, however, silent on the functions of the atoms. The doctrine of *Maṇimēkalai*, that atoms combine in fixed proportions, with its apparent corollary that no element may exist in its pure state, is similar to that of the Buddhists. Buddhist atomic theory also agrees with that of the Ājīvikas in attributing the function of cohesion to one element only, although in the former system this is water, and in the latter air.

Of all the theories so far discussed that of Pakudha Kaccāyana seems to be the most primitive, the parent of the theories of later times, unless indeed the theory outlined in the *Sāmañña-phala Sutta* is itself the refinement of an earlier theory which admitted only four elements.[3] Pakudha's atomic system was preserved in its purest form by the Ājīvikas, who at all periods of their history seem to have maintained the material nature of the soul, and who are more than once referred to in the Pāli Scriptures as holding Pakudha's theory. It has been suggested that Jaina, Vaiśeṣika, and Buddhist theories all look back to Pakudha,[4] and hence to Ājīvikism. This view is probably correct. The subtleties and refinements are the work of the philosophers of the respective sects ; but the conception of the world as divided into an enormous number of indivisible entities is the heritage

[1] Keith, *Buddhist Philosophy*, p. 161.
[2] McGovern, op. cit., pp. 127–8. Keith, op. cit., p. 161.
[3] V. supra, p. 25.
[4] Ui, *The Vaiśeṣika Philosophy*, p. 25.

of Pakudha, and of other nameless contemporaries and predecessors of the Buddha, who were loosely called Ājīvikas, and whose spiritual descendants merged with the school of Makkhali Gosāla.

The Soul

Nīlakēci's criticism of Ājīvika doctrines contains a verse giving surprising information about the nature of the soul (*uyir*, Skt. *jīva*). As we have seen, the material atoms were thought of as being too minute to be visible to mortal eyes.[1] *Jīva*, however, was the colour of a *pālai* fruit, and reached to the height of 500 *yojanas*.[2] We are nowhere told how the Ājīvikas justified this bizarre theory, which is quickly and easily disposed of by Nīlakeci as being inconsistent with reason and common sense. The strange doctrine is not found in other Tamil sources, and we would be tempted to dismiss it as a fantastic invention of the Ājīvikas' opponents, if it were not for the fact that the identical theory is to be found in a statement of heretical doctrine in the Pāli scriptures.

In the Buddha's day speculation about the nature of the soul was widespread. The *Brahmajāla Sutta* of the *Dīgha* refers to heretics who declare the soul to have form and to be unharmed after death, while others maintain its formlessness.[3] Buddhaghosa declares the Ājīvikas and others to be in the former category, while the Niganṭhas or Jainas were in the latter.[4] His obscure phrase *ādisu kasiṇa-rūpam attā*, may imply that the former school thought of the soul as having a complete form, or that Ājīvikas on the lower levels of spiritual development endowed it with form as a *kasiṇa*, or help to meditation. We have seen already that the Ājīvika soul theory did in fact differ from that of the Jainas in the manner stated by Buddhaghosa.[5] The *Petavatthu* passage, which we have already mentioned in various contexts,[6] confirms his statement.

[1] V. supra, p. 265.

[2] *Pālai-ppaḷattiṉ iṟattaṉa vāy ppala māṭṭ' oṭu kaṇ*
Nālē-t tuṇaiy um ak aṉṟ' aintu nūṟum pukai-y uyarntu
Ñālatt' iyaṉ ṟana nall-uyir eṉpatu nāṭṭukiṉṟay.
Nīl. 712. The *pālai* is blue (Chakravarti, *Neelakesi*, p. 240).

[3] *Rūpī attā hoti arogo param maraṇā saññī. Dīgha*, i, p. 31.

[4] *Sum. Vil.* i, p. 119.

[5] V. supra, p. 267.

[6] *Petavatthu*, iv, 3, p. 57. V. supra, pp. 20, 146.

This passage contains reminiscences of the fatalism of Makkhali Gosāla, the antinomianism of Pūraṇa, and the positivism of Ajita; it also contains a reference to the seven-element theory elsewhere ascribed to Pakudha. It is impossible to slay another being, because the sword-cut passes between the interstices of the seven (*scil.* elements), which are thus literally atomic in structure. Life (*jīva*) cannot be cut or split, it is of eight parts, or octagonal (*aṭṭhaṃso*), circular, and 500 *yojanas* in extent.[1] Thus we find the enormous size of the soul according to the Tamil text confirmed by an independent source from a different sectarian tradition. Since the doctrine is not mentioned in other parts of the Pāli canon, and only occurs in one of the three chief Tamil sources, we may infer that it was only held by a small sub-sect of the community. If it had been widely held this fantastic theory would surely have attracted more attention than it actually did.

The term *aṭṭhaṃso* is rendered "octagonal" in the English translation of the text.[2] No corresponding word or phrase occurs in the Tamil source; and it will be seen that it involves contradiction, since the soul is in the next word said to be *gūḷa-parimaṇḍalo*, which must mean "round like a ball". The commentary to the *Petavatthu* tries to solve the paradox by explaining that according to this theory the soul is sometimes octagonal and sometimes circular.[3] The commentary further states that the immense size of the *jīva* is found only in souls in their last stage before *nirvāṇa*.[4] It is possible that the author of *Nīlakēci* intended to express this by the *nall'* (good), which is prefixed to the word *uyir* in the relevant verse.[5] A further contradiction is to be found in the Pāli reference in the word *-aṃso*, which implies divisibility, while in the same line the soul is said to be indivisible (*acchejjabhejjo*). The Ājīvika soul theory

[1] *Acchejjabhejjo jīvo aṭṭhaṃso gūḷaparimaṇḍalo*
Yojanāni satā pañca. Ko jīvaṃ chetum arahati?
Petavatthu, iv, 3, v. 29, p. 57.

[2] *Vimānavatthu and Petavatthu*, tr. J. Kennedy and H. S. Gehman, p. 233.

[3] *Aṭṭhaṃso gūḷaparimaṇḍalo ti eso pana jīvo kadāci aṭṭhaṃso hoti, kadāci guḷaparimaṇḍalo. Paramattha-dīpanī*, iii, p. 253.

[4] *Yojanāni satā pañca ti kevalī-bhāvaṃ patto pañca yojana-sat'-ubbhedo hoti.* Ibid.

[5] V. supra, p. 270, n. 2.

is so strange that it may indeed have included these paradoxes, but since they are only to be found in one source they must be accepted with great caution.

Equally questionable is the Tamil statement of the soul's blue colour, which is not confirmed by the Pāli text. That the *jīva* should have a permanent colour is scarcely compatible with the doctrine of the six spiritual colours, especially as blue, according to *Nīlakēci* the soul's natural colour, occurs very low in the list of *abhijātis*.[1]

The enormous size of the soul, whether at all times or in the last stages of its progress, is identical in both sources, and may therefore be accepted. *Jīva* seems to have been thought of as an aura, extending far beyond the individual's body. Its structure was atomic, and, as we have seen, atoms could not interpenetrate. It is difficult to suggest how the Ājīvikas accounted for the fact that living bodies were capable of approaching one another; doubtless some answer was found to this problem, but it is now lost to us.

The Gods

The *Bhagavatī Sūtra* names two divinities who were worshipped by the simpler folk of North-Eastern India at the time of the great teachers, and who filled a comparatively humble place in the pantheons of the greater communities, but who seem to have been given a special status by the Ājīvikas. These are Punnabhadda and Māṇibhadda, or, in their Sanskrit forms, Pūrṇabhadra and Maṇibhadra. We meet them first as the divinities whose duty it is to test the dying ascetic on the last night of his final penance; if he yields to their caresses he is born again, if he resists he is saved.[2] The same two appear again as the generals of the fierce Ājīvika king, Mahāpaüma, the reincarnation of Gosāla Maṅkhaliputta.[3] The Tamil text *Nīlakēci* mentions two *devas*, Okkali and Ōkali, who, according to the mythology of the Dravidian Ājīvikas, are said to have instructed men in the scriptures, presumably having received them from the divine Maṟkali.[4]

[1] V. supra, p. 243. [2] V. supra, p. 128. [3] V. supra, p. 142.
[4] *Nīl.* v, 681. V. supra, p. 215.

Pūrṇabhadra and Maṇibhadra are well known *yakṣas*, popular divinities of the period in the Ganges valley. The *Mahāniddesa* refers to worshippers of Vāsudeva, Baladeva, Puṇṇabhadda, and Maṇibhadda.[1] Thus they appear to have been coupled in popular devotion with the rising Vaiṣṇavite heroes. In Jainism they are chiefs of the demigods, Pūrṇabhadra of the Southern horde of *yakṣas* and Maṇibhadra of the Northern.[2] The *Mahābhārata* refers to Maṇibhadra as a king of the *yakṣas*, and he seems to have been a tutelary deity of travellers.[3] In the epic his companion Pūrṇabhadra does not appear as a *yakṣa*, but as a *nāga*, one of the hundred sons of Kadru.[4] Despite this discrepancy, it is clear that the two demigods were popular objects of worship among the inhabitants of a wide area of Northern India. A relic of the cult is a large statue of Maṇibhadra, set up by a guild of his worshippers at Pāwayā, Gwalior, in the first century B.C., which is among the earliest examples of Indian sculpture in the round.[5] Okkali and Ōkali, the Tamil counterparts of the two *devas* of the Northern Ājīvikas, were probably popular local Dravidian demigods of a similar type, other record of whom has now vanished, who took the place of Pūrṇabhadra and Maṇibhadra when Ājīvikism spread to the south.

As well as of these two there is every reason to believe that Ājīvikism, like Buddhism and Jainism, accepted the reality of the chief Hindu deities. Gosāla, in defining the Ājīvika heavens, in each of which the soul resides during its last transmigrations, mentions Brahmaloka among the Māṇasas and Māṇusuttaras.[6] This indicates that he recognized the existence of the god Brahma, and we may infer that the rest of the Hindu pantheon of the time was accepted by Ājīvikism.

Dr. Barua would go further than this. " The same chapter " (of the *Bhagavatī Sūtra*), he writes, " also points to an age when many Vedic and non-Āryan deities were affiliated to the Ājīviya pantheon, e.g. Punnabhadda, and Māṇibhadda, Sohamma,

[1] *Mahāniddesa*, i, pp. 89, 92.

[2] *Sthānāṅga*, 9, teste *Abh. Rāj.* s.vv. *Punnabhadda*, *Māṇibhadda*.

[3] *Vana*, 61, 123 (Poona edn.), and refs. in Sörensen, *Index of Names in the Mbh.*, s.v. *Maṇibhadra*.

[4] *Ādi*, 35, 12 (Kumbhakonam edn.). The Poona edn. (*Ādi*, 31, 12) gives the name as Pūrṇadaṃṣṭra.

[5] Coomaraswamy, *Yakṣas*, pt. i, p. 38, and pl. 1.

[6] V. supra, p. 250.

Sanakkumāra, Bambha, Mahāsukka, Āṇaya, and Āraṇa." [1] We can only agree with him as regards the first two names, and that of Bambha or Brahma. Admittedly these names and some others do occur in the relevant chapter of the *Bhagavatī Sūtra*, but they are there spoken not by Gosāla, but by Mahāvīra,[2] who, after Gosāla's death, prophesies that the soul of his renegade disciple will, after a long period of births in purgatories, attain divinity in the Jaina heavens; the names mentioned by Barua are merely those of some of the twelve Jaina *Kalpas*,[3] and give no indication whatever of the divinities worshipped by the Ājīvikas. We have already seen that the Ājīvika classification of the heavens was very different. Therefore our attempts at reconstructing an Ājīvika pantheon must stop with Pūrṇabhadra, Maṇibhadra, and Brahma. Other gods there must have been, but we have no evidence of their names.

Ājīvika Logic

The evidence of the Jaina commentators shows that the Ājīvikas had their own epistemology and logic, which had much in common with that of the Jaina sect of Trairāśikas.[4]

The distinctive characteristic of the Ājīvika system of epistemology, like that of the Trairāśika Jainas, was the division of propositions into three categories, in contrast to the orthodox Jaina system, which allowed seven. Some information on this system may be gathered from the commentaries to the *Nandi Sūtra* and to the *Samavāyâṅga*, which do not significantly differ :—

"The Ājīvika heretics founded by Gośāla are likewise called Trairāśikas, since they declare everything to be of triple character, viz.: living, not living, and both living and not living; world, not world, and both world and not world; real, unreal, and both real and unreal. In considering standpoints (*naya*) (they postulate that an entity may be) of the nature of substance, of mode, or of both. Thus, since they maintain three heaps (*rāśi*), they are called Trairāśikas." [5]

[1] *JDL.* ii, pp. 58–9.
[2] *Bh. Sū.* xv, *sū.* 560, fol. 693.
[3] V. supra, p. 250, n. 3.
[4] V. supra, pp. 174 ff.
[5] *Tathā ta eva Gośāla-pravarttitā' Ājīvikāḥ pāṣaṇḍinas Trairāśikā ucyante, yatas te sarvaṃ vastu tryātmakam icchanti, tad yathā jīvo 'jīvo jīvâjīvaś ca, loko*

The Ājīvikas thus seem to have accepted the basic principle of Jaina epistemology, without going to the over-refined extreme of *saptabhaṅgi*, as in the orthodox Jaina *syādvāda* and *nayavāda*. The Ājīvika postulate of a third possibility, neither being nor not being, must have formed a convenient logical basis for the unusual doctrine that some souls were compelled to return even from *nirvāṇa*.[1] These would be classified in the third category, *sadasat*—emancipated from *saṃsāra* and yet not emancipated.

The Status of Makkhali Gosāla

In the course of the *Bhagavatī Sūtra's* account of his last days Gosāla is twice said to have claimed for himself the status of the twenty-fourth and last *tīrthaṅkara* of the current *Avasarpiṇī* age.[2] The terminology of the phrase is distinctly Jaina, and the same words might equally well be applied to Mahāvīra. The Ājīvika system of chronometry, outlined elsewhere in the *Bhagavatī*,[3] makes no mention of the Jaina *Utsarpiṇī* and *Avasarpiṇī*, or phases of universal development and decline. Furthermore the Buddhist description of the Ājīvika *abhijātis*, or spiritual colours, places only three individuals, not twenty-four, in the highest rank.[4] Yet Jainism and Ājīvikism were so close in their origins, that it is possible that the two held a theory of *tīrthaṅkaras* in common. It is unlikely that the Ājīvikas, with their doctrine of immensely long *mahākalpas*, were content with only three *tīrthaṅkaras*, and twenty-four seems a more probable figure.

Whatever the total number of *tīrthaṅkaras* it is evident that Gosāla enjoyed a status among his followers comparable to that of Mahāvīra among the Jainas, and was treated with great respect. Like Mahāvīra, he seems to have been considered omniscient by his devotees, for Ayampula, who visited him in his last delirium, refers to him as such.[5] Already in the

'loko lokâlokaś ca, sad asat sadasat. Naya-cintāyāṃ dravy'-âstikaṃ paryāyâstikam ubhayâstikaṃ ca. Tatas tribhī rāśibhiś carant' îti Trairāśikāḥ. Nandi comm., fol. 113, quoted Weber *Verzeichniss*, ii, p. 685. Cf. *Samavāya* comm., fol. 129.

[1] V. supra, p. 259.
[2] V. supra, pp. 64, 68.
[3] V. supra, pp. 253–54.
[4] V. supra, pp. 243 ff.
[5] V. supra, p. 62.

Bhagavatī Sūtra certain pious Ājīvikas are referred to as *arihanta-devatā-gā*, which possibly implies that they invested their *arhants*, Makkhali and others, with divine status.[1]

The earliest of our Tamil sources, *Maṇimēkalai*, mentions Maṟkali only as the author of the Ājīvika scriptures. *Civañāṉa-cittiyār* refers to him as omniscient,[2] and the commentator Tattuvappirakācar describes him as the *arukaṉ* or *arhant*. The latter text does not mention him by name, but it is evident that only Maṟkali can be meant. In these two sources his status is still that of a Jaina *tīrthaṅkara*.

Nīlakēci, however, seems to represent another school of Ājīvikism, wherein the hagiology has become a theology. Maṟkali, the *Āptaṉ*, is, as in the other sources, the all-knowing Lord. He is perfectly motionless and silent, lest he injure minute living creatures by his speech.[3] He is free from age and decay, his form is incomprehensible (*terivill-uruvam*), and he is like the rainbow.[4] Yet he seems to be by no means completely removed from his followers, as were the Jaina *arhants*, but to appear to them from time to time, as unexpectedly and unpredictably as the rainbow,[5] if we are to accept Vāmanamuni's very probable interpretation of the obscure passage in the text. The latter also refers to Maṟkali as *tēvaṉ*, the God. With this we must compare the verse quoted by the Jaina commentator Malliṣeṇa, which declared that the Ājīvikas believe that the *tīrthaṅkaras* return to earth when their doctrine is in danger.[6]

The *Vāyu Purāṇa* shows us Ājīvikas worshipping *Piśācas* with costly ceremonies,[7] while *Nīlakēci* depicts Maṟkali as a sort of god, manifesting himself to his devotees in sudden and brilliant theophanies. Both Śīlâṅka and Malliṣeṇa, as well as the *Civañaṉa-cittiyār* suggest that, like Viṣṇu, he was thought of as occasionally performing *avatāras*.[8] We have here evidence of a school of Ājīvikism which had developed a devotional cult, which may have had much in common with the less orthodox sects of Vaiṣṇavism, such as the Pāñcarātras.[9]

[1] *Bh. Sū.* viii, *sū.* 329, fol. 369. V. supra, p. 140.
[2] *Arampilā-v aṟivaṉ. CÑC.* p. 255, v. 2.
[3] *Nīl.*, 672.
[4] *Vāṉ-iṭu-vill-aṉaiyaṉ.* Ibid., v. 673.
[5] *Intira-tanucu-p-pōla-t toṉṟum.* Comm. to above.
[6] V. supra, pp. 222, 260.
[7] V. supra., pp. 162 ff.
[8] V. supra, p. 260.
[9] V. infra, pp. 280–82.

The Ājīvikism represented by *Maṇimēkalai*, and also by *Civañāṉa-cittiyār*, if we exclude the verse of the latter text referred to above, would seem to be that of a purer school, wherein the importance of Maṟkali is like that of Mahāvīra in Jainism and of Buddha in Hīnayāna Buddhism. The more orthodox terminology in the latter text, for instance the employment of the word *viṉai*, or *karma*,[1] and the absence of emphasis on determinism in this, the most recent connected account of Ājīvika teaching, suggest that one branch of the small Ājīvika community was in the fourteenth century merging with the Jainas. This is the substratum of truth in Hoernle's theory, that the Ājīvikas and Digambaras were identical, and is the basis of the belief of such Tamil scholars as Schomerus, who, quoting Pope, believed that the Ājīvika atomic doctrines expressed in *Civañāṉa-cittiyār* were the product of an heretical Jaina sect.[2] We have reason to believe that other Ājīvikas were, from the days of Utpala onwards,[3] drawing close to Vaiṣṇavism. No doubt the last followers of Makkhali Gosāla, the heretic of Sāvatthi, forgot their master for either Kṛṣṇa or Mahāvīra, according to the branch of Ājīvikism to which they belonged.

[1] V. supra, pp. 238–39, 266.
[2] *Der Śaivasiddhanta*, pp. 104–5.
[3] V. supra, pp. 168 ff.

CHAPTER XV

CONCLUSION

SUMMARY

In the preceding pages we have traced as far as we can the history and doctrines of the Ājīvikas. Great lacunae and serious uncertainties remain, but the main outlines of the story are clear.

Out of the philosophical ferment of the sixth century B.C. at least three unorthodox sects developed in the same region, all seeking more satisfying explanations of the cosmic mystery than those of sacrificial brāhmaṇism and the Upaniṣadic gnosis. These sects were built around the doctrines of Buddha, Mahāvīra, and Gosāla, about each of whom a great body of legend accumulated. From this unreliable material, it would seem that Gosāla was at one time closely associated with Mahāvīra, the Jaina *tīrthaṅkara*, but that later their partnership was broken. Closely allied to Gosāla were Pūraṇa Kassapa the antinomian, and probably Pakudha Kaccāyana the atomist, whose doctrines were adopted by the later Ājīvikas. Gosāla's fatalism inspired the new sect, which developed around groups of naked wanderers, devoted to asceticism, but accused by their opponents of secret licentiousness. A vigorous lay community supported the Ājīvika sect, which held its own until the Mauryan period, when it appears to have reached its zenith and to have received the patronage of Aśoka and of his successor Daśaratha. After this, however, the Ājīvika community in Northern India dwindled rapidly, and soon became insignificant.

In South India it survived longer. Ājīvika ascetics reached the Tamil country probably in the Mauryan period, and the communities which they founded survived at least until the fourteenth century, though often heavily taxed by orthodox kings and village communities. The one fifteenth century reference of

Vaidyanātha Dīkṣita is the last we hear of them.[1] We may infer that by this time or soon after they had ceased to exist.

Dr. Barua's Three Questions

In concluding his valuable paper on the Ājīvikas, Dr. B. M. Barua asks certain pertinent questions, which, though stated by the author to be two in number, are in fact three :—

" . . . The simultaneous process of absorption and assimilation which seems so largely accountable for the disappearance of the Ājīvikas involve (*sic*) two questions of far-reaching importance, which are :—

" (1) Where are the Ājīvikas who maintained their existence among the rival sects up till (*sic*) the fourteenth century A.D., if not later ?

" (2) Is it that the Ājivika (*sic*) system dwindled into insignificance without enriching the systems which supplanted and supplemented it ?

" Finally if it be admitted that truth never dies and that the Ājīvikas had a distinct message for Indian peoples, the history of the Ājīvikas cannot be concluded without a general reflection on the course of Indian history, nor can the historian discharge his true function without determining the place of the Ājīvikas in the general scheme of Indian history as a whole." [2]

Dr. Barua's first question is quickly answered by all who have even cursorily examined the foregoing pages, or any other work on Ājīvikism. The Ājīvikas have ceased to exist. Answers to the second and third questions are less easy, but we conclude by attempting to give them. Our conclusions must be tentative, but we submit them as our own inferences from and interpretations of the facts which we have gathered.

The Influence of the Ājīvikas

It has already been suggested that two schools of thought or sub-sects existed within the Dravidian Ājīvika community. The first retained, with modifications, the seven element theory of the *Sāmañña-phala Sutta*.[3] As far as we can gather it did not remem-

[1] V. supra, p. 184. [2] *JDL.* ii, pp. 79–80. [3] V. supra, pp. 262 ff.

ber Pūraṇa Kassapa. In its later stages it seems to have adopted orthodox terminology,[1] and when we last hear of it it is apparently in the process of assimilation with Jainism.[2] This school is that referred to in *Maṇimēkalai* and in *Civañāṉa-cittiyār*.

The second sub-sect had moved far from early Ājīvikism. It taught the existence of only five elements,[3] and the theory of *avicalita-nityatavam*,[4] which, in its collorary of the illusoriness of all phenomena, represents a step in the direction of monism. This school remembered the early teacher Pūraṇa,[5] and believed that its founder, Maṟkali, was a divine being, manifesting visions of himself to his devotees and incarnating himself for the restoration of the Ājīvika faith.[6] This is the Ājīvikism of *Nīlakēci*.

These two schools may be compared to Hīnayāna and Mahāyāna Buddhism. The tendency towards monism, theism, and *bhakti*, which is evident in the later schools, both of Ājīvikism and Buddhism, was part of the profound religious and cultural movements at work in the India of the time, which culminated in the popular devotional Hinduism of the Middle Ages.

With the Ājīvikas that tendency may have manifested itself quite early, for it is already suggested in the *Vāyu Purāṇa.*[7] As this branch of the sect decayed we may suggest that its members drew more and more closely to Vaiṣṇavism, with its similar doctrines of theism and *avatāras*. From Utpala's commentary to Varāhamihira [8] it seems that this process had commenced as early as the tenth century A.D.

It is likely that former Ājīvikas would not at first find a spiritual home with the more reputable Vaiṣṇavite sects, but rather with a sect on the fringes of orthodoxy, such as the Pāñcarātras, and there are features of Pāñcarātra teaching which are very reminiscent of that of the Ājīvikas. The doctrine of *avatāras* or divine incarnations is one such feature ; others, though less obvious, are equally significant. For instance the Pāñcarātra, like the Jaina and the Ājīvika, uses the term *jīva* for the soul,[9] in preference to *ātmā*. As with the Ājīvikas, the soul, according

[1] V. supra, pp. 238–39, 266, 277. [2] V. supra, p. 277. [3] V. supra, p. 265.
[4] V. supra, pp. 235 ff. [5] V. supra, pp. 80–81. [6] V. supra, p. 276.
[7] V. supra, pp. 162 ff. [8] V. supra, pp. 168 ff.
[9] Schrader, *Introduction to Pāñcarātra*, p. 56.

to Pāñcarātra theory, is in some sense atomic,[1] and liberated souls are of two classes, *nityas* and *muktas*, the former of which can incarnate themselves at will, just as Viṣṇu himself.[2] We recall the *maṇḍalas* and *sambodhakas* of *Civañāṉa-cittiyār*.[3]

Like Ājīvikism the Pāñcaratra system has a doctrine of *niyati*, although in the latter it is not so important as in the theory of Makkhali Gosāla. "In the foetus like condition of the *manus* in the energy (*śakti*) of God there springs up from time-energy (*kāla-śakti*) the subtle destiny (*niyati*) which represents the universal ordering element (*sarva-niyāmakaḥ*)." [4] *Niyati* is "not only what the Vaiśeṣikas call Diś, to wit the regulator of positions in space . . . but . . . it also regulates, as karmic necessity, the intellectual capacity, inclinations, and practical ability of every being".[5] *Kāla*, "the mysterious power existing in time which urges everything on . . . is looked upon as originating from *niyati*." [6]

These similarities are by no means conclusive, but they suggest mutual influence. The doctrine of *Niyati*, as propounded by Makkhali Gosāla, is to be found recorded in texts much earlier than the *Pāñcarātra Saṃhitās*, the earliest quotation from which is as late as the tenth century A.D.,[7] although they are thought to have been written some centuries earlier.[8] It is therefore possible that the Pāñcarātras borrowed the doctrine of *Niyati* from the Ājīvikas, giving it a theistic basis by converting it into a secondary principle emerging from their god.

Similarities may also be found between Ājīvikism and other Vaiṣṇavite schools, especially those of Southern India, where the Ājīvika sect survived longest. Thus the Āḻvār Vaiṣṇavite hymn-writers believed "that the grace of God was spontaneous and did not depend on any effort on the part of the devotee".[9] We recall the words of Makkhali: "There is no question of bringing unripe *karma* to fruition . . . by virtuous conduct, by vows, by penance, or by chastity." [10] Contact with the Ājīvikas may have

[1] Ibid., p. 57. [2] Ibid., pp. 56–8. [3] V. supra, p. 260.

[4] Das Gupta, *History of Indian Philosophy*, vol. iii, p. 45.

[5] Schrader, *Introduction to Pāñcarātra*, p. 64.

[6] Ibid., loc. cit. South Indian Śaivism also gives *kāla* and *niyati* minor positions in its metaphysical scheme, as the 7th and 8th *tattvas*, through which the soul is controlled by *karma*. Schomerus, *Der Çaiva-Siddhānta*, p. 137.

[7] Ibid., p. 18. [8] Ibid., p. 19.

[9] Das Gupta, *History of Indian Philosophy*, vol. iii, p. 85. [10] V. supra, p. 14.

developed this theistic *akriyāvāda*, or doctrine of salvation by grace.

It is also possible that Ājīvikism influenced the doctrines of Madhva and the Dvaita school of Vaiṣṇavism. Madhva has been said to owe much to early Dravidian Christianity,[1] and the parallels between Christianity and some of Madhva's doctrines are certainly close. But we do not believe that the Syrian Christians of Malabar have ever maintained a rigid Calvinism which classed all souls in three groups, those destined for salvation, perpetual transmigration, and damnation respectively.[2] For this doctrine we can find no more likely prototype than the rigid determinism of Makkhali, especially when combined with the later Ājīvika doctrine of the *maṇḍala* and *sambodhaka* forms of salvation.[3] Madhva seems to have taken Ājīvika determinism and recast it in a theistic mould. In fact it might be suggested that the whole school of salvation "on the analogy of the cat" (*pūṉai-campantam*), which arose in the Dravidian country with the growth of *bhakti*, owed much in inspiration to the originally atheistic Ājīvika doctrine of *Niyati*.

The influence of the Ājīvikas on the doctrines of the Pāñcarātras, Āḻvārs, and followers of Madhva cannot be proved, but it may be inferred as a valid probability. A further line of influence may also be suggested.

As we have shown, the *Mahābhārata* proves that fatalist views, implying a far more complete determinism than the orthodox doctrine of *karma*, were widespread in Northern India at a very early period.[4] Further evidence, from the Epic onwards, shows that the small Ājīvika community of later days was not alone in its fatalism. Thus Manu instructs the Āryan not to rely on Destiny but to act for himself.[5] Bhartṛhari's *Nītiśataka* contains ten verses in honour of Fate.[6] Like Manu, the *Hitôpadeśa* bears witness to and deplores the existence of fatalist views.[7] Even in later times we can still hear echoes of Makkhali Gosāla's despairing cry, *N' atthi purisakāra*. The Ājīvikas survived until the late medieval period in the Tamil country, and certain later Tamil proverbs seem to show

[1] Grierson, *ERE*. viii, p. 234. [2] Ibid., loc. cit. [3] V. supra, p. 260.
[4] V. supra, p. 218. [5] vii, 205. [6] *Nītiśataka*, vv. 81–90.
[7] *Hitôpadeśa*, i, 29. V. supra, p. 222, n. 2.

traces of their teaching. We quote a few examples from Jensen's collection :—

"That which does not exist will not come into existence, and that which exists will not be annihilated."[1] This is the Ājīvika doctrine of *avicalita-nityatvam.*

"Even if a man do penance on the point of a needle he will not get more than was destined for him."[2]

"One may bathe so as to wash off oil, but who can rub so as to free himself from fate."[3]

"Though a man exert himself over and over again he shall only get what comes on the appointed day."[4] This reminds us once more of Gosāla's original teaching : "There is no strength, no courage, no human endurance."

As the propagator of the doctrine of the futility of human effort and of the all-embracing power of Destiny, Ājīvikism cannot have failed to "enrich the systems which supplanted and supplemented it". It would indeed be an error of over-caution to assert that this system, in the two thousand years of its existence, had no influence on the development of wide-spread and popular theories in agreement with its fundamental doctrine of determinism.

The Place of the Ājīvikas in Indian History

The position of the Ājīvikas in "the general scheme of Indian history as a whole" can best be understood by again looking at their origins. They emerged at a time when the whole civilized world was in intellectual ferment, which was expressed in India in the heretical non-brāhmaṇic sects, and the gnosis of the Upaniṣads. The reaction was in part a revival and restatement of pre-Āryan and pre-polytheist animism—an animism adapted to the high degree of material civilization already reached by its adoption of ethical standards and of speculative world-views, which were later worked up into metaphysical systems of great complexity and subtlety. Buddhism moved furthest away from

[1] *Illatu varātu, uḷḷatu pokātu.* Jensen, *Classified Collection of Tamil Proverbs,* p. 5, no. 48.

[2] *Ūci muṉaiyil tavam ceytālum uḷḷatu tāṉ kiṭaikkum.* Ibid., p. 5, no. 49.

[3] *Eṇṇey pōka muḷukiṉālum eḻuttu-p pōka-t tēy-p pāruṇṭā.* Jensen, op. cit., p. 5, no. 51.

[4] *Aṭuttu muyaṉṟulum ākum nāḷ tāṉ ākum.* Ibid., p. 5, no. 65.

this primitive animist background, but its humble ancestry may perhaps be traced in the doctrine of transmigration which it shared with all sects, and which appears by this time to have become a fundamental axiom of all Indian creeds. With the other creeds and sects the animist origins are clearer. The impersonal *brahman* of the Upaniṣads is probably derived not from the anthropomorphic polytheism of the Āryans, but from the belief in impersonal magical power, or *mana*, common to most primitive peoples. The doctrines of the Jainas and the Ājīvikas show further and stronger traces of the animist heritage. The conception of *dharma*, *adharma*, *sukha*, and *duḥkha* as in some sense material [1] is surely a survival of the primitive mentality, which is scarcely capable of conceiving an abstract entity.

The Ājīvikas show an even closer relationship to animism in their doctrine of the atomic nature of the soul, a theory but little removed from the soul-stuff theories of the savage, who viewed even the life of man as a solid substance. It is to the credit of the Ājīvikas that on this primitive basis they developed what was probably the earliest atomic theory of India; the concept of invisible and unchanging atoms is surely a manifestation of a rationally controlled imagination of a high order, and for this we must give credit to Pakudha Kaccāyana, the doctrines of whom, if not the name, were preserved by the Ājīvika sect.

Similarly the Ājīvikas deserve credit for their doctrine of *Niyati*. This represents a very real recognition of orderliness in a universe on the human level apparently wholly unpredictable and disorderly. The same, it is true, may be said of the other new sects of the period, all of which, reviving in one way or another the Vedic concept of *ṛta*, but incorporating with it an atheistic or impersonal first principle, posited a framework of *karmic* cause and effect, within which the soul moved. It was for the Ājīvikas to drive this doctrine to its extreme conclusion, and replace the chain of causation, new links of which might be forged by the free will of the individual, by the single determining principle, *Niyati*, which denied free will altogether. The pragmatic value of this doctrine was slight, or even negative, but at least Makkhali Gosāla may claim the doubtful honour of

[1] V. supra, pp. 263, 267.

anticipating by over two thousand years the now rather unfashionable world view of the nineteenth century physicist.

It is nowadays not unheard of for the historian to attempt to find economic and material counterparts to philosophic and religious developments, and to give logical priority to the former. Thus the development of philosophy in Ancient Greece has been ascribed to the replacement of the tribal warlords of the Homeric age by a community of city states ; with the disappearance of the chieftains and tribal kings the gods, who were their heavenly counterparts, appeared obsolete to the best minds of the times, and new speculative systems were devised to replace them. Similarly the rise of Protestantism in Europe in the sixteenth and seventeenth centuries has been attributed to the growth of a powerful commercial middle class, antagonistic to the ruling aristocracies, and demanding a new order in religion as in politics.

While we cannot share the view that this theory of the development of philosophy and religion contains the whole truth, it may be conceded that the philosopher and the religious reformer may often be inspired, consciously or unconsciously, in their search for deeper insight by social, economic, and political change. It is possible to suggest a social and economic counterpart to the great wave of spiritual unrest which swept the Ganges valley in the sixth century B.C.

The thirty-three great gods of the Āryans, and the lesser earth-spirits of the aboriginals, were too motley a company to correspond to the orderly civilization which had already emerged, while the martial and capricious character of the former, and the chthonic nature of the latter group of divinities, were inadequate to meet the spiritual needs of the rising class of merchants, to the existence of which both Buddhist and Jaina texts testify. We will concede to the historical materialist that Buddhism, Jainism, and Ājīvikism were to this extent a reflection of the changes in the social and economic pattern of the times.

Among the three new cults Ājīvikism stands out for its thoroughgoing recognition of order in the universe. The cosmos of Makkhali Gosāla is immense in space and time, and ordered in every detail. The traditional cosmology, on the other hand, is an untidy confusion, wherein, for instance, the immediate cause of the monsoon is the victory of Indra over the cloud-dragon, and its ultimate cause the satisfactory performance of the sacrifices whereby Indra and the other gods are maintained. The earlier conception is only appropriate to a half-civilized tribal society. The efforts of the poets of the philosophical hymns in the *Ṛg* and *Atharva Vedas*, and of the brāhmaṇic thinkers who attempted to systematize the theory of the sacrificial cult, probably took place at the same time as comparable developments in the sphere of political and economic organization. The great efflorescence of religious thought coincided with the growth of large well-organized kingdoms in Magadha, Kosala, Kosambi, and Avanti.

Of the various new doctrines propounded in the sixth century B.C., that of Ājīvikism, with its rigidly controlled cosmos, seems the most appropriate to a closely knit autocracy, and it is significant that it appears to have reached its period of greatest influence in the time of the Mauryas, when Indian government attained a higher degree of centralization over a larger area than at any other period before the nineteenth century. With the decline of centralized control, and the growth of smaller loosely knit kingdoms, to which lesser states were linked in quasi-feudal relationship, the sect waned in power, and ultimately vanished. The more orthodox concept of *karma*, which allows some scope for human initiative, seems more appropriate to such conditions than does the rigid determinism of *Niyati*. After the Maurya period central governments were by no means all-powerful; often indeed they were unable to maintain control in their outlying provinces; and the political unity of Bhāratavarṣa had vanished. The rapid decline of popular support for Ājīvikism, which seems to have taken place after the Maurya period, may perhaps be attributed to the unconscious conviction that Ājīvika cosmology did not fit the facts as they appeared on earth. It will be remembered that the sect survived longest in districts ruled by the Cola kingdom, where the political machine seems to have functioned more smoothly and efficiently than in most other parts of India.

A further religious development, which affected the Ājīvikas, also shows a correspondence to contemporary political changes. While no monarch after Aśoka exerted so much power as he, the status of kingship rose from Mauryan times onwards. Aśoka, although " dear to the Gods ", was a simple *rājā*. The Guptas, on the other hand, were emperors (*mahārājâdhirāja*). In the succeeding epoch almost every independent king, however small his kingdom, adopted this or some such magniloquent title. The theory of the king's divinity gained ground from Kushān times onwards. In the smaller kingdoms which succeeded the Mauryas, especially as the standards of bureaucratic administration declined, kings claimed a more exalted status and at the same time, owing to the smaller size of their kingdoms, their presence must have been felt more directly by their subjects. The impersonal principles of the heretical sects may have been appropriate to the less personal bureaucratic machine of the Mauryas, but they did not resemble the actual situation of later times, when power was usually vested in a single very exalted individual. Theism would be better suited to such a state of affairs, and theism did in fact begin to manifest itself as a significant element in the Indian religious situation at about the time of the break-up of the Maurya empire. Strengthened perhaps by survivals from popular chthonic cults, or even by ideas from the West, it developed throughout the Hindu period of India's history, and, as we have seen, Ājīvikism itself was not unaffected by it.[1] Indian theism reached its final form when much of the land was in the control of alien monarchs, and when simple people must have been craving for the milder paternal despotism of such legendary rulers as Rāma and Vikramâditya. Thus the growth of devotional monotheism fits into the perspective of India's political vicissitudes.

We would not by this analysis maintain that the rise and decline of religious systems and sects are mere reflections of social conditions. They are, however, manifestations of human need. If they can no longer fully satisfy the needs of their adherents they will stagnate and die. But a religion is long in dying. It may obtain a new lease of life by a restatement of old verities in a more modern form, or by the introduction of new elements of belief. It may retain an attenuated and local existence long after it has outlived its period of general usefulness. And even when it is dead, some of its features may survive in a disguised form, incorporated into other systems, or maintained as folklore or superstition. Thus for a while Ājīvikism met the needs of

[1] V. supra, pp. 276–77.

a large body of adherents, but soon began to lose its vitality; it survived long in one region of India, incorporating new features into its doctrine; and it does not seem to have vanished without leaving some faint traces upon later Indian religion.

So, tentatively, we answer Dr. Barua's questions, and conclude our study of the Ājīvikas. Their long, but by no means glorious existence, has left but few traces, and we have only been able to reconstruct their history and doctrines in faint outline by extracting every possible hint from the material available to us. Even now it has been necessary to leave many questions unanswered, and large gaps in the structure of the history of the Ājīvikas are unfilled. But new information may yet come to light which may enable the structure to be strengthened. No work of history can have more than a provisional conclusion—the remainder of the History and Doctrines of the Ājīvikas is yet to be written.

BIBLIOGRAPHY OF WORKS MENTIONED IN THE TEXT

I. Original Sources

A. *Pāli Texts*

Aṅguttara Nikāya. Ed. R. Morris and E. Hardy, 5 vols., PTS. London, 1885–1900.

Tr. F. L. Woodward and E. M. Hare, *The Book of the Gradual Sayings*, 5 vols., PTS. London, 1932–36.

Buddhaghosa. *Dhammapad'-aṭṭha-kathā*, ed. H. C. Norman and L. S. Tailang, 5 vols., PTS. London, 1906–15.

Tr. E. W. Burlinghame, *Buddhist Legends*, 3 vols., Harvard Oriental Series, vols. xxviii–xxx. Cambridge, Mass., 1921.

Papañca-Sūdanī (Comm. to *Majjhima Nikāya*), ed. J. H. Woods, D. Kosambi, and I. B. Horner, 5 vols., PTS. London, 1922–38.

Paramattha-Jotikā II (Comm. to *Sutta Nipāta*), ed. H. Smith, 3 vols., PTS. London, 1916–18.

Samanta-Pāsādikā (Comm. to *Vinaya Piṭaka*), ed. J. Takakusu and M. Nagai, 7 vols., in progress. PTS. London, 1924–47.

Sumaṅgala-Vilāsinī (Comm. to *Dīgha Nikāya*), ed. T. W. Rhys Davids, J. Estlin Carpenter, and W. Stede, 3 vols., PTS. London, 1886–1932.

Dhammapāla. *Paramattha-Dīpanī* (Comm. to *Khuddaka Nikāya*), part iii (to *Petavatthu*), ed. E. Hardy, PTS. London, 1894.

Idem, part v (to *Therīgāthā*), ed. E. Müller, PTS. London, 1893.

Dīgha Nikāya. Ed. T. W. Rhys Davids and J. Estlin Carpenter, 3 vols., PTS. London, 1890–1911.

Tr. T. W. and C. A. F. Rhys Davids, *Dialogues of the Buddha*, 3 vols., PTS. London, 1899–1921.

Dīgha Nikāya Tr. R. Otto Franke, *Dīgha Nikāya . . . in Auswahl Übersetzt*. Göttingen, 1913.

Jātaka. Ed. V. Fausböll, 6 vols. and index. London, 1877–97.

Tr. by various hands, ed. E. B. Cowell, 6 vols. and index. Cambridge, 1895–1907.

Mahābodhivaṃsa. Ed. S. A. Strong, PTS. London, 1891.

Mahāniddesa. Ed. L. de la Vallée Poussin and E. J. Thomas, 2 vols., PTS. London, 1916–17.

Mahāvaṃsa. Ed. W. Geiger, PTS. London, 1908.

Tr. W. Geiger and M. H. Bode. London, 1912.

Majjhima Nikāya. Ed. V. Trenckner and Lord Chalmers, 3 vols., PTS. London, 1888–99.

Tr. Lord Chalmers, *Further Dialogues of the Buddha*, 2 vols., PTS. London, 1926–27.

Petavatthu. Ed. Minayeff, PTS. London, 1888.

Tr. H. S. Gehman, PTS. London, 1942.

Saṃyutta Nikāya. Ed. L. Feer, 6 vols., PTS. London, 1884–1904.

Tr. C. A. F. Rhys Davids and F. L. Woodward, *The Book of Kindred Sayings*, 5 vols. London, 1917–30.

Sutta Nipāta. Ed. V. Fausböll, 2 vols., PTS. London, 1885–94.

Tr. V. Fausböll, *SBE*. x, part 2. Oxford, 1881.

Therīgāthā. Ed. H. Oldenberg and R. Pischel, *Thera and Therī Gāthā*, PTS. London, 1883.

Tr. C. A. F. Rhys Davids, *Psalms of the Early Buddhists*, 2 vols., PTS. London, 1909–13.

Vaṃsatthappakāsinī. (Comm. to *Mahāvaṃsa*), ed. G. P. Malalasekera, 2 vols. London, 1935.

Vinaya Piṭaka. Ed. H. Oldenberg, 5 vols. London, 1879–83.

Tr. T. W. Rhys Davids and H. Oldenberg, *SBE*., vols. xiii, xvii, and xx. Oxford, 1881–85.

B. *Prākrit Texts*

Ācārāṅga Sūtra. Ed. H. Jacobi, PTS. London, 1882.

With Śīlâṅka's Commentary, 2 vols. Bombay, 1916.

Ācārāṅga Sūtra Tr. H. Jacobi, in *SBE*. xxii. Oxford, 1884.

Antakṛd-daśāḥ (Antagaḍa Dasāo). Ed. M. C. Modi. Ahmedabad, 1932.
Tr. L. D. Barnett. London, 1907.

Aupapātika Sūtra. Ed. Hema Sāgara. Bombay, n.d.

Āvaśyaka Sūtra. With *Cūrṇī* of Jinadāsa Gaṇi, 2 vols. Ratlam, 1928–9.
V. *Abhidhāna Rājendra*, infra, p. xxvii.

Bhadrabāhu. *Kalpa Sūtra*, ed. H. Jacobi. Leipzig, 1879.
With Vinayavijaya's comm. Bombay, 1915.
Tr. H. Jacobi, *SBE*. xxii. Oxford, 1884.

Bhagavatī Sūtra. With the comm. of Abhayadeva, 3 vols. Bombay, 1918–21.
India Office MSS., Catalogue Nos. 7446–47.

Jinadāsa Gaṇi. V. *Āvaśyaka Sūtra* above.

Jinaprabha Sūri. *Vihimagga-pavā.* V. Weber, *Verzeichniss*, vol. ii, no. 1944.

Kālakâcārya. V. Varāhamihira, infra, p. xxvi.

Nandi Sūtra. With the comms. of Jinadāsa and Haribhadra, ed. Vijayadāna Sūri. Bombay, 1931.

Nemicandra. *Pravacanasāroddharaṇa*, with the comm. of Siddhasena, ed. Jīvanacandra Sākaracandra, 2 vols. Bombay, 1922–25.

Nirayāvalikā Sūtra. Ed. with translation by A. S. Gopani and V. J. Chokshi, Ahmedabad, 1934.

Praśnavyākaraṇa Sūtra. With the commentary of Jñānavimala. Ahmedabad, 1935.

Samavāyâṅga. With Abhayadeva's commentary, ed. Veṇīcandra Suracandra. Bombay, 1918.

Sthānâṅga Sūtra. With Abhayadeva's commentary, ed. Veṇīcandra Suracandra, 2 vols. Bombay, 1918–20.

Sūtrakṛtâṅga. With Śīlâṅka's commentary, ed. Veṇīcandra Suracandra. Bombay, 1917.
Tr. H. Jacobi, *SBE*. xlv. Oxford, 1895.

Upāsaka Daśāḥ (Uvāsaga Dasāo). Ed. and tr. A. F. R. Hoernle, with the commentary of Abhayadeva, 2 vols. Calcutta, 1889–90.

Uttarâdhyayana Sūtra. Ed. Vijayomaṅga. Bombay, 1937.
Tr. H. Jacobi, *SBE*. xlv. Oxford, 1895.

Vaṭṭakerâcārya. *Mūlâcāra*, ed. P. Soni, 2 vols. Bombay, 1921.

C. *Sanskrit Texts*

Abhayadeva. V. *Bhagavatī Sūtra, Samavāyânga, Sthānânga Sūtra* and *Upāsaka Daśāh*, above.

Ajayapāla. *Nānârthasaṅgraha*, ed. T. R. Chintamani. Madras, 1937.

Āśvalāyana Śrauta Sūtra. Ed. G. S. Gokhale. Poona, 1917.

Bāṇa. *Harṣacarita*, ed. A. A. Führer. Bombay, 1909.

Bhāgavata Purāṇa. Ed. V. Śarma. Bombay, 1905.

Bhartṛhari. *Śatakatrayam*, ed. D. D. Kosambi. Bombay, 1946.

Bhaṭṭi. *Bhaṭṭikāvya*, ed. K. P. Trivedi, 2 vols. Bombay, 1898.

Caraka. *Caraka Saṃhitā*, ed. N. N. Sastri, vol. i. Lahore, 1929.

Divyâvadāna. Ed. E. B. Cowell and R. A. Neil. Cambridge, 1886.

Guṇaratna. V. Haribhadra.

Halâyudha. *Abhidhāna-ratnamālā*, ed. Th. Aufrecht. London, 1861.

Haribhadra. *Ṣaḍdarśana-samuccaya*, with Guṇaratna's commentary, *Tarkarahasya-dīpikā*. Ed. L. Suali, Calcutta, 1905.

Hemacandra. *Abhidhāna-cintāmaṇi*, ed. O. Böhtlinck and C. Rieu. St. Petersburg, 1847.

Anekârtha-saṅgraha, ed. Th. Zachariae. Vienna, 1893.

Sthavirāvalī or *Pariśiṣṭaparvan*, ed. H. Jacobi. Calcutta, 1883–91.

Hitopadeśa. ed. P. Peterson. Bombay, 1887.

Jñānavimala. V. *Praśnavyākaraṇa Sūtra.*

Kalhaṇa. *Rājataraṅgiṇī*, ed. M. A. Stein. Bombay, 1892.

Tr. M. A. Stein, *Kalhaṇa's Chronicle of the Kings of Kashmīr*, 2 vols. Westminster, 1900.

Kālidāsa. *Meghadūta*. ed. K. B. Parab, 5th edn. Bombay, 1902.

Kauṭilya. *Arthaśāstra*, ed. R. Shamashastry. Mysore, 1924.

Kumāradāsa. *Jānakī-haraṇa*, ed. H. Sastri. Calcutta, 1893.

Lalitavistara.	Ed. S. Lefmann, 2 vols. Halle, 1902.
Mādhavacandra.	V. s.v. Pathak, infra, p. xxix.
Māhābhārata.	(*Ādi* to *Bhīṣma Parvans*), ed. V. S. Sukthankar and others. Poona, 1927– (in progress).
	Ed. T. R. Kṛṣṇâcārya and T. R. Vyāsâcārya (Kumbhakonam edition), 6 vols. Bombay, 1906.
	2 vols. Calcutta, 1834–39.
Mahāvastu.	Ed. E. Senart, 3 vols. Paris, 1882–97.
Mahendra Vikrama Varmā.	*Mattavilāsa*, ed. T. Ganapati Sastri. Trivandrum, 1917.
Malliṣeṇa.	*Syādvādamañjarī*, ed. A. B. Dhruva. Bombay, 1933.
Mānava Dharma Śāstra.	Ed. Gangānātha Jhā, 3 vols. Calcutta, 1932–39.
Matsya Purāṇa.	Ānandâśrama Series No. 54. Poona, 1907.
Pāṇini.	*Aṣṭâdhyāyī.* V. s.v. Patañjali.
Paramahaṃsa Upaniṣad.	V. s.v. Weber, *Analyse* . . . infra, p. xxx.
Patañjali.	*Vyākaraṇa Mahābhāṣya*, ed. F. Kielhorn, 3 vols. Bombay, 1892.
Praśna Upaniṣad.	With Śaṅkara's commentary, ed. H. N. Apte. Poona, 1911.
Ṛg Veda.	Ed. F. Max Müller, 2nd edn., 4 vols. London, 1890–92.
Saddharma-puṇḍarīka.	Ed. H. Kern and Bunyiu Nanjio. St. Petersburg, 1912.
	Tr. F. Burnouf, *Le Lotus de la Bonne Loi*, 2nd edn. by S. Levi, 2 vols. Paris, 1925.
Śaṅkara.	V. s.v. *Praśna* and *Śvetāśvatara Upaniṣads.*
Śatapatha Brāhmaṇa.	Ed. A. Chinnaswami Sastry. Benares, 1937.
Sāyaṇa Mādhava.	*Sarvadarśana-saṃgraha*, ed. V. S. Abhyankar. Poona, 1924.
Śīlâṅka.	V. s.vv. *Ācārâṅga Sūtra* and *Sūtrakṛtâṅga.* supra, pp. xx–xxi.
Somadeva.	*Kathā-sarit-sāgara*, ed. H. Brockhaus, 2 vols, Leipzig, 1839–62.
Suśruta.	*The Suśruta*, 2 vols. Calcutta, 1835–86.
Śvetâśvatara Upaniṣad.	Ed. S. V. Shastri. Allahabad, 1916.

Utpala. V. s.v. Varāhamihira below.

Vaidyanātha Dīkṣita. *Jātaka-pārijāta*, ed. and trans. V. Subrahmanya Sastri, 2 vols. Bangalore, 1932–33.

Vāmana and Jayâditya. *Kāśikā*, ed. Bala Sastri, 2nd edn. Benares, 1898.

Varāhamihira. *Bṛhajjātaka*, with Utpala's commentary. Bombay, 1863.

Vasubandhu. *Abhidharmakośa*, tr. L. de la Vallée Poussin, 6 vols. Paris, 1923–26.

Vāyu Purāṇa. Ed. H. N. Apte. Poona, 1905.
Ed. R. L. Mitra, 2 vols. Calcutta, 1880.

Vīranandi. *Acārasāra*, ed. Indralal. Bombay, 1917.

Viśākhadatta. *Mudrārākṣasa*, ed. P. D. Karmakar. Poona, 1940.

Viṣṇuśarman. *Pañcatantra*, ed. F. Kielhorn and G. Bühler, 3 vols. Bombay, 1891–96.

Yādavaprakāśa. *Vaijayantī*, ed. G. Oppert. Madras, 1893.

Yaśomitra. *Abhidharmakośa-vyākhyā*, ed. U. Wogihara. Tokyo, 1932–36.

D. *Tamil Texts*

Aruṇandi. *Civañāṉa-cittiyār Parapakṣam*, with the commentary of Tattuvappirakācar, ed. M. Aḻagappa Mudaliyār. Madras, 1911.
Tr. J. M. Nallaswami Pillai, '*Śivajñāna Siddhiyār*.' Madras, 1913.

Cāttaṉ. *Maṇimēkalai*, ed. U. V. Saminath Aiyar. Madras, 1898.
Tr. Krishnaswami Aiyangar, *Maṇimekhalai in its Historical Setting*. London, 1928.

Iḷaṅkōvaṭikaḷ. *Cilappatikāram*, ed. U. V. Saminath Aiyar. 3rd edn. Madras, 1927.
Tr. V. R. R. Dikshitar, "*Śilappadikāram*." Madras, 1939.

Jensen, H. *A Classified Collection of Tamil Proverbs*. London, 1897.

Nacciṉārkkiṉiyar. "*Tholkāppiyam Porulathikāram*," with the commentaries of Nacciṉārkkiṉiyar and Pērāciriyar, ed. S. Buvanandam Pillai, 4 vols. Madras, 1916–17.

Nīlakēci. ‘*Neelakesi*’—*the Original Text and the Commentary of Samaya-Divākara-Vāmana-Muni,* ed. A. Chakravarti. Madras, 1936.

Tattuvappirakācar. V. s.v. Aruṇandi.

Tiruvaḷḷuvar. *Tirukkuṟaḷ,* ed. and tr. V. R. R. Dikshitar. Adyar, 1949.

Vāmanamuni. V. s.v. *Nīlakēci.*

E. *Inscriptions*

General

Sircar, D. C. *Select Inscriptions Bearing on Indian History and Civilization,* vol. i. Calcutta, 1942.

Maurya Inscriptions

Bühler, G. *The Barābar and Nāgârjunī Hill Cave Inscriptions of Asoka and Dasaratha. IA.* xx, 1891, pp. 361–65.

Pillar Edicts of Asoka. Epi. Ind. ii, 1894, pp. 245–74.

Hultzsch, E. *Corpus Inscriptionum Indicarum,* vol. i, new edn. Oxford, 1925.

Senart, E. *Les Inscriptions de Piyadasi,* 2 vols. Paris, 1881–86.

Khāravela Inscription

Barua, B. M. *Hāthīgumphā Inscription of Khāravela. IHQ.* xiv, 1938, pp. 459–85.

Jayaswal, K. P. *Hāthīgumphā Inscription of the Emperor Khāravela. JBORS.* iii, 1917, pp. 425–85.

The Hāthīgumphā Inscription. JBORS. iv, 1918, pp. 364–403.

The Hāthīgumphā Inscription of Khāravela. Epi. Ind. xx, 1929–30, pp. 71–89.

Konow, S. *Some Problems Raised by the Khāravela Inscription. Acta Orientalia* i, 1923, pp. 12–42.

Maukhari Inscriptions

Fleet, J. F. *Corpus Inscriptionum Indicarum,* vol. iii. Calcutta, 1888.

Govindacandra Inscription

Sahni, D. R. *Saheth Maheth Plate of Govindacandra. Epi. Ind.* xi, pp. 20–26.

South Indian Inscriptions

Hultzsch, E. *South Indian Inscriptions*, 11 vols. Madras, 1890–1940.

Krishnamacharlu, C. R. *Viḷavatti Grant of Pallava Siṃhavarman. Epi. Ind.* xxiv, 1937–38, pp. 296–300.

Krishnarao, B. V. *Tāṇḍikoṇḍa Grant of Ammarāja II. Epi. Ind.* xxiii, 1935–36, pp. 161–170.

Narasimhachar, R. *Epigraphia Carnatica*, vol. ii, 2nd edn. Bangalore, 1923.

Rice, L. *Epigraphia Carnatica*, 12 vols. Bangalore, 1886–1904.

F. *Miscellaneous*

Athenaeus. V. *CII.* i.

Homer. *Iliad.*

Das Nibelungenlied. Ed. K. Bartsch, 3rd edn. Leipzig, 1887.

Táin Bó Cúalnge. Ed. with translation by E. Windisch. Leipzig, 1905.

II. Secondary Authorities

A. *Reference Books, etc.*

Annual Reports on South Indian Eipgraphy. Madras, 1887–

Böhtlinck, O. and Roth, R. *Sanskrit Wörterbuch.* 7 vols. St. Petersburg, 1855–75.

Eggeling, J. and Windisch, E. *Catalogue of Sanskrit and Prākrit MSS. in the India Office Library*, vol. i, 1887–99.

Hastings, J., ed. *Encyclopædia of Religion and Ethics*, 12 vols. Edinburgh, 1908–26.

A Gazetteer of the Bombay Presidency, 27 vols. Bombay, 1877–1904.

Keith, A. B., and Thomas, F. W. *Catalogue of the Sanskrit and Prākrit MSS. in the Library of the India Office*, vol. ii, 2 parts. Oxford, 1935.

Kittel, F. *Kannada–English Dictionary.* Mangalore, 1894.

Tamil Lexicon. Madras University, 6 vols. Madras, 1926–1936.

Malalasekera, G. P. *Dictionary of Pāli Proper Names*, 2 vols. London, 1937–38.

Monier Williams, M. *Sanskrit–English Dictionary*, new edn. Oxford, 1899.

Ratnacandraji, Muni Śrī. *An Illustrated Ardha Māgadhī Dictionary*, 4 vols. Ajmer, 1923–32.

Rhys Davids, T. W., and Stede, W. *Pāli–English Dictionary*. PTS. Chipstead, 1925.

Seṭh, H. D. T. *Paia-sadda-mahaṇṇavo*. Calcutta, 1928.

Sörensen, S. *An Index to the Names in the Mahābhārata*. London, 1904.

Vijayarājendra Sūri. *Abhidhāna Rājendra*, 7 vols. Ratlam, 1913–25.

Weber, A. *Verzeichniss der Sanskrit und Prākrit Handschriften im Königliche Bibliotek, Berlin*, 2 vols., 1853–92.

B. *Monographs*

Aiyangar, S. K. *Maṇimekhalai in its Historical Setting*. London, 1928.

Barua, B. M. *Pre-Buddhistic Indian Philosophy*. Calcutta, 1921.

Brown, P. *Indian Architecture*. Bombay, n.d.

Coomaraswamy, A. *Yakṣas*, 2 vols. Washington, 1928–31.

Cunningham, A. *Coins of Mediæval India*. London, 1894.

Four Reports made during . . . 1862–5. ASI. Reports, vol. i. Simla, 1871.

Das Gupta, S. N. *History of Indian Philosophy*, 4 vols. Cambridge, 1922–48.

Fergusson, J. *History of Indian and Eastern Architecture*, revised by J. Burgess and R. P. Spiers. London, 1910.

—— and Burgess, J. *The Cave Temples of India*. London, 1880.

Foucher, A. *L'Art Gréco-Bouddhique du Gandhara*, 2 vols. Paris, 1905–18.

Glasenapp, H. von. *Der Jainismus*. Berlin, 1925.

Grünwedel, A. *Alt Buddhistische Kultstätten in Chinesisch Turkestan*. Berlin, 1912.

Alt Kutscha. Berlin, 1920.

Guérinot, A. *La Religion Djaïna*. Paris, 1926.

Hauer, J. W. *Der Vrātya*. Stuttgart, 1927.

Hoernle, A. F. R. *Studies in the Medicine of Ancient India*, part i. Oxford, 1907.

Iyengar, P. T. S. *History of the Tamils to 600 A.D.* Madras, 1929.

Jain, J. C. *Life in Ancient India as Depicted in the Jain Canons*. Bombay, 1947.

Keith, A. B. *Buddhist Philosophy*. Oxford, 1923.
History of Sanskrit Literature. Oxford, 1938.
Indian Logic and Atomism. Oxford, 1921.

Kern, H. *Der Buddhismus und seine Geschichte in Indien*, tr. H. Jacobi, 2 vols. Leipzig, 1882–84.

Krom, N. J. *Barabuḍur—an Archæological Description*, 2 vols. The Hague, 1927.
The Life of the Buddha on the Stupa of Barabuḍur. The Hague, 1926.

Lassen, C. *Indische Alterthumskunde*, 4 vols. Leipzig, 1858–74.

Macdonnell, A. A. *A History of Sanskrit Literature*, 7th impression, London, 1928.

Majumdar, R. C. (ed.). *History of Bengal*, vol. i. Dacca, 1943.

McGovern, W. M. *A Manual of Buddhist Philosophy*, vol. i. London, 1923.

Pires, E. A. *The Maukharis*. Madras, 1934.

Prasad, Ishwari. *History of Medieval India*. Allahabad, 1925.

Rapson, E. J. *Indian Coins*. Strassburg, 1897.
(ed.) *Cambridge History of India*, vol. i. 1922.

Ratna-Prabha Vijaya. *Śramaṇa Bhagavān Mahāvīra*, 5 vols., 8 pts. Ahmedabad, 1948.

Raychaudhuri, H. C. *Political History of Ancient India*, 4th edn. Calcutta, 1938.

Rockhill, W. W. *The Life of the Buddha*. London, 1884.

Saletore, B. A. *Mediæval Jainism*. Bombay, 1938.

Sastri, K. A. N. *The Colas*, 2 vols. Madras, 1935–37.

Schomerus, H. W. *Der Śaiva Siddhānta*. Leipzig, 1912.

Schrader, F. O. *Introduction to Pāñcarātra and the Ahirbudhnya Saṃhitā*. Adyar, 1916.

Schubring, W. *Die Lehre der Jainas*. Berlin, 1935.

Sewell, R. *The Historical Inscriptions of South India*, ed. S. Krishnaswami Aiyangar. Madras, 1932.

Shah, C. J. *Jainism in North India, 800* B.C.—A.D. *526*. London, 1932.

Smith, V. A. *Early History of India*. 4th edn. Oxford, 1924.

Sugiura, S. *Hindu Logic as Preserved in China and Japan.* Philadelphia, 1900.

Ui, H. *The Vaiśeṣika Philosophy.* London, 1917.

De la Vallée Poussin, L. *Dynasties et Histoire de l'Inde Depuis Kanishka jusqu'aux Invasions Musulmanes.* Paris, 1935.

L'Inde aux Temps des Mauryas. Paris, 1930.

Indo-Européens et Indo-Iraniens. L'Inde jusqu'en 300 avant J.C. New edn. Paris, 1936.

Winternitz, M. *Geschichte der Indischen Literatur,* 3 vols. Leipzig, 1909–20.

C. *Articles*

Banerji Sastri, A. *The Ājīvikas. JBORS.* xii, 1926, pp. 53–62.

Barua, B. M. *The Ājīvikas. JDL.* ii, 1920, pp. 1–80.

Ājīvika—What it Means. ABORI. viii, 1927, pp. 183–88.

Bhandarkar, D. R. *Ājīvakas. IA.* xli, 1912, pp. 286–90.

Charpentier, J. *Ājīvika. JRAS.* 1913, pp. 669–74.

Dorner, A. *Fate. ERE.* v, pp. 771–78.

Fleet, J. F. *The Meaning of Adhakosikya in the 7th Pillar Edict of Asoka. JRAS.,* 1906, pp. 401–17.

Foucher, A. *Le "Grand Miracle" du Buddha à Çrāvasti. JA.,* 1909, pp. 1–77.

Gopani, A. S. *Ājīvika Sect—a New Interpretation. Bhāratīya Vidyā* ii, pp. 201–10, and iii, pp. 47–59, 1941.

Grierson, G. A. *Madhvas. ERE.* viii, pp. 232–35.

Hoernle, A. F. R. *Ājīvikas. ERE.* i, pp. 259–69.

Jackson, V. H. *Two New Inscriptions from the Barabar Hills and an Identification of Gorathagiri. JBORS.* i, 1915, pp. 159–71.

Jacobi, H. *Atomic Theory (Indian). ERE.* ii, pp. 199–200.

Jainism. ERE. vii, pp. 465–74.

Jolly, J. *Fate (Hindu). ERE.* v, 790–92.

Keith, A. B. *The Authenticity of the Arthaśāstra. Asutosh Mookerji Commemoration Volume,* pt. i, 1926, pp. 8–22.

King, L. W. *Fate (Babylonian). ERE.* v, pp. 778–80.

Pathak, K. B. *The Ājīvikas, a Sect of Buddhist Bhikkhus. IA.* xli, 1912, pp. 88–90.

Srinivasan, K. R. *The Megalithic Burials and Urn Fields of South India in the Light of Tamil Literature and Tradition*. *Ancient India*, ii, 1946, pp. 9–16.

Vogel, J. P. *Le Makara dans la Sculpture de l'Inde*. *Revue des Arts Asiatiques* vi, 1930, pp. 133–47.

Weber, A. *Analyse der in Anquetil du Perrons Übersetzung enthalten Upanishaden. Vierter Artikel*. *IS*. ii, 1853, pp. 170–236.

Über die Heiligen Schriften der Jaina. *IS*. xvi, 1883, pp. 211–479, and xvii, 1884, pp. 1–90.

INDEX

In addition to those on pp. xxxi–ii, the following abbreviations are used in the index; Ā.: Ājīvika; esp.: especially; k.: king; M.G.: Makkhali Gosāla; n.: note; n.pr.: proper name; Pkt.: Prākrit; pl.: place name, whether of a town or district; Skt.: Sanskrit; Tam.: Tamil.

ā, Skt. particle, 103
Abhassarā, Buddhist heaven, 261
Abhayadeva, Jaina commentator, 35, 40, 48 n. 1, 63, 68, 111–12, 127, 129, 140, 178, 213–14, 220–1, 242, 249–250, 254 n. 1, 255; quoted, 35 n. 3, 40 n. 5, 51 n. 1, 63 nn. 2, 3, 68 nn. 2, 3, 111 nn. 3, 4, 5, 112 n. 1, 117 n. 3, 128 nn. 1, 2, 3, 4, 221 n. 1, 222 n. 2, 249 n. 3, 255 n. 4.
Abhidhāna-cintāmaṇi, lexicon of Hemacandra, 35, 182
Abhidharma-kośa, Yaśomitra's comm. on, 241
abhijātis, six classes of men, 14, 20, 27, 80, 84, 106, 109, 139, **243–6**, 272, 275
abrahmacariyavāsā, *v.* antitheses
Ācārāṅga Sūtra, Jaina scripture, 41, 46
Ācārasāra, Jaina text, 186, 203
Ācārya Śrī Yogânanda, n.pr., 155
Acchidda, *disācara*, 56, 57
Accua-kappa (Pkt.), Jaina heaven, *v.* Acyuta-kalpa
acelaka, a naked ascetic, 96–7, 107–8, 118–19, 121, 123, 132, 139, 217, 243
Achilles, 7
Āciva(ka)-kācu (Tam.), 189
ācu (Tam.), 192
Ācuva, Tam. form of Ājīvika, 191
Ācuva-k-kaṭamai (Tam.), 189–191
Ācuvikaḷ-kācu (Tam.), 188–9, 194
Ācuvi-makkaḷ (Tam.), 188, 192
Ācuvula-paṟṟu, pl., 156, 187–8
Acyuta-kalpa, Jaina heaven, 140, 142, 204, 261
Adda, n.pr., 53–4, 114, 121, 129
Addapura, pl., 54
adharma, Skt., sin, 266
adhyāya, Skt., lesson, chapter of a text, 39
Aggivesāyaṇa, *disācara*, 56–8
Aggivessana, n.pr., 27, 57, 58, 118–19
Agni, the fire-god, 81, 93 n. 2
Agniveśa, legendary physician, 57–8
agnosticism, 17
agrahāra, a grant of land, usually to brāhmaṇas or temples, 206
ahetukavādin, one maintaining the doctrine of causelessness, 18, 227
ahiṃsā, the doctrine of non-violence, 18, 61, 123, 126; Ājīvika, 122
Aiyangar, K., 192, 197
Ajantā frescos, 107
Ajātasattu, k. of Magadha, 5, 11, 13, 67–77, 89; war with Licchavis, 69–70
Ajayapāla, lexicographer, 182–4
ājīva (Skt.), profession, 247
Ājīva, form of Ājīvika, 162–3, 182–3
Ājīvakinī, Ājīvinī, an Ājīvika nun, 139, 243
Ājīvik-a, -ism, *passim*; an A. announces Buddha's death, 136; asceticism, **109–115**; atomism, **262–6**; before M.G., **94–101**; begging and dietary practices, **118–123**; Buddhists, relations with, **134–8**; cosmology, **ch. xiii**, *passim*; Dravidian, southern, 108, 115–16, 124–5, 174, **ch. x**, *passim*, 236, 255, 259, 262, 272, 279; epistemology, **274–5**; etymology, **101–4**; final penance, **127–38**; influence, 279–283; initiation, **104–7**; Jainas, relations with, **138–141**; language, 219–220; last references to, 184–6; laymen, 131–6; leaders, before M.G., **27–34**; in Nanda and Maurya periods, **ch. viii**, *passim*; nudity, 107–9; origin, 94–101; place in Indian History, 283–8; *-sabhā*, 52–3, 115–17, 156; schools of, 239, 279–280; scriptures, 51, ch. xi, *passim*; *-seyyam*, 125; solitary ascetics, 114; in Tamil literature, 196–203; worldliness and immorality, 123–7
Ajita Kesakambalī, n.pr., 11, 17–23, 25, 55, 93, 218, 228; doctrine, 15
Ajjunna Gomāyuputta, n.pr., 56–7
Ajjuṇa Goyamaputta, n.pr., 32, 34, 57
ajñānavādin, a sceptic, 174
Akanāṉūṟu, Tamil anthology, 197
ākāśa, space, ether, 268

akriyavād-a, the doctrine of the fruitlessness of works; *-in*, a believer in this doctrine, 174, 226–7, 281
akṣara, a syllabic letter of any Hindu script, 151
Ālabhiyā, pl., 32–3, 44, 133 n. 1
Ālavi, pl., 33
Āḻvārs, Dravidian Vaiṣṇavite hymnodists, 281–2
Amara, lexicographer, 182
Ammarāja II, E. Cālukya k., 187
anāgāmī, one who will not be reborn on earth, 95
anaïkkamaṇijjāiṃ (Pkt.), inevitables, 254–6
Ānanda, disciple of Buddha, 18–20, 27, 133
Āṇanda, disciple of Mahāvīra, 59, 140, 216
Anantamānasa, Buddhist heaven, 135 n. 2, 261
Anantavarman Maukhari, chieftain, 153–5, 158
anassāsikāni brahmacariyāni (Pāli), *v.* vocations
anātma, soullessness, 199
Āndhra, pl., 196
anekântavāda, a doctrine of epistemological relativity, 202
Anekârtha-saṅgraha, lexicon, 182
Aṅga, pl., 5
aṅga, text of Jaina canon, 178
Aṅgamaṇḍira, pl., 32
Aṅgiras, n.pr., 30
Aṅguttara Nikāya, Pāli scripture, 20, 27, 54, 106, 133, 135, 243; quoted, 133 n. 2
animism, 5, 283–4
annihilationist, 95
Anotatta, lake, 251
antara-kappa, lesser æon, 243
Antariñjikā, pl., 177
Anthologies, Tamil, 196–7
antinomian-ism, 18–19, 21–2, 168, 228, 239, 261, 271
antitheses to the higher life, 18, 228
aṇu, atom, 265, 268
Anurādhapura, pl., 146
apāṇagāiṃ (Pkt.), *v.* substitutes for drink
apsaras, a celestial nymph, 249
Āpta-ṇ, title of M.G., 79, 125, 244, 276
Āpūraṇa, son of Kaśyapa, 90
ārāma, a park or garden, 135
Āraṇyaka, Brāhmaṇic scripture, 98
Arcot Dist. of Madras, 188–190
Ardha-māgadhī, the dialect of Pkt. in which the Śvetâmbara Jaina scriptures are written, 25, 35, 252
Ardhanārīśvara, god, 155
arhant, an Ājīvika, Jaina, or Buddhist saint of the highest rank; Ā., 28, 29, 56, 79, 140, 244, 259; Jaina, 168, 201
Arjuna, mathematician, 34; hero, 57
Arkacandra, n.pr. 199
Arthaśāstra, text on polity, 120, 127, 161; quoted, 161 n. 1
Aruṇandi Śivâcārya, Tamil Śaivite author, 203
Āryans, 4–6, 8, 44, 162, 196, 284–5
Āryâvarta, pl., 8
asaññi-gabbha (Pāli), unconscious births, 248–9
asceticism, 12; Ājīvika, 4, 104–115; *v.* also penance
ascetics, types of, 165, 169–171, 181, 184
Ashibika, Japanese form of Ā., 112
Aśoka, emperor, 53, 97, 127, 136, 138–9, 146–154, 156–7, 159, 161, 193, 196, 278, 286
āśrama, hermitage, 98; stage of life, 99, 162
Assagutta, n.pr., 147
astrolog-y, -er, 7, 127, 168–170, 184–5
asura, a type of demon, 70, 163; modes of existence as, 256
Āśvalāyana Śrauta Sūtra, Brāhmaṇic text, 103
Atharva Veda, 286
atom-ism, Ā., 17, 19, 91, 232, 238, **262–6**, 284; Ā., in relation to other Indian atomic doctrines, 267–270 (Jaina, 267; Vaiśeṣika, 267–8; Buddhist, 268–9)
Atreya, n.pr., 57
aulambalam, *avalambalam*, tax, 190
Aupapātika Sūtra, Jaina scripture, 111, 119–120, 140, 204, 261
Āvaṇi, pl., inscription, 188, 191–2, 195
Avanti, pl., 286
Avasarpiṇī, an era of decline (Jainism), 27, 64, 68, 144, 254, 275
Āvaśyaka Sūtra, Jaina scripture, 267; *cūrṇī*, 41, 70
avatāra, the incarnation of a god, 172, 260–1, 276, 280
āvatīgaṅgā, Ā. measurement of time, 253
Āvattā, pl., 44
avicalita-nityatvam, unchanging permanence, **236–240**, 262, 280, 283
Avīci, Buddhist hell, 86

Avīha, Buddhist heaven, 95
Ayampula, n.pr., 62–4, 117, 132, 140
ayurveda, the science of medicine, 58

Babylonians, 6
Bahula, n.pr., 39
bahuvrīhi, type of compound noun, 105
Baladeva, god, 44–5, 47, 273
Bambhaloga (Pkt.) = Brahmaloka (q.v.), a heaven, 250
Bambhaṇagāma, pl., 42
Bāṇa, author, 99, 163, 168, 208
Bāṇārasī, pl. (Pkt.) = Vāṇārasī, Kāsī, Benares, q.v., 133 n. 1
Banerji Sastri, A., 158.
Barābar, caves, 148, **150–160**, 210; hill, 151
Barua, B. M., 11–12, 17, 28–30, 32, 40–1, 47 n. 4, 57, 61, 65, 92, 100, 119, 133, 141–3, 145, 167–8, 172, 214, 219–220, 247, 252, 258; quoted, 97–8, 120, 129–130, 142 n. 3, 173, 273, 279
Battle, Last, with large stones, 68, 74
Bebhela, pl., 83
begging, Ā. practice, **118–123**; bowl, 121
Belagāmi, Mysore, 105
Benares, 18, 29, *v.* also Bāṇārasī, Kāsī, Vāṇārasī
Bengal, 5, 41, 44, 202
Bhaddā, n.pr., mother of M.G., 35–6, 78; queen, 142
Bhaddiyā, pl., 44
Bhadrabāhu, Jaina pontiff, 193, 196, 214
Bhāgavata, a devotee of Viṣṇu, 171, 173
Bhagavatī Sūtra, Jaina scripture, 27, chs. iii and iv, *passim*, 83, 88–9, 94–5, 103, 116, 122, 127, 131, 140, 142–5, 154, 213–14, 216, 219, 242, 244, 249–251, 253–7, 272, 274–6; quoted, 37 n. 4, 40 nn. 1, 4, 47 n. 4, 48 nn. 1, 4, 56 n. 2, 60 n. 3, 61 n. 1, 62 n. 9, 63 n. 1, 122 n. 3, 128 n. 5, 219 n. 2, 249 n. 2, 250 n. 5, 253 n. 3
Bhairavâcārya, n.pr., 167
bhakti, devotion to a personal deity, 47, 280, 282
Bhandarkar, D. R., 149, 167, 173; quoted, 166, 172
Bhāraddāi, n.pr. (Pkt.) = Bhāradvāja, 32–3, 58
Bharadvāja, sage, 58
Bhāradvāja, *gotra*, 33
Bhāratavarṣa, Hindu name of India, 286
Bhartṛhari, poet, 282
Bhaṭṭi-kāvya, poem, 99, 166–7
Bhaṭṭiprolu Casket, 196
Bhaṭṭotpala, commentator, *v.* Utpala
Bhāva, nature, 225–7, 232
Bhavānī, goddess, 154
Bhela, n.pr., 58
bhikkhu (Pāli), a monk; Buddhist, 11, 18, 75, 95–6, 124, 135–7, 139–140, 146, 194, 243; Jaina, 214
bhikṣu (Skt.) = *bhikkhu*, 169, 184, 204
bhikkhunī (Pāli), a nun, 116, 124–5
Bhīma, hero, 218
Bhogavatī, city of *nāgas*, 90
Bhūtapati, god = Śiva, 155
bhūtavādī, materialist, 200
Bihār, pl., 5
Bilhaṇa, poet, 205
Bimbisāra, k. of Magadha, 5, 51, 67, 73, 76–7, 85, 89, 120, 124, 132, 136
Bindusāra, emperor, 127, 131, 146–7, 151
births, Ā. categories of, chief forms, 241; conscious, 250; divine, 249; from knots, 14, 248; sentient, 14, 219, 248–250; unconscious, 14, 248; uterine, 14, 241, 248
biruda, a secondary name or royal title, 205
Bodhisatta (Pāli), in Hīnayāna Buddhism, a previous incarnation of a Buddha, 29, 84, 110, 114, 165
Bodhisattva (Skt.), in Mahāyāna Buddhism, a being who voluntarily postpones his Buddhahood to work for the welfare of the world, 165, 261
Bodhi Tree, the tree near Gayā under which Buddha gained enlightenment, 95
Bombay Gazetteer, 170
Borobodūr, pl., 106–8
Boṭikas, Digambara Jainas, 175–6
Brahmā, god, 162, 164 n. 3, 274
Brahmadatta, k. of Kāsī, 18, 29
Brahmajāla Sutta, 270
Brahmakalpa, Jaina heaven = Brahmaloka, 204
Brahmaloka, heaven, 30, 261, 273
Brahman, the impersonal world-spirit, 284
Brāhmaṇa, the priestly class, 12, 15, 21, 29, 131, 196; scripture, 98
Brāhmaṇism, 10, 100
Brāhmī, the earliest Indian alphabetic script, 157, 159
Bṛhajjātaka, astrological text, 169, 171

Buddha, 5, 10–12, 20, 28, 34, 53–5, 57, 59, 66–7, 71–2, 74–7, 80–1, 83, 85, 89, 93–7, 100, 102, 108, 118–19, 122, 132, 134–7, 198–200, 242, 277–8
Buddhaghosa, Buddhist commentator, 27, 35, 37, 52, 71–2, 79, 82, 91–2, 96–7, 102–3, 105–6, 118 n. 1, 120, 125, 135 n. 2, 139, 220, 225, 240, 242–3, 246–9, 251–2, 254, 260–1, 270; quoted, 13 n. 2, 14 n. 2, 15 nn. 1, 2, 3, 16 nn. 2, 3, 19 n. 7, 27 n. 7, 71 n. 5, 92 n. 2, 107 n. 1, 125 n. 1, 139 nn. 5, 6, 7, 241 nn. 1, 3, 4, 243 n. 5, 248 nn. 2, 5, 261 n. 4
Buddh-ism, -ist, 3, 6, 12, 25, 30, 35, 101, 124, 131, 172, 183, 200, 268–9, 280, 283; confused with Ās., 107, 135; relations with Ās. **134–38**; scriptures, 5–6, 27–8, 33, 285
Bühler, G., 149, 151, 170, 173
burial, ritual, in Ā. initiation and penance, 106, 112
Burnouf, E., 101

Caitanya, n.pr., 117
caitya, a sacred spot in popular religion, usually a tree or mound, 31–3, 60–1, 67, 154, 162
cakradhara, type of ascetic, 169
cakravartī, a universal emperor, 144
Cālukya, dynasty, 205
Calvinism, 282
Camara, Indra of the *asuras*, 70
Camataṇṭa, pl., 201
Campā, pl., 32, 42, 73, 95, 133 n. 1
Cāṇakya, n.pr., 145, 167
Canarese, 204
Candalā, n.pr., 205, 208
Candoyaraṇa, *caitya*, 32
Candra Gupta I, 75
Candragupta Maurya, emperor, 77, 151, 167, 193
Cāpā, n.pr., 95
caraka, type of ascetic, 169
Caraka Saṃhitā, medical text, 57
carimāiṃ, *v.* last things
Cārvāka, a materialist sect, 3, 17, 25, 165, 184, 204; *v.* also *Lokāyata*, materialism, *nāstika*
categories, Ā., ch. xiii, *passim*; seven elementary, 16, 262–6
Cāttaṉ, Tam. poet, 197–8
Catuṣkanāyika, school of Jainism, 178–9
causation, European doctrine, 227
causelessness, doctrine, of, 227
caves, Ā., **150–160**; Buddhist, 156; Jaina, 159
Ceḍaga (Pkt. = Skt. Ceṭaka), chieftain of Vesāli, 69–70, 73, 76, 133 n. 1
cempōtakar (Tam. = Skt. *sambodhaka*), 260–1, 281–2
Central Asia, frescos, 108
Ceylon, 166; Ās. in, 145
Chakravarti, A., 192, 200; quoted, 191
chance, *v.* *Saṅgati*
Chalmers, Lord, 15 n. 3, 19 n. 7, 118 n. 1
Charpentier, J., 36, 74, 94
chastity, vow of, 126
Chin-a, -ese, Buddhist literature, 112; version of *Sāmañña-phala Sutta*, 21, 23, 91
Christianity, 82 n. 1; Syrian, 282
chronometry, Ā., 252–3, 275
Cilappatikāram, Tam. poem, 134, 197; quoted, 197 n. 4
Civañāna-cittiyār Parapakṣam, Tam. Śaivite text, 81, 91, 106, 112, 186–7, 198, 200, 202, 204, 238, 244–5, 256, 260–1, 264–6, 276–7, 280; quoted, 91 n. 10, 238 nn. 4, 5, 260 n. 2, 264 n. 5, 265 n. 9, 266 n. 6
classes of men, *v.* *abhijāti*
coins, of Harṣa of Kashmīr, 205, 209
Cola, kingdom, 194, 208
Coḷamaṇḍalam, pl., 108
commentators, quotations from Ā. literature by, **220–3**
Conscious Births, seven, 249
Coraga, pl., 42
Corāya, pl., 44
cosmology, Ā., ch. xiii, *passim*, 285–6
Cuchullain Saga, 7
Cuṇḍa, n.pr., 75
Cunningham, A., 33, 152–5
cūrṇi, commentary, to *Āvaśyaka Sūtra*, 41
cuvai (Tam.), sweetness, sensual pleasure, 125, 202

Daḍhapaīnna, n.pr., 142
Dance, Last, 68, 117
dancing, ritual, 194
Daṇḍabhukti, pl., 202
Daṇḍaki, k., 29
daṇḍin, type of ascetic, 170–1
darbha, a grass, 128–131
daridda-thera, type of ascetic, 43, 47

Daśaratha, k., 150–1, 154–5, 157, 159, 278
Das Gupta, S. N., quoted, 225, 281
Deccan, 208
De la Vallée Poussin, L., 74 n. 1
Delhi-Topra Pillar, 148
Destiny, 7, 222, 282–3 ; v. also Fate, *Niyati*
determinism, 3, 8, 17, 19, 22, 96, ch. xii, *passim*
deva, a god, 42, 133, 142, 219, 251, 258, 272–3 ; Ā., 218, 222, 229, 272–4
Devānampiya Tissa, k. of Ceylon, 146
devaputta, demigod, 216
Devaseṇa, n.pr., 142–3
Dhamma (Pāli) = Skt. *dharma*, 19
Dhammapada Commentary, Pāli text, 85, 96–7, 105, 107, 113, 201
dhanu, a measure, about 6 feet, 253
dharma, good conduct, righteousness, virtue, 266–7
dialectic, 228–235
diet, Ā., 118–123
Digambara, the branch of Jainism whose ascetics practised nudity, 107, 121, 167–8, 170, 174–6, 181, 183–4, 186, 203–4, 277
Dīghanakha, n.pr., 57
Dīgha Nikāya, Pāli scripture, 11, 23, 102, 256 ; quoted, 72 n. 3, 73 n. 5 ; v. also *Brahmajāla Sutta*, *Mahāparinibbāna Sutta*, *Sāmaññaphala Sutta*
Dikshitar, V. R. R., 134
Diṅnāga, Buddhist logician, 197
disācaras, 51, **56–8**, 64, 70, 117, 213, 255
Divine Births, seven, 249
Divyâvadāna, Buddhist Skt. text, 83, 85–6, 97, 109, 138, 146–7, 207 ; quoted, 87 nn. 1, 2
Doāb, pl., 4
dreams, 14, 252
Drink-s, four, 62, 127–130, 254 ; last, 68
Dṛṣṭivāda, Jaina scripture, 178–181
dugharantariya, type of Ā. ascetic, 111, 119
duḥkha, suffering, 91
Dulva, Tibetan Buddhist scriptures, 21, 24
Dvaita, school of Vaiṣṇavism, 282
dvandva, type of compound noun, 105, 225

ekadaṇḍin, type of Vaiṣṇavite ascetic, 47, 79, 100, 114, 166–7, **169–172**, 174, 184–6, 204
Eleatics, 238, 262
elements, 91, 215, **262–6** ; characteristics of, 265, 268
elephant, 153, 209 ; v. also Sprinkling Elephant
Eṇejjaga, n.pr., 31–2
epic, literature, 7 ; tradition, 132 ; Tam. 197
evolution (*pariṇāma*), 82

faculties, 14, 248
fatalism, 19, 21, 132 ; Āryan, 8 ; Ā., ch. xii, *passim* ; v. also determinism, *niyativāda*
Fate, 6, 221, ch. xii, *passim*, 256 ; v. also Destiny, *Niyati*
Ferdiad, n.pr., 7
Fergusson, J., 153
Finalities, eight ; v. Last Things
Fleet, J. F., 153
fortune-telling, 127, 147, 168
Foucher, A., 107
Franke, R. O., 24, 248
free will, 229–230, 233, 284
funerary urns, 111

Gāhaḍavāla, dynasty, 208
gairuka, type of ascetic, 181
gaṇarājas, tribal chieftains, 70
Gaṇḍa, n.pr., 85
gandhabhaṇḍa (Pāli), scented substance, 71–2
gandha-hatthī (Pkt.), scent-elephant, 72
Gandhāra, pl., 205 ; sculptures, 108
gaṅgā, Ā. measurement of time, 253
Ganges, river, 4, 5, 9–10, 13, 33, 51, 72, 133, 285
Garuḍa, a mythical bird ; species of, 256
Gautama, *gotra*, 34
gautama, type of ascetic, 165
Gayā, pl., 150
Geiger, W., 74 n. 1
gharasamudāṇiya, type of Ā. ascetic, 111
Gijjhakūṭa, hill, 72
Gobahula, n.pr., 36
goblins, 162, 251 ; v. also *piśāca*
Gobhūmi, pl., 45
Godhāvari, river, 29
gods, Ā., **272–4**
Gommateśvara, Jaina temple, 125
Gopani, A. S., 28, 65
Gopikā, cave, 152, 154, 157–8
goputthae, one of the " Four Drinks ", 131

Gorathagiri, hill, 158
Gosāla, Gośāla, Gośālaka; v. Makkhali Gosāla
gotra, a brāhmaṇical sept, 33–4, 57
govālikā, grass, 63
Govindacandra, k., 208
grace, salvation by, 281
grahaṇa, definition of, 173
Greece, 285
Greeting, Last, 68
Grünwedel, A., 108
Guḍihalli, pl., inscription, 190
Gujarāt, 182
Guṇa, n.pr., ascetic teacher, 20, 104–5, 217, 263; ascetic of Kashmīr, 206, 210
guṇa, quality, 199, 265; the three basic qualities of Sāṅkhya philosophy, 39; *rajo-g.*, the second or fiery quality of Sāṅkhya, 248
Guṇaratna, Jaina commentator, 80–2, 174, 176–7, 185, 221–2, 226, 235; quoted, 222 n. 4, 226 n. 2, 235 n. 2
Guntupaḷḷi, pl., 156
Gupta, dynasty, 134, 152–4, 159, 162–3, 165, 185, 286
guru, a religious teacher; type of ascetic, 184

Hagen, n.pr., 7
hair, extraction of, 106
Haladhara, n.pr., 206, 209
Hālāhalā, n.pr., 32, 51, 53, 56, 59, 61–2, 116, 124, 132, 134
Halâyudha, lexicographer, 100, 182–4; quoted, 182
Haledutā, pl., 43
hallā, insect, 62–3, 117
Hare, E. M., 139 nn. 6, 7, 243
Haribhadra, Jaina philosopher, 81, 178, 185, 222
Hārīta, n.pr., 58
Harṣa, k. of Kanauj, 167–8; k. of Kashmīr, 148, 154, 185, **205–210**
Harṣacarita of Bāṇa, 167–8; quoted, 167 n. 4
Hastināpura, pl., 199
Hāthīgumphā, cave inscription, 145, 158
heavens, Ā., 250; Jaina, 250 n. 3, 274; salvation in, 261
Hebrew, monotheism, 7
Hector, n.pr., 7
Hemacandra, Jaina polymath, 8, 35, 74, 77, 144, 182
Heretics, six, ch. ii, *passim*, 67, 85, 92–3, 108, 138
hermits, 98, 110
hero, doomed, 7
Himālaya, 143, 201
Hīnayāna, the form of Buddhism now practised in Ceylon and Burma, 277, 280
Hindu-ism, 3; devotional, 117, 280, 287; literature, 228; scriptures, 33
Hitopadeśa, Skt. text, 282; quoted, 222 n. 2
Hoernle, A. F. R., 11, 28, 33, 35–6, 40, 47 n. 4, 61, 69, 76–8, 109, 114, 121, 133 n. 1, 139 n. 6, 142 n. 3, 143–4, 172, 178, 180–1, 186, 190, 214, 226, 245, 254 n. 1, 255, 259, 277; quoted, 38, 65, 68, 78, 99, 101–2, 175, 183
Homeric Age, 285
Hoysala, dynasty, 189–190, 194
Hultzsch, E., 148, 150, 158, 190–1, 193; quoted, 151
Hūṇas, 168
hupeyya, Pāli verbal form, 220

iconoclasm, 147, 185, 205–210
idealism, Berkeleyan, 230
Iliad, 7
Indabhūi Goyama, disciple of Mahāvīra, 35, 47, 58
Indo-European peoples, 7
Indra, god, 69, 285
indriya, faculty, 247
Indus Civilization, 4
Inevitables, six, 255–6
infinity of souls, 260
initiation, Ā., 104–7
Ionian philosophers, 6
Islām, 207
issarakāraṇavādi, a believer in the doctrine of the creation of the world by a personal god, 18
iyalpu (Tam.), quality, 265

Jacobi, H., 17, 28, 74, 76–7, 121 n. 5
Jain-a, -ism, 3, 6, 10, 12, 17, 30, 35, 119, 121–2, 131; categories, 266; literature, 24; scriptures, 6, 17, 27, 34, 56, 133, 285; tradition, 144
Jambuka, n.pr., 97, 105–6, 109, 113, 137–8
Jambusanda, pl., 44
Janaka, k., 4, 5
Jānakī-haraṇa, poem of Kumāradāsa, 97, 106, 165–7; quoted, 165 n. 4
Janasāna, n.pr., 131, 138, 146–7, 149

Japanese Buddhist literature, 106, 112
Jātaka, a folk-tale or other story which has been adapted to Buddhist purposes by making the principal character the *bodhisatta*, or the Buddha in a previous birth; 28–30, 51, 59, 92, 105, 113, 165, 209–210; quoted, 81 n. 6, 104 nn. 4, 5, 7, 112 n. 6, 113 n. 1, 228 n. 1; *Lomahaṃsa*, 110, 113; *Mahābodhi*, 18, 217; quoted, 18 nn. 2, 3, 4; *Mahānāradakassapa*, 20, 104, 217, 263; *Nakkhatta*, 127; *Naṅguṭṭha*, 110; *Neru*, 95; *Paṇḍara*, 102; *Sarabhaṅga*, 29; *Tittira*, 99, 104, 112
Jātaka-pārijāta, astrological text, 184
jāti, caste, 188
jaṭila, type of ascetic, 181
Jatūkarṇa, n.pr., 58
Java, island, 108
Jayaswal, K. P., 158–9
Jensen, H., 282
Jesus, 36
Jetavana, park at Sāvatthi, 86, 110–11, 153
jina (Skt.), *jiṇa* (Pkt.), a teacher whose soul has reached perfection, especially with the Jainas and Ās., 56, 60, 64–8, 79, 84, 90, 145, 246, 260
Jinadāsa Gaṇī, Jaina commentator, 41, 45–6, 48 n. 2, 50 n. 1, 70; quoted, 42 n. 3, 44 n. 5
Jinapaha Sūri, Jaina writer, 54, 122, 256–7; quoted, 257 n. 1
jīva, lit. life; the soul; Ā., 63, 260, **270–2**; Jaina, 267; Pañcarātra, 280
Jīvaka, n.pr., a physician, 11; = Ājīvika, 101, 182–4
Jiyasattu, k., 45, 133 n. 1
Jñānavimala, Jaina commentator, 220–1, 226; quoted, 221 nn. 1, 2, 226 n. 1
Johnson, Dr., 230
Jotipāla, n.pr., 29–30

Kabandhin Kātyāyana, n.pr., 92–3
kācu. Tam., gold coin, 188, 194
Kadalī, pl., 44
Kadru, n.pr., 273
Kaivāra, Mysore, inscriptions, 190, 195
Kākanti, pl., 199
Kakuda Kātyāyana = Pakudha, 21–2, 92
Kāla, n.pr., prince, 69; = Upaka, 95
kāla, time, 257; Pāñcarātra doctrine of, 281; *v.* also time
Kālakācārya, Jaina teacher, 169–171, 174, 214; quoted, 171 n. 1
kālakaṇṇi, scapegoat, 29
Kalanda, *disācara*, 56–7
Kalaśa, k. of Kashmīr, 205
Kālāya, pl., 42
Kalhaṇa, Kashmīr historian, 205–210
Kālī, goddess, 193, 198
Kaliṅga, pl., 145
kalpa, Skt., æon, 14, 31, 135; *v.* also *kappa*
Kalpa Sūtra, Jaina scripture, 41, 46, 74, 177 n. 3
Kaluhaḷḷi, pl., inscription, 189
kāma, passion, desire, 241–2
Kāmamahāvaṇa, *caitya*, 32
kamma (Pāli and Pkt.), types of action, 219, 241–2; *v.* also *karma*
Kampilla (Pkt.), Kāmpilya (Skt.), pl., 133, 199
Kaṇāda, Vaiśeṣika philosopher, 57
Kaṇanda, n.pr., 57
Kanauj, pl., 33
Kāñcī, pl., 186
Kandara-masuka, n.pr., 102–3
kaṇḍaka-vuttika (Pāli), interpretation of, 243
Kaṇiyāra, *disācara*, 56–7
kāñji-ya, rice gruel, 92, 204
Kaṇṇaki, n.pr., 134, 197
Kaṇṇamuṇḍa, Lake, 251
kapālin, type of ascetic, 169
Kapila-pura, -vastu, pl., 34, 199, 202
kappa (Pāli and Pkt.), æon, 243; *v.* also *kalpa*
Karambiya, pl., 102
karma (Skt.), the effect of one's actions on one's future condition, whether in this life or another, 5, 8, 18, 23, 79, 96, 102, 135, 175, 196, 199, 203, 224–5, 229, 235, 238–9, 266–7, 277, 281–2, 284, 286; Ā., 14, 241; *v.* also *kamma*
Karṇa, hero, 37
Karṇa Chopār, cave, 152, 157
Kārttikeya, god, 37
Kashmīr, 36, 185, 205–210
Kāsī (Pāli), Kāśī (Skt.) = Benares, 5
Kāśikā, grammar; quoted, 79 n. 3
kasiṇa (Pāli), help to meditation, 270
Kassapa, Buddha, 146
Kaśyapa, sage, 30
Kataṅgala, pl., 43
Kathā-sarit-sāgara, Skt. text, 143; quoted, 144 n. 1
Kātyāyanī, goddess, 154

Kauṇḍinya, n.pr., 30
Kāvanūr, inscription at, 188
Kaviṭṭha, forest, 29
kāya (lit. body), element, 262–3
Keith, A. B., 161
Kerala, pl., 198
Kern, H., 103, 149, 170, 173
Keśin the Karṇāṭa, n.pr., 205
kevalin = *arhant*, 56, 79
Khalatika, hill, 150, 158
Khāravela, k., 145, 158 ; date, 159
khattavijjavādi, one maintaining a form of antinomianism, 18
Kīlūr, inscription at, 188
Kisa Saṅkicca, n.pr., 19–20, **27–30**, 84, 90, 94, 98, 118, 139, 244
Kisa Vaccha, n.pr., 29–30
Kistna, river, 156
Koḍiya, *maṭh*, 105
Kolar, district of Mysore ; inscriptions at, 189–191
Kollāga, pl., 39–41
Kondañña, n.pr., 29–30
Kondīvte, pl., 156
Koṇḍiyāyaṇa, n.pr., 32
Koṅgudeśa, pl., 206
Konow, S., 158
Kosala, pl., 5, 51, 73, 86, 89, 95, 133, 286
Kosambi, pl., 133, 286
Koṭṭhaga, *caitya*, 60–1, 67
kriyāvādin, a believer in the efficiency of works, 174
Kṛṣṇa, god, 154, 277
Kṛṣṇa III, Rāṣṭrakūṭa k., 188
kṣaṇikavāda, the Buddhist doctrine of momentariness, the impermanence of all things, 199
kṣapaṇaka, a Jaina ascetic, 105, 167–8, 170, 182–3
kṣattriya, the warrior class, 21
Kṣūrapāṇi, n.pr., 58
Kukkuṭanagara, pl., 81, 199, 201
Kūlavālaya, ascetic, 70
Kulottuṅga Coladeva, k., 188
kulūpaga, an ascetic maintained by a single household, 127, 131, 138, 146
Kumāradāsa, poet, 99, 106, 165–6
Kumāradevī, queen, 75
Kumāraya, pl., 42
Kumbhavatī, pl., 29
Kummāragāma, 47, 49, 51
Kuṇāladaha, lake, 251
Kuṇḍaga, pl., 45
Kuṇḍaggāma, pl., 49
Kuṇḍakoliya, n.pr., 133, 141, 218, 222, 229
Kuṇḍalakeśī, n.pr., 199
Kūṇiya, Ajātasattu, k. of Magadha, 70, 73–6
Kurukṣetra, pl., 4
Kusinārā, pl., 136
Kūṭâgāra-sālā, at Vesāli, 57
Kushān, dynasty, 287

Lāḍha, pl., 41, 44–6
Lalita-vistara, Buddhist Skt. text, 34, 165
Lakes, great, 14, 251
Lambuya, pl., 44
Lassen, C., 101
Last Things, eight, 62–3, 68, 127, 209, **254–5**
Leśyās, Jaina classification of psychic types, 139, 245
lexicographers, 100–1, 163, 182–4
Licchavi, tribe, 20, 69–71, 74–6
liṅga, the phallic emblem of Śiva, 183
liṅgī, ascetic carrying a *liṅga*, 183
logic, A., **274–5** ; Buddhist, 197
Lohaggala, pl., 45
lohiyagaṅgā, Ā. measure of time, 253
Lokāyata, materialism, 3, 232 ; *v.* also *Cārvāka*, materialism, *nāstika*
Lomas Ṛṣi, cave, 153, 156, 159, 209
Loṣṭadhara, n.pr., 206, 209
lotus, 111
Luke, St., Gospel of, 36
lump, grasping a heated, 104, 209

maccugaṅgā, Ā. measure of time, 253
Maddaṇā, pl., 45
Mādhavacandra, Jaina commentator, 204, 261 ; quoted, 204 n. 4
Madhva, Hindu theologian, 282
Maḍivāḷa, pl., inscriptions, 189–190
Madurā, pl., 195, 197
Magadha-n, pl., 4–5, 8, 11, 26, 35, 44, 47, 51, 67, 70–6, 78, 89, 95, 133, 143, 145, 147, 150, 157, 159, 160, 286
māgadha, bard, 8, 35
Māgadhī, dialect of Pkt., 24–5, 216, 220
Maggas, Pkt. paths, of song and dance, 56, 64, 117, 213–14, 216
magic, 51, 60, 62, 131, 186, 194, 209 ; Ā. rites, 112–13
Mahābhārata, Skt. epic, 7–9, 34, 38, 90, 132, 158, 162, 218, 273, 282 ; quoted, 90 n. 2, 218
Mahābodhi-vaṃsa, Pāli text, 143
mahāgaṅgā, Ā. measure of time, 253
Mahāgiri, Jaina *sthavira*, 177 n. 3
mahā-kalpa (Skt.), *-kappa* (Pāli and Pkt.), a great æon, 219, 225, 249, 252–4, 258, 263, 275

Mahākassapa, disciple of Buddha, 108, 136
Mahāli, n.pr., 20
mahā-māhaṇa, a great brāhmaṇa, 52
mahāmāṇasa, Ā. measure of time, 254, 257
mahā-mātra (Skt.), *-matta* (Pāli), a minister or government official, 132, 136, 148–9
Mahāmoggalāna, disciple of Buddha, 126
māhaṇa (Pkt.), a brāhmaṇa, 52 n. 6
Mahānandin, k., 144
Mahāniddesa, Pāli text, 273
Mahāṇimittas, Ā. scriptures, 56, 117, **213–16**
Mahāpadma Nanda, k., 142–4
Mahāpaüma (Pkt.), k., 142–4, 148, 272
Mahāparinibbāna Sutta, 71, 77
mahāpuruṣas, eight, 256
Mahāsaccaka Sutta, 118, 123–4
Mahāsilākaṇṭae, battle, 69
Mahāvaṃsa, Sinhalese chronicle, 73–4, 89, 145; quoted, 73 n. 2; comm., 131, 145–7
Mahāvastu, Buddhist Skt. text, 34, 78, 83
Mahāvīra, founder of Jainism, 8, 12, 17, 22, 31–5, 40–54, 58–62, 64, 66, 69–71, 75–7, 83, 89, 96, 100, 108–9, 114, 127, 130, 133, 138, 140–2, 174, 229–230, 234, 236, 254, 274–5, 277–8; meeting with M.G., 39; illness, 67
Mahāyāna, the form of Buddhism now practised in the Far East and Tibet, 280; literature, 165
Maheśvara, god = Śiva, 170
Maḥmūd of Ghaznī, 207
Majjhima Nikāya, Pāli scripture, 18, 20, 23–4, 27–8, 91, 96, 118–120, 126, 134, 228; quoted, 19 n. 7, 96 n. 2, 118 n. 1, 123 n. 4, 135 n. 1, 229 n. 1
makara, a fabulous sea monster, 154
Makkhali Gosāla, chief leader of the Ās., *passim*; doctrine, **13**; predecessors, **27–34**; life, **34–66**; birth, **35–9**; meeting with Mahāvīra, **39**; peregrinations, **41–7**; and sesamum plant, **47–9**; and Vesiyāyaṇa, **49–50**; attains magic power, **50**; leader of Ās., **51**; taciturnity, 52; compared to fisherman, 54; compared to hair blanket, 55; last days, **56–66**; exposed by Mahāvīra, **58**; visits Mahāvīra, **60**; delirium, **61**; repentance and death, **64–6**; date of death, **66–78**; name and titles, **78–9**; reincarnations of, 142; status, **275–7**; deified, **276**; etymology of name, **36–8**
Malabar, pl., 195, 198, 282
Malalasekera, G. P., 89, 92
Mallarāma, n.pr., 32
Mallinātha, commentator, 166; quoted, 166 n. 4
Malliṣeṇa, Jaina commentator, 184, 222, 260, 276; quoted, 222 n. 5
mana, impersonal magical power, 284
Māṇasa, Ā. heavens, 250–1, 273
mānāykaṉ (Tam.), captain, 134
maṇḍalar (Tam.), *v. maṇṭalar*
maṇḍala-mokṣa, the Ā. doctrine of cyclic salvation, 124, 174, **257–261**
mandārava, a heavenly flower, 136
Maṇḍiya, n.pr., 32
Maṇḍiyakucchi, *caitya*, 31
Maṅgala, pl., 43
mango, 64, 85, 130; stone, 61, 63, 86
Māṇibhadda (Pkt.), Maṇibhadra (Skt.), Ā. god, a *yakṣa*, 123, 131, 142, 247, 257, 272–4
Maṇimēkalai, Tam. poem and its heroine, 81, 91, 187, 197, 200, 215, 238–9, 244, 263–6, 269, 276–7, 280; quoted, 81 n. 5, 91 nn. 6, 9, 238 n. 3, 244 n. 5, 263 nn. 2–6, 264 nn. 1–4, 265 nn. 2–4
Maṅkha, n.pr., 36
maṅkha, type of mendicant, 8, 35–7, 50, 78, 208
Maṅkhali, father of M.G., 36, 78–9
Maṅkhaliputta, patronymic of M.G., 78
Maṅki, n.pr., 9, 34, 38, 162, 218
maṇṭalar (Tam.), saints who return from *nirvāṇa*, **260–1**, 281–2
Manu, lawbook of, 282
Mānusa, seven, 14, 251
Māṇusuttara, Ā. heavens, 250–1, 273
Māra, god, the tempter of Buddhism, 86, 198
mārga (Skt.), *v. magga*
Maṟkali, Tam. form of name of M.G., 34, 52, 78–9, 81, 115, 125, 172, 215, 242, 272, 276–7, 280; *-nūl*, Book of M., 215–16, 263
Maskarin Gośāla, Gośālikāputra, Gośālīputra, Skt. form of name of M.G., q.v.
maskarin, an ascetic bearing a staff, 79, 99–100, 165–7, 171, 182
material-ism, -ist, 5, 18, 23, 200, 267; *v.* also *Cārvāka*, *Lokāyata*, *nāstika*

math, a Hindu monastery, 105
Mattavilāsa, Skt. farce, 126
matter, 267
Maudgalyāyana, disciple of Buddha, 80, 199, 200
Maukhari, clan, 155, 158
Maurya, dynasty, 138, **145–162**, 193, 196, 278, 286–7
meat, eating, by Ās., 122; by Buddha and Mahāvīra, 123
Menander, Greco-Bactrian k., 67
Meṇḍhiyagāma, pl., 67
mendicants, wandering, 94–107; types of Ā., 111, 119
merchants, story of, 59; class, 285
Mercury, planet, 169–171, 184; metal, 185
metempsychosis, 5
Migāra, n.pr., 97, 132, 137–8
Milinda-pañha, Pāli text, 10, 21, 67; quoted, 21 nn. 1, 2
Mīmāṃsaka, school of Hindu philosophy, 229
miracle contest, at Sāvatthi, 84–90
mokṣa, salvation, 176, 180, 259
molecules, 267, 269
monastery, Ā., 81, 201–2
monism, 6, 280
monotheism, Hebrew, 7
Moses, 37
Mucalinda, lake, 251
Mudrārākṣasa, drama, 35, 167–8; quoted, 35 n. 7
Mukta, n.pr., 206
mukta, a soul released from transmigration (in Pāñcarātra system), 281
Mūlācāra, Jaina text, 204
muni, sage, 49, 198
Muslim, 154–5, 157, 192, 207
mystery cults, 96

Naccinārkkiniyar, Tam. commentator, 111, 196; quoted, 111 n. 6
nāgas, divine serpents, 90, 247; worlds of, 14, 247, 258
Nāgârjunī, hill, 148, 150–1
nāgâvāsa, worlds of serpents, 247
nagga-bhogga (Pāli), naked and crippled, 102, 105, 208
nagga-samaṇa (Pāli), a naked ascetic, 97
nagna (Skt.), naked, a type of ascetic, 163–5
nagna-bhagna (Skt.), naked and crippled, a type of ascetic, 105, 208
nagn'-âṭa, -ka, a naked wandering ascetic, 168, 184, 208–210
Nāla, pl., 95
Nālandā, pl., 39, 41, 46
Nanda, dynasty, 143–5
Nandaka, *peta*, 20
Nanda Vaccha, n.pr., 19–20, **27–30**, 84, 90, 94, 98, 118, 139, 244
Nandi Sūtra, Jaina scripture, 178, 180–1, 274; commentary quoted, 274 n. 5
Nārāyaṇa, god = Viṣṇu, 170, 172–3
Nāriśvara, god = Śiva, 81
Nāstika-vādin, a materialist, 25, 218; *v.* also *Cārvāka*, *Lokāyata*, materialism.
nature, 225; *v.* also *Bhāva*
naya, in Jaina epistemology, standpoints of predication, *-vāda*, the doctrine of *nayas*, 179–180, 274–5
Neil, R.A., 113
Nellore District, inscriptions, 187, 190
Nemicandra, Jaina writer, 181, 204; quoted, 181 n. 2
Nepāl, 70
Newal, pl., 33
Nibelungenlied, 7
nigaṇṭha (Pāli), *nirgrantha* (Skt.), heterodox ascetic, esp. a Jaina, 16, 27, 96–7, 102, 109, 112, 118–19, 138–9, 147–150, 161, 163, 165, 169, 181–4, 243–4, 256, 270
Nigaṇṭha Nātaputta = Mahāvīra, 11, 16–18, 21–23, 61, 75, 80, 91–3, 96, 138, 217; doctrine, 16
nigaṇṭhi-gabbha, birth from knots (?), 248–250, 256
Nigoha, cave, 150, 152
nikendabtra, Japanese form of *nigaṇṭha*, 112
Nīlakēci, Tam. poem and its heroine, 52, 80–1, 84, 91, 122, 125, 186–7, 191, 198–202, 215, 236–9, 257, 259–260, 265–272, 276, 280; quoted, 81 n. 1, 115 nn. 1, 2, 122 n. 5, 125 n. 2, 201 n. 4, 202 nn. 2–4, 236, 237 n. 4, 260 n. 1, 265 nn. 5, 7, 270 n. 2, 276 n. 4
niraya, purgatory, 248
Nirayâvalikā Sūtra, Jaina scripture, 68, 71–3, 76–7
Nirgrantha Jñātrīputra (Skt.) = Nigaṇṭha Nātaputta (Pāli), q.v.
nirvāṇa, the highest bliss of the soul, 68; Ā., 219, 250, 253, 255, 258–261, 271, 275; Jaina, 204; = death, *parinirvāṇa*, Buddha's, 73–4, 76, 89, 108; Mahāvīra's, 75–7
niryukti, Jaina commentary, 54
Nītiśataka, poem, 282

niṭṭhā (Pāli), condition of perfection, 135 n. 2, 261
nitya, type of perfected soul, capable of incarnation at will (in Pāñcarātra philosophy), 281
Niyati, the cosmic principle of the Ās., Fate, 3, 6, 8, 26, 42, 60, 172, 174, 203, ch. xii, *passim*, 240–1, 257–8, 260–3, 266, 284, 286; in Pāñcarātra philosophy, 281; in Śaivism, 281 n. 6; *v.* also Destiny, determinism, Fate
niyativāda, doctrine of *Niyati*, 17, 82, 185, 220, 222, **226–235**; development of doctrine, **235–9**
non-Āryan, influence on Indian religion, 4–5; countries, 45
nudity, religious, 83, 107–9, 114, 202

Okkali and Ōkali, Dravidian Ā. gods, 215, 272–3
oligarchies, 5
omniscience, 19; of M.G., 275–6
Oṉpatu-katir, Tam. Ā. scripture, 215–16, 222
outcastes, 21

paccayas, requisites of Buddhist *bhikkhu*, 243
Paḍaveḍu, pl., inscription at, 189, 192
Padmaprabha Traividya, Jaina commentator, 204; quoted, 204 n. 5
Padmapura, pl., 199
Pakudha Kaccāyana, n.pr., 11, 17–20, 23–6, 80, **90–3**, 168, 217, 228, 256, 262–4, 266–7, 269, 271, 278, 284; doctrine, 16
Palar, river, 186
Pāli, sacred language of Hīnayāna Buddhists, 25, 33, 71; canon, scriptures, 10–13, 18, 34, 40, 54, 81, 99, 116
Pāli Text Society, Dictionary of the, 56, 105, 116 n. 2
Pallava, dynasty, 194
paṇa, silver coin, 161
Pāṇagāiṃ, *v.* Drinks
Pāñcarātra, a Vaiṣṇava religious system, 276, 280–2; *Saṃhitās*, 281
Pañcatantra, Skt. text, 167, 170 n. 5, 172
Pañcika, *yakṣa*, 86
Paṇḍas, land of the, 142
Pāṇḍu, n.pr., 57
Paṇḍukābhaya, k. of Ceylon, 146
Pāṇḍuputta, n.pr., 57, 126, 131, 133
Pāṇḍya, dynasty, 196
Pāṇini, grammarian, 36, 78–9, 99; quoted, 78 n. 6
Paṇiyabhūmī, pl., 40–1, 46, 51
Panjab, 4
pāpa, sin, evil, 91
Papañca Sūdanī, comm. of Buddhaghosa to *Majjh.*, quoted, 19 n. 7, 27 n. 7
papāta, precipice, 252
paramahaṃsa, type of ascetic, 105, 114
paramâṇu, atom, 267
Paramattha Dīpanī, Dhammapāla's comm. to *Khuddaka Nikāya*, quoted, 271, nn. 3, 4
paramâvati, Ā. measure of time, 253
Parāśara, n.pr., 58, 80–1, 177, 199, 200
paribbājaka (Pāli) = *parivrājaka* (Skt.), q.v.
parikammāiṃ, Jaina term of uncertain significance, 178
pariṇāma, evolution, 82
parinirvāṇa, of Buddha = death, 136
Pariśiṣṭa-parvan, Skt. Jaina text, 74, 144
parivrājaka, wandering ascetic, 57, 97, 100, 146, 165, 204, 247
Parmāḍi, Parmāṇḍi, *biruda* of Vikramâditya VI, 205
Parmenides, 17, 236
Pārśva Nātha, 23rd *tīrthaṅkara* of Jainism, 42, 44, 108
Pasenadi (Pāli), Prasenajit (Skt.), k. of Kosala, 5, 51, 85, 89
Pāṭaligāma, early name of Pāṭaliputra, 72–3
Pāṭaliputra, pl., 143, 147
Patañjali, grammarian, 78–9; quoted, 79 n. 1
Pathak, K. B., 183, 204
Paths, two, *v. Maggas*; sixty-two, *v. paṭipadā.*
paṭipadā, paths, 14, 242
Pattakālaya, pl., 42
Pattakālagaya, *caitya*, 32
paṭuvā, Ā. category, 251–2, 256
paüṭṭa-parihāra, abandonment of transmigration, 31, 48–9, 57–8, 219, 250–2
Pāwayā, pl., 273
Pāvā, pl., 75, 136
penance, Ā., 88, **110 12**, 202–3; bat-p., 110; p. of five fires, 110; in jars, 111, 242; final p., **127–131**, 247, 250; Jaina, 128–9
penance-ground, 111, 116
per, *pēr* (Tam.), name, person, 194–5
permanence, unchanging, *v. avicalita-nityatvam*

pesāca, births as goblins, 14, 251
peta (Pāli), a ghost, 20, 146
Petavatthu, Pāli text, 20, 146, 217, 270–1 ; quoted, 271 n. 1
Pillar Edict, Seventh, of Aśoka, 148–9, 161 ; quoted, 148 n. 4
Piṇḍola Bhāradvāja, disciple of Buddha, 85
Piṅgala, k., 146
Piṅgalavatsa, Ā. ascetic, 146
Pippalāda, n.pr., 92–3
piśāca, a goblin, 14, 134, 162, 165, 210, 276 ; births as, 14, 251
Piśācaka, n.pr., 200
Piṭṭhicampā, pl., 43
Piyadasi = Aśoka, 150–1
Polāsapura, pl., 52, 115–16, 132–3
poll tax, on Ās., 194–5
polytheism, 4, 6, 284
Pope, G. U., 277
pots, 46, 88, 111, 134
potters, 134, 193
Poygai, pl., inscriptions at, 189–190, 192
Prabhākaravardhana, k., 167–8
Prajāpati, god, 93
prakṛti, in Sāṅkhya philosophy, matter, 81
pralaya, dissolution of the universe, 258
Praśnavyākaraṇa Sūtra, Jaina scripture, 25, 221 ; quoted, 218
Pravacana-sār'-oddhāra, Jaina text, 181 ; quoted, 181 n. 2
Pravaragiri, hill, 158
Prayāga, n.pr., 206
Pre-Buddhistic Indian Philosophy of B. M. Barua, 12
precipices, 14, 252
predication, principles of, 177, *v.* also *naya*
Priyadarśin (Skt.) = Piyadasi (Pkt.), q.v.
" proofs," Ā. category, 256
prostitute, 87, 209
Protestantism, 285
proverbs, Tam., quoted, 283
pubbekatavādi, one who maintains the orthodox doctrine of *karma*, 18
pudgala, in Jaina philosophy, matter, 267
Puṇḍas, land of, 143
Puṇḍra, -vardhana, pl., 143, 147–8, 198
Punnabhadda, Ā. god, 128, 131, 142, 247, 257, 272–4
Punnakalasā, pl., 44
puṇya, virtue, merit, 91
Purāṇas, Hindu scriptures, 143–4, 177 ; *Bhāgavata*, 144 ; *Vāyu*, 113, 122–3, 134, 162–5, 276, 280 ; quoted, 163 n. 1, 164 n. 1
Pūraṇa Kassapa, Ā. leader, 11, 17–24, 26–8, **80–90**, 92–3, 97, 102, 107, 109, 115, 138, 168, 174, 185, 198–9, 201, 216–17, 221, 228, 243, 262, 271, 278, 280 ; death, 84–90 ; doctrine, 13
Purāṇaṉ (Tam.), elder, 81, 202
Puṟanāṉūṟu, Tam. anthology, 197
" Pure Drink," Ā. penance, 128–9, 250
purgatories, Ā., 14, 248
Purimatāla, pl., 45
purisa-bhūmi, stages of life, 14, 246, 256
Pūrṇabhadra (Skt.) = Punnabhadda (Pkt.), q.v.
Pūrṇa Kāśyapa (Skt.) = Pūraṇa Kassapa (Pāli), q.v.
Puruṣa, in Sāṅkhya philosophy, the soul, 199, 229
Pūrvagatam, section of *Dṛṣṭivāda*, 180
Pūrvas, earliest Jaina scriptures, now lost, 56, 117, 175, 180–1, 213–15
Puṣyabhūti, n.pr., 167
Puttūr, pl., 189
Puvvas (Pkt.) = *Pūrvas* (Skt.), q.v.
Pyrrhonists, 17

quarters, six, of Indian cosmology, 58

Rahamusala, battle, 69–70
Rājagaha (Pāli), Rājagṛha (Skt.), Rāyagiha (Pkt.), pl., 11, 31, 39, 40, 72–3, 85, 126, 158
Rājarāja III, Cola k., 188–9
Rājataraṅgiṇī, Kashmīr chronicle, 36, 105, 125, 205–210 ; quoted, 205 n. 5, 206 n. 7, 207 n. 1, 209 n. 7, 210 n. 2
Rājendra Coladeva, k., 188
rajo-dhātu, Ā. category, 248
Rājyavardhana, k., 168
rākṣasa, demon, 144
raktapaṭa, type of ascetic, 169
Rāma, hero, 287
Rāmanātha Deva, k., 189–190
Rāmânuja, philosopher, 200, 208
" ranks," kinds of, 256
Rapson, E. J., 206
Raseśvara-darśana, system of philosophy, 185
Rathakāra, lake, 251
rationalist, 19
Ratnacandrajī, *Ardha-māgadhī Dictionary*, 56

Ratna Prabha Vijaya, Muni, 45 n. 1
Rāvaṇa, n.pr., 165–6
Rāyagiha, *v.* Rājagaha
Raychaudhuri, H. C., 71, 72, 133 n. 1
reanimations, of M.G., 28, **31–3**, 49 ; *v.* also *paütta-parihāra*
regression, infinite, 234
restraint, fourfold, 16, 23
Ṛg Veda, the most ancient Hindu scripture, 7, 131, 286
Rhys Davids, T. W., 242, 247–8, 252
Rice, L., 105 n. 5
rice-gruel, *v. kañji*
robbers, M.G. captured by, 44
Rockhill, W. W., 21–2, 89, 247, 256
Roha, n.pr., 32
Rohagupta, n.pr., 177–8, 267–8
Roman Empire, 96
ṛṣi, a legendary sage, 30, 126
ṛta, the order of nature, 284
rugṇa-nagnâṭaka, type of ascetic, 105

sabhā, meeting place, of Ās., *v.* Ājīvika
Saccaka, n.pr., 27, 57, 118, 123
Saddālaputta, n.pr., 52, 53–4, 115, 132–4, 140–1, 229–230, 234. 236
Ṣaddarśana-samuccaya, Skt. philosophical text, 81, 185, 222, 235
Saddharma Puṇḍarīka, Buddhist Skt. text, 165
sādīṇagaṅgā, Ā., measurement of time, 253
sāgarovama, Jaina measurement of time, 142, 250
Sahasrāra-kalpa, Jaina heaven, 203–4
Śāhi, dynasty, 205
St. Petersburg Skt. Lexicon, 56
Śaivism, cult of the god Śiva, 124, 170, 200, 266 ; ascetics, 100, 166–7
Sākala, pl., 67
Sāketa, pl., 135
Sakka, god = Indra, 44, 86
Śākya, Buddhist, 161, 164, 169, 181, 184 ; tribe, 5, 34
Saletore, B. A., 105 n. 5, 191, 194
samaṇa (Pkt.) = *śramaṇa* (Skt.), q.v.
Sāmañña-phala Sutta, Pāli scripture, ch. ii, *passim*, 34, 35, 37, 67, 79, 80, 84, 89, 91, 162, 217–220, 224–5, 227, 236, 240, 254 n. 1, 256, 262, 267, 269, 279 ; quoted, 13 n. 1, 14 n. 3, 15 n. 4, 16 nn. 1, 4, 17 n. 1, 217, 224 nn. 2–4, 262 nn. 3–5
Samataṭa, pl., 201–2
Samavāyâṅga, Jaina Scripture, 178–181, 274 ; quoted, 178 n. 4, 215 n. 1 ; comm., 178 ; quoted, 179 nn. 2, 3, 5
sambodhaka (Skt.) = *cempotaka* (Tam.), q.v.
saṃhitā, a compilation, 281
Sammuti, k., 142, 144
Saṃyutta Nikāya, Pāli scripture, 52, 67, 80, 91, 216 ; quoted, 20, 67 nn. 4, 5, 216 n. 5, 217 nn. 1, 2
saṃsāra, the cycle of transmigration, 14, 122, 241, 244, 257–9, 261, 275
saṃsāra-suddhi, purification by transmigration, 228
Sāṇa, *disācara*, 56–7
sand, mound of, 92
Sandaka, n.pr., 18–19, 28, 39, 80, 138
Sandaka Sutta, of *Majjh.*, Pāli scripture, 18, 28, 96, 228 ; quoted, 19 n. 7
saṅgati, chance, 225–7, 232
saṅgha, an unorthodox religious community, 3, 56, 100–1 ; Ā., 111, 113, 115, 149 ; Buddhist, 103, 120, 136–8
saṅgulikā, a cluster (?), 48 n. 1
Sañjaya Belatthiputta, Sañjayin, sceptic teacher, 11, 17, 19, 21–2, 86, 93 ; doctrine, 16
sañjūha (Pkt.), group (of demigods), 249–251
Śaṅkara, philosopher, 93 n. 2, 200, 229
Sāṅkhya, system of orthodox philosophy, 81, 199, 225, 229, 248
Saṅkicca, n.pr., 29–30
saññi-gabbha, conscious births, 14, 248–251
sannyāsī, an ascetic, 108, 169
Sanskrit, drama, 24 ; literature, references to Ās. in, ch. ix, *passim*
Śānti Parvan, book of *Mbh.*, 38
saptabhaṅgi, Jaina epistemological system, 275
sara (Pāli), lake, Ā. category, 251 ; Ā. measurement of time, 252–3
Sarabhaṅga, n.pr., 29–30
Śarada, season, 46, 47
Saravaṇa, pl., 36–8
Śārdūlavarman, chieftain, 154
Śārdūla-vikrīḍita, Skt. metre, 171
Sāriputta, 57
Sarva-darśana-saṅgraha, Skt. philosophical text, 185, 198
Sarvâstivādin, sect of Buddhism, 268
sassatavādi, " eternalist," 95
Sastri, K. A. N., 191
sattagharantariya, type of Ā. ascetic, 111, 119

Savvāṇubhūti, n.pr., 60, 141
Sāvatthi, pl., 31, 32, 43, 50–3, 56, 58, 59, 62, 64–6, 71, 72, 75, 84–6, 88, 95, 97, 107, 110–11, 124, 132, 133 n. 1, 135, 138, 140–1, 143, 201
Sayaduvāra, pl., 142–3
sceptic, 19
Schomerus, H. W., 277
Schrader, F. O., quoted, 281
scriptures, Ā., ch. xi, *passim*
Semites, 6
Senart, E., 150–1
Seṇiya, k. = Bimbisāra, 69, 73, 77, 144
senses, seven, 256
serpents, regions of, 247
serpenthood, work of, 128, 131
sesamum plant, M.G. and, 45, 47–9
seṭṭhī, a wealthy merchant, 85, 132–3
Sewell, R., 192
sexual laxity, of Ās., 124–6
Siddhatthagāma, pl., 42, 45, 47
Sīhappapāta, lake, 251
śikhin, type of ascetic, 166
Sikhism, 172
Śīlâṅka, Jaina commentator, 41, 121, 124, 170, **174–181**, 220, 228, 259, 261, 276; quoted, 174 n. 6, 175 nn. 1–3, 176 nn. 1, 4, 221 n. 1, 227 n. 2, 230 n. 1, 231 nn. 1, 2, 232 nn. 1, 2, 233 nn. 1, 4, 234 nn. 1, 3, 4, 235 n. 1, 259 n. 3, 261 n. 2
silence, of M.G., 52, 242
Siṃhavarman, Pallava k., 187, 191–3
Sinhalese Chronicle, *v. Mahāvaṃsa*
Sītā, n.pr., 166
Śiva, god, 36, 155, 170
skandhas, five, of Buddhism, 199; molecules, 267
Soma, god, 81, 93 n. 2
Somânanda, n.pr., 209–210
Someśvara, type of god, 209–210
Song, Last, 68, 117; song and dance, 116–17, 214, *v. Maggas*
soul, Ā. doctrine of, 270–2
Sprinkling Elephant, Last, 68–9, 154, 209
śrāddha, ceremony in commemoration of ancestors, 120, 163–4
śramaṇa, an ascetic, esp. Jaina, 96, 183, 203
Śravaṇa Beḷgoḷā, pl., 125, 193, 214
Śrāvasti (Skt.), *v.* Sāvatthi (Pāli)
Śrīnagara, pl., 206
Srinivasan, K. R., 111
staff, of ascetic, 99–100
stages of life, *v. purisa-bhūmi*
standpoints, *v. naya*
static universe, Ā. doctrine of, 236
Stein, M. A., 207
Sthānakavāsī, sect of Jainism, 207
Sthānâṅga Sūtra, Jaina scripture, 112, 214; quoted, 112 n. 2
Sthānvīśvara, pl., 168
sthavira, elder of Jaina or Buddhist *saṅgha*, 177 n. 3
Stormcloud, Last Great, 68
stūpa, a sacred mound, esp. in Buddhism, 108, 156
Subhadda, n.pr., 95
Subhadrāṅgī, n.pr., 146
Subhakiṇhā, Buddhist heaven, 261
Substitutes for Drink, four, 62–3, 127–130, 254
Sudāma, cave, 152–3, 156–7
Śūdra, the lowest, servile, class, 21, 134
Sugiura, S., quoted, 112 n. 3
suicide, of Ceḍaga, 70; of Pūraṇa, 84–90; ritual, 64, 127–131
sukha, joy, happiness, 91
Sumālya, n.pr., 144
Sumaṅgala, n.pr., 142
Sumaṅgala Vilāsinī, comm. of Buddhaghosa to *Dīgha*, quoted, 13 n. 2, 14 n. 2, 15 nn. 1–3, 16 nn. 3–4; *v.* Buddhaghosa
Sumati, n.pr., 144
Suṇakkhatta, disciple of Mahāvīra, 60, 141
Sunakkhatta, Licchavi, 141 n. 4
Śuṅga, dynasty, 185
Sunīḍha, n.pr., 72
śūnyavāda, the doctrine of "emptiness", the illusoriness of the material world, 199
supina (Pāli), a dream, 220, 252
Suraṭṭha, pl., 146
Sūrya, god, 171
Suśruta, physician, 228
sūtra, a concisely expressed rule, 36; a text of religious or technical type, 58; of Trairāśikas, 175, 180–1; of *Dṛṣṭivāda*, 179
Sūtrakṛtâṅga, Jaina scripture, 53, 114, 121, 124, 174, 176, 226, 230, 232, 234, 261; quoted, 53 nn. 3, 4, 54 n. 1, 114 n. 8, 121 nn. 3, 5, 6, 124, 227 n. 1, 233 nn. 3, 5, 259
sutta (Pāli and Pkt.) = *sūtra* (Skt.), q.v.
Sutta Nipāta, Pāli scripture, quoted, 96 n. 3; comm. quoted, 220
Suvaṇṇakhalaya, pl., 42
Svabhāva, nature, 226; *v.* also *Bhāva*

svabhāvavādin, a believer in Nature as first principle, 226, 232
Śvetâmbara, the sect of Jainism whose ascetics wear white robes, 176, 183–4
Syādvāda, Jaina doctrine of epistemological relativity, 275
Syādvādamañjarī, Jaina philosophical text, 184, 222

tāḻi (Tam.), funerary urn, 111
Tambāya, pl., 44
Tamil literature, Ās. in, 34, 123, **196–203**, 262
Tāmralipti, pl., 202
tapas, ascetic penance, 112
tāpasa, type of ascetic, 97, 100, 181
tapasvin, type of ascetic = *tāpasa*, 100, 169
taṟi-iṟai (Tam.), tax, 190, 194
Tarka-rahasya-dīpikā, comm. to *Ṣaddarśana-samuccaya*, 80, 235; quoted, 81–2
Tattuvappirakācar, Tam. commentator, 239, 276
tattvas, basic categories, 199
tax, on Ās., 134, 187–196, 278
temple, Vaiṣṇavite, 46
Terāsiya (Pkt.), *v.* Trairāśika (Skt.)
tēvaṉ (Tam.), god, *arhant*, 201
tēvar, plural of above, title of Tiruvaḷḷuvar, 200
theism, 23, 231–2, 280–2, 287
Theravāda, Hīnayāna Buddhism, 239
Therīgātha, Pāli text, 95
Thullanandā, n.pr., 125
Tibetan, version of *Sāmañña-phala Sutta*, 21, 23, 247, 249 n. 1, 256; version of death of Pūraṇa, 85, 87, 89
tigharantariya, type of Ā. mendicant, 111, 119
time, 81, 231, 233, 257, 281; *v.* also *kāla*
tīrthaṅkara, a fully perfected teacher of an unorthodox sect, esp. of Jainism, 12, 27–8, 64, 68, 79, 97, 108, 143 n. 3, 144, 244, 255, 260–1, 275–6, 278
Tirukkuṟaḷ, Tam. text, 196, 201
Tiruvaḷḷuvar, Tam. poet, 201
Tiruvoṟṟiyūr, pl., inscription at, 188–9, 192
Tiyaggaḷa, lake, 251
Tolkāppiyam, Tam. grammar, 111, 196
traditionalist, 19
Trairāśika, unorthodox Jaina sect, **174–181**, 259, 267, 274
transmigration, 5, 21, 284; abandonment of, *v.* *paüṭṭa-parihāra*
tridaṇḍin, type of ascetic, 166–7, 204
Trilokasāra, Jaina text, 204
truth, double standard of, 230, 241
Turk, Turuṣka, 82, 207

Uccala, n.pr., 206, 209
ucchedavāda, doctrine denying survival after death, 18, 95, 263
Udāi Kuṇḍiyāyaṇa, n.pr., 30–3, 57–8, 60, 95, 244
Uddaṇḍapura, pl., 32
Udayagiri, pl., 159
Udayarāja, n.pr., 206
Udāyi, *bhikkhu*, 135–6
Ugrasena, k. = Mahāpadma, 143
Ujjain, pl., 199, 214
Upaka, Ā. mendicant, **94**, 98–9, 104, 108–9, 133, 138, 220
upalakṣana, connotation, 172–3
Upananda, *bhikkhu*, 136
Upaniṣad, Hindu mystical texts, 4–6, 99, 100, 283–4; *Paramahaṃsa*, 114; *Praśna*, 92; quoted, 93 n. 1; *Śvetāśvatara*, 98, 228; quoted, 229 n. 1
uppala-beṇṭiya, type of Ā. mendicant, 111, 120
Uraiyūr, pl. = Trichinopoly, 201
Uruvilvā, pl., 83
Utpala, commentator, 100, 166–7, **168–174**, 186, 277, 280; quoted, 170 n. 1, 171 n. 2
Utsarpiṇī, an era of progress (Jainism), 143 n. 3, 144, 275
Uttarâdhyayana Sūtra, Jaina scripture, 70 n. 2, 214
Uttar Pradesh, formerly United Provinces, 5
uṭṭiyā-samaṇa, type of Ā. ascetic, 111, 120
Uvacca, Uvaicca (Tam.), 189, 192–3
Uvananda, n.pr., 42
Uvāsaga Dasāo, Jaina scripture, 52, 115, 121, 133, 141, 156, 222, 229; quoted, 218, 229 n. 4

Vacchagotta, n.pr., 134
Vaccha Kisa, n.pr., *v.* Kisa Vaccha
Vaḍathikā, cave, 152, 155, 157
Vahiyakā, cave, 151, 155, 157
Vaidyanātha Dīkṣita, astrologer, 101, 124, 184–5, 191; quoted, 184 n. 9

Vaijayantī, lexicon, 183
vaikhānasa, type of ascetic, 98, 100
vainayika, a believer in the doctrine of salvation by good conduct, 174, 176–7, 261
Vaiśeṣika, school of orthodox Hindu philosophy, 57, 177–8, 180, 199, 267–9, 281
Vaiṣṇav-a, -ism, cult of the god Viṣṇu, 149, 169, 170–2, 174, 177, 186, 209, 261, 273, 276–7, 280–2; ascetics, 166–7
Vaiśya, the third, mercantile class, 21
Vaitāḍhya, mountain, 143
Vajjabhūmī (Pkt.), Vajrabhūmi (Skt.), pl., 41, 45–6
Vajji, tribe, 5, 69, 72, 74–5, 77–8
Valabhī, pl., 166
Vālmīki, poet, 177
Vāmana, grammarian, 79
Vāmanamunī, Tam. commentator, 122, 201–2, 215, 237–8, 260, 265; quoted, 122 n. 6, 202 n. 5, 237 n. 2, 276 n. 5
Vaṃsa, pl., 133
vānaprastha, type of ascetic, 98, 100, 184
Vāṇārasī (Pkt.), pl. = Bāṇārasī, Benares, Kāsī, q.v., 32
Vāṇiyagāma, pl., 133 n. 1
Vañji, pl., 197–8
vanyāśana, type of ascetic, 169
Varāhamihira, astrologer, **168–174**, 184, 280; quoted, 169 n. 1
varṇas, four, classes of Hindu society, 5, 134, 162
Vasiṣṭha, legendary sage, 177
Vassakāra, n.pr., 72–4
Vāsudeva, god = Kṛṣṇa, 43, 45–6, 273
Vaṭṭakera, Jaina writer, 204
Veda, the earliest and most sacred Hindu scriptures, 33, 98, 199, 248, 284
Vedānta, system of orthodox Hindu philosophy, 200
Vehalla, n.pr., 69
Vesāli, pl., 20, 32, 34, 44, 57, 69, 71–4, 76, 102, 133 n. 1, 136; siege, 70
Vesiyāyaṇa, ascetic, 49–50
Viḍavalūra, pl., 187
Videha, pl., 4, 95
Viḍūḍabha, n.pr., 5
vihāra, a monastery, esp. Buddhist, 47, 101, 116
Vihimaggapavā, Jaina text, 54, 122, 256; quoted, 54 n. 4
Vijaya, n.pr., 39
vijjuantariya, type of Ā. mendicant, 111, 120
Vikramāditya, legendary k., 287
Vikramāditya VI, Cālukya k., 205
Vimalavāhaṇa, title of k. Mahāpaüma, 142–3
vīṇā, musical instrument, 63–4, 117
Vinaya Piṭaka, Pāli text, 116, 120, 124, 132, 135–7; quoted, 136 n. 5
vinayavāda, the doctrine of the *vinayavādins* or *vainayikas*, q.v.
Vinayavijaya, Jaina commentator, 41, 46
Vindhya, mountains, 142
Vindusāra, k. = Bindusāra, q.v.
Vīranandi, Jaina writer, 203–4
Visākhā, n.pr., 135, 138
Viśākhadatta, dramatist, 35, 168
viśiṣṭādvaita, school of orthodox philosophy, 200
Viṣṇu, god, 170–1, 276, 281
Viśvāmitra, cave, 153, 156–7
Vītāśoka, prince, 148
vivāsas, type of ascetic, 184–5
vocations, comfortless, 19
vrātya, renegade Āryan, 8
vṛddha, *vṛddhaśrāvaka*, type of ascetic, 165, 169–170
Vyantara, type of Jaina god, 42 n. 2
Vyāsa, legendary sage, 177

wagon maker, 131
war-engines, 69–70
weaving-shed, 39
Weber, A., 114
wind-eater, type of ascetic, 97
women, in Ā. order, 106
writing, kinds of, 256

Yādava, lexicographer, 182–4; quoted, 183
yakṣa, type of demigod, 86, 249, 273
Yama, god, 35
Yama-cloth, 35
Yaśomitra, Buddhist commentator, 241
yati, type of ascetic, 170
yoni-pamukha, chief sorts of birth, 14, 241, 248–9
yojana, league, a measure of length varying from 4 to 8 miles, 253, 270, 271

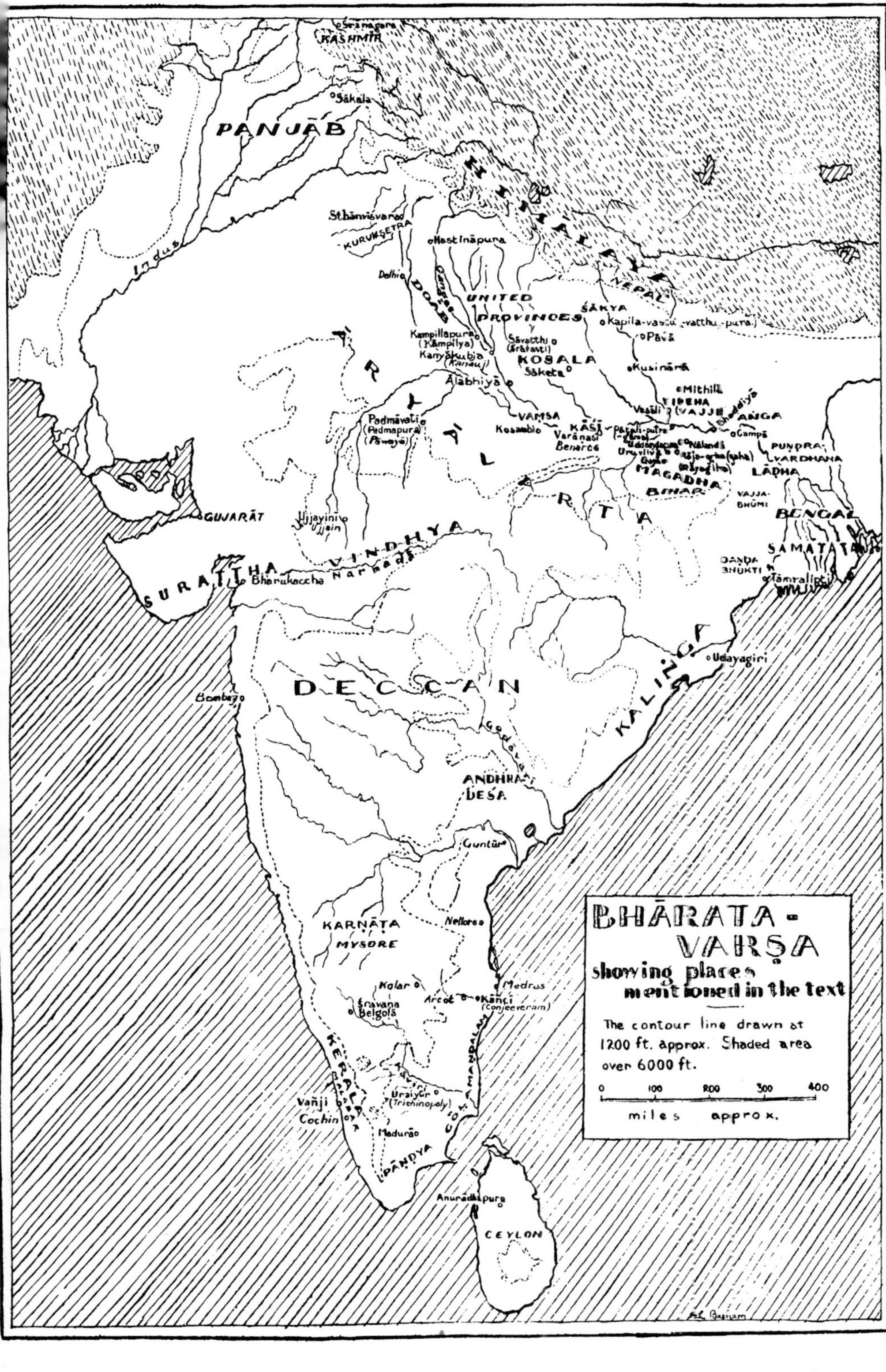

BHĀRATA-VARṢA
showing places mentioned in the text
The contour line drawn at 1200 ft. approx. Shaded area over 6000 ft.
0 100 200 300 400
miles approx.
Śrīnagara
KASHMĪR
Sākala
PANJĀB
Indus
Sthānvīśvara
KURUKṢETRA
Hastināpura
Delhi
DOAB
Ganges
UNITED PROVINCES
NEPĀL
ŚĀKYA
Kapila-vastu (-vatthu-pura)
Pāvā
Kusinārā
Kampillapura (Kāmpilya)
Kanyākubja (Kanauj)
Sāvatthi (Śrāvastī)
KOSALA
Sāketa
Ālabhiyā
Padmāvatī (Padmapura) (Pawayā)
VAMSA
Kosambi
KĀŚĪ
Vārāṇasī
Benares
Mithilā
VIDEHA (VAJJI)
Vesālī
Bhaddiya
AṄGA
Campā
Nālandā
Uruvilvā
Gayā
MAGADHA
BIHAR
PUṆḌRA-VARDHANA
LĀḌHA
VAJJA-BHŪMI
BENGAL
SAMATATA
DAṆḌA BHUKTI
Tāmralipti
GUJARĀT
Ujjayinī
Ujjain
VINDHYA
Narmadā
SURAṬṬHA
Bharukaccha
DECCAN
Bombay
Godāvarī
KALIṄGA
Udayagiri
ANDHRA DEŚA
Guntūr
Nellore
KARṆĀṬA
MYSORE
Madras
Kolar
Arcot
Kāñcī (Conjeeveram)
Śravana Belgolā
KERALA
Vañji
Cochin
Uraiyūr (Trichinopoly)
Madurāo
PĀṆḌYA
Anurādhapura
CEYLON